REALITY THERAPY
FOR
THE 21st CENTURY

REALITY THERAPY FOR THE 21ST CENTURY

Robert E. Wubbolding, Ed.D.

USA	Publishing Office:	BRUNNER-ROUTLEDGE
		A member of the Taylor & Francis Group
		325 Chestnut Street
		Philadelphia, PA 19106
		Tel: (215) 625-8900
		Fax: (215) 625-2940
	Distribution Center:	BRUNNER-ROUTLEDGE
		A member of the Taylor & Francis Group
		7625 Empire Drive
		Florence, KY 41042
		Tel: 1 (800) 634-7064
		Fax: 1(800) 248-4724
UK		BRUNNER-ROUTLEDGE
		A member of the Taylor & Francis Group
		27 Church Road
		Hove
		East Sussex, BN3 2FA
		Tel: +44 (0) 1273 207411
		Fax: +44 (0) 1273 205612

REALITY THERAPY FOR THE 21ST CENTURY

7 8 9 0

Printed by George H Buchanan Co., Bridgeport, NJ, 2002.
Cover design by Curtis Tow.

A CIP catalog record for this book is available from the British Library.
∞ The paper in this publication meets the requirements of the ANSI Standard Z39.48-1984 (Permanence of Paper).

Library of Congress Cataloging-in-Publication Data
Wubbolding, Robert E.
   Reality therapy for the 21st century / Robert E. Wubbolding.
     p. cm.
   Includes bibliographical references and index.
   ISBN 1-56032-886-X (pbk.)
     1. Reality therapy. I. Title: Reality Therapy for the twenty-first century. II. Title.
RC489.R37 W827 2000
616.89'14—dc21   00-035561
                                                                 CIP

For Sandie, my wife and best friend, who has worked with me through every paragraph and sentence of this book. Together, we spent hundreds of hours pouring over the comments of reviewers and jointly positioned everything from ideas to commas. Many such projects drive a wedge between partners, but it has been the opposite for us. This project, accomplishing exactly what reality therapy should do, has been an occasion for celebrating and increasing our closeness and mutual respect. To my true love I say, "Unto Eternity."

This book, *Reality Therapy for the 21st Century*, contains several sections that are an expansion of the chapter "Reality Therapy" written by William Glasser and Robert E. Wubbolding, which appeared in R. Corsini and D. Wedding, eds., *Current Psychotherapies* (Peacock Publishers, Itasca, IL, 1995). These sections have been updated and significantly expanded and are reprinted with permission from Peacock Publishers.

CONTENTS

continued

ACKNOWLEDGMENTS

A 7-year process of teaching, practicing, and studying reality therapy has culminated in this seminal text. Learning the implications of this system and its underlying theory helped me enhance the difficult skill of listening. I learned from colleagues, instructors, students, and workshop participants from around the world, as well as the rich literature from hundreds of sources. I thank all of you for your many contributions.

Equally important were individuals who reviewed the manuscript and provided help for integrating the ideas and presenting them in a comprehensive and lucid manner.

Linda Harshman, administrator of The William Glasser Institute, continues to play a major role in propelling reality therapy into the 21st century. A colleague and friend, she provided many ideas and continues to support me in every way.

A special thank you is due to Jerry Corey, who has encouraged and inspired me in all my projects. Tom Bratter, always frank and unequivocal, provided specific and useful input. Larry Palmatier's fine-tooth comb never wore out as he assisted me with my phraseology and writing style. I am deeply indebted to him. Bob Cockrum, a close friend, confidant, and reviewer, provided invaluable help in arranging the ideas and constant encouragement throughout the entire project. Brian Lennon's insight, supportive comments, and pointed suggestions helped me clarify many ideas. My sister, Joan Walsh, who with her superb computer skills entered the ideas and prepared them for many revisions, deserves my deep gratitude.

Margie Burns has been like a sister to Sandie and me. Her unflagging loyalty and support for us and for reality therapy is her hallmark. My wife Sandie, to whom this book is dedicated, knows her many valued contributions. My thanks to you is offered daily.

Carleen Glasser's repeated comment, "Who better to write this book than you who have been with Bill for so long and have been a rudder for the Institute," came as a continuous reminder of the need to follow through even when feeling the occasional fatigue and frustration with such a project. A thousand thank yous for the confidence you have placed in me.

The inadequacy of words characterizes my effort to thank Bill Glasser. A friend for decades, he has encouraged me to write this book. He originated the ideas; he is the architect and builder of the house. This book adds a coat of paint. Full credit for founding and developing reality therapy belongs to him. To teach the principles of reality therapy is to teach his ideas. The number of lives enriched by this method is uncountable. This book is my way of thanking him for his support, friendship, and encouragement to answer my calling.

Tim Julet and Jill Osowa of Brunner-Routledge, Taylor and Francis Group, provided highly professional support beyond what I expected. Much gratitude to you.

FOREWORD

Reality therapy will enter the first year of the 21st century with two major books. *Reality Therapy for the 21st Century* is the complete and definitive book on the subject. It contains the most up-to-date material on all aspects of these ideas from their historical beginning to the latest practices. I am deeply grateful to Dr. Wubbolding for writing this seminal book. It is something I could not write but I knew needed writing. The other book, *Reality Therapy in Action*, is mine. It brings together both the practice and the art of the therapy, as I do it and envision it, 35 years after the first *Reality Therapy* was published in 1965.

I feel privileged to have been associated with Bob Wubbolding for almost 30 years. Every creator of ideas needs a colleague and advocate like him to keep the records, integrate the practice, present the research, and add his own creativity in a way that is supportive and still retains a stamp of originality and authenticity. This book speaks for itself. When you read it you will not be able to avoid seeing what I have tried all my life to bring to the world's attention. Reality therapy is far more than a method of counseling. Over the years, with the addition of choice theory, it has become for me and my wife, Carleen, for Bob Wubbolding and countless others, a way of life.

William Glasser, MD,
Founder of reality therapy
and president of
the William Glasser Institute

INTRODUCTION

Does your work cause you stress? Does traffic cause you aggravation? Does inclement weather cause you (or anyone else) anxiety?

If you answered "yes" to any of the above questions, this book is for you. If you counsel anyone or teach anyone or manage anyone who would answer "yes" to these questions, this book is for you. This book will help you deal with people who see the causes of their behavior originating outside themselves. A diligent study of the theory and delivery system presented in this book will help you discover a path leading to more internal happiness, increased peace of mind, and more harmonious human relationships. It requires consistent hard work and there is no absolute guarantee. Though the skills presented in this book are intended to be used in your professional capacity as a leader, counselor, therapist, or manager, they also apply to your personal growth and well being.

Revolutionary since its inception, reality therapy, a method of counseling, psychotherapy, and education, was founded by William Glasser, MD, who developed and practiced it in a mental hospital and a correctional institution. Now used in virtually every kind of institution and in many cultures, it applies to all types of relationships: therapy, teaching, managing, marriage, parenting, family, friendship, and professional consultation among colleagues.

A system of brain functioning called choice theory, which is a major development of a similar theory known as control theory or control system theory, serves as its basis. Choice theory states that human beings are motivated to fulfill the psychological needs of belonging, power or achievement, fun or enjoyment, and freedom or independence as well as one physiological need of survival or self-preservation. Behavior is seen as a choice. And so, neither the external world nor past history needs to determine present behavior. For example, as William Glasser frequently points out, the ringing telephone does not *cause* a person to answer it. Nor does poor parenting *cause* a child to be dysfunctional when he or she attains adulthood. The answering of the phone as well as healthy or unhealthy adult behavior are both fundamentally *caused* by a current unmet need and more proximately by specific wants. Thus we answer the ringing phone because of the need for belonging. An adult chooses functional or dysfunctional behaviors to fulfill a currently unmet need.

Reality therapy is the system that helps people define specific wants related to their generic needs, also known as genetic instructions, evaluate their behaviors, and make concrete plans for fulfilling their needs. For the most part, this counseling method is free of obscure psychological terminology, a characteristic leading to the false belief that, after all, it is just common sense and therefore easy to put into practice. And though the methodology is summarized in an easy-to-remember acronym WDEP (wants, doing, evaluation, and planning), it cannot easily be capsulized because it is far more intricate than it appears (chapter 9). Because the techniques of reality therapy are so numerous, it is practical and useful to therapists, counselors, managers, supervisors, teachers, parents, and others who can select what is relevant at a given moment.

More specifically, this book extends the principles and practices of reality therapy beyond earlier descriptions. I have also provided my interpretation of choice theory, adding a nuance here and there, especially in the degree of precision in the definitions of the five basic needs or genetic instructions.

A significant contribution of this book is the chapter on research, which refutes the charge that little empirical work exists to validate the use of reality therapy. As the research chapter documents, this counseling method has been studied in relation to diverse populations in many contexts: with addicts, offenders, students, handicapped persons, teachers, and parents. Topics for research have included school achievement, discipline, self-esteem, locus of control, teacher education, among many others. The controlled research in multicultural settings extends from Hong Kong to Spain to Australia to Korea, to mention a few.

Even though reality therapy has been validated by research studies and authenticated by the informal testimony of thousands of practitioners, it is unethical to make an absolute guarantee that a specific person or persons will achieve the outcome of a cure. Reality therapy is practical and useable and applicable to virtually any human behavior, but the ultimate choice for outcomes rests with the client, student, or person being helped.

It is important to note that in June of 1996, William Glasser made a dramatic change in the name designation of the theory underlying reality therapy. He changed the name from "control theory" to "choice theory," giving as his main rationale that behavior as a choice had become the centerpiece of the theory. Behavior is seen not as a direct result of early childhood conflicts nor as something thrust upon us from external stimuli, but as originating inside of us. The word "choice" is a fitting word for the theory. "Control theory" serves as the backdrop for choice theory, but it is no longer accurate to designate the theoretical underpinnings of reality therapy by the word "control."

Still, the brain can be seen as a control system analogous to a thermostat, which maneuvers or "controls" its own behavior. The heating and air-conditioning units behave by impacting the external world, i.e., changing the room temperature. Occasionally, I refer to the brain as a "control system" and sometimes as a "choice system." The two phrases refer to the same process—the workings of the brain—with slightly different emphases: impacting the external world or choosing behavior. Control refers to aligning the external world with what we want as well as closing the gap between what we want and what we have. But it does not describe the role of choice in the process. This is Glasser's distinguishing contribution.

When referring to "counseling" and "therapy," I have used the words with studied indifference. For me no difference exists. The real distinction rests on political turf and involves an argument that does not affect the day-to-day use of reality therapy. I ask readers who identify themselves as therapists to read "therapy" throughout the book. If you are a counselor, please read these words in line with your professional responsibilities. If you are a teacher, parent, or manager you can use the same principles in your human relationships. Please read the appropriate term into the examples and into the text as a whole. This book is intended for you.

I have extended the WDEP formulation of reality therapy in many ways. Self-*evalu*ation now includes 22 ways for clients, students, and helpers to examine their own behavior, make noncritical judgments about it, and then make more effective guilt-free plans for improvement.

The multicultural applications represent and demonstrate the fact that choice theory is universal and not culture bound. Everyone has needs or genetic instructions, a quality world collection of specific wants and core beliefs, as well as behaviors designed to fulfill wants and needs. Further, the practice of reality therapy is shown to be useful in the cultures of North America and around the world.

In the chapter on multicultural applications, I have referred to sources other than the typical therapy and educational ones. Hardly a day goes by without some mention of an aspect of a cross-cultural, multicultural, transcultural, or diversity issue in the media. Consequently, I have tried to connect reality therapy with what most people experience in their "real worlds."

Throughout the book, I generally use language that includes both genders avoiding the she/he and he/she forms whenever possible. It is not possible, however, to accurately present a vast amount of information without, at times, using the cumbersome formulations relating to gender.

The central point of this book is that reality therapy is a method inherently designed for the exigencies of the 21st century. The planet today, growing in awareness of cultural differences coupled with instant communication and a desire for both speedy and demonstrable results, is a very different place than that of 1900 or even 1990. Whereas the cold war mentality has dominated our thinking since 1945, the buzzword and mind-set for the 21st century will be "globalization." Thomas Friedman, author of *The Lexus and the Olive Tree* (1999) stated, "We are all one river. If we didn't fully understand that in 1989, when the Berlin Wall came down, we sure understood it a decade later" (p. xiii). *Reality Therapy for the 21st Century* connects reality therapy with an ever-expanding and ever-shrinking world. To meet these changing expectations reality therapy will include elements that exist now in their early stages of development.

1. The full implications of choice theory and globalization will be developed in years to come. Also, the degree of moral, legal, and psychological responsibility will be defined.
2. The importance of relationships as the root of most long-term psychological problems will be emphasized. At the turn of the century there is much evidence that improving relationships can have profoundly positive effects on a person. The social implications of networking and interpersonal influence will be part of real-

ity therapy. In chapter 9 I have presented a significant expansion of the procedures of reality therapy illustrating how their use improves relationships.

3. Reality therapy will be research based. It is insufficient for proponents of any theory and method to function merely as advocates. "Show me the data" will be addressed by a results-centered body of literature. In chapter 12 of this book I have summarized a sampling of research studies. Some are more persuasive than others. Future users of reality therapy will be able to justify their practice with convincing data.

4. Reality therapy will be a developmental model. Effective behaviors and regressive behaviors are described in chapter 5. I have also presented a workable model in chapter 7 for counseling applied to relationships: the "red room," self-esteem skills, quality time, specific communications skills, as well as the "solving circle" described by Glasser in *Choice Theory* (1998a) constitute a flexible series of interventions. Each one is intended to build on the previous one.

5. The cultural adaptations of reality therapy will be more emphasized in the early part of the 21st century. Instructors for The William Glasser Institute teach currently around the world, and many countries now have their own indigenous instructors. The theory and method must be seen in a different light in Asia, in Africa, and in the Middle East than when dealing with the majority group in North America. In a more authoritarian culture it is best taught and practiced differently than in a democratic culture. I have spelled out these variations in an introductory way in chapter 11.

6. Applications will be made to management and supervision. The use of the WDEP formulation in business, industry, government, and agencies as a management tool is in its infancy. As organizations use the tools of quality and performance improvement they also need a coaching and motivational system. Many managers ask, "How do I help the employees become more responsible and buy into the goals of the organization?" There are tools available and they will be used on a more widespread scale in the 21st century.

7. The practice of reality therapy can be used to meet the demands of managed care. I have not written extensively about managed care itself because, while the trend is clear, the details are continually changing. Selecting appropriate self-evaluation questions helps clients learn the process as well as make a commitment to rapid change. This is followed by treatment planning geared to the five needs summarized in chapter 8. The advantage of reality therapy for managed care is that the pathways for plans are clear and they present alternatives to the ineffective and destructive behaviors described in the *Diagnostic and Statistical Manual* (American Psychiatric Association, 1994).

8. Glasser's most recent effort to add to the quality of human relationships is the "choice community project." He alludes to this in chapter 4. Schools improve, crime decreases, and the general well being of people improves when the entire community makes the commitment to learn the ideas and to implement them in their relationships. Corning, New York is at present committed to such implementation and the leaders have set the above goals. In the 21st century choice theory will, more than likely, be adapted by other communities.

9. Reality therapy will be seen as an open system firmly rooted in credible theory. As such, it allows for the use of techniques borrowed from other theories and

methods: disputing ineffective self-talk with consequent cognitive restructuring, visualization, self-affirmations, relaxation techniques, and many others.

10. Total behavior will be seen not only as a means to maneuver the external world for the purpose of need satisfaction but as a way to communicate a message. Thus behavior is both outcome centered and process centered. The twofold teleology of total behavior is explained in chapter 2.

My hope is that reality therapy in the 21st century will be extended and further developed. It will be adapted, validated, and more widely used than in the 20th century. The vanguard of "pioneers" and "hunters" who teach reality therapy will be followed by "settlers" and "developers" who contribute to the building of a more humane society and globalized world.

CHAPTER

Getting Down to Cases:
How Would I Handle Conflicts?

Tom

Tom, 47, father of three teenagers and a middle-level manager for a large company, walks into his office at 8:00 a.m. The day seems to begin as every day has for the past 16½ years. At 8:15 an upper level manager walks into Tom's office and asks him to come immediately to a brief meeting. In the other, more elaborately decorated office sit three high-level executives and one of the company lawyers. Tom is told the company is downsizing and he is one of many middle-level managers who is being "released from the company." Tom experiences a sinking feeling in his stomach, which gets worse as he is told he has 1 hour to clean out his desk with two witnesses to watch. He feels this adds insult to injury as he has been a trusted, dedicated worker for many years and thought of himself as advancing upward in the company.

When he goes home to break the news to the family he begins to cry and then gets angry. The family is supportive of him, but he believes he has let them down, begins to wonder what he did wrong at work, and has deep feelings of inadequacy and personal rejection.

As the weeks go by he feels more and more depressed and spends most of the day watching television. The only energy he seems to demonstrate overtly is criticizing the children and fighting with his wife.

Questions

- Why is he depressed, angry, and upset? What caused him to be depressed?
- How do you think most people would answer the above questions?
- What is missing in his life?
- How would you counsel him?

Keep in mind the answers might not be as simple as they appear.

Lenore

Lenore, 33, mother of three preteens, lives in a housing project in a poor neighborhood. She has an entry-level seasonal job at a retail store. She is periodically on public assistance, but because she desperately wants to be independent and make more money, she has enrolled in GED classes. She explains that her attendance has been sporadic because of the children. Lately she has developed what she labels anxiety attacks: fast heartbeat, perspiring palms, and a generalized sense of impending doom. Insomnia has become a problem because of her worries and her fear of drug dealers in the neighborhood. Someone has suggested she come to the mental health center to talk to one of the workers. But most of the mental health workers are of a race different from hers. She believes this is a barrier and that they will not understand her problems.

Questions

- Why is she fearful, worried, and panicky?
- What other information would you want to know about her?
- If a physician told her she could find nothing wrong with her, what would you say to Lenore?
- What would be some goals for therapy if you had eight sessions to see her?
- How would you deal with her thinking and feelings about racial issues?
- Formulate a tentative treatment plan for her.

Martha

Martha, 24, has worked for a travel agency since graduating from college 3 years ago. Women manage many of the offices in other cities, but the home office has just announced the promotion of a man from another city to manage her office. She believes she has been discriminated against because she is a woman. Feeling resentment because of this perceived affront, she ventilates her anger in front of the other employees who also believe she is qualified to manage. They add that she might be discriminated against because of her age and color. She becomes more infuriated and says that she is going to go to the home office, adding that the meeting will be "an intergalactic star war shoot out at the less than OK Corral."

Questions

- Why is Martha upset?
- How would you describe her behavior?
- What do you think she is telling herself?
- What would you say to her about her behavior in the office and her decision to confront the top people at the home office?
- What would you say to her about her feelings of discrimination?
- What other questions would you ask her about the "intergalactic star war shoot out"?

Tyrone

Tyrone, 13, is a student in his first year at a junior high school. His teachers gave him a "social promotion" last year as they believed it would accomplish nothing to have him repeat the year. He wants to be an actor and has been in *all* the school plays. He tells other students they are stupid for studying because he passed much easier than they did without even studying. "Boring" and "stupid" are his favorite adjectives whenever he talks about school. Tyrone's mother is upset but doesn't know what to do except ground him and revoke his privileges. She says, "He has not seen the outside world after dinner except through the windows for 2 years, and the 'G' for his middle initial stands for 'Grounded.'"

Questions

- Why doesn't Tyrone study?
- How would you counsel him?
- What would you say to the mother? How would you work with the parents if they were together? If they were divorced or not together?
- If you consulted with Tyrone's teachers, what would be your agenda?
- What would be some "dos" and "don'ts" for the teachers?

John and Mary

John and Mary Bickerson come for counseling. Each complains about the other. In summary, each says that if the other person would change, life would be much better. They have one child, 10, who is quiet and generally well behaved, but the subject of many arguments. Other topics for arguments include money, priorities, in-laws, holidays, sex, and the lack of it.

Questions

- Why do they argue?
- In counseling them, where would you start?
- What would you want to talk to them about, other than the ever-present criticizing and arguing?
- Would you let them ventilate their feelings in the office? Why? Why not?

Caroline

Caroline has trouble relating to men. At 35, she wants to marry, but has almost given up on the idea because she is fearful. She says that this is due to continual abuse by several relatives as a child and even into her teenage years. Her guilt feelings remain even now because in her mind she caused the abuse, especially in her teenage years. She attends a support group in which the members relive and describe in detail the abuse they suffered.

Questions

- How would you deal with the abuse issue?
- Would you allow, encourage, or discourage more discussion of the abuse in counseling?

- Would you encourage, discourage, or remain neutral about her attendance at the support group?
- Outline your treatment plan for her.

The above cases and questions are intended to provide a background for the subsequent explanation of choice theory and the method of counseling known as reality therapy. I suggest you revisit these cases while reading this book to see if your answers change in any way.

2

CHAPTER

Choice Theory: What Is It?

The purpose of psychotherapy, according to some, is to gain insight, to see connections, and to come to a higher level of self-awareness. While these goals are not in opposition to reality therapy, they receive less attention in therapist–client discussions. The goal of reality therapy is neither insight about underlying causes of problems nor resolution of unconscious conflicts. Rather, the desired outcome is a change in behavior resulting in need satisfaction and greater happiness. People enter psychotherapy because they feel that something has gone wrong in their lives or that there is need for improvement. The reality therapist believes that when clients are not fulfilling their needs effectively they feel discomfort, anxiety, depression, guilt, fear, and shame. Others act out negatively or develop psychosomatic symptoms. If they are comfortable in tolerating or ignoring their problems but others believe they have problems, they are often coerced into therapy. Often such persons do not want to change, at least in the beginning of the therapy process. And yet, through the skillful use of the procedures of reality therapy, they can see the benefit of evaluating whether change is desirable and possible and whether adjusting to the demands of the "real world" would be appropriate and need-satisfying. If clients decide that change is beneficial to them, they are helped to make better choices designed to maintain or increase their sense of need fulfillment.

☐ Overview

Reality therapy is based on a system of brain functioning that has been known for many years (MacColl, 1946; Powers 1973; Wiener, 1948, 1952). William Glasser (1981, 1985), the founder of reality therapy, has adapted this theory to clinical work and education. He has formulated it in a way that makes it useful to therapists, counselors, teachers, clergy, and others. Called "control theory," it states that the human brain functions like a control system such as a thermostat, which seeks to regulate its own behavior (furnace or air conditioning) with the desired result of changing the world around it. Expanding on the highly theoretical work of Powers (1973), Glasser injects the notion that five internal forces, or needs, motivate human beings. These human needs are innate, not learned; general, not specific; and universal, not limited to any specific race or culture. William Glasser (1998a) frequently refers to them as "genetic instructions." In all their actions, people seek to maintain or add to a need for belonging, power or achievement, fun or enjoyment, freedom or independence, and survival. The result of the effective satisfaction of these needs is a sense of control or what other theories might refer to as self-actualization, self-fulfillment, or a fully functioning person. Because of the additions made by Dr. Glasser, he changed the name of the theory to *choice theory* in 1996 to fit its clinical and educational use and because of its emphasis on human behavior as a choice. These changes are more than mere accessories or appendages. They are described in his book, *Choice Theory* (Glasser, 1998a) and summarized below.

☐ Human Needs

As you read the description of the need system below, you will note a similarity with hierarchy of needs described by Maslow (1970). However, only two needs are identical with those on Maslow's list. Also, in choice theory, needs are not seen as a hierarchy. Rather they are analogous to the legs of a chair, which functions most effectively when the chair is balanced on all its legs.

Survival or Self-Preservation

First and foremost, all biological sensate creatures from primitive life forms to human beings have a need to stay alive and to reproduce. Many behaviors are related to this need, such as the inner functioning of the organism. The working of the autonomic nervous system, as it controls the motor functions of the heart, glands, digestion, and all the internal organs, attempts to maintain life and satisfy the need for survival. Sometimes labeled the "old brain," it keeps our body machinery functioning. It can function as an independent unit warding off invading diseases. Yet, for many of its functions, it requires the help of the cerebral cortex, or "new brain," so called because of its more recent development in the history of humankind. The old brain sends a help-me signal to the new brain when we need water, air, food, warmth, or sex.

The cerebral cortex, or "new brain," houses the psychological needs. It functions for the most part at the level of awareness and regulates our voluntary behaviors as well as some routine behaviors that are less consciously attended to, for example, walking.

Belonging

Survival, like the other needs, is seen as a genetic instruction written into the genes of all living creatures. However, creatures high on the evolutionary scale attempt to congregate and have a need for belonging. Because of this need, they learn to cooperate and function as a unit. Thus the family unit, the school, the workplace, the social club, and the religious organizations are among the settings where people currently attempt to find belonging. Currently, love and belonging are seen with an additional element: the two-way nature of this need. W. Glasser (1998a) states, "Both love and friendship are two way streets" (p. 36). Mothers and fathers love a child without expecting much in return for a long time, but once that child becomes older, parents usually want their love returned. Consequently, one goal of psychotherapy is to help clients fulfill this basic human drive. And in those parts of the world where survival is taken for granted, belonging becomes a prominent area for discussion by clients. Thus the job of the therapist is to help clients love and be loved. This includes teaching them how to reach out to others and how to make themselves attractive so as to get love from each other. An excess in one direction results in a kind of self-absorbed "neediness" and in the other direction, in an insecure do-goodism. No longer are we living in a society consumed with mere survival. Rather, we are seeking to fulfill our identity needs, an effort that differentiates one human being from another (W. Glasser, 1972).

Furthermore, the need for belonging is fulfilled and violated in many ways. We customarily say that part of belonging, or perhaps power, is recognition. Most people want to be acknowledged for their achievements. And though it is generally legitimate to provide such attention, some people don't want to be singled out. They become embarrassed and shamed by recognition. Such a person rarely enters politics as a candidate for public office! Thus, providing recognition can be quite subtle and the praise given to people can have undesirable consequences.

> *Motivation for behavior originates in the here and now*

Moreover, cultural elements can make fulfillment of these needs even more subtle. Sister Josephine, a workshop participant in a Singapore training session, described to me how important the concept of "face" is in Asian cultures. She said that people are often hesitant to take credit for a success. To claim credit or to be given credit could, ironically, cause them to lose face. They would be set apart from the group. Group membership is so important that they would lose face by receiving and especially by claiming credit even if they deserved it. Thus in attempting to help someone fulfill a need for belonging or for power, the reverse could occur.

Nevertheless, in his current teaching William Glasser (1998a, 1998b) emphasizes the importance of focusing on relationships in virtually all counseling. Others have emphasized the significance of relationships also. Adams (1992) states that the importance of relationships is reflected in the numbers of friends and the durability of friendships. Parents of teenagers have an average of 4.7 friends. On the other hand, people beginning their retirement report having 6 special friends. The older the adults are, the less likely they are to terminate friendships and they tend to believe that faded friendships can be revived.

Central to the successful use of reality therapy in counseling, applied to schools, practiced by parents, or adapted to the workplace is the quality of human relationships. As the reader learns the procedures of reality therapy described in this book there is a danger of thinking that successful therapy is the result of merely "technique-ing" one's clients. Nothing could be farther from the intent of this book. The techniques are a *means* for establishing relationships and, paradoxically, they can also be an outgrowth of the relationship. The physician–patient *relationship* is crucial to the effective practice of medicine, but physicians need more than empathy, congruence, and positive regard as medical tools. They require knowledge, skills, and techniques. Still, I am in complete agreement with Corey (2000a) that "techniques are far less important than the quality of the therapeutic relationship that they develop." Also, "the kind of person a therapist is, or the ways of being that he or she models, is the most critical factor affecting the client and promoting change. If practitioners possess wide knowledge, both theoretical and practical, yet lack human qualities of compassion, caring, good faith, honesty, realness, and sensitivity, they are merely technicians . . . [and they] do not make a significant difference in the lives of their clients" (p. 5). The environmental suggestions and the procedures described in this book should be seen in the context of genuine relationships.

The importance of healthy relationships as preventive medicine and as the royal road to effective living is indicated by the finding that when there is a significant disruption in relationships with parents a major depression could result (Stivers, 1998). According to Hammond and Romney (1995), "a number of studies report that family adversity, parental discord, and friendship difficulties all exert direct provoking effects on the risk of depression" (p. 668). Moreover, as many as 1 in 50 school-age children have symptoms of major depression (Lamarine, 1995). Silver, Stein, and Dadds (1996) measured children's adjustment related to dependency, anxiety/depression, and withdrawal. They found that children from two-parent families had the highest level of adjustment, followed by children living with mother alone. The poorest adjustment was seen in children living with mother and an unrelated adult. Also, on scales measuring aggression, noncompliance, rule breaking, and lying the lowest scores were those of children living in two-parent families. In the language of choice theory and reality therapy it is clear that the environment set by a two-parent family where opportunities for healthy relationships are present enables children to make healthier choices.

Healthy relationships are externalized in many ways such as parents modeling appropriate behaviors and providing a materially secure atmosphere for children. Teachman and Paasch (1998) concluded that parents who give their children encouragement about schooling impact their children's desire for education. Both role modeling and providing economic resources have an effect on the attitudes of their children toward education.

It is clear that the need for belonging occupies a central place in human motivation. In other words, a wide range of behaviors springs from the desire of people to connect with each other. Also, the development of healthy human relationships provides the basis for a healthy society. Living together in harmony, the result of satisfying human interaction, will become even more important in our 21st century globalized and multicultural world.

Power

Human beings seek to gain power, achievement, competence, and accomplishment. Exploitation of others and competition can be paths to the fulfillment of this need, but more humane, and therefore more appropriate, ways to satisfy power exist. This need should be seen in a wide context. "Power" is derived from the French word *pouvoir* meaning "to be able." To think that when someone fulfills a need for power, someone else automatically loses power is inaccurate. Satisfying power should be seen as accomplishment or achievement. No power "pie" has ever appeared in the world to somehow imply that power is limited for those seeking more of it. A better approach is to see power as an internal quality. When power increases, no one else's honest efforts are necessarily diminished. Similar to a batting skill in baseball, an increase in one player's average does not lessen another player's average (Wubbolding, 1991a).

Nevertheless, the fulfillment of this "distinctively human need" (W. Glasser, 1998a, p. 37) for power is a major source of conflict in our society. It creates conflict in families, schools, agencies, neighborhoods, and even among nations. In a society in which men have unnecessarily seen their identity as protector, dominator, and even exploiter of women, we now see conflict when women are no longer satisfied with fulfilling their need for power in traditional ways or even in denying their need for power. Thus, another goal of psychotherapy and reality therapy in other areas of life such as education is to assist people to fulfill their need for power without diminishing another's right to do the same.

Another aspect of power is the need to feel inner control of our lives. If our lives are overly regulated from the outside we will frequently rebel through antisocial behavior, apathy, or other negative symptoms described in chapter 5. Joy Smith, a graduate student of mine, told me a story that illustrates the need for power and freedom. One of her employees in a rehabilitation program was a student worker. The young woman was clearly working below her capacity. Because of lateness, sloppy work, and procrastination, the hallmarks of her behavior, she was about to be dismissed from the program. But Joy decided to make one more effort. She wondered if allowing the woman to alter the allotted 30-minute lunch period would be helpful. The young woman chose to have two 15-minute lunch periods in order to eat and then spend a few minutes with her friends. Any change in her work would be easily measured because she did piece-work. The result was that her productivity increased by 60%. She then moved to another site and Joy stated, "I can't find enough to keep her busy." Tom Peters, the management expert, has frequently remarked that workers' productivity increases when they feel even a modicum of control over their lives.

Belonging and Power Applied to Gangs. Because of the importance of these two needs and their conflictual nature, I wish to make a special application to gangs. From 1985 to 1991 the annual rate of murders for males between the ages of 15 and 19 increased 154%. Thus even though gangs have existed since the late 19th century, their increasing destructiveness is evident.

According to Lawson and Lawson (1994), gangs constitute a new family for many lonely and alienated youth. The reasons young people give for their attraction to gangs are given in the left column of Table 1. On the right is a listing of relevant needs as seen in choice theory.

The gang member seeks to fulfill needs, as does anyone. The motivation originates within each person. Still, the environment places many restrictions on a person's ability to fulfill personal needs. Limiting the ability of gang members to achieve inner need satisfaction include socioeconomic status, community norms, cultural and prejudicial barriers, lack of employment and educational opportunities, and protection from other gang members. As always when considering need fulfillment, the environment and systems within which people live should not be underestimated.

Significantly, Lawson and Lawson (1994) suggest that prevention and early inter-

TABLE 1.

Reasons for the attraction of gangs	Relevant needs
Need for affiliation; adolescents joining with people of similar backgrounds	Belonging, involvement, relationships
Gangs offer the possibility of "making it"	Power, achievement
Lack of openness to outside influence	Belonging
Do not turn to parents for help; peers become important	Belonging
Learned helplessness: failure leads to gangs as the only hope	Achievement, power, belonging
Risk-taking behavior; belief that gang members are invincible	Power
Low self-esteem	Power
Lack of positive role models; inability of parents to show them how to achieve the good life	Power, recognition, fame, and belonging
Boredom; few ways to use leisure time productively	Fun, enjoyment

vention efforts should emphasize parent education designed to help parents become more active in the lives of their children as well as helping children discover the choices available to them. Community intervention on a systemic basis where study groups are established in businesses, church groups, community centers, and even in homes can raise the consciousness and skill level of the entire political and social community. Though not in response to a community-wide gang problem, Corning, New York, under the leadership of Mary Hayes-O'Brien, has responded to this challenge by learning choice theory and implementing it in their institutions.

Freedom or Independence

The next psychological need is that for freedom, independence, or autonomy. The need for freedom implies that if we are to function in a fully human manner, we must have the opportunity to choose among various possibilities and to act on our own without unreasonable restraints. We are born with the urge to choose. Many who seek counseling do not see that they can make choices, no matter how dreadful their circumstances. Finding satisfactory options is a primary goal of reality therapy applied to counseling, education, and society in general. As with the other needs, the external world puts natural and circumstantial limits on ways this need can be fulfilled. But no matter how dire the conditions of a person's life, the user of reality therapy and choice theory believes "there is always a choice." William Glasser (1998a) also stated that the need for freedom provides a balance between our ability to choose and the attempt of others to impose their wishes on us.

The need for freedom is in some ways connected to power. Though freedom is connected to choosing, it is not limited to making choices from among various possibilities. Nor is it only a sense of independence. It has many other nuances, some of which overlap with power. The following illustrates the connection between power and freedom.

Several years ago, Gil McDougal was interviewed on *Good Morning America*. It would not be unusual for a former baseball player, a Yankee, from the 1950s to be interviewed on a national TV show, even though he had been rendered deaf as a result of being hit in the head with a line drive in practice many years ago. What made his situation unusual was that, in the fall of 1994, he had an operation in which an implant restored his hearing after more than 30 years of deafness. The surge of power that he must have felt had to have been indescribable. I would imagine that superimposed on this sense of power was a feeling of freedom, and liberation from the burden of deafness. The five core needs overlap, and yet each one has its own variants and nuances.

Fun or Enjoyment

Human beings also have a need for fun or enjoyment. Infants seek to find ways to enjoy a sense of comfort. They later spend a major part of their time having fun. Effective fulfillment of this need results in the opposite of boredom, apathy, and depression. Aristotle defined a human being as a creature that is "risible." It can laugh. The word "fun" as used here does not refer to "silliness." Rather, it refers to enjoyment.

William Glasser (1998a) connects fun with human learning:

> We are the only land-based creatures who play all our lives. And because we learn all our lives, the day we stop playing is the day we stop learning. People who fall in love are learning a lot about each other and they find themselves laughing almost continually. One of the first times infants laugh is when someone plays peek-a-boo with them. I believe they laugh because that game teaches them something very useful. They learn, I am I and you are you. (p. 41)

> *The shortest distance between two people is a laugh*

Thus the developmental task of differentiating oneself from others involves the deep inner need for fun.

Fun is also connected to relationship building. A couple needs to plan to have fun together. And if they have achieved a high degree of intimacy, they have spent time together learning. A therapist, using reality therapy, helps clients have fun together, do enjoyable activities as a couple, laugh at themselves and at the foibles of others. Victor Borge, the comedian, has said that the shortest distance between two people is a laugh. Having fun together is an intimacy-increasing behavior. Couples seeking a more advanced level of intimacy can spend time discussing activities that are mutually need satisfying, especially fun activities. Additionally, educators are well advised to incorporate and enhance fun in the learning process. Maria Montessori once remarked that what is learned through play is there to stay.

We should avoid believing that fun is a superficial, shallow idea and that it does not touch a deeper level of intimacy because it does not involve a more intense level of shared feelings. The opposite is actually true. Fun provides common ground for couples to build upon when the time comes for deeper sharing. Also, the so-called deeper level of sharing does not by itself increase intimacy. If the solid groundwork of quality time, enjoyable activities, and individual need satisfaction are present, less time is needed for affective discussions.

Our lives should include fun or enjoyable activities. Partaking in activities that are not at least tolerable can lead to their abandonment or replacement by harmful compensating behaviors. Many people who find a relationship intolerable, a job unbearable, or their lifestyles totally unacceptable (e.g., feeling coerced to live in prison or even in an undesired place), can depress themselves, act out in a destructive way, or develop psychosomatic aches and pains. Consequently, one of the goals of reality therapy is to help people fulfill the need for fun or enjoyment within reason and without infringing on the rights of others.

I wish to reemphasize that it would be easy to misconstrue the needs, as described in reality therapy, as a hierarchy similar to that described by Maslow (1970). For example, it might appear that survival is more fundamental than the other needs. Indeed, a person must first be alive in order to have a sense of belonging, to have fun, etc. But people often commit suicide when their needs are not fulfilled. Others risk their lives for a loved one, to gain power, to feel an exhilarating sense of freedom, or simply for fun. The reader is invited to think of other specific examples. As stated earlier, the need system in choice theory is analogous to a five-legged chair: survival, belonging, power, freedom, and fun. Just as one leg of the chair might be thicker, so too, one or the other need might be more prominent. But, for the most part, the person who is mentally healthy, whose personality is developing in a sound manner, maintains balance among the needs.

Intraneed Conflict

McNamara (1997) expanded the need system to include intraneed conflict. Not only can one need conflict with another, but one aspect of a need can exist in a state of tension with another aspect of the same need. The need for survival can include the motivation to be safe and the urge toward growth. Belonging embraces both altruistic love and eros or sensuous love. Power includes the dialectic of a static sense of achievement and the drive toward a more dynamic quality: discovery. Freedom *from* means escape, and freedom *to* implies the urge to explore. And finally, fun, he stated rather arbitrarily, includes the conflict between static satisfaction and continuing desire.

These additions to the need schema can be useful for teachers and therapists to explore with students and clients. Yet the true conflict is expressed in what we term *the quality world*, i.e., among the specific wants. I would place the conflict, for instance, between having a feeling of achievement and the urge to continue to maintain a sense of discovery in the quality world. Clearly some astronauts and winners of Nobel Peace prizes bask in their accomplishments rather than pursuing other adventures. This, however, represents a decision to fulfill a specific want. Nevertheless,

McNamara (1997) has provided us with a flash of information that is useful for educational purposes.

☐ The Quality World: Wants

We interact with our environment and find that some parts of the world satisfy our needs, and other parts of the world do not fulfill the four psychological needs. Consequently, we take this information and build inside of our minds a file of wants. These are specific images of people, activities, treasured possessions, events, beliefs, or situations that are need fulfilling. Because they are appealing, they are said to have high quality. The conglomerate of these *wants* is the world in which we would like to live (W. Glasser, 1998a). Hence the phrase *quality world* aptly describes the collection of wants related to the five needs. Each of these quality images or wants is specific. So we can call these *pictures* and can refer to the conglomerate as the *mental picture album* (W. Glasser, 1985). Palmatier (1998) added, "We control ourselves from a mental file or a picture album that shows us, moment to moment, what we need and what we are attempting to match through our senses" (p. 32). More specifically, we have ideas and beliefs about people who fulfill our need for belonging. Some people prefer relationships with quiet, nonassertive partners. Others believe that the ideal partner is an uninhibited extrovert.

Ideas about specific ways to gain power range from maintaining a reasonable weight to maintaining a high level of political office or reigning over a financial empire. Donald Trump's idea of a satisfying life is vastly different from the late Mother Theresa's picture. Specific pictures of freedom are also unique to each person. Satisfying to some persons is the structure of a 9-to-5 job with clear guidelines and routine responsibilities. Such people often feel free of the ambiguities and uncertainties that a lone entrepreneur feels. On the other hand, a daily schedule can be very restrictive for people who view freedom differently. Similarly, perceptions of fun vary from person to person. One person sees sky diving as fun. Another, terrified even by watching it on television, finds a casual walk to be exciting enough or even the epitome of enjoyment. Still another likes to play professional football, while his opposite thinks exercise means filling the bathtub, sitting for a half hour, pulling the plug, and fighting the current as the water rushes out.

In describing the importance as well as the elusiveness of the quality world, W. Glasser (1998a) wrote, "Throughout our lives, we will be in closer contact with this world than with anything else we know. Most of us know what's in it to the minutest detail but very few of us know that it, itself, exists. . . . If we knew it existed and understood the vital role it plays in our lives, we would be able to get along much better with each other than most of us do now" (pp. 46–47).

Thus we incorporate need-satisfying pictures or wants from the world around us. People raised in China usually speak Chinese. People raised in Boston have a different accent from people in New Orleans (or "Nyawrlins"). Many children of physicians choose medical careers. A woman in Batavia, New York told me that her parents took her to art galleries beginning when she was 3 weeks old. By the time she was 5 years old, she loved art, and today she is a dedicated art teacher.

Quality worlds are not only diverse, that is, unique to each person, they are also dynamic. They change as a person grows. The wants of a child change in adolescence and again in adulthood. They also exist as a set of priorities. In fact, much time can be spent in counseling and therapy and in education helping clients and students determine their priorities, that is, what is most desirable and what is less important to them. Many people raised in tumultuous and dysfunctional families where there is much inconsistency encounter difficulties setting priorities and knowing the relative importance of various wants.

Quality world wants can also be in conflict. People often agonize over decisions about whom to marry or not marry, which job to take, where to go for a vacation, or which TV show to select. Furthermore, pictures of what is need satisfying are often linked together. Advertisers try to identify a national hero as a spokesperson for their product. The reason is that they hope the public will insert the product into their quality worlds next to the hero. As soon as any of these public figures falls from grace, companies quickly abandon them as representatives for products.

A person's quality world wants can not only be in conflict with each other, but these pictures can be in conflict with other people's wants. This explains, for example, how one person cheers for one team, and another individual cheers for the other team. Such conflicts provide the substance for relationship therapy, couple counseling, family therapy, and any other form of counseling. These differences in pictures form a basis for political campaigns, diplomacy, international boundary disputes, and even warfare.

The educational implications include the necessity of teachers to exert unrelenting efforts to become part of the students' quality world, with the result that students also insert the content, or course, material taught by their teachers.

In describing the quality world, William Glasser (1998a) stressed that living in the quality world exclusively is not possible. We fulfill our wants in the real world: "No matter how good a reason you have to keep someone in your quality world, if you can't be with him or her the way you want to, you suffer. Romeo and Juliet might have been better off separating for a while until they got older, but their quality worlds did not give them that choice" (p. 48).

Fortunately, pictures or wants contained in the quality world are not only unique, dynamic, and conflictual, they are also removable. The new, shiny, comfortable automobile soon enough becomes an old, drab, rattle trap to be sold or traded. The owner replaces the earlier picture from the quality world. We can even remove people who are seen as important and who are loved intensely. Fifty percent of marriages end in divorce because one or the other partner has altered quality world pictures of the spouse.

Another characteristic of the quality world is that pictures or wants exist in priority; some are more important than others. Often a major task of a therapist is to help clients determine priorities about what they would find need satisfying not merely for the moment but on a more permanent basis. A major developmental task in recovering from addictions, for both the addict and the family members, is to recognize that the fulfillment of some wants is more appropriately delayed. Dealing with the pattern of clinging rigidly to wants is part of the inner self-evaluation, which is a skill that can be refined. "I want what I want when I want it, and I want it now." So goes the motto of many persons choosing addictive substances as they put off learning that some wants might not be immediately achievable.

Though some practitioners of reality therapy disagree, my belief is that some wants show up as blurred in people's brains. A photograph is an image of a specific person, object, or event. The photo can be blurred. So too, people may appear tentative or dogged in certain counterproductive behaviors because their wants are sketchy or foggy. The exact kind of desirable residence, job, or friend can be unclear to someone struggling with an addiction or emotional upset. Counselors of adolescents ask them what they want to do upon graduation, or during the next summer vacation, or even over the weekend. The translation of the answer, "I dunno," may be, "My quality world picture is blurred right now."

Pictures or wants can also be realistically attainable, totally unachievable, or some-where in between. In an earlier book on reality therapy (Wubbolding, 1985a), I wrote, "Frequently adolescent clients have a burning desire to 'get my parents off my back.' A parent sometimes wishes the child would act the way he or she did before becoming a teenager . . . " (p. 29). These unrealistic pictures are not abnormal. The helper assists such people to evaluate their competence to attain the particular want or quality picture at this moment.

In this approach to counseling and therapy, the first goal of the helper is to become part of the client's quality world. If clients see their therapist as part of their quality world, a relationship is formed and change can occur. Still, it is useful to realize that what psychiatrist and Cistercian monk Dom Thomas Verner Moore said of adults is true of all people. "(They) cannot be helped by others unless they want to be, and even then, it is a difficult task" (1943, p. 121). While the goal of connection is similar in other theories, reality therapy practitioners do not stop with good intentions about rapport building. Specific skills are employed which we discuss in chapter 9.

Material Success and the Quality World

The impact of effective need satisfaction cuts across most aspects of life. In 1946 Harold Burson founded what is now the world's largest public relations company. It has of-fices in 35 countries and retains 2,200 employees. In an interview with *Executive Strategies* (1997, p. 3), though not using the language of need satisfaction and the quality world, Burson referred to the primacy of effective behaviors related to the powerful motivators of belonging and power or achievement:

ES: Do you think there is one skill that ensures career success?

Burson: *The No. 1 skill anyone needs is the ability to get along with people. And I'm not just talking about your co-workers. It's equally important that you learn to get along with those under you as well as those above you.*

ES: If you can work well with others, will you rise higher than someone who's just as ca-pable as you but who lacks people skills?

Burson: *You have to have an inborn will to move ahead. You cannot be content to stay where you are. In our business, creativity is very important. The people who do best are never content to rest on their creative laurels. They keep pushing themselves to be better.*

ES: How can you tell if someone has that will to succeed?

Burson: *We can spot a winner after two or three weeks on the job. These are the people who immediately start producing great work. And then they find the next thing to do rather than being told what to do.*

Clearly, if you want to succeed in a highly competitive world, human motivation is important. Also required is a repertoire or internal suitcase of positive, habitual, and goal-centered behaviors aimed at satisfying the inner motivational needs and wants. We achieve success, even in the material arena, not by gaining external rewards or by avoiding punishments, but through the exercise of highly satisfying skills in overcoming a feeling of frustration and obtaining a desired goal at a particular moment.

Culture and the Quality World

When large groups develop similar quality worlds the commonality often takes on the dimension of culture. Such wants are deeply rooted and widespread among people in a particular geographical area or ethnic group. Because thousands of ethnic groups inhabit the planet in extremely diverse geographical areas, many varying sets of quality worlds appear in people's minds. Such diversity can be seen as enriching the country and the world or as having the opposite effect—threatening one's own culture. When we adopt a view that others' diversity contributes to our losses, the result is a sense of quality world superiority, that is, "my quality world is better than your quality world." This attitude, in turn, leads to quality world imperialism or self-righteousness, where one group demeans the wants of another group and attempts to impose a supposedly better set of quality world pictures. You can describe to yourself specific examples of this rigid thinking about cross-cultural differences. Applying reality therapy to cross-cultural work is the main subject of chapter 11.

Out-of-Balance Scales and Behavior

When you perceive that you are getting what you desire from the external world, your immediate want and basic need is satisfied. But when you see a difference between what you desire and the input you receive by way of the perceptual system, you are motivated to generate a choice, a behavior that directly affects the external world. From this perspective, behavior serves a purpose, which is to close the gap between what a person wants and what a person has at a given moment.

Watzlawick (1988) described how W. Ross Ashby, one of the founders of cybernetics, observed that a tightrope walker could maintain balance only by constant random movements with the balancing pole.

We can see this high-wire situation and conclude that quite an opposite explanation is true. The gymnast's movements are not random. Every movement, in fact, has a clear purpose: staying in balance and thus remaining on the tightrope. The behaviors appear to be random to an observer but are in actuality precise and purposeful to the high stepper. The multitude of gross and fine motor skills might be almost automatic, with little thought required. But like driving a car, which requires practiced movements and steering adjustments, or like writing or walking, we can see that the programmed behaviors are not random, but quite purposeful.

Total Behavior

The behavior generated to fulfill quality world wants is always composed of four elements: actions, thinking, feeling, and physiology. Thus, all behaviors are *total behaviors* having four components. In this way, total behavior is teleological or purposeful. The complexity of total behavior is designed to maneuver the external world so that wants and needs are met. We can all benefit from a close look at a profound truth in the age-old vaudeville joke, "Why did the chicken cross the road?" "To get to the other side." The chicken, wanting to be on the other side of the road, generated the total behavior of walking. Accompanying this action step is the self-talk that most of us practice: "I wanted to be on the other side of the road and I have a feeling of immense satisfaction at having dodged the traffic."

Moreover, behavior is "total" because all behaviors are composed of action, thinking, feelings, and physiology. Various theories of psychotherapy emphasize various components of this system. Reality therapy states that they are all important but that we have the most direct control over the action component. The handle of the suitcase of total behavior is attached to the action ingredient. Transporting a suitcase is most dexterously accomplished by lifting the handle. So too, when we make the conscious choice to change our actions the other components follow.

> *Change what we do and we change what we view*

This was most vividly brought home to me on December 15, 1998 when I underwent a colonoscopy, a test determining whether there is cancer or other complications. A full anesthetic is administered and so the procedure is completely painless. Nevertheless I felt completely out of control, that is, my scales were out of balance as I lay on the hospital bed in the endoscopy room waiting for the doctor, who was unavoidably detained. The much-desired good news about the results would come about an hour later. Two nurses sat with me as I watched the sphygmomanometer measure the rise of my systolic blood pressure to 149. I decided to take control of my total behavior and to see if I could bring the level back to its accustomed level of 130 to 135. I embarked on a series of questions about the nurses' careers, how long they had worked in the endoscopy unit, what they liked about their jobs, etc. As I predicted to myself, they began to reciprocate with their own questions. This enabled me to tell them about my practice of teaching reality therapy around the world. As usual, I began to get excited about the topic and grew quite animated when they showed sincere interest. In a few minutes I looked at the blood pressure and it had dropped to 113.

There could hardly be a more vivid demonstration of the fact that when we establish even short-term but satisfying relationships there are measurable physiological behaviors which are congruent with effective, in-control choices.

Perception

To understand perception we first need to know that a perceptual outcome results from blending two elements: levels of perception and the perceived world. The input we desire from the world first enters our brain through our sensory system and then through two special filters by which we recognize the perception (knowledge filter) and then give it a value (valuing filter). The thousands of perceptions that each of us stores in our mind and keeps in our perceived world we call the "all-we-know world." When we compare a desired perception or want with a current perception of what we have, we generate behavior if the two are not aligned. Thus the output and input loop is complete. We apply a behavior to the world around us for the purpose of gaining a specific perceptual input. This loop continues to function as long as we are alive.

☐ Using the Perceptual System

Our perceptual system and its filters that tell us we have an unmet need or have not yet satisfied our picture have practical implications.

Sumiye Kakitani, instructor for The William Glasser Institute Japan, related a story about an incident that happened near a Buddhist temple in Tokyo. She was visiting the shrine with her children and all three were feeding the many pigeons always present in public squares, religious sites, and temples. These persistent birds seemed to be on special assignment. She and other parents observed one pigeon standing on its only leg and eating heartily as it hobbled to and fro around the plaza. Sumiye heard two comments from the parents. One said to her child, "Look at that poor pigeon. Isn't it sad to see such a sight. The poor thing!" A second parent remarked to her child, "Now there is a courageous bird. Look at the way it goes after the food. It keeps up with the other pigeons in spite of its handicap. Is there a lesson here for you and me?"

I invite you to think about these two comments and how they relate to the skillful application of reality therapy. Several discussion questions follow.

Questions

1. What do you think about these two comments? How do these different ways to describe an observation of aviary behavior touch your life?
2. How would you relate the incident to the levels of perception?
3. Evaluate the following statement in light of the incident: "Whether you think you can or whether you think you can't, you're right."

Ken Lyons, of The William Glasser Institute Ireland, told me the following riddle. It illustrates several aspects of the perceptual system. A physician receives an invitation to attend a lawn party. Upon arrival, the host pours her a small drink, whereupon someone immediately tells her she has an emergency at the hospital. She hurriedly downs her drink, and then goes to the hospital for a few hours. She returns to the party later, only to discover all the guests sprawled all over the floor dead. Because of her skillful observation of the bodies, she knows instantly that each person has been poisoned.

Question: Why did she not die?

Answer: The poison was in the ice.

In the above riddle, all the facts were presented or implicit in the narrative. Yet to some, the explanation might not have been evident. We don't always perceive what is truly presented to our senses. We need to perceive connections or relationships in order to have a proper context in mind. Thus I suggest that we consider the possibility of a third level of perception, that of an "understanding filter." In the riddle above, the physician perceived the connection between the dead guests and the unseen poison.

Questions

1. Can you see other applications of the perceptual system to this riddle?
2. Can you think of similar examples where you missed relationships or connections that were "obvious"?
3. How would the principles illustrated in this riddle and its answer relate to cultural differences? Do human behaviors contain meanings that are not immediately evident to someone unskilled in observing them?

Functions of Perception

Perception creates reality. If you have a back injury, you may very well say that a hard surface feels very soothing. For others, the same surface might be uncomfortable or even painful. Some people like summer, while others prefer spring or autumn, and I have even heard that some designate winter as their favorite season. Several years ago a local newsman reported that the owner of the Howdy Car Wash had a sign on the wall, "Pray for Snow." The owner told the reporter, "In the winter there is no substitute for slush. Some see slush, we see gravy."

Perception is the umpire. The arbiter of a baseball game creates the reality. The pitch is only a pitch until the umpire says it is a ball or a strike. Interestingly, whether a player's line drive hit down the foul line is fair or foul depends on the umpire's call, a subjective judgment we know as a perception. The umpire creates the reality even if a videotape later proves him "wrong."

Moreover, our perceptions not only determine external events, they create an inner reality. In fact, these perceptions *are* our inner reality. While conducting a choice theory workshop in Japan, I witnessed a participant, Yoki Nasada, illustrate how perception creates reality. She asked 10 people in the group to close their eyes and extend their hands forward with the palms up. She stated, "In the right hand you have a thick phone book. It is heavy, very heavy. As you hold the book, it seems to get even heavier. Tied to your left hand are five balloons all lighter than air. These balloons are light, so light that they seem to want to float higher and higher into the air." She continued this theme for approximately 2 minutes. Upon opening our eyes, we discovered that the hand with the imaginary phone book had sunken lower than the starting position and the hand with the balloons was noticeably elevated. I personally report that I felt the hand with the phone book get heavier and sink involuntarily as if it had a heavy weight on it. Our brains chose to perceive an experience and our perception created a reality.

In seeking to control our behavior and to shape the world around us to match our inner wants or quality world, we seek to gain perceptions. Human beings want specific perceptions related to each need; a relationship that satisfies belonging, a skill that satisfies power, a joke that satisfies fun, and a type of food that satisfies survival. But we never insert these *real* objects into our brain. Rather, we insert a mental image. We want, for example, a perception that a particular person likes us, a perception that we are good at a sport, a perception that our stomach is full, etc. We can even seek to maintain current perceptions to the degree of blocking out information. Do you really want to know *everything* your teenagers are doing? Do you want to know every last detail about how an autopsy is performed? Is it really useful to see the blood, guts, and gore graphically presented in horror movies? It's been said that the reason drive throughs were invented is so that we don't have to know what happens in restaurant kitchens!

Two Perceptual Filters, and a Third

Images enter our brain through two filters or lenses, the low-level filter and the high-level filter. The low-level filter is that of recognition by which we merely label the world around us. Our mind seems to have a prototype of a chair stamped in it as a perception. The same applies to a person, a car, a dish, or a flower. When we see such an object in our environment we recognize it and give it the appropriate name.

Through the high-level valuing filter we assign a value to the incoming image. According to W. Glasser (1985), we determine a positive, a negative, or a neutral value. Thus, for example, we assign a positive value to a chair that is a family heirloom. On the other hand, a visitor's tour of the state penitentiary might reveal a chair that, for most people, has a very negative value. Furthermore, according to W. Glasser (1985), the chair could receive a neutral value if it falls between the plus of need-fulfillment and the minus of need-violation.

William Glasser (1981) described several ways in which we understand relationships. We perceive shapes, sequences, transitions, detailed programs, principles, and systems as various levels of perception. Later, Glasser (1985), simplified his explanation of perception by retaining only two levels.

To explain cognition and to account for experiences that remain unexplained by two levels of perception, I suggest that a middle level be utilized in order to clarify an element omitted from the low and high levels of perception. This middle-level filter is the understanding filter, used to perceive connections and relationships.

In the understanding filter, more intricate cognition occurs. If the recognition filter is the beginning of cognition, this filter extends cognition. As stated above, by means of the low-level filter, we merely recognize and label objects in the external world. In the middle level of cognition the object is described further. Attributes are more explicitly defined and their interconnectedness understood. Through the middle-level filter, we see connections linking an object and an attribution.

> The chair is large.
> The man is short.
> The woman is tall.
> The car is a compact.

Also, an even more intricate cognition occurs with the use of metaphors. The explanation of choice theory is replete with metaphors: quality world, behavioral car, suitcase of behavior, filters, etc. Intrinsic to the explanation and understanding of choice theory is the use of metaphors. A metaphor is a figure of speech, a comparison, in which one phenomenon is understood in terms of another. Height and depth are used to understand feelings. The word depression means "a lowering or pressing down." Connections or relationships are thus understood.

> "I'm feeling down today."
> "I was up yesterday."
> "I'd like to get high, but I then fall into a deep depression."

Distance is used to describe progress:

"You've come a long way."
"We're right back where we started from."

Another recurrent metaphor, used by Lakoff and Johnson (1985), is that of "war" to explain the concept of argument. Though the following example is overstated, the cognition required to grasp the explanation is clear. "I defended my point, but I had to give ground when my opponent attacked my rationale. Of course, some of my ideas went over my adversary's head. He never did surrender and so I didn't win. Finally, when we reached stalemate, we agreed to an armistice." Now, argument is a building: "I buttressed my argument with facts, and though he tried to knock down my supports my rationale was unshakable because I was on solid ground."

And so the ability to see relationships becomes complicated and in some ways intuitive. Some metaphors do not require a detailed explanation but are instantly figured out because of the person's previous experience. A German friend told me of a proverb about a soldier who threw his gun into a cornfield. This means "to give up." Though I had never heard the analogy, little explanation was necessary because of past perceptions and memories or associations that I stored in my perceived world.

Thus, through the understanding filter we perceive more complicated relationships and we put only a neutral value on various understandings and cognitions.

Another significant function of the understanding filter is our ability to see meaning or purpose. The Greek philosophers and other pioneers of human thought have described nature as "teleological" or "final," meaning that nature has a purpose, aim, or goal. A highly developed understanding filter enables us to see the purpose in the events of our lives and in the world around us. A person trained in a discipline, a science, or an art can see purposes when others overlook them. When I open the hood of my car, I see a maze of belts, hoses, gadgets, and contraptions that make little sense and seem to have no purpose. However, a skilled observer with a repertoire of mechanical behaviors has a corresponding highly developed understanding of the interconnectedness of the parts and the purposes served.

A talented artist may look at an ordinary situation and see the very soul of a person, including the relationships that the ordinary person misses and meanings in events that escape a more superficial observer. Similarly, the skilled physician looks at physical symptoms and can interpret their significance. Such skilled people have a highly developed understanding filter or lens relative to the workings of the human body. *When you see the world through the eyes of choice theory and reality therapy, you see ways to help people more quickly and efficiently.*

Carrying the discussion to another plane regarding the understanding filter, it can safely be said that while the specific meanings or purposes might not be understood, the fact that one can find purpose and meaning is often taken on faith. When I look at the aggregate of parts under the hood of my car, I *believe*, based on some experience and minimal knowledge, that they have purpose and in fact are more than an aggregate of separate parts. They function in unison for a purpose.

When a person turns on a light switch, he or she understands the specific purpose as well as the concept of "purpose." However, a sophisticated knowledge of electricity might be lacking. The skilled electrician, however, sees further implications of the purposeful throwing of the switch and understands many relationships.

☐ Faith and Spirituality

Related to the understanding filter, therefore, is faith, which refers to a belief in things outside oneself and which overlaps with the valuing filter. Faith gives meaning to experiences not easily understood. This could be a belief in a "cause" or it could have a more spiritual aspect. It also relates to the total behavior of believing.

Frankl (1984) described his own faith, which sustained him for 3 years at Auschwitz during World War II. It gave a sense of purpose and meaning that enabled him and others to survive. He even contended that those who survived were not the most athletic people but those who could perceive purpose and meaning in the dreadful experience. Not everyone had such a highly developed understanding filter and thus some were less capable of facing such barbaric circumstances. They often died from giving up more than from physical causes.

More specifically, reality therapy has been applied to spirituality (Carleton, 1994; Linnenberg, 1997; Tabata, 1999; Wubbolding, 1992). The search for love, the desire for accomplishment, the quest of individuals and even of nations to be free and autonomous—these are profoundly spiritual adventures. We are spiritual beings with specifically local experiences. In my view, choice, purpose, and responsibility are indisputably spiritual.

Linking spirituality to family relationships, Mickel and Liddie-Hamilton (1996) stated, "If we are to be effective, we must deal with spirituality as a component of some families' world view" (p. 97).

☐ High-Level Perception: The Valuing Filter

The valuing filter puts a positive or negative value on perceptions. Thus

> The larger chair is uncomfortable.
> The short man is the robber.
> The tall woman is attractive.
> The compact car is economical to operate.

It should be noted that cognition, thinking, and self-talk are used at each level. Also, the filters do not exist as totally separate in their functioning. A useful diagram for understanding the three levels of perception, or the three filters, is seen in Figure 1.

Practical Implications

The discussion of three levels of perception is not mere theory without useful applications. Quite the contrary: We can always draw practical conclusions from this discussion.

1. Many people see the world around them from a high level of perception and put excessively negative values on their perceptions. Even though they often say they are being "realistic," I have labeled it excessive because they are unhappy and often admit that their needs are not being fulfilled. They see everything as a crisis or a threat.
2. Some people see the world around them from the opposite end of the telescope.

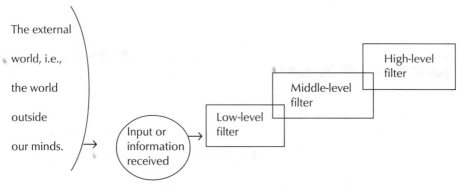

FIGURE 1. Three Perceptual Filters.

They view the world indifferently and passively. The student who flunks all courses and believe that "it doesn't make any difference" perceives his world from a low level of perception. The work of the reality therapist is to help such people raise their level of perception.

3. By means of the *evaluation* component of reality therapy, clients are helped to gain insight into the connection between what they want and what they are doing to get it. They learn to see this very important connection. Also, because of the current emphasis on relationships (W. Glasser, 1998a), this level of perception is even more meaningful.

I once counseled an adolescent who was flunking in school, breaking his curfew, and continually talking back to his mother. He had stated clearly that he wanted to move out of his mother's house and into his father's. I asked him, "Is what you're doing helping you to get what you want? Is it helping you to get the approval you need to move in with your father?" At first there was no sound except the thud of his jaw hitting his chest in amazement. Then he said, "I never thought of it that way." This connection that a counselor so easily made (as it should be!), was suddenly understood by the client. The person made the connection, saw the relationship, and easily formulated plans. His understanding took a quantum leap forward.

4. The use of metaphor can facilitate the counseling processes as well as our own personal growth (Witmer, 1985). Listening for metaphors, analogies, similes, and figures of speech can help the client perceive experiences in a different, more useful way. To see a marriage as having "a case of the flu" helps a married couple to reframe criticism, blame, and finger pointing into a more neutral and therefore more manageable problem.

5. It is helpful to facilitate some insight by using reality therapy. Helping clients reach the understanding that current behavior is ineffective, that a want is unrealistic, that a specific problem or event is not totally harmful or negative can be a very helpful insight.

6. Since faith can be part of the middle-level filter of the perceptual system, clients can be helped to explore how they see their purpose in life and what they believe in. Because the issue of faith links the understanding filter with the valuing filter, faith often relates to what clients see as important or unimportant, meaningful or senseless.

In summary, the three levels of perception and their practical implications serve to put reality therapy in the cognitive school of counseling theories. Much of the effective reality therapist's effort is expended on helping clients, students, and workers change how they view the world around them.

Changing Our Viewpoint

It is difficult to change a perception, a viewpoint, or an opinion directly or merely by fiat. Only through a change in behavior, i.e., acting differently, or thinking differently, do we gain new experience or new information which will result in a changed world view. An illustration of this was the one-hour documentary "Return to Iwo Jima" shown as part of *Our Century* on the Arts and Entertainment cable TV channel on May 27, 1990. The show documented the reunion of Japanese and American troops who had fought there over 40 years ago. In this gripping episode the theme expressed was "my job is done." Some Americans who were interviewed expressed hesitancy at reconciling, but they all agreed that this event was a good idea. One veteran said that he was able to lay to rest the demons haunting him since he fought on Iwo Jima. At the end of the reunion a ceremony was held dedicating a monument commemorating the bravery of men on both sides.

Those men were able to change their perceptions of one another by choosing a new behavior: returning to Iwo Jima, encountering the former enemy, conducting a ceremony that brought them face to face with the past, and thereby confronting the lingering perceptions that had been a need-attacking experience for many years. Discarding these painful perceptions, held in place at great cost, was the result of positive action and choices taken by these former enemies.

The lesson of this World War II postscript for counselors is the importance of replacing a current negative perception by making a new, dramatic behavioral choice. Changing long-standing perceptions is not easy, but it can be done.

Exercises

You are invited to apply the principles of perception and total behavior to the cases below, which illustrate the input–output loop of choice theory and the levels of perception.

- Leslie walks to the kitchen and takes a drink of water. This ordinary event, like more complicated behaviors, can be seen in the context of needs, wants, behaviors, and perception. Leslie has a need for survival, which involves quenching his thirst. This drive prompts Leslie to take action. He compares his present condition of thirst with his want for comfort. Thus his mental scale is out of balance, and through his internal motivation, he chooses a total behavior: walking to the kitchen to get a glass of water. His behavior is described as "total" because, as in all human behaviors, we see four elements: action, such as walking; thinking or the internal self-talk, "I want a drink"; feeling, such as the satisfaction of quenching the thirst; and the physiological behavior of swallowing. Having completed this effective total behavior, his perception of what he has now matches what he wants and he ends up with a condition of balance or homeostasis.
- Lee is an unemployed military veteran who is an alcoholic and who directs anger

toward his wife and children to the extent that he physically abuses them. He also suffers from nightmares about combat and flashbacks to the battlefield. In the context of choice theory, the most obvious elements of his control system are his abusive actions and the entire array of ineffective and harmful "total behaviors." The origin of these behaviors is an attempt to fulfill his seriously unmet power need. He wants his environment to be structured in ways that are unattainable. His wife and children live in ways congruent with their own wants, not his. He rigidly clings to his unattainable wants. In fact, the alcoholic dictum, "I want what I want when I want it and I want it now," is his underlying chronic and pervading negative thought. The primary feelings are irritation, anger, and rage, along with fear and insecurity. Among the ineffective physiological behaviors accompanying this destructive lifestyle are ulcers and high blood pressure. These behaviors are habitually generated because he has chronically out-of-balance scales and has not yet developed more effective behaviors for putting them in balance. His repeated attempts to gain the perception of having power become less and less effective as he increases his effort. Desperately in need of intervention, he could change the direction of his life if he were helped to conduct a searching self-evaluation. Such inner self-evaluation is the core of reality therapy.

Questions

1. In terms of levels of perception, what is the difference between these two cases?
2. Describe the four components of the total behavior of Leslie and Lee.
3. How do you think the total behaviors of Leslie and Lee differ in their effectiveness? What is the purpose of their behaviors?
4. Based on what you know about Lee and about choice theory, how would you counsel him?

Social Implications

Because the theory and practice of reality therapy are based on the conscious behavior, wants, needs, and perceptions of human beings, they are applicable in every setting. People marry and form intimate relationships initially to fulfill their needs, especially those for survival and belonging, at the most personal and intense level. Often, after a while, conflict arises over the need for power. In this age of relative equality between genders, wants and behaviors related to the power need become more evident and pronounced within intimate relationships. In male–female and other relationships, each person is asked to examine his or her own wants, behaviors, and perceptions, to evaluate them, and to make more effective plans. More specifically, they compare their ratings of their need strength (W. Glasser, 1995).

Parenting is also rendered more effective when adults and children learn the futility of coercion and punishment as well as communication skills based on the principles of reality therapy and choice theory. Wubbolding (1984) states, "Families are held together if there is cohesion, that is, a feeling that the members genuinely are interested in each other" (p. 6).

Another application of the principles is to relationships in the world of work (W. Glasser, 1994; W. Glasser & Karrass, 1980). Techniques for measuring the perceptions of need-fulfillment of employees are widely used (Mintz, 1992). Wubbolding

(1996a) has identified specific types of employee behaviors and how the system is applied effectively to enhance the quality of the workplace and the need satisfaction of both the worker and the employer.

Reality therapy and choice theory have been applied to the classroom (C. Glasser, 1990, 1996; W. Glasser, 1968, 1993), to educational reform (Crawford, Bodine, & Hoglund, 1993; Glasser, 1990a; Green, 1994; Palmatier, 1998), to relationships (Ford, 1980, 1983; W. Glasser, 1988, 1995), to alcoholism and drug abuse (T. Bratter, 1974; Carey, Farrell-Jones, & Rowan, 1996; Hallock-Bannigan, 1994; Mickel, 1993, 1996; Wubbolding & Brickell, 1995), to violence (Mickel, 1994), and family mediation (Mickel, 1995) to working with the deaf (Burns, Barth, Stevens, & Burns, 1998), to mood control and cancer (Akahori, 1999), to stress management (Brickell, 1992; Watanabe, 1999), to aging issues (Wubbolding, 1989), to counseling in schools (Fates, 1989; Hammel 1989), and to difficult adolescent behavior (Richardson, in press).

Most recently, William Glasser (1998a) has developed an application to the community at large. He calls it the "choice community project." This is an unparalleled effort to teach the entire community the principles of choice theory. It is in its early stages of development and several communities have shown interest, most notably Corning, New York, where a massive training program is underway (Hayes-O'Brien, 1998a, 1998b).

☐ Summary

Choice theory provides a comprehensive explanation of human behavior. William Glasser has presented a brief but workable overview of this system:

> Choice theory explains that we all are motivated by pleasure which, in practice, means that whether or not we feel pain, we always want to learn how to behave to feel better. In the same sense, we all are motivated to avoid painful situations as soon as we recognize they may be painful. But choice theory also explains in detail that all pleasure and pain is derived from our efforts to satisfy *five basic needs* built into our genes. These needs are the following: *survival, love and belonging, power, freedom,* and *fun.* All behavior that satisfies one or more of these needs is pleasurable. All behavior that attempts, but fails, to satisfy one or more of these needs is painful. (W. Glasser, 1998a, p. 3)
>
> Choice theory also explains that *all we can do from birth to death is behave, that we choose all behavior that attempts to satisfy our needs, and that all behavior should be considered total behavior.* Total because it is always made up of four components: *acting, thinking, feeling,* and the *physiology* that accompanies our actions, thoughts, and feelings. But of these four components, only two, acting and thinking, are *voluntary.* The other two, feelings and physiology, are *involuntary;* they depend on how successful our actions and thoughts are in satisfying our needs.

This theory (choice theory) and method (reality therapy) now comprise a comprehensive system for both understanding human behavior and enhancing relationships. Its universal appeal, its transcultural application, and its 21st-century significance will be evident from the chapters that follow.

Other Systems: How Is Reality Therapy Different?

Central to the understanding of reality therapy is whether it is an effective and efficient method, empirically validated, and teachable to a wide variety of professionals and helpers as well as to the public at large. Many students in the helping professions as well as seasoned therapists and theoreticians also ask how reality therapy differs from other theories and methods. The purpose of this book is to demonstrate the first point—that reality therapy is an effective and efficient method. This chapter contains a summary of how reality therapy differs from other theories.

☐ Rational Emotive Behavioral Therapy

Reality therapy is seen by some as similar to the rational emotive behavioral therapy (REBT) of Albert Ellis (Sewall, 1982). While there are many similarities, there are more significant differences. Reality therapy and REBT share the principle that outside forces do not cause stress, depression, anxiety, or any other disturbance. Ellis is fond of quoting the first century Roman Stoic Epictetus: "Men are disturbed not by things, but by the views they take of them." The theories overlap in their belief that the current life of the client is paramount and endless scrutinizing of every past experience is useless. Reality therapists, however, make explicit and emphasize that the action and thinking parts of total behavior are chosen. And so, just as ineffective, harmful behaviors have been selected to satisfy a specific want related to a need, so too, alternative choices can be made in the future. Reality therapists emphasize choice as a means to more effective living rather than implying that a change in thinking is a prerequisite. Reality therapists see thinking as only one component of the behavioral totality.

Some of the techniques used in REBT, however, are congruent with choice theory: rational imaging, in vivo practice, use of humor, bibliotherapy, cognitive distraction, and others. These are seen as planning techniques in reality therapy and are effective to the degree that these help a person satisfy needs.

Also, these tactics work only if the client has evaluated that such steps are worth taking, are better than previous attempts at a solution, and if the client has evaluated past modes of behaviors as now unwanted and unsatisfying to one or more needs. Reality therapy emphasizes the important client self-evaluation component with its many forms of self-assessment. "Is your current, overall direction helping or hurting you?" "Did your actions yesterday get you where you wanted to be?" "Is what you are telling yourself a help or a hindrance?"

Another major difference is that choice theory, the basis of reality therapy, is not based on Greek philosophy or Eastern philosophy, as REBT claims to be. Choice theory is based on a psychological theory of brain functioning that applies to all human beings over time and across cultures. Along with the practice of reality therapy, it transcends the confines of any particular value system and applies equally to the "indirect" cultures of the Far East, the Middle East, the Southern Hemisphere, and Africa.

Still another significant difference lies in the clear explanation of human motivation that choice theory and reality therapy provide. Human beings never fulfill their innate needs completely. Rather, we are attempting to fulfill these inner drives from moment to moment. REBT is based on the principle that we are human because we can think, and when disturbed we are not thinking rationally. Reality therapy, on the other hand, states that thinking is a behavior generated from within and is accompanied by actions, feelings, and physiology. This "total behavior," of which thinking is only one part, has a clear purpose: to fulfill the five needs; therefore, thinking by itself does not cause actions.

Ellis, on the other hand, repeatedly states that if human beings needed love they would always have it. Since they don't always have it, they clearly don't need it, even though it might be advantageous to be loved and feel belonging. But in choice theory and reality therapy love and belonging as well as the other needs are defined not as "absolutistic musts" (in the language of Ellis), but as motivators or sources of behavior. When we don't have love, we are motivated to get love because we inherently desire it. (The "it" is the specific want related to the needs.)

Moreover, how does a person decide that "rational" thinking is better if it doesn't satisfy a need? The source of behavior, therefore, whether effective or ineffective, rational or irrational, springs from deep inside a human being, and the irrational thinking is a symptom, not the cause, of human problems.

Still, reality therapy logically belongs among the generic cognitive-behavioral systems of therapy. As Palmatier (1996) stated, "One well known cognitive-behavioral therapy is, of course, reality therapy with its balanced emphasis on the way people *think* about their goals and the way they *manage to get* what they want in everyday practice. Thinking and acting are the main levers for making change in this method of counseling" (p. 80).

☐ Behaviorism

Reality therapy, based on choice theory, is quite different from the operant conditioning of Skinner and the classical psychoanalytic approach of Freud. From the perspective of a reality therapist, operant conditioning and, to some extent, the other behavioristic theories, fail to give enough attention to the inner control that clients may have and the choices they may make. These other external control explanations deny the existence of human needs. Bandura (1997) allows for the cognitive processes, especially in his revised expression of "goal theory." He stated, "Motivation based on personal standards involves a process of cognitive comparison of perceived performance to an adopted personal standard. By making self-satisfaction conditional on matching the standard, people give direction to their actions and create self-incentives to persist in their efforts until their performances match their goals" (p. 128). The effectiveness of the treatment techniques of systematic desensitization and flooding can be used by reality therapists, because clients may thereby gain a sense of control over a symptom and then let it go. Thus they discover that surrendering a symptom becomes more need-satisfying than working hard to retain it.

The cognitive behaviorism of Meichenbaum and others is similar to reality therapy in that it embraces both thinking and actions as important components of change. Yet change in any component of the behavioral system, from the perspective of reality therapy, requires an honest and searching self-inventory or self-evaluation that one's current way of living is not helping. Thus, those consulting a reality therapist are helped to genuinely restructure their thinking by changing their judgment about some aspect of their lives, especially the way they interact with others. In the end, any change they choose to make in their routines is for the purpose of satisfying a specific want and a general need.

☐ Psychoanalytic Theory

Reality therapy is a radical alternative to many of the basic assumptions of psychoanalysis and the psychoanalytic method. Because reality therapists see behavior as a person's best attempt to fulfill current human needs, this counseling method rejects the notions of internal compulsions and repression that come from psychoanalytic theory. Reality therapists, therefore, do not accept what they see as a reactive mindset that attributes disturbances to outside forces, as in behaviorism, or to past events, as in psychoanalytic theory. In reality therapy, anxiety, phobias, and even psychoses are the result of unmet needs and wants. Many people from the same family and from the same environment choose opposite behaviors. One is a picture of mental health. The other spends a lifetime on the back ward of a mental hospital. In reality therapy, attributing these behaviors to the unconscious or to past experiences is simplistic. Even though some limited discussion of past experiences is acceptable, the reality therapist encourages clients to discuss what they can control: their current actions, thinking, and feelings, but especially their actions.

Just because all current behaviors are choices, it does not follow that another choice is readily available to the client. Quite the contrary is true. Clients raised in a dysfunctional family, for example, often incorporate what they see in the environment. Such incorporation might be their only choice available at the time, and so this decision is their best attempt to fulfill wants and needs. A therapist's role is to help clients develop more satisfying choices. If they could easily choose alternative behaviors, they would not need a therapist.

The reality therapist is aware of how he or she feels about the client, but the importance of transference and countertransference is considered minimal. The reality therapist accepts the clients' perceptions at face value and does not search for hidden meanings in their comments. Clients always try to satisfy their needs, and in therapy sessions they often meet their need for belonging by feeling close to the therapist. Similarly, if reality therapists function as persons whose wants and needs are being met, they can handle their own attractions and dislikes for clients. Their own self-evaluation facilitates their healthy, ethical behaviors toward clients. As in any theory, whenever feelings run high, the counselors would seek consultation with an objective and experienced professional.

Unlike the conventional analytic approach, the reality therapist deals with what the patient or client presents rather than with unconscious processes. Dreams are behaviors designed to get the mental scales in balance. Choice and actions are discussed, whereas free association and slips of the tongue, though interesting, are of little value in assisting with conscious self-assessment and action planning aimed at effective need-fulfillment and more effective relationships.

Contrary to what has occasionally been stated about reality therapy, persons using reality therapy accurately in any setting such as counseling or education are not moralistic or dogmatic. They are not upholders of the standards of a sectarian or political group or system. The reality therapist helps clients recognize that each of us has personal standards, as does society at large. These standards are considered when clients judge the effectiveness of their behavior to satisfy their needs. If they choose behaviors that differ from any of these standards, the reality therapist helps them become aware that they risk serious problems when they attempt behavior contrary to their own or society's values. Consequently, reality therapy can be used by clergy, pastoral counselors, believers, agnostics, or atheists.

☐ Adlerian Therapy

It has been said that reality therapy has its roots in Adlerian therapy. Indeed, Glasser has acknowledged some similarities between the two theories (Evans, 1982) and there have been some attempts to link the two theories (Whitehouse, 1984). There are many areas of agreement and, conversely, many ways in which the two theories differ. Mosak (1989) stated that Adlerian therapy changes the question, "How do heredity and environment shape the individual?" to "How does the individual use heredity and environment?" (p. 77). Reality therapy is in complete agreement with this latter form of the question and extends it to "How can the individual make better choices to fulfill the five needs without infringing on the rights of others who also seek to fulfill their wants and needs?" Encouragement, paradoxical intention, role reversal, establishment of goals, and the resolution of conflict (Dinkmeyer & Dinkmeyer, 1991) emphasized in Adlerian theory and practice are congruent with choice theory and the WDEP (wants, doing, evaluation, and planning) system of reality therapy. Paradoxical techniques, used in many theories, enjoy an especially prominent place in reality therapy. Adlerians study the family constellation and how the child interacts from early on, but birth order is not important to the reality therapist. The current wants, perceptions, and behaviors of the client vis-à-vis the other family members are of paramount importance irrespective of how they were developed in the past. Reality therapy focuses on current relationships.

The reality therapist helps the client search out the ways in which he or she fulfills the five human needs, one of which is power. It appears that the Adlerian view of a person seeking significance is similar. Even in childhood, we seek to excel, to gain

> *The more you do what you're doing the more you'll get what you got*

recognition, and to be competent. These efforts fulfill the need for power or achievement as seen in reality therapy.

The process of therapy also differs for reality therapists and Adlerians. Reality therapists see dreams as behaviors, but these are of little use in that they are not directly controllable. The insight clients gain in reality therapy is not that there is some underlying dynamic to their behavior, but the more profound and far-reaching discernment that "I am responsible for my behaviors"; "I can change myself, but I cannot change other people"; and "My current behavior is or is not effective in helping me get to my goal," to name only three possibilities.

Accentuating the positive is central to reality therapy in view of the fact that it is impossible to build a more effective series of choices upon something that is absent. Thus, if a person will commit only 10% of his or her energy to change, the user of reality therapy can choose to ask, "What would you be doing tonight that would be within that 10%?" In reality therapy, the 10% is seen as having more useful potential for change than the 90% that is absent. Role playing, behavior rehearsal, and Adler's idea of "acting as if" can be used in this context.

Adlerians accept that insight is useful if not necessary, and reality therapists minimize its importance. If insight occurs, it is often the result of changing one's actions; therefore, insight often follows change in behavior.

☐ Person-Centered Theory

On a superficial level, reality therapy appears to be at odds with person-centered therapy. One emphasizes action and questions and is a therapist-led approach. The other stresses feelings, reflective listening, and a client-initiated agenda. The style of a reality therapist is directive in that the therapist takes the lead and actively encourages specific changes. Though it is not heavy handed or coercive, it is markedly different from the style of a person-centered therapist. The latter follows the lead of the clients and is more inclined to wait for them to decide to change. While therapy sessions conducted by a reality therapist sound much different from those conducted by a person-centered therapist, on a more profound level, the theories share a common bedrock. Among the common principles are the following:

1. Human nature is seen from an optimistic point of view. People are essentially good and aim for what they believe elevates them.
2. People are responsible for their behavior. They choose behavior and are not coerced by past experience or external stimuli from their environment.
3. Behavior has a purpose. Choices are made to accomplish a goal. For person-centered therapists, the goal is self-actualization. Reality therapists aim to assist clients in achieving more effective control or need-fulfillment.
4. Effective therapy is based on trust and the therapist must be healthy as well as

authentic. Therapists have an overall basic trust for people and yet can allow for this trust to be verified; therapists have clients' best interests at heart and work toward achieving an inner wholeness and enhanced mental health (effective need-fulfillment).

5. Human relationships are at the heart of both theories as well as at the center of effective living.

In general, reality therapy is most similar to systems of therapy that see human beings as inner and currently directed. By contrast, it does not ignore the influence of parents, past experience, and the environment, all of which can play a facilitative or restrictive role in the life of the client.

The core of the practice of reality therapy is the ability of the therapist to connect with clients and help them evaluate the attainability of their wants and both the appropriateness and effectiveness of their behavior. Unlike many theories, this system, as well as the underlying theory of brain functioning, choice theory, is expressed in terminology that requires little elucidation. A glossary of obscure technical terms would be a short list.

CHAPTER

History: What Are the Origins?

This chapter contains an overview of the development of choice theory and reality therapy and The William Glasser Institute. The first part presents a dispassionate account of how the ideas and the organization have developed. The second part of the chapter is a verbatim interview that I conducted with William Glasser in which I introduce the reader to the man himself by describing in print his conversational and engaging tone as he recounts his own development, struggles, and history. In the third part of the chapter I chronicle my own involvement with reality therapy, which formally began in 1972. I have included this portrait to answer a question frequently asked in my training sessions throughout the world, "When and how did you get involved with reality therapy, choice theory, and William Glasser?"

☐ Who Were the Forerunners?

William Glasser (1965) created reality therapy out of his experience with clients. Almost all of his early training, however, was in conventional psychoanalysis. As reality therapy concepts began to cross his mind, he rejected much of his formal training and observed that many of his instructors did not practice what they taught. As they interacted with patients, success did not seem to fit with the theories that they professed. It was more reality centered.

One of his few nonanalytical teachers, G. L. Harrington, encouraged Glasser to implement his ideas and to discuss them. Harrington became his mentor and helped him to formalize reality therapy in the early 1960s. Harrington was influenced by Helmuth Kaiser, a psychoanalyst who had worked in the 1950s at the Menninger Clinic, and who, himself, had begun to turn away from conventional analysis. Kaiser, too, had a direct effect upon Glasser. He provided psychiatric therapy for his own clients out of Glasser's Los Angeles office for one year.

The roots of reality therapy are seen in the words of Kaiser (1955): "It is the analyst's task to make the patient feel responsible for his own words and his own actions. . . . If making the patient feel responsible for his own words is equal to curing the patient, then one must be able to read the equation in reverse, anything that increases the patient's feeling of responsibility for his own words must tend to cure him" (p. 4).

☐ How Did It Start?

Reality therapy began when Glasser became dissatisfied with psychoanalytic psychiatry as taught at the Veterans Administration Brentwood Hospital and at the University of California at Los Angeles. The endless ruminations about patients' problems being "caused" by the family or by a "harsh" world resulted, he believed, in the perception of victimhood and helplessness. The analyst was supposed to have the skills to help the patient access the unconscious motivations and, if this occurred appropriately, transference would free the patient from the internal restraining forces. Such discussions were interesting but Glasser did not believe they accomplished anything. Patients gained many insights and transferences were worked through, but little progress was made and patients often did not make better choices.

On his own, Glasser began to emphasize present behavior and helped patients realize that they were responsible for what they did and that they had to change themselves. They could not count on others to change, and insight, by itself, could accomplish very little. For example, one woman had been attending the clinic for 3 years and had spent most of that time blaming her nervousness and depression on her deceased grandfather. When Glasser began to see her, the therapy took a new direction. He told her that he would see her only on the condition that she could never again mention her grandfather in therapy. She was shocked and responded, "If I don't talk about my grandfather, what will I talk about?" Glasser told her to talk about what she was doing now to solve her problems, that her grandfather was dead and no longer had anything to do with her life. In a few short months, even with this early crude version of reality therapy, she stopped depress-ing and anxiety-ing (choice theory behavior terms) and started doing many things to fulfill her needs. She had taken control of her life. For 3 years traditional therapy had deprived her of the chance to help herself.

O'Donnell (1987) described how Glasser timidly explained his unorthodox move to his residency consultant, Harrington. Instead of being reprimanded as he feared, Harrington shook his hand and said, "Join the club." This started a 7-year relationship during which Harrington continued to consult with Glasser and helped him formulate the ideas that became reality therapy. Harrington had been working along these lines for many years, but he had not published or promoted his ideas even though he did teach them to those who showed interest.

Donald O'Donnell, school administrator (personal communication, 1999), whom I frequently refer to as "present at the creation" because of his very early association with Glasser, provided a site for Glasser to develop his early ideas about schools: Pershing Elementary School near Sacramento, California in 1963 and later in Ventura Elementary School in Palo Alto, California. I asked Donald, "What was Glasser like in those days?" He said, "He was always open to trying things. He did not feel he had all the answers and he was very easy to work with. He became a very good friend."

Al Katz, another original associate of Glasser, became acquainted with reality therapy in 1967 and quickly experienced "fire in the belly" research. After taking a class at the

Ferkauf Graduate School of Yeshiva University, he used the principles with one student who made a 180-degree turnaround and became a model student. The student wrote his own clinical report saying that he was able to alter his own behavior because of his agreement with Mr. Katz. In spite of such success, the administrators of the child guidance clinic disallowed the practice of reality therapy because it was too radical (Katz, personal communications, 1999). This book is a testimony to the vast changes that have taken place in the worlds of mental health and education since that time.

> *The only thing*
>
> *new is*
>
> *the history*
>
> *you don't know*
>
> –Harry Truman

In 1965 Glasser became consultant to the Ventura School (which had no connection to the elementary school mentioned earlier), a California Youth Authority institution for delinquent girls. There he also found that the young women had all been told that they were emotionally disturbed and were not responsible for their law-breaking. The people who ran the school were upset at this irresponsible viewpoint and supported Glasser in his attempt to introduce the beginnings of reality therapy into this and other Youth Authority institutions.

As interest in this approach grew, Glasser was invited to speak at the 1962 meeting of the National Association of Youth Training Schools. There he presented the new ideas that he called *reality psychiatry*. The response was phenomenal. Evidently many people in the field of treating emotionally disturbed adolescents doubted the effectiveness of any therapy that did not ask people to accept responsibility for what they chose to do with their lives. Several months later, while presenting these ideas to the British Columbia Correctional Association, he changed the name of the approach to *reality therapy* and this name has been used since. From this start reality therapy has grown to the point where it is now accepted as a major therapeutic approach.

At the 1990 international convention of the Institute for Reality Therapy, the silver jubilee anniversary of the publication *Reality Therapy* (W. Glasser, 1965), Bea Dolan, the superintendent of the Ventura School from 1961 to 1976, though too ill to attend, sent a message epitomizing the beginning of reality therapy. "We, at Ventura, started every treatment program the department had; citizens advisory groups, ward advisory committees, small- and large-group counseling, off-campus services, etc. And what did we get? Each other! A reward beyond compare."

☐ What Is Its Current Status?

At present reality therapy is recognized as a widely used therapeutic modality and educational medium. According to an unpublished document of the Department of Defense used at a 1981 conference on drug abuse in the armed forces, as of 1981, over 90% of the more than 200 armed forces clinics which treated drug and alcohol abuse were using reality therapy as their preferred therapeutic approach. As of 1997 reality therapy constituted a major part of the instruction for the Naval Corrections Academy at Lackland Air Force Base in San Antonio, Texas. More recently, survey results showed that in the state of Arkansas, 90% of substance abuse programs using group therapy followed a reality therapy model. Individual alcohol and drug abuse counselors ranked only the 12-step model higher than reality therapy (Whisnant, Hammond, & Tilmon, 1999).

The Institute for Reality Therapy, now called The William Glasser Institute, founded in 1968, promotes the teaching of reality therapy applied to psychotherapy, counseling, schools, agencies, and management. In 1975, it held its first certification week or test-out session for certifying persons in the practice of reality therapy. I was privileged to attend this session with approximately 30 other participants.

The reason for the change in the name of the Institute in 1996 from the Institute for Control Theory, Reality Therapy and Lead Management to The William Glasser Institute was to reflect more accurately the changing mission and work of the Institute, which is to promote the ideas of William Glasser and reality therapy. Formerly, persons attending the training programs were therapists and counselors, but there has been a growing trend to train teachers, supervisors and managers in both choice theory and reality therapy. The teachings of William Glasser occupy a central place in the certification process. And because of the vast numbers of teachers and therapists, as well as the increasing numbers of professionals who work with "involuntary" clients, it was felt that this new name reflects the de facto work of the Institute: to apply the principles originated by William Glasser to as wide an audience as possible.

The title "Reality Therapy Certified" (RTC) is given to persons completing an 18-month training program. This program consists of attending a 1-week course conducted by a qualified Basic Week instructor. In this workshop, choice theory and reality therapy are introduced and taught through lectures, demonstrations by the leader, small-group practice with feedback provided by the leader, viewing and critiquing video tapes, and other experiences. During this time participants discuss their practice sessions in the context of choice theory and reality therapy (Wubbolding & Glasser, 1992). If the candidates wish to pursue certification, they undergo a 6-month practicum with a qualified Institute supervisor in which they practice and study the ideas further. When they reach a predetermined level of competence, their supervisor recommends them for the Advanced Week. During this experience, they are expected to understand and practice the ideas in greater depth with the help of an Advanced Week instructor. Then, another practicum period is completed before Certification Week. During this third week, participants are expected to demonstrate skills and knowledge to an instructor who did not instruct them previously.

The William Glasser Institute in Chatsworth, California (near Los Angeles) administers this certification process, and in 1988, Dr. Glasser asked me to become the first director of training for the Institute. In this capacity, I continue to monitor the certification process and the faculty training programs.

Much of the work of practitioners of reality therapy extends beyond the world of psychotherapy. In 1968, Glasser wrote *Schools Without Failure*, in which he asserted that when children are unable to control their world successfully, that is, to succeed in school, it hurts so much that they often stop trying to learn. While Glasser was not aware of choice theory when he wrote the book, the accuracy of his educational approach has been confirmed by the theory. The purpose of a school without failure is to help children gain adequate control over their learning, something most cannot do if they fail in school. For many years it has become almost impossible to satisfy our needs without, at minimum, a high school education, and in a globalized society this trend will hardly be reversed. When students fail, they give up on learning and school and they turn to disruption, drugs, or many other negative symptoms in an attempt to gain a sense of satisfaction, however transient (Glasser, 1986). Small (1977) showed that school failure, more than a poor home environment, is the cause of young people entering prison.

In 1994, the Institute name was changed on an interim basis to The Institute for Control Theory, Reality Therapy & Quality Management, and its instructors were asked to teach Dr. Glasser's *The Quality School* (1990c) to schools in the United States and elsewhere. In this ground-breaking work, he has applied the work of W. Edwards Deming (1986) to education. The major problem underlying the educational system is not the disruption of the students, poorly paid teachers, unused computers, lack of community involvement, or dozens of other problems. Rather, these weaknesses are symptomatic of the simple but overlooked fact that we have settled on mediocre work, behavior, and effort on the part of students. If the nation is at risk, the main problem is a lack of quality education. Glasser (1990c, 1993) believes that choice theory and reality therapy, if taught properly, can enhance the quality of students' performance in schools. In a quality school, everyone receives training to use the principles of Deming and Glasser. For instance, all professionals learn what quality is and also to evaluate their own work, determining what is quality effort for them. A major goal is to make letter grades unnecessary and to make coercion and boss management gradually vanish in favor of lead management. In the Apollo School, Simi, California, where the above ideas were pilot tested, one student, named Jeremy, stated, "I have learned good enough is not good enough" (Glasser, 1991).

In the quality school consortium, nearly 262 schools have committed themselves to the process of becoming quality schools. In each of these schools, self-evaluation by the students is a major instrument for enhancing curriculum, instruction, counseling, and administration.

Still, reality therapy remains the counseling, therapy, and managing tool that it was from the very beginning. It is now taught in many countries besides the United States and Canada, and the Institute is developing firm roots in Croatia, Slovenia, Japan, Korea, Ireland, Norway, Israel, the United Kingdom, Germany, Spain, Columbia, Russia, Kuwait, Australia, New Zealand, Hong Kong, Singapore, and Italy.

Glasser began teaching choice theory to the general public in 1982 and since the publication of *Stations of the Mind* (1981) and *Control Theory* (1985), thousands of persons have learned about this model as well as the ongoing developments of the delivery system, reality therapy. Moreover, he has reconceptualized the essentials of reality therapy under two general categories: environment and procedures (Glasser, 1990a). Wubbolding (1996b, 1999b) has extended these ideas by describing them as a cycle of therapy and the WDEP (wants, doing, evaluation, and planning) system. This acronym is a useful pedagogical tool for summarizing the concepts that form the main part of this book. The WDEP summary describes a system with each letter standing not for one idea, but a cluster of ideas and skills. This cluster does not represent a series of rote steps and should not be seen as a simplistic cookbook. The system represents a teaching tool, which helps the learner remember the overall methodology. In her resource materials for classroom use, Carleen Glasser (1990, 1996) suggests that the formulation be simplified for primary school students. She has changed the E, for evaluation, to H, because the concept of evaluation is too abstract for primary

school students. H indicates help or hurt, a more concrete way to express self-evaluation. Cockrum (1989) states, "William Glasser has never been content to allow his
theories to be taught or used without constant scrutiny, addition and sometimes even
major changes" (p. 15).

Central to the effective practice of reality therapy is the core philosophical belief
that most long-standing psychological problems are rooted in human relationships.
Even if the presenting problem is not explicitly an interpersonal one, the therapist
can focus on how clients have become disconnected from people around them and
how they can enhance their relationships. Educators, too, can focus on their own
relationship with students, the peer relationships among students, and their professional connections within the school building and even within the district (Chance, E.
& Chance, P., 1989). This process constitutes a major component of the journey to
quality for an institution.

Consequently, the WDEP system is not a recipe to be blindly applied. Rather, it is a
method for building relationships with clients and for helping them relate better to
their individual worlds. It serves also as a tool for organizational development when
agencies, businesses, and schools ask themselves what they want to achieve, examine
the effectiveness of their current organizational behaviors, and formulate specific strategies and tactics for implementation.

In 1981 *The International Journal of Reality Therapy* was launched and has been ed-
ited by Dr. Lawrence Litwack of Northeastern University in Boston. Since that time,
hundreds of essays, articles, and research studies have been published on the multitude of applications of reality therapy including Franklin's (1993) bibliography, "Eighty-
Two Reality Therapy Doctoral Dissertations Written Between 1970 and 1990."

Nearly 6,000 people have completed the certification process worldwide and the
numbers increase each year. Reality therapy has enjoyed a slow but steady increase in
acceptance as a viable and respected psychotherapy theory and educational system.
It is frequently misunderstood and sometimes ignored in the professional world, but
when understood and used in its entirety, it is useful in the counseling office, the
school, the therapy clinic, the plant, the manager's office, and the home.

☐ Interview With William Glasser

Below is a verbatim interview that I conducted with Dr. William (Bill) Glasser. A summary of the history of reality therapy has already been provided, but the interview is
included in its entirety so that the reader might gain a sense of the man's personality,
style, and background as told in his own words.

Bob: *It's nice to be here with you Bill, and I have a couple of questions. Many people over
55 are looking forward to retirement. Some individuals with a legacy more modest than
yours have taken up the fishing pole at this stage of their lives. Yet you are constantly reig-
niting yourself and taking on a new project. My question to you is, how would you describe
what really motivates you? Leaving the five needs aside, what do you do that reignites yourself?*

Bill: *Well, I basically retired when I was around 35 or 40 years of age because to me retirement is having no pressure to do anything but what you want to do. When I began to get
involved in reality therapy I said, "This is what I want to do for the rest of my life." I've*

expanded the ideas and clarified them, but I want to teach them to as many people as possible and therefore I'm going to keep teaching them until I can no longer physically go about my business. And I do it because I enjoy it so much. I just finished a seminar which I conducted here with you in Cincinnati for a couple of hundred people demonstrating and explaining my new book Choice Theory. *It was a tremendously enjoyable experience. And so I'm not going to quit doing what I enjoy, and certainly there's none of the so-called occupations of the retired that have any interest to me. When I'm home I write and when I travel I teach and lecture. That's what I want to do. I'll always write and I'll always teach and lecture.*

Bob: *Just carrying these questions a little bit further, what is it about teaching and lecturing that you like?*

Bill: *I believe the audiences are very very interested in what I have to say and they ask questions and they show kindness to me. My power need is satisfied when people listen to what I have to say. And I have found large groups of people and individuals who hear what I have to say, and it feels very good. I'm not going to give up that good feeling and I can't think of anything that I know that could even begin to replace it. After I'm home for sometimes 5 or 6 weeks around Christmas and I haven't really been doing much teaching, I start to miss it and I am very happy to get back to doing what I like to do.*

Bob: *You don't seem to fit the stages of development—when people get about 55 they sort of level off and watch TV.*

Bill: *Fifty-five, as you know, is 18 years ago going on 19 years ago . . .* [laughs]

Bob: [Laughing] *Well if you don't tell people they won't know.*

Bill: *I was just beginning to be involved with what I called in those days control theory and that's certainly taken up my time. Now that I have changed it to choice theory, expanded it, and clarified it, I really want to start teaching it even more. So I don't look at the clock or the calendar. I do what I want to do but not to the extent of hurting anyone. I'm married to a woman who wants to do it with me and that's what we're going to do for the next 20 years anyway.*

Bob: *The people who will listen to these tapes are going to be saying that we hope you will be doing this for the next 30 years.* [This interview will also be available as an audiotape recording.]

Bill: *Well 30's a little extreme but maybe 20.* [laughs].

Bob: *Let's talk a little about your early professional life. In fact, let's even go back before that. You were born and raised in Cleveland. Tell us a little about the atmosphere; talk about family atmosphere, classroom atmosphere, community atmosphere. What was the climate like in your family and in your community? I think these are the kinds of things people want to know about.*

Bill: *I grew up during the depression in a neighborhood with a lot of families on the street. Nobody worked, but in my neighborhood nobody was starving either. Even though in my school we did take up a collection around Thanksgiving and Christmas for the poor. We collected canned goods and other things. There were poor people, hungry people attending that school. And my family, my father actually, had a business. We weren't rich, but we never really suffered from anything that I can think of. We didn't live luxuriously. My father wasn't educated at all. He didn't have any education in the United States except a few courses at Cooper Union in New York when he was just a very young boy. He went to work at 13. And he quit at 56 when he retired. He worked 43 years and that was enough for him. He didn't enjoy what he was doing very much, and so he was looking forward to retirement. My* *mother was educated. She finished high school and graduated, my guess is around 1912. And the young women, unless they came from families more affluent than hers, rarely graduated from high school. I think she was the only high school graduate in both families. My father came from 8 children, and my mother came from 8 children. I think she was the only high school graduate. But from what she said she got quite an education in that high school. She was always a reader and took me to museums, parks, and other places to look at things and talk about them. My mother had a lot of flaws, but in terms of intellectual interests she never really lost it. So, she encouraged me to read. We all read, my brother and my sister and I read. My father read the newspaper, my mother read books. But we didn't have any lofty intellectual achievements. There was no university influence or anything like that.*

Bob: *You saw people reading and that must have influenced you to read.*

Bill: *I liked to read. My first-grade teacher taught me to read. I mean I just was so happy. And I had the library fairly accessible and I literally read my way through the library. I read the encyclopedia, I read everything in sight. Even today I'm still a great reader. I read, read, read, read all the time.*

Bob: *Your father came from Russia? Was he actually born there?*

Bill: *Yes, he came to this country in 1905. He was born in 1892. And he came from a very, very wealthy family in Russia, wealth beyond my dreams. As soon as a child was born they would have a servant that would take care of that child exclusively plus all the other servants. It's a long story which I really don't want to go through. They decided to leave Russia, which was politically unstable, in 1905. There were a lot of pogroms against the Jews and they were Jewish and they left. And no one was ever wealthy like that again. And my grandmother whom I never met died when she got to New York. She couldn't live without her accustomed luxury. My father was the oldest at 13 and he went to work. When the others reached 13, they went to work, and they made it pretty well.*

Bob: *You mentioned that you're an avid reader. What kind of books would you say have been the most influential in your life?*

Bill: *That's hard to say. I like books that interest me and I'm interested in a lot of things, and I certainly have read a tremendous amount of nonfiction. I don't read textbooks and I never read the great books or anything like that. They're mostly pretty boring, although I have read a few of them my daughter introduced me to. When I graduated high school I thought I'd become an engineer. My brother and sister had graduated college by that time but they took nothing in college that they would ever use, even though they attended pretty good colleges. And so my father said to take something that I could use. So I thought engineering was for me and I got my degree in engineering. I worked for a year as a chemical engineer but I really began to get restless and I thought I wanted to become a psychologist. I didn't think I would get into medical school because I didn't have good grades in college so I went back to become a psychologist. I got good grades in psychology although I didn't particularly like the psychology I was being taught. It was heavily Freudian and it didn't really make a great deal of sense to me. And then I met a teacher who was the dean of the school at Western Reserve Men's School, which was what they called it in those days. Case Western Reserve was separate. I took a course from him called experimental psychology and we talked about a guy whose name was Wundt, or somebody like that.*

Bob: *Wundt?*

Bill: *Yes, Wundt and other people like him. They did experimental things and the course was pretty boring, but I liked the teacher and I did well. Once I got into psychology I always* *did really well. And the teacher took a liking to me. It was the first time in school that I would say—in all the years I was in school, and I went to school for many years—that any teacher ever took a real personal interest in me, after my elementary school, where a few teachers did. He said to me, "What do you plan to do with your life?" And I said, "I plan to become a clinical psychologist." We're now talking 1946, right after the war. He said, "That's a good plan but instead of becoming a clinical psychologist, why don't you become a psychiatrist?" I said, "To become a psychiatrist you have to get into medical school and since I had poor grades, I think my average in engineering school was about C plus when I graduated, I don't think I could get in because they look at undergraduate grades. They won't just look at my graduate school grades." We talked about 10 or 12 minutes and he said, "I think you should give it a try." He said that he didn't think from the little he knew about me that I had the personality to be a psychologist. He added there are other people who are psychiatrists who have much more say about things than you do. [Bob laughs.] I thought he was a moderately perceptive man. He said I should give it a try and maybe I'd make it. I added the two biology classes that I needed, along with botany and zoology. Otherwise I had everything from chemical engineering with the math and the science; not very good grades, but I had most of the courses. And then I applied to medical school that year and I got turned down by 6 or 7 schools. But I didn't apply to Case Reserve Medical School that year because, . . . I don't know why I didn't apply that year, but I had a couple of friends whose parents were doctors and they wrote letters for me to their medical schools at McGill University and New York University. I didn't get in so I decided to try my own college. And I never knew what I got on the medical aptitude test but I think I did pretty well. A lot of the questions required general knowledge, but since I was an avid reader, I had a lot of*

> *"Bill, when you don't know what to say to a patient, ask, 'What's your plan?'"*

such knowledge. I also knew that even though I didn't get good grades in engineering school I still had a lot more technical knowledge than most of the people applying for medical school. So I handled the questions pretty well. And the math, I knew the math. It was simple math. I probably did very well on the test because shortly I got a letter from Western Reserve saying they wanted to interview me. And so I went in and discovered that the dean was interested in me. I found out later that he was allowed to take about 6 or 7 in a class of 85 who under normal circumstances would never be admitted to medical school [chuckling] and I was one of those 6 or 7. He shared that information with me later on, after I became a member of Who's Who in America. He said he thought it was a good thing to admit me. Anyway, back then, I had an interview with him and I promised him I'd be a psychiatrist. After this he decided that he could eliminate any fear that I might be out there killing people [Bob and Bill laugh] so they let me in. And it was a marvelous medical school. It's really a model for all the work I do in schools. It was a school without failure. It was definitely a school where they didn't try to do anything except teach you, very few tests, no threats, they told you right off the bat, "If you come here you'll become a doctor."

Bob: *They didn't tell you to look at the person on the left and on the right, etc.?*

Bill: *No, no they said everybody's gonna graduate. The only thing is you gotta come. They said if you don't attend, we can't graduate you. We'll teach you if you come.*

Bob: *That's an unusual professional school!*

Bill: *Very unusual, very unusual. And it was just a pleasure those 4 years, and I learned a lot of medicine and still know it actually. In medical school, I never really changed my mind about what I believed, although the psychiatry that was taught to us as medical students was almost totally Freudian. At that point I had no interest in it at all, and so I never attended any of the medical school psychiatric classes because they all seemed to me to be just gibberish. But I still wanted to be psychiatrist. Then when I graduated from medical school I wanted to move to California. It seemed to be a good time to make the move. I was going to live in California, take my training out there, and make contacts. I took my internship at the Veterans Administration Hospital in West Los Angeles. But even in those days, some internships were more prestigious and people were fighting about who would get into the fancy internships, and I didn't have any interest in that. The Veterans Administration had about 120 openings and they only succeeded in getting about 80 people, so I didn't have any problem getting in there. It was a good internship. It was much better than that of some of my other friends whom I talked to later. I learned a lot, had great teachers and then from there finished . . .*

Bob: [Interrupting] *What attracted you to California?*

Bill: *My parents traveled a lot and I had been twice in California and I really loved it, and I had gone to school in Palo Alto, California. My brother was at Stanford and my mother suspected he wasn't going to graduate and so she came out there the last year and she was right. He didn't graduate, but she stayed with him through summer school and he later graduated. And so during that time, I attended David Star Jordan Junior High School in Palo Alto and really loved it. I mean, really, It wasn't the school that was so good, but it was the outside. It was beautiful weather and I had some good friends there. And then after I finished my medical school, my cousin with whom I was very close in Cleveland had moved to Los Angeles and my best friend for many years had also moved to Los Angeles too, and my wife's best friend had moved to Los Angeles. So with those three people, we decided we would move there too. We kept in touch and are still very close to all those people, almost 50 years later.*

Bob: *You know, the rumor is that when you were young, you weren't quite as outgoing as you are now.*

Bill: *I'm still not outgoing, but I can act outgoing* [Bob laughs], *when I give talks and everything like that. Basically I was very shy when I was young, felt inadequate as compared to other people. I was a good enough student in high school, I graduated 55th in a class of 550. So that makes me in the upper 10%. And we had some prominent people graduate in my class, I guess moderately prominent people. But anyway, I went to college and I didn't really quite understand engineering. I understood it to some degree, but it wasn't for me and I knew it. It was during the war and technical people were getting deferred and my brother was out fighting and getting wounded in the war and my mother said to stay in college and I did. She said, "Your brother is doing all the fighting for the family." He was a mildly decorated soldier. And after the war I was drafted when the thing was over, but by that time I had started my psychology work and I went on to get a masters in psychology and then I worked on my doctorate, including my preliminary exams. I didn't have the thesis and I wrote one, but it wasn't very good. I don't blame them for saying I had to work on it, but by that time I was in medical school and I had no more incentive. I have asked my college if they would grant me* *a degree based on the 13 or 14 books that I have written, but they won't do that.* [Bob laughs.] *But now recently—this is interesting—the Dean of the College of Arts and Sciences, a man named John Bassett, a very nice man, came to my house to visit me and I thought for sure he was coming for money because it is not unusual.*

Bob: *It is not unknown that that would happen.*

Bill: *Yeah* [laughs], *and I was going to bring up the fact that maybe he should have at least granted me my doctorate degree, but nothing like that ever came up. He wasn't coming for money. He heard about my work and he wanted me to come back to Case as a visiting scholar, etc., for a couple of days or a week or so, and I have arranged to do that in the fall of this year. And he is very interested in my book,* Choice Theory, *which I have mailed to him. It was just a wonderful, supportive interview. It is nice to have people in your home town recognize you.*

Bob: *That's not easy to accomplish.*

Bill: *But I told him, I do give money every year, I give a substantial sum to the medical school, but he didn't represent the medical school, so I said I am not being a tightwad or anything, but the only real college I enjoyed in this particular university was the medical school and I appreciate that they let me in and I give them a good sum of money every single year. But he said he didn't come for money* [laughs]. *Anyway, to get back to my original point, I finished college and moved to California, took my internship at the Veterans Administration, went into psychiatry at the Veterans Administration, which is under the aegis of UCLA Department of Psychiatry. They interviewed me at the Department of Psychiatry and accepted me in the Veterans Administration Program. I never really thought they wouldn't. There was no reason for them to turn me down. I had some psychological knowledge. I spent my 3 years, 2 years at the Veterans and 1 year at UCLA. It was at UCLA in the outpatient division that several things happened. I began my break with tradition, when I met Dr. Harrington whom I knew slightly because he worked at the mental hospital where I had worked, but I didn't know him well. He became one of my supervisors of my third year of outpatient psychiatry, and we became very close. He had a large influence on my continued break with tradition because he himself had broken with tradition. And I also met a man, who subsequently used my office for a while, Hellmuth Kaiser, who is quite well known in the field, but he also was a psychiatrist who had broken with Freudian psychiatry.*

Bob: *He wrote a wonderful book called* Effective Psychotherapy. *In that book, he talks about the analyst's job being to get the client to be responsible. I quote that book every chance I have.*

Bill: *I met Kaiser and I interacted with him, because he came to me and said he needed an office to practice. I said, "Look, I don't use my office 2 days a week at all," so he used my office for about a year and then I guess he passed away. I don't remember it exactly. He influenced Harrington and Harrington influenced me. That's what it really amounts to.*

Bob: *What was it about Harrington that really attracted you? It must have been not only his ideas, but his style, his personality, his total behavior.*

Bill: *Well, Harrington was a very nonpushy person. And if I had wanted supervision in what they would call in those days (maybe they still do) psychodynamic psychology, he knew enough about it to supervise me. But, when I got to UCLA as an outpatient psychiatrist, they had a clinic there and they started you out with some patients. They had the patients waiting for you, six or seven patients that I would be starting to see. And most of the patients I saw there had been in treatment the previous year with other residents, and they* *were just being transferred to me with maybe a short interval of a couple of weeks between the time I came on board and the others left. One patient I recall in particular was named Pat. I have no idea of what her last name was and wouldn't say it anyway, but her name was Pat. She immediately started telling me about her grandfather and how her grandfather was really the source of her problems. I hardly could believe my ears. This woman had been 3 years at that clinic. It was the 4th year of psychotherapy with four different psychotherapists and she is still talking about her grandfather. I thought I had got into some kind of a time warp or something. And so I said to her, "You have seen psychiatrists and you have told them about your grandfather." "Oh yes, my grandfather is a big part of my life." "And is he alive?" I wondered. The woman looked like 30 years of age. "No he has been dead for a number of years." And so I said, "I can tell you that if you want to see me, I don't have any interest in your grandfather. There is nothing I can do about what went on with him, nothing you can do about what went on with him. He's dead. Rest in peace. But if that's what you want, then you'll have to say you want a new psychiatrist because I think you have some problems, but you have been avoiding them for a number of years by talking about your grandfather, and I want to talk about what's wrong in your life right now. I have no interest in what was wrong yesterday. I deal with what's going on right now." By that time, I had made up my mind, after 2 years of training, that's what I want to do. Although when I told that to Harrington he reached over and shook my hand and said, "Join the club."*

Bob: *Now that's a famous line in your teaching. "Join the club."*

Bill: *It was a very small club at that particular time. Because Harrington had the personality and was good friends with psychoanalysts; they supported him and sent him patients. If they couldn't deal with a patient, they sent him to Harrington knowing he could. And he was one of those people—I've never been able to do that—who had enough of a presence and a skill to do a different kind of thing from what most psychiatrists were doing, but still gain their respect. Besides, he was trained at the Menninger Clinic. Actually, the Menninger Clinic started in his basement. His father, who had been a renowned surgeon in Kansas, decided to become a psychiatrist. So he took the train from Topeka, Kansas where they lived, to Chicago and underwent psychoanalysis, I think by Franz Alexander, and became a psychoanalyst. Then when the young Menningers were trying to found their clinic, they used his basement. When Harrington finished up and got into psychiatry, he went to work at Menninger and I met him 2 or 3 years after he left Menninger. He had by that time officially broken with psychoanalysis, and the Menninger Clinic was still psychoanalytic at that point. It may still be, for all I know. So that's the background. Harrington took a liking to me and what I was doing. During the course of that third year of residency, I began to work in the Ventura School for Girls. He became very interested in that. The Ventura School for Girls had no psychiatrist. The one they had left.*

Bob: *I want to ask you: In your lectures you still refer to Harrington as "my teacher."*

Bill: *I stayed with him for 7 years. Once a week I came to his office and talked over my patients and my struggles. He was like a supervisor. But we never really became personally very friendly. I didn't see him socially. I did persuade him to help write the book I was working on about psychotic people, Reality Therapy. He wrote a chapter in that book. I don't know exactly what happened next. I don't remember why I stopped seeing him. Whether I got too busy or he got too busy or whatever it was, but I saw him for 7 years from '57 through about '65, until the book Reality Therapy was published. It became a bestseller. We kind of separated and I don't know exactly why.*

Bob: *Can you say anything at all about why you separated?*

Bill: *I have some remembrance of why, but it had nothing to do with Harrington and my-self. There were other people that were putting pressure on him not to be associated with me, and I don't want to say what that was but it was just happening, that's all.*

Bob: *Tell the story about the artist. Harrington had a very good comment about the patient who was the artist. It seems that it had an impact on you.*

Bill: *In those days, all the patients were diagnosed schizophrenic of four various kinds: catatonic, paranoid, simple, maybe there is another kind, I don't know. He dealt with them by engaging them in hard work, mixing cement and building sidewalks around the Veterans Hospital, which evidently had to be built. But he used the patient labor to build them and occasionally, even though it was a Veterans Hospital, a prominent person would get sent there. Some very prominent artist, I don't remember his name, was sent to the Veterans Hospital because he was, as Harrington would say, crazy. He never used the word schizo-phrenic. I don't believe in mental illness per se, but whether there is such a thing as craziness I don't know, but he certainly was acting way off the norm and had gotten the diagnosis of being crazy. He might have even had hallucinations, delusions. But, the newspaper found out that he was in the Veterans Hospital and sent a reporter out to talk to his doctor about what kind of a treatment this very famous man was getting. Harrington said he is on the cement mixing gang, building sidewalks. The newspaper reporter asked whether there was some-thing like an art studio in the hospital with art therapy, where people can paint? And Harrington, "Oh, yes, we have a very good studio." The reporter asked, "Why isn't he in it?" Harrington's famous remark that really affected me and I guess a lot of other people was, "He knows how to paint, we are teaching him how to build sidewalks." [Bill laughs.] And the man, like all the others, got sane. It is almost impossible to be insane and do hard work. And I think that's as valid in 1956 as it is now. And one of the main difficulties with the treat-ment of so-called psychotic people today is that the lawyers have gotten into the act and said you are exploiting them and you are forcing them to do things they don't want to. Harrington didn't really force the people to do work on the sidewalks, he offered it to them and said your chances of getting out of the hospital if you do this are a lot better than if you don't. Harrington used to talk straight to them. "You are crazy right now, but that's no big problem. A lot of people are crazy and our job is to help you become sane. And you become sane when you do work and you feel good about doing the work. I don't let crazy people have the privilege of walking around the hospital. And so if you want to get sane and have the privileges to walk around and partake in some of the activities of the hospital that are kind of fun things, then you got to mix cement."*

Bob: *I remember you saying that you would go up to the patients and say, "Will you stop acting crazy so I can talk to you?"*

Bill: *I continually rediscover just as I did a few weeks ago at a session in Montreal, that there is no reason, as far as I know from my experience, that a person who doesn't know me has to talk crazy with me. Because if you understand choice theory, it will not help him to talk crazy. And so I used to tell the people that I don't know what's wrong with them, but I think they know how to talk sane and I would like them to talk sane with me and if they are not talking sane, I will remind them. I will talk sane with them and this will help both of us. I hardly found anybody at all in my dealings with many, many people who wouldn't talk reasonably sane when approached in that way. Even if they were hearing voices, I'd say, "Just pay attention to me not to the voices." And so I am not a big believer in mental illness. There may be such a thing as mental illness, but I like to see a definite organic component in the brain like something is eating up your brain. I don't believe there is such a thing as* *schizophrenia in the sense it is now diagnosed and dealt with. Certainly there is craziness. People do act so far off the norm that they can certainly be called crazy.*

Bob: *Your explanation is that these are behaviors, that people are choosing what they are doing. Behaviors are generated. They are not static conditions.*

Bill: *Everybody chooses what he or she does.*

Bob: *How did you get to that point?*

Bill: *Not easily or initially. This came out of my discussions with Dr. Harrington. I've thought a great deal about choice. And because if Harrington was correct, and if he was going to teach people to be sane, then he can only present the teaching to them. They still have to make the choice to be sane. I saw 15, 20 people leaving the Veterans Hospital every month in taxicabs because they finished being crazy. That was impressive.*

Bob: *That was one of my questions. There is the study that you did where so many people left the hospital, like half in a ward of 200 left the hospital.*

Bill: *That was in the women's ward. My own experience there was on the women's ward. When I got there, I was given, I think, 40 patients to deal with. And in a 4-month period, I discharged 36 of them. I couldn't just do it on my own. It had to be approved by the doctor who was above me. By dealing with them, talking to them, making plans for using reality therapy, they literally chose not to be crazy. I can't say I did it alone. I had help from the nurses, the attendants, they all began to see that this was a good way to work with people.*

Bob: *So it was a total program that you had?*

Bill: *Yes. And there was a doctor running it, I won't mention his name, but he was a very good psychiatrist. He supported me thoroughly.*

Bob: *What were the political impacts on other people, on other wards? Was there any kind of ripple that was negative or positive as a result of that?*

Bill: *Well, by that time, Harrington was in the hospital and already discharging people. He wasn't my supervisor then, but he was in the hospital. And I had some interaction with him and he was supportive in what I was doing. And the other doctor was also very supportive. Besides, the program was working. And I don't think at that point there was any problem. Harrington ran into some difficulty, as when a patient would strike other people, become hostile or aggressive. Harrington preferred not to give them drugs to sedate them and not to wrap them up in a sheet like they sometimes did, but to just put them in leather cuffs on their wrists. Some professors from UCLA came over to see him and saw patients with cuffs on and they thought cuffs were wrong and we should never put cuffs on people. But Harrington didn't think they were cruel at all. He thought it was more cruel to give them drugs that would knock them out. They went up to one of the guys wearing cuffs and they said to him, "I see you've got cuffs on. Who put the cuffs on?" And the patient pointed to the "big guy." Harrington was the "big guy." "He put me in these cuffs." " Do you like being in the cuffs?" " No," he said, "why would I like being in cuffs? It's terrible to be in cuffs." "Would you like to get out of the cuffs?" "Oh, no" the patient said, "I'm not ready to get out of the cuffs." They said, "How come?" And he said, "Because Dr. Harrington explained to me that I've got hand trouble." [Bob laughs.] They said, "What's hand trouble?" He said, "Well, when I'm not in the cuffs, my hands are always in other people's faces." [Bob laughs.] "And he said as long as I do that, I'll never get out of this hospital. The big guy also told me, 'When you are ready to get out of the cuffs, tell me and I'll think about it seriously.' And I'm not ready yet, so I am staying in the cuffs and that is okay with me." That is a great story. The man was obviously hitting people and hard to control, but he recognized he needed the help and he recognized*

Harrington was his friend, not a persecutor trying to treat him cruelly. And that is the basis of reality therapy. I realized before I even wrote the book that a good relationship is at the core of all psychiatric or psychological help. And now I believe and teach that good relationships are at the core of everything and bad relationships are at the core of all psychological problems.

Bob: *Bill, in a short paragraph, how would you contrast your ideas now with the way they were when you first developed reality therapy?*

Bill: *This leads to my experience at the Ventura School. In the chapter on the quality community in the book* Choice Theory, *I discuss what we did at the Ventura School for Girls and I liken it to a small quality community. It was not merely a school. The girls lived there. And they went to school there, and they worked there. They had the opportunity to interact with other people when volunteers visited to take them out into the surrounding community. I talk about what we did there and how we treated the girls. I will give you an example to get the flavor of what I am trying to say. The girls came to the Ventura School and were angry because it is a prison. They'd be locked up and so we had a rule. They had their own little room and their own bed and they had to make their bed. And I think what we did there was unique. Occasionally a girl would say that she's not going to make the bed and she would add a few invectives for emphasis. She would add, "It's your bed, you can take your bed and shove it." In most places it would never occur to them not to punish her. And at the Ventura School, if a girl wouldn't make her bed, the house mother would come up and say, "We really want you to make your bed, you know, but if you won't, then we have girls in this cottage come here and help you make it. The last thing I want to do is punish you." The new resident would come downstairs and say, "If someone wants to make my bed, fine, bring her over." But the other residents would come in and say, "Look it is not pleasant being locked in like this. I came here like you. I was angry and everything else, but I'll tell you this is a pretty good place and they don't believe much in punishment. It is hard to get punished around here. But, I'd like to help you make the bed and when we get it done then let's go and meet some of the other girls. I think you'll find this is a pretty good place." The girl would say, "I'm not making the bed. You want the bed made, make it yourself." And the girl would say, "It's okay, I'll make it, I'll make it for you and then we'll go down and meet the other people here." And by the time the girl started making the bed, the other girl would chip in and make it with her. Rarely did we ever have a girl just not make the bed. Yet, there was no punishment. We said, "We're not going to hurt you. We only want to help, we want to be with you, we want to support you. We realize you are upset, we realize you are away from home, locked up behind two-inch steel doors at night." And when she would go downstairs, the other girls would welcome her and say, "Look, it's okay, you are going to have friends here." And then we would have no more trouble. We would go months without even a discipline problem with these really terribly so-called delinquent girls. When you'd visit the school, you wouldn't think they were delinquent girls. You'd say there were some nice young ladies going to a private school, which it certainly was. So this is how we dealt with the girls. Ordinarily, in the girl's whole life prior to coming here, whenever she resisted, she was punished. Punishment for resistance wasn't used here and so the girl had nothing else to do. I mean, if it doesn't work, she had no other behavior. And when the girls offered her friendship and support, she took it. In fact, I had some feedback from Corning, New York, which I'll discuss later, that this is one of the things in the chapter that people are having a hard time dealing with (Glasser, 1998a). They don't think it is right to do away with punishment.*

Bob: *Right, many people fear what will happen if there is no punishment.*

Bill: *But, the thinking behind it is right. You see many kids get into big trouble and cost communities lots of dollars. And all their behavior stems from rejection and punishment, even though the community's rejection and punishment didn't start until the kids started acting up. I'm not saying the community went out in the street and punished them. They committed their little offenses and did their thing. Choice theory is all about trying to get away from the thinking that the universal right thing has to apply to all situations and the right thing is to punish. Well, punishing might be the right thing in some belief systems, but it is wrong in the sense of trying to help that child become a good citizen. As much as people insist they won't learn unless we punish them, what they learn from punishment is to resist and be harder to get along with, and there are like 16 million opinions of research that back this statement up. It's been my experience that the first time you deal with someone without punishment, they start to change. We did it in the Schwab school in Cincinnati, where by the end of the year the kids who had been quite hard to get along with were learning. But the main thing was that they got tremendously polite. It was "please" and "thank you." "I appreciate it." We didn't teach courtesy or good language. Every child knows courtesy and knows good language, but he won't use it if he feels that you are treating him in a way that he or she doesn't want to be treated. So it is hard to treat people sans angst, and as the Bible says to turn the other cheek. That's hard to do. But in my experience, it is reasonably accurate and so I really* am *teaching people that when we deal with kids, we better get used to turning the other cheek or we will fill our jails with even more prisoners.*

Bob: *Let's get back to Ventura for a moment. What kind of follow-up did you get years later? Give some examples.*

Bill: *I got supportive letters, and I used to meet these girls around California when I was giving lectures. They would show up. I remember riding in a Cadillac car with a woman, formerly of the Ventura School, who said, "Oh, Dr. Glasser I'm a real estate agent now. I'm doing very well in this community. And I really owe a lot of it to you." Our recidivism rate was really significantly lower than the other schools which were for males only. But we had a very low recurrence rate. This just made a big impact on my life. The experience has remained with me.*

Bob: *It must be gratifying to be able to have that kind of an experience that these people change their lives.*

Bill: *I also ran into trouble at the California facility. And this is an interesting part of my life too. When they found out that I was really into helping these girls, that things started to change, they tried to get rid of me. Which hasn't been an uncommon experience.* [Bob laughs.] *Because I was making trouble.*

Bob: *It happens that way!*

Bill: *You don't want to rock the boat. We were rocking the hell out of that boat. And so they didn't pay me for 2½ years. By that time, they had raised my salary, and when I finished my residency I became a full-fledged psychiatrist. They raised my salary from $35 a day to $75 a day. I still had to drive the 60 miles back and forth.*

Bob: *No travel pay?*

Bill: [Laugh] *No travel pay, no travel time. But at least I didn't have to punch a clock. I got to the school about 10:00 a.m. and left about 4:00 p.m. I didn't work from 8 to 5 or anything. I just worked without pay and kept sending my bills. It was a contract. I wasn't on salary. I was a contract consultant and Mrs. Dolan would say, "You keep working, they'll pay eventually." And I got a check for several thousand dollars.* [Bob laughs.] *I don't know what hap-*

pened, but she must have told them that they can't have the guy working and not pay him. "At $75 a day, we're not being overcharged." [Bob laughs.] *And so I got my money and after that I always got paid. But I never earned more than $75 a day. That was the maximum I ever earned there, but I said to myself, I am earning thousands of dollars a day because I am getting vast experience. I'm getting known all over the world. I'm doing a good job. My book* Reality Therapy *is based on this experience. And the girls helped me with the book. The book* Schools Without Failure *was typed in part by the girls. And then in 1967 I left.*

Bob: *I'd like to ask you about the orthopedic hospital.*

Bill: *That was a totally different experience.*

Bob: *You worked there concomitantly with some of these other places.*

Bill: *Right. I had my private office. I worked a day at the Ventura School, I worked a half a day at the orthopedic hospital. Also, I was doing lecturing around the state for the youth authority. And I was getting other work also.*

Bob: *What was the significance of the hospital experience, the most important impact on your development?*

Bill: *Like the Ventura School, they called the UCLA Department of Psychiatry and said they had an opening for a psychiatrist. Nobody was interested and I said I'm interested because there was a $200 a month fee for a half day, once a week—about $50 a day. To me that was a huge amount of money considering I was seeing patients in my office for $10 or $15 an hour.*

Bob: *Sometimes even collecting the fee!*

Bill: *No, no, I was collecting. I don't think anyone stiffed me. But my income then was probably in the neighborhood of maybe less than $100 a day. It was $25,000 a year. It wasn't that much money, but on the other hand, it was okay. I was not crying about it. But the orthopedic hospital turned out to be quite lucrative. When I left the orthopedic hospital, I was making about $1000 for that morning, which is a fantastic sum of money in those days. Because the orthopedic hospital said they just pay $50 for coming in and doing what they want me to do, but anything I bill here, I bill to the insurance companies who pay for the patients. I didn't learn that for about a year.* [Bob laughs.] *Nobody told me. But then the psychologist who was running the unit I was on, a guy named Jim, said, "You ought to bill these people." I said, "What do you mean?" He said, "We bill them for all our work." And so he showed me. By the time I left, I was earning at least $1000 a morning there. When I left there, I was working with mostly industrial accidents involving Workman's Compensation, but with other accidents also: quadriplegics, paraplegics, and people with back pain. I think I became the world's leading expert on lower back pain when I was there. If the first operation did not provide the desired relief from pain, the doctors would ask me whether they should operate again. I was pretty well able to predict when the second operation wouldn't succeed by the patient's psychological condition: They were usually very lonely people, alienated with low self-worth.*

Bob: *Being sick was pretty much their identity.*

Bill: *The worth of their life is being sick. And so I developed one question to use for deciding if the second operation would work. It is not a question you'd throw around easily but I did it carefully. I would ask the people, "When did you last have a really good time?" If they couldn't answer that question rather quickly and specifically, the operation wouldn't work. If they could answer, "Oh, about 2, 3 weeks ago or a month ago or even 6 months before I was injured, I had a good time, socializing, having fun, and being with family," then the operation* *would work. I knew they had a physical problem. Otherwise they were doing what I would call "back aching." And there is no surgery that is going to cure "back aching." "Back aching" is choosing a pain to deal with a life that is not in effective control, as I would say today. I learned about those things while I worked there. In fact, I appeared in various courts, as a witness. I gained a little bit of experience with people suing and it was a very interesting time for me.*

Bob: *What would be an example of a case that sticks out in your mind, a situation where this happened?*

Bill: *There are some funny ones. There was a guy who couldn't walk. We thought that he could walk and that he had an hysterical condition and he was choosing not to walk. So I called an anesthesiologist and we gave him some sodium amytal. And under amytal, he would walk, do splits, jumping jacks, high jumps, and scary things. [Bob laughs.] We made a little video of it. Actually, it was a movie in those days. But finally we stopped doing that because it didn't do any good really. It proved to us that, yes, he could walk, which we probably pretty well knew anyway. But when we showed it to him or explained it to him, he would say, "Look, you gave me that medicine. I can do anything. Just keep giving me that medicine." But, you can't give a person sodium amytal all the time. That was a very interesting experience. Most of the patients were people who had injuries and no satisfying life. If you have little happiness and you are injured, then the injury becomes a life. If you had no good close relationships, and you didn't really like your work, and you thought you were badly treated by your employer . . . all of these things were pathogenic of long-term injuries. I would be told by the insurance companies to settle it as well as I could. I was able to tell the person, "I think if you go back to work you are going to be better off even if it hurts." After being injured for a long time many of them were looking for an excuse to get out, go back to work, and get a settlement from the insurance company. They didn't pay much in those days. Now they pay more. But I learned about pain; in fact, I became an expert on pain. I learned about a drug called Phenergan, which is an antihistamine and has nothing to do with pain. When you take it, you feel you took something. You feel like you got a drug inside you. And so I got the idea to give the people Phenergan and tell them it will help their back pain. I also believe you should never ever be deceitful with people, so I told them that basically I was giving them a placebo. They asked, "What is a placebo?" They had never heard the word placebo. I said, "Placebo is a drug or sometimes just a sugar pill, although in your case I am giving you a little drug." I explained it was an antihistamine and would probably help their pain. And how it would help their pain and why, I didn't know, but I believed it would. And if they would take it, fine, if they didn't want to take it, fine. They were hurting and all of them wanted narcotics, which I didn't want to give them. I never did give narcotics. There were doctors who could give them narcotics. But I never had a narcotics license, so I have never been able to give narcotics. I never wanted to have a narcotics license because I always wanted to tell people, I can't provide them with narcotics. If you really need narcotics, there are doctors who will give them to you. I'm just not one of them. I'm not against you having them, but I can't give them. As it turned out the drug Phenergan worked remarkably well. A lot of people I dealt with took Phenergan orally. I would usually start with a shot, but afterwards I gave it to them orally. I said, "It is not going to work forever, so you better think about getting your life together and going back to work." So the combination of the suggestion, the Phenergan, and telling them it was a placebo, not a medication that would numb them, helped them deal with their pain. And I can't say I was tremendously successful at the orthopedic hospital because in most of the cases, the pain didn't go away until the case itself was settled legally.*

Bob: *Well you learned, it seems to me, that at least some pain in behavior is at least partially a choice.*

Bill: *Absolutely. I also learned that people who chose pain really didn't want it. They'd rather get back on their feet and could with professionals who gave warmth, good treatment, and listening. The doctors who treated these people were very busy, and they couldn't give them the psychological attention I gave them. And the lawyers' psychologists, many of whom they had seen, were more interested in preserving the pain. And I was the insurance company's psychologist. So I told them, "I'm being paid by the insurance company to help you get rid of the pain." I said, "I'm not completely neutral here, but I am neutral to the extent that I'm not doing anything differently with you than if you or your attorney paid me directly. I would do exactly the same thing." I had one dramatic incident at a Workman's Compensation hearing about a guy under my care. I testified that I thought he was able to go back to work, but that he still had some pain. The other side testified next. Then the guy stood up and said, "The only one whom I've ever seen since I got that injury that cared about me was Dr. Glasser. And what he says I believe. As for the rest of you, I don't believe a word of what you say."*

Bob: *Way to go Bill.*

Bill: *That really caused a commotion, I'll tell you.*

Bob: *I'll bet it did.* [Bill laughs.]

Bill: *All the lawyers started arguing. My lawyer for the insurance company told me just sit down and keep quiet, which I did. And in no time at all they settled the case. And so I said, "Did I hurt the case?" The lawyer immediately said, "No, you didn't hurt the guy. We gave him what we were going to give him anyway, but that's all we are going to give him. " And the client was very happy and so I felt it was okay. So I had varied experiences with a lot of unusual cases. Eventually, though, I left the hospital for a job working in the L.A. City Schools for $100 for the whole day. So I took a $900 cut* [Bob laughs] *for a job a hell of a lot harder too.*

Bob: *I'd say so.*

Bill: *But, I was by that time involved in the schools and I wanted to work in them full time. I would have stayed at the hospital, but more and more I was being given the paraplegics and quadraplegics to deal with and that was more than I had the psychological strength to deal with. These people begged me to kill them—life isn't worth living, why are we seeing a psychiatrist? I did okay with them, but I was getting to the point where I didn't want to go into the room to see them, and when I got to that point, I left. It wasn't fair to them for me to stay; I was too discouraged. I worked there for about 2 or 3 years and then I had to leave. By that time I had accepted an offer from the L.A. City Schools for 2 days a week, so I just quit the hospital job.*

Bob: *I think that's a good lesson for anybody. When a job is too much or you just don't feel like you can contribute, it's time to leave.*

Bill: *Especially when other people's lives and health depend on your being upbeat, positive, and energetic. By then, I was losing my steam. I didn't feel I had the right to stay anymore and I quit.*

Bob: *In 1965, you wrote the book* Reality Therapy. *Now this was a ground-breaking book. I know you've told stories about the impact this had and the impact on you. Could you talk a little bit about that? Tell us how your colleagues responded to this book.*

Bill: *Well, the book was obviously highly critical of what I call traditional psychiatry. Go-*

ing back into people's past, believing in mental illness, giving people medication. I didn't deal with any of these things. I dealt with the here and now and made a relationship part of the counseling. I thought they were all very lonely people. That was true of almost everyone that came to my office. If they didn't come to my office, I saw them in institutions or in hospitals. It was all the same thing. I was a very good psychiatric resident. I had a lot of successes and I became well known in the hospital. And one of the honors you get when you leave your residency is to be appointed a member of the clinical faculty. I received such an appointment and I thought this must be an open-minded place. They are willing to bring in someone with new ideas and I would be teaching my ideas, not the standard ones, and I was very happy about that. We are talking about 1957 now, because I was already starting with these ideas at that time. I hadn't fleshed them out until 1965, of course. The worst thing that ever happened to me because I didn't go along with traditional psychology was when I got a call from a doctor who I had thought was really supportive of me, an older doctor, from Ohio. He was well known in Ohio and he came to Los Angeles. I don't want to mention his name or what he was well known for, but he was one of my other supervisors during my third-year residency. He was very interested in my way of treatment. He taught a little bit but was pretty much retired on the job, as many of the old people do in this profession. He asked me if I would like to become a member of the clinical faculty? I said yes. And then when it was all set, he called me at home and said that they didn't realize that they hired two people for the job and they gave the other guy the offer first. I said I understood and let's not talk about it any longer. And that was it. So those things were disappointing, as when I now try new ideas in schools or anyplace else where people don't want them and don't want me. Progress is made very slowly, at least in the mental health field and the educational field. I'm now more aware of why there is so little progress, but certainly that was an indication that if I wanted to get ahead in the world, I would have to do it on my own. No one was going to be helping me. So when you say, "What was the reaction to the book?" There wasn't much reaction to it.

Bob: It was widely accepted by many people, but I was wondering about the kind of reception by your colleagues.

Bill: Over the years, I had probably gotten about half a dozen psychiatric consultations. A few psychiatrists wrote to me and used my stuff. But none has ever gone so far as to take my training. Maybe one did, I forget his name, he was from Santa Barbara, but I forget who he was now. He never really followed it up. The psychiatrists dealt with me by ignoring me rather than trying to discredit me.

Hardly anybody actively tried to discredit me. But ignoring me and my work was rather common. And then, interestingly enough, I became more and more known in the schools, and by 1966 my name was widely known in education. I had been working in Watts for about a year. I worked in four elementary schools half a day a week in each school, which adds up to two whole days a week. I got some recognition for that almost immediately. As a psychiatrist I was well known. They never had a psychiatrist there before. I was teaching teachers and demonstrating classroom meetings and talking about no failure and let's stop punishing kids and other things. And interestingly enough, I got a letter from the W. Clement Stone Foundation of Chicago. Clement Stone was a very well known and very wealthy man in the country, one of Nixon's big financial supporters. He sold insurance and his foundation asked if I would like some money from the Foundation to continue my work. My wife, Naomi, said, "I don't want anything to do with these people; something is wrong."

Bob: Somebody wants to give you money! [Bob laughs.]

'd to at least talk with them. I told them, "If you want to give me money, ... I said to Naomi, "If they are genuinely interested, they will come to the ...ch they did. They came and I invited my friend Donald O'Donnell to be present. ...nted a neutral party present, and he was very much involved with my school work. Also at that time I was teaching an extension course through UCLA to which teachers could come but they had to bring their principals. The foundation representatives asked how much I wanted. I replied that I didn't know how much money I needed or what to do with it. They insisted they would provide some money. That's when I decided what I would do with the money. I would start the Institute for Reality Therapy and the Educator Training Center, which was a branch of the Institute working with schools. Doug Naylor, who had attended my course at UCLA, became the head of the Educator Training Center until it dissolved in 1997.

The amount they provided was $300,000 over a period of 3 years, which was a lot of money. We then started training all over the country in "Schools Without Failure." We developed such a school in Palo Alto, California, where Donald O'Donnell was principal. And we also made a lot of money through the training. This kept us going and we had qualified instructors, and the Institute for Reality Therapy became a big deal, at that time, not so much in counseling as in education. When we ran out of money, I asked them for more money. I remember going to the meeting to get more money and Dr. Carl Menninger was there. They were also giving him money. During the course of the meeting he stood up and spoke against giving me more money. He didn't know me, but he made a statement to the effect that they ought to really support real psychiatry, not this stuff that is being taught through my institute. He never mentioned my name nor shook my hand, though we were sitting right in the same room. By that time Stone's daughter was pretty much in charge of the foundation. She liked me and said we don't care about that old guy, we will give you the money. And so she gave me another $75,000 in checks made out to William Glasser, and asked for no accountability on my part. I could have taken the money and put it my bank or run away on it. They had complete faith. In fact, I wasn't in my office one day when a check arrived by certified mail and the pharmacist signed for it. For some reason he opened it. When he called me later he told me, "There is a check here for $40,000. Gee, that's pretty good. How come you get $40,000?" I said, "From the Stone Foundation? They sent it to me?" And from that time on we kept careful track. We had a bookkeeper and sent reports to the foundation about how we used the money. The foundation reported we were the only organization that ever did what we said we would do and reported that it really did work. And so they would have continued to give me money, but the Foundation ran out of funds. I was on very good terms with them, however. I did remember them telling me, "You are the only one that told us what you'd do. You'd start a school, you'd teach people 'schools without failure.'" And we had data that it was effective.

Bob: Let's move to another discussion. I think the history of what you used to call control theory is pretty well known and written about very thoroughly. Let's go to the current moment and talk a little about your thoughts about the quality community and choice theory as far as how you want to saturate a community with it.

Bill: I have to go back a little tiny bit. While in Australia in the spring of 1996, due to the audiences dealing with my ideas, I decided to change the control theory that I had been working on since 1979, almost 20 years. I always disliked that name of the theory, "control theory." By 1996, Powers and I had major disagreements. He didn't believe in the basic needs or total behavior, or any of the things that I was now teaching. I could see that to the audi-

ences in Australia, a country founded on convict labor, the word "control" had a bad name like it has everywhere. So I got rid of the word "control." I changed the name of the organization from the Institute for Reality Therapy, Control Theory and Quality Management to The William Glasser Institute. There are many such institutes. I'm not dead, and I decided to change it while I'm still alive. Most of my people support it highly, and I've been told by many people I should have done that years ago.

I began to think about choice theory and how different it was from what I had been teaching. I have written a book about major improvements and changes in the ideas. Many schools found it very hard to convert all the way to what would be a quality school. For a long time, we had only one school, the school in Michigan, that went all the way. We now have other schools, such as the ones in Boston and in Florida. It's still a slow process and I came to the conclusion that we are never going to get quality schools, which are schools really based on choice theory and acceptance, on sensible work, no failure, a lot of interaction, and never allowing a student to get credit for anything except competent work. I laid it out very clearly in my 1998 book Choice Theory. *And then I was asked back to Corning, New York to work with their schools. I have this feeling in my heart about Corning, having been there 35 years ago. I said I would be willing to come.*

By this time my wife, Carleen, and I had developed a little talk to give to communities about marriage and staying together. I wrote a book called Staying Together *about how to put choice theory into marriage relationships. And I heard from the people in the community that I have been corresponding with that it looked like there would be a huge crowd. When we got there, 650 people showed up. This is a lot of people in any town and this is a small town. It wasn't that they remembered me from the previous conference, 35 years earlier. I had no idea why that many people showed up. I didn't know if they knew me. Maybe it was just something different, an article in the newspaper might have helped too. And besides anybody who focuses on schools might have something interesting to say. Then I made the marriage presentation and told them mostly about choice theory. I told them choice theory is the difference in succeeding in the things you want to do with people or not succeeding. And to tell you the honest-to-goodness truth, I told them they seemed amazingly interested in the idea of applying it to marriage and that it also applies to school, to work, to family, and to life. I said that in none of these places is it going to be as successful as it could be unless we teach choice theory to the whole community and create a quality community. I just said it right out like that and they were listening. And I told them that I would help them do this. "Why don't we move Corning toward a quality community?" They said, "When can we talk further?" I said, "I'm only going to be here one more day, tomorrow. Come at lunchtime tomorrow if you are interested." Thirty people showed up and they were the leaders in the community, from the Corning Glass Company, the Foundation, the medical field, the newspaper, TV and radio. The police were there, including the police chief. This is a sophisticated community with a lot of educated people. The glass company headquarters is there. They said maybe they would do this, but how? We went back and forth with ideas and did not decide anything definite. A week later I wrote and told them they won't need a lot of training. They would need to do it themselves based on reading the book. And as far as cost, it would be negligible. People have to buy the book and get together and read it. That's the only way it is going to work. And they talked about it further, and then they said they would try it. Later I would go to Corning to a meeting with at least 100 people from the community. Probably a lot more would have read the book* Choice Theory, *and then we would talk about how we could move toward a quality community. I said I can't do it. It's* your *community. I'll consult.*

I'll help. I'll do everything possible. The Corning Medical Foundation, Corning College, the YMCA, and several other major sponsors are really behind it. Since then they have hired a person full-time to direct what they call the Choice Community Project, which is teaching choice theory to the whole community.

Bob: *In outline form, what do you envision this quality community to look like?*

Bill: *Well, it won't look any different. On the surface it will look like any other community, but the people in it will know choice theory and begin to practice it in their everyday lives and in their work.*

Bob: *And how will the outsider know that people are practicing it?*

Bill: *The outsider won't really know, but we'll keep statistics. I said I'll only do it and put my name on it if you will hire some reputable researcher to look at several factors in the community, such as crime, domestic violence, etc. We'll look at school success and failure. We'll look at delinquency. We'll look at drug use. We'll look at dropouts. We'll look at referrals to juvenile court. All of the statistics that the community normally keeps should be reduced as this theory begins to be learned. When parents and community members use it in their lives, they will become more effective, as would professional people who use the ideas. And if those people want training, then they are going to have to get training like everybody else. I told them, "I won't charge for my work. I am not doing this for money. I'm doing this because I believe in it wholeheartedly, and if you are good enough to give me the community who will cooperate with me and get it started, I certainly am not going to charge anything for my contribution." If a segment of people in the community need training and hires some of our trainers, they can pay for it. And so they began to see that I really wasn't in this for the money. There is some intimation, I'm in it for the prestige, and I don't deny that. But Corning isn't the only community interested. We have four or five other communities already seriously interested. In my book, I wrote a chapter, with their permission, about what we are planning to do at Corning.*

Bob: *One of my questions is, "What is your next project?" and I think you just answered it. I think it is the quality community.*

Bill: *The quality community. Unless it completely fades away, I will be spending the rest of my life doing that. I'm not sure I will do it free of charge to every community that is interested, but I will certainly do it at Corning free of charge. And my idea is to learn enough in Corning so we have a model that we can pass along to other cities.*

Bob: *What size city would this be most applicable to?*

Bill: *I can picture cities in the neighborhood of 25,000, 30,000, 40,000 people. I can picture schools that are trying to be quality schools using their school as focal point. The man that gave me the original interest and start in Corning is a man that appeared that night, Vince Capolla, the superintendent of schools. He is an important man in Corning and he showed his enthusiasm and said he was convinced that what Dr. Glasser is trying to do in our schools is exceedingly important. I don't think anyone has ever developed a psychological idea and carried it to this point. It certainly is something that I am interested in. I work for money and I make money, but at this point in my life, I have a large retirement fund. Financially, I can live on what I have.*

Bob: *Another important issue is multiculturalism. There is a current movement expressing the opinion that the counseling theories, the interactional theories that people have developed, have been developed by what they call "EuroAmerican men." That phrase is often used with a kind of a negative connotation, meaning that because they are developed in this West-*

ern Civilization, they are not applicable to minority groups. In fact, they are not applicable to any cultures that are non-Western. I know you feel very strongly, as indeed I feel very strongly, about this point regarding reality therapy and choice theory. Would you comment about that now?

Bill: *I'd be happy to. First of all, choice theory is strongly based on the idea that built into our genetic structure are five basic human needs, and that all people on earth today, regardless of their size, shape, color, or anything else, have exactly the same genetic structure. We are all one race.*

Bob: *Right.*

Bill: *This theory says we have five needs. Now, we have no choice but to try to satisfy these needs because we get pleasure when we satisfy them and pain when we don't. And those are the most accurate ways of knowing the needs are being satisfied. If you feel good, you are satisfying your needs unless you have taken some chemical into your body that bypasses the system by giving you the chemically induced good feelings, like morphine or something. If you feel good, you have done something to satisfy a need. If you feel good for a long period of time, you are probably doing things to satisfy all your needs. And your shape, size, color, background, race, or your community or wherever you come from doesn't excuse you from trying to do this. So the differences we have found around the world are the differences that people themselves have learned and practiced. These are not genetic. And so I feel that what I am doing is trying to get down to the fundamentals of helping people satisfy their needs. And whether I am a White person whose father came from Europe originally or whether I am another kind of a person, this is what I would be teaching because it is what I believe. And my teachings seem to have worked with every possible variation of human being. They certainly work with African Americans whom I've had a lot of experience with working in schools. There were Americans of Mexican and Spanish origin because I worked with those people a great deal in school. They work with Asians because we have a large component of reality therapy and choice theory working in Japan. They work in Korea with another group of Asian people, quite different from the Japanese culturally speaking.*

Bob: *I've taught in the Middle East, which is again another very different world.*

Bill: *Kuwait. It works in Australia, Singapore, which is mostly Chinese, and in Hong Kong these ideas are used. People from our Institute have gone up to northern Canada and into Alaska and worked with Native Americans, both Canadian and American. The Native Americans, more than any other group, say that choice theory is more congruent with their culture than any other ideas they have ever run into. They say, "We have been practicing choice theory for a thousand years." And one of the difficulties Native Americans have in getting along with external control culture which we live in is that their culture is so different and their way of resisting it and getting rid of the pain of living in the culture is different. It doesn't allow them to effectively satisfy their needs in a way they would like to. These are cultural differences, not genetic differences. So many of them turn to alcohol as a way to get rid of the pain of a society that really doesn't quite allow them to satisfy their needs in a way they would like. The ability to satisfy needs has a lot to do with the society in which we live. And so the criticism that this theory is limited because of its origins, I don't agree with. Many people have contributed to choice theory even though I don't know these people. And a lot of cultures say this seems to work for them. I don't know much about European cultures. My father hated the country he came from, Russia, and never would even speak a word of Russian once he got here and would never talk to me about it. What he emphasized was, "Forget about it, we're in the United States now, we are Americans." And so I never had any* *idea that Europe was better than America in my house. My mother, who was born on the boat coming over from Austria, certainly didn't feel that Europe was better than this country. So I am American and this is a multicultural country. I can get along with most anybody and I have an organization of people who teach from a whole variety of cultures and countries. You and I just presented a workshop and a Pakistani man who follows our ideas was there. That's another very different culture. Have you ever worked in that part of the world?*

Bob: *Yes, I've been to India, but not Pakistan and the ideas were very well received.*

Bill: *All right, so there. I mean that is a very different culture.*

Bob: *It is. Yet, as you say, they love the ideas. There are many cultures on the Subcontinent.*

Bill: *It is easy to say, just because you are not like me, you can't understand me. The history of the world shows that the greatest harm that has been done to various cultures and racial groups has been done to them by people of their own race and culture. There is all kinds of evidence to back up the fact that's just because the guy running your deal is the same race as you are, and the same culture, doesn't mean he is going to treat you well. I can back that up if people want me to. Man's inhumanity to man is well known.*

Bob: *There is a long history of cultures borrowing from each other and taking ideas from each other. That is also well documented.*

Bill: *Look at what's happening in Europe now. They're really trying to create the United States of Europe, the European Community.*

Bob: *Sure.*

Bill: *Because our thing here has worked pretty well. And they are very serious about what they're doing.*

Bob: *Well, we are hoping that you will teach these ideas for the next 30 to 40 years and never take up the fishing pole. About the year, say, 2075, what would you like to be remembered for?*

Bill: *I would like to be remembered for bringing forth ideas that people took seriously enough to try in their communities. Before I die, if we can get 15 or 20 communities really moving in this direction in the United States, we can get them all over the world. The world looks to the United States, looks to us for good things and looks to us for bad things. In the long run, I'm not so much worried about the bad things as long as we get some of the good things going.*

Bob: *Well, anybody listening to you, I know, has the idea that we are listening to a man that teaches the good things, so I want to personally thank you for what you have contributed to me and I think I can speak for a few million people who will say the same thing.*

Bill: *Well, I appreciate it.*

Exercise

After gaining an overview of the historical development of reality therapy, the following questions will help you reflect on the work of William Glasser and the evolution of theory and practice thus far.

1. What idea impresses you as the most significant?
2. Is there anything in the philosophy of choice theory that you disagree with? Why?
3. Evaluate how choice theory compares with other theories.
4. What do you project the future of choice theory and reality therapy will be in the first quarter of the 21st century?

☐ My Own Involvement in Reality Therapy

My involvement with reality therapy spans nearly 30 years of learning, teaching, writing, creating, and mentoring, as well as observing trainees and monitoring the training programs of The William Glasser Institute. My workshop training sessions and requests for lectures increase steadily, and during these programs very often the question is asked, "How did you get involved in reality therapy and with Dr. Glasser?" At first I was surprised that this topic would be of interest to audiences. But as years pass the question is asked more and more frequently. So I have included here a brief history of my own connection with the reality therapy movement.

My early training in counseling focused on the client- or person-centered tradition in which I learned that counselors need to "get to the feeling level" of the clients' problems. Somehow I believed that if clients described how they felt, not merely what they thought, that this would be enough to help them make changes and that other kinds of interactions with clients were superficial or mere problem-solving sessions. Unless clients identified the underlying emotion, problem solving was doomed to be unsuccessful because these real problems were not addressed. We emphasized that a thought is a statement. A feeling is a word such as anger, loneliness, depression, disappointment, sadness, and, of course, shame. Until clients "got in touch with these feelings," labeled them, admitted them, and thus took responsibility for them, nothing would change. And if any alteration were to occur in their behaviors it would be temporary and shallow. If counselors did not help clients reach a level of the affective expression, they were timid, reluctant, and perhaps afraid of their own such feelings.

This approach meant that clients took the lead in the discussion and the counselors followed. After all, clients knew best. And the job of therapists was to listen, reflect, and demonstrate accurate, genuine empathy and positive regard. If this happened, change would result. As a high school teacher I employed this method in the classroom. And it had the beneficial result of getting close to the students and having better relationships with them. I have never felt ashamed or regretful of this training, nor do I even now look down upon it in any way. In fact, I honor and treasure it. It has been invaluable to me to this day and it continues to help me in both my personal and my professional life.

My experience as a high school counselor and an elementary school counselor was the occasion for a more directive approach. My instincts told me that there were other, more efficient ways to work with clients. Still, the person-centered approach was later emphasized in my doctoral program, and I even critiqued masters-level therapists and counselors' work as if it were the only valid form of counseling.

But after completing my doctoral studies I hoped to achieve a deeper level of knowledge and skills in various methods which I had been studying: Adlerian, behavioral, and rational. Consequently, I attended short-term seminars on various theories, including the first international conference on Rational Emotive Therapy in Glen Ellen, Illinois in 1975. By this time, however, I had initiated study in reality therapy, which had piqued my interest in a workshop I attended in Cleveland, Ohio in 1972 conducted by Ed Ford and sponsored by the Case Western Reserve Department of Social Work. I had read Glasser's *Reality Therapy* in 1969 and it made sense. Ed Ford made the system come alive, and even the exaggerated self-confidence of Albert Ellis and his imitators could not shake my belief that it was the work and ideas of Dr. William

Glasser that struck a chord with me. This theory explained human nature, human behavior, and human motivation. I had to know more.

Making myself known to Ed Ford helped me put a human face on the theory. He said that Dr. Glasser conducted 4½-day workshops in Los Angeles and that he had a group of close associates who helped him conduct these programs: Dick Hawes, Glen Weist, Mary Ann Dancy, Gary Applegate, Fitz-George Peters, Al Katz, and himself, Ed Ford. I began to attend these workshops and was able to do so inexpensively, as my brother and sister-in-law Ed and Irene Wubbolding, lived in Northridge, about 45 minutes from the site of the training, which took place on West Olympic Boulevard at the now-defunct Educator Training Center, a subsidiary of the Institute for Reality Therapy. This training began in 1972, and I was among 25 people who were certified at the first certification week in August 1975, just before I went to Japan to teach for a year.

It was during this 3-year period that for me reality therapy progressed from a chord to a theme song. Choosing reality therapy as an obvious option occurred after I was a "client" in a role play with Dr. Glasser. At that time I was working as a group therapist at a halfway house for women ex-offenders. In the 30-minute role play I used every manipulative behavior previously used on me: anger, helplessness, blaming others, seduction, and avoidance. Throughout the session he gently but firmly removed any payoff for each of these attempts, on my part, to avoid taking responsibility for my actions. When we were finished the only choice for me in my role was to confront myself, to face my behavior, and to deal with my own current choices.

More significant was the impact of this single 30-minute experience outside the simulation period. The eye-opening realization that there was more to this system than superficial problem solving was genuine "fire in the belly research" (cf. chapter 12). It was, and is even more so today, a system for helping people look at their lives and make profound change. As a result of a mere half-hour simulation I changed the entire direction of my professional life and became convinced that I had a mission to teach reality therapy.

Upon returning from my year in Japan, I reconnected with the Institute, attending many training weeks, four in a year. Glasser began to notice that there was one person who continued to appear at these workshops, and he asked me to be one of his group leaders. He then created a category for ancillary instructors, "Field Faculty." This meant I could conduct the basic 4½-day workshop with small numbers of attendees outside Los Angeles.

In 1983, Dr. Glasser restructured his teaching organization and required all his instructors to submit videotapes to demonstrate that we understood reality therapy and could use the skills that he believed were essential for a senior faculty member. In part, his letter to me of June 14, 1983, said:

> I was totally satisfied with everything you did (on your videotape). You seem to have an excellent understanding of control (choice) theory and how to integrate it into reality therapy. I was especially impressed with your critique of the (other) person who did the role play. . . . You brought out so much good teaching material as you talked, even briefly, and I was extremely impressed with your ability to teach. . . . You have the honor of being the first level II (senior) instructor to pass the tape requirements.

By 1985 and 1986, I was deeply involved in the teaching of reality therapy. The publication of many journal articles in *The Journal of Reality Therapy* and elsewhere, including one (1979) in the first issue of the *Journal of the American Mental Health Counselors Association,* established my name as someone who taught and practiced reality therapy.

Glasser then formed a professional development committee whose mission was to monitor the rapidly advancing certification process. I was assistant chair, but this being a highly political committee, I was often even unaware of when the meetings were held. However, I did not create a confrontation about this, a behavior which has always appealed to Glasser. In 1988, he asked me to be the first "director of training." The primary responsibility was, and remains to this day, chairing the faculty development committee and monitoring the certification process. When asked about what he expected of me, he simply said, "Don't make a big deal out of it." Over the years, because of increasing interest and numbers of trainees, it has become a "bigger deal" with more responsibility. However, the vast majority of work and responsibility remains with the Institute office in Chatsworth, California under the direction of Linda Harshman, Administrator, who has been a close friend and colleague during the vicissitudes of Institute history. In my 13 years working with her, I have found her to be a paragon of integrity, reasonableness, and wisdom.

In 1992, Naomi Glasser died, and both my wife Sandie and I lost a good friend. After a while, Bill Glasser recovered from this painful loss and married another good friend of ours, Carleen Floyd. Together they are an incomparable team leading The William Glasser Institute into the 21st century.

It has been not only the ideas of William Glasser, but his nonpompous, engaging personality and wit that have been part of my quality world and that have made it easy to be part of this Institute. As in any organization, there are politics, rivalries, and disputes, but the quality of relationships has been a sustaining influence for those of us who have chosen to remain part of the Institute and demonstrate leadership.

As we enter the 21st century, my hope is that an increasing number of people throughout the world will learn choice theory and reality therapy. I hope to continue to play a vital role in the spread of these ideas, which are humane, liberating, and deeply spiritual.

CHAPTER

Personality: Why and How Do People Do What They Do?

Reality therapy, based on choice theory, the explanation of the human brain as a system that seeks to mold the external world, explains the development of human personality as an attempt to fulfill innate drives: survival, belonging, power, freedom, and fun. From the cradle to the grave we generate behaviors, and through experimentation we find them need-satisfying or need-threatening. As these behaviors impact our external world we learn that other persons, events, objects, and situations are either need-satisfying, need-attacking, or neutral.

☐ Choice and Discovery

Choice theory and reality therapy teach that individuals choose behaviors and that the only behavior we can control is our own. When choices are made, people discover that the result attained is desirable or undesirable. They thus discover that their behaviors are effective or ineffective in satisfying their needs. They also discover the many aspects of the external world as pleasurable (need-satisfying), painful (not need-satisfying), or neutral.

Infants "choose" the only behavior available in attempting to fulfill a physiological need related to survival, more specifically, comfort and sustenance. Since infants are unable to forage for food or change their own diapers, they reach into their suitcase of rather limited behaviors and discover what is possibly one of the few innate total behaviors: crying, accompanied by angry or at least irritable feelings, as well as various facial expressions. They thus send out their best signal to the persons in the external world, that is, their immediate environment, in an attempt to get what they want relative to their needs. As children grow and develop language, they discover through their creative behavioral system that other behaviors are available. They see other people smiling, talking, walking, reaching, touching, and playing. They choose to attempt these behaviors at appropriate developmental and maturational points as more effective ways to fulfill their needs.

The word "choice," predicated for an infant's behavior, is not used with the same meaning as a fully voluntary selection made by an adult. "Choice" as used in reality therapy means that the behavior is generated from within the person for the purpose of need satisfaction. Choice, therefore, is not *caused* by environmental stimuli. As a person grows and develops, choices become more conscious and explicit and adults become more clearly aware of choices. All behaviors are treated "as if" they are choices.

☐ Role of the Outside World

Even though behavior is seen as internally caused, still the influence of the "real world" is not ignored. A person growing up in an English-speaking environment with no exposure to other languages chooses the only option available in the suitcase of behavior. Nevertheless, it is useful to see even this selection as a choice. Similarly, a person living in a schizophrenic family, an abusive or drug-dependent family, or a neighborhood characterized by crime *might* be inclined to choose similar behaviors. Indeed, some correlation exists between having been abused as a child and abusing one's own children, but not everyone who has experienced abuse as a child chooses similar behaviors as a parent. Many people have found other behaviors that are need-satisfying. And so, while the environment is important, our physical surroundings are not the source of human behavior.

Furthermore, to say that behavior is self-generated and even chosen is not to say that it is easily changed or that other options are always accessible. Critics of reality therapy have erroneously concluded that it simplistically states that human beings should be blamed or criticized for their ineffective or harmful choices and that change is easy to accomplish. On the contrary, reality therapy is in agreement with Aristotle, who stated that people can choose only the good or the apparent good. Every choice is seen by its originator as effective at the time of the choice. Second, because we have a limited number of behaviors in our suitcases, it often takes time, practice, and therapy to develop other choices. Thus the reality therapist continually assists clients to evaluate the helpfulness, effectiveness, and appropriateness of their behavior.

☐ Personality Development and Identity

William Glasser (1972, 1986) described two general types of human personality. These are explained primarily in the context of how individuals see themselves and secondarily in how others see them. As stated previously, all persons generate behaviors in order to fulfill human needs. As people attempt to accomplish various developmental tasks, they either succeed or fail. When they habitually fail to fulfill their needs effectively, they develop a failure identity (W. Glasser, 1972, 1986) characterized by ineffective or out-of-control behaviors (W. Glasser, 1985).

Glasser has recently discarded the term "failure identity" in that all people have what is for them a success identity, but often they choose less effective behaviors. The goal of the helper is to assist these misguided people choose more effective quality world pictures and behaviors, which will help them fulfill their pictures or wants. Thus a true "success identity" or collection of effective behaviors is determined not only by the individual but, from a systems perspective, by society at large.

Less Effective Life Direction

Three stages of less effective behavior are characterized by identifiable total behaviors. A specific case example helps to illuminate the stages.

Stage 1: Giving Up. Shelby, a student in elementary school, attempts to learn the material his teacher is presenting. In making the effort to learn, Shelby is attempting to fulfill the need for power or achievement and possibly fun. Successful efforts result in need-satisfaction for the other children, but Shelby is unable to find adequate behaviors that result in learning. While others succeed and attain need-satisfaction, Shelby feels frustrated, powerless, and bored. Feelings of isolation result, and the need for belonging is unmet. School is painful, not enjoyable, and Shelby feels trapped in ineffective behaviors. The thinking behavior "I give up" is manifest in actions that are evident to many observers.

Stage 2: Subsequent Choices. Shelby does not remain in the "give up" stage of ineffective behavior. In fact, the bridge to the second stage is often indiscernible. In this stage Shelby is characterized by one or more total behaviors. As time passes these behaviors can become quite pronounced and can significantly interfere with his life direction and that of other people.

Acting Out Behaviors. The inability to meet his needs effectively might result in antisocial behaviors. As Shelby journeys to adulthood, acting out could intensify to seriously destructive actions toward himself or toward others. In school he becomes argumentative and even violent. His lack of cooperation with even the reasonable expectations of school, family, and society eventually results in dropping out of school. The number of such students, like Shelby, leaving school before high school graduation ranges from 10% to 20%. Such individuals are characterized by an inordinate number of contacts with the criminal justice system.

Ineffective Thinking Behaviors. The thinking component of total behavior could become the most prominent. Chronic, ineffective self-talk might be most characteristic of his behavior: "I can't," "I'm no good," "I'm worthless," "I'm powerless," "I'm bored with life," "No one is going to tell me what to do," "I'm going to do whatever I please regardless of what others tell me," and the statement which is central to failure, "Even though what I'm doing is not helping me, I'm going to continue to do it." Even more serious, Shelby might withdraw from his external world, and may even develop more serious psychological problems. Other behaviors, such as anorexia and bulimia, are attempts to gain control, to achieve perfection, and to fulfill an intense need for power. The reality therapy goal for people showing such behaviors is to help them fulfill other needs such as belonging and fun as well as to help them continually evaluate other more successful and positive behaviors.

Ineffective Feeling Behaviors. Acting out, or harmful cognition, is likely to be accompanied by mild or intense emotional behaviors. Clearly, hostile actions involve anger and even rage at the external world. When mental scales are out of balance, i.e., when people are unable to get what they want to meet their five needs, they often generate feelings of annoyance, impatience, and anger. When they wish their actions in their past history to be different and when this wish is intense, they often generate regret, embarrassment, shame, or guilt. When someone is rejected by another person or persons, the primary emotion they resort to is typically that of feeling hurt. This can progress to resentment, anger, and even revenge, which can be followed by retaliatory actions. When fun and enjoyment are lacking, the person generates boredom and apathy. Depression is an all-encompassing category that often accompanies passive actions and ineffective self-talk, such as "I can't," "I'm not in control of my life," and "I have no choices." Depression can exist along with actions ranging from procrastination and aimlessness to long-term inability to search out need-satisfying actions. Fear and panic accompany the perceived present or future inability to satisfy the need for power. This powerful negative emotion of misery can also be related to the perceived loss of control, which is a failure to adequately satisfy the entire need system.

Most importantly, the emotions are not static conditions, but active components of behaviors. Similarly, emotions are not the sources of other actions. Anger, for example, does not cause actions, but accompanies aggression and a myriad of other actions. The causes of anger are unmet wants and unfulfilled needs. Consequently, to "get in touch" with anger and other feelings, to label them, and to talk about them, is of limited value, but is only a beginning. Relating our feelings to actions is important because we have more direct control of actions than feelings. People who depress themselves can only make plans to *do* something new and different. They cannot simply decide to feel better. Yet, because all components of behavior are connected, a change in action ripples through the other components of behavior. And, in time, these also change. Thus, accompanying Shelby's acting out and self-destructive thinking are feelings of anger, rejection, alienation, self-pity, among others.

A reality therapist would help Shelby decide what exactly he wants related to his five needs, examine his actions designed to fulfill them, and, most importantly, evaluate all aspects of the behavioral system, especially actions. Building upon the essential self-evaluation, the therapist would assist Shelby to abandon self-destructive actions and to make alternative action plans designed to enhance his sense of belonging, power, freedom, and fun. Only then will feelings change, for these do not exist in a vacuum, separate from the other components of behavior. And we do not change our feelings directly through discussions, as if these were the cause of other behaviors.

Less Effective Physiological Behaviors. Because behavior is "total," i.e., comprised of actions, thinking, feelings, and physiology, a person who has gone beyond the "give up" stage is characterized by physiology that is not effective for satisfying needs. When a person feels out of control, the physiological component can be the most obvious symptom. Heart attacks, strokes, ulcers, high blood pressure, and other problems are sometimes due to the impossibility of fulfilling the quality world wants. The practitioner of reality therapy refers such clients for medical assistance, in addition to helping them to gain more control of their diet and exercise. But the emphasis is on assisting clients gain overall control by helping them change their wants and/or choose more effective behaviors.

If Shelby were to develop physical problems, such as flu symptoms, skin problems, or stomach aches, an effective reality therapist would see such behaviors as similar to feelings. These are similar to the lights on the dashboard of a car, which when lit indicate to the driver that the automobile needs attention. Getting to the root of the cause, however, means more than merely talking about it. It can mean getting one's life under control, i.e., fulfilling needs. The reality therapist would help Shelby get proper medical attention, but would also use the WDEP system to deal with his "total behavior."

These behaviors, while significantly less effective than their opposites, are the clients' best efforts at a given moment to fulfill wants. The role of the therapist or any user of reality therapy is to help individuals choose the opposite of these ineffective behaviors. This occurs after helping them define their *wants*, describe what they are *doing* (total behavior), *evaluate* their behaviors and wants, and *plan* for a better future.

Stage 3. Addictions. Some persons choose noxious behaviors and perceive them to be need-satisfying. These behaviors produce, at least in their early stages, an illusion of immediate need-satisfaction. They provide a "high," which can include a short term and groundless sense of be-

> *Heredity is not predestination*
> -Ashley Montague
> *We choose our behavior*

longing, power, freedom, and fun. Alcohol, drugs, gambling, food, sex, even the addiction to work, can, each in its own way, provide the user with a distorted and momentary sense of popularity, power, excitement, or liberation from stress and pain.

Depending on the stage of recovery, the reality therapist works in diverse ways. In the early stages, such as pretreatment, stabilization, and early recovery (Gorski, 1985), the application is more directive than in the subsequent middle, late, and maintenance stages, in which the relational and life issues are discussed after a history of sobriety has been established and a firm program of day-to-day living is well in place.

If Shelby turns to drugs, and early detection and intervention is available to help him, he may choose more effective behaviors and thus more effective control. Such intervention could take many forms, which might be confrontational (Johnson, 1980; Johnson Institute, 1996) or supportive (Gorski, 1985). If drug treatment or 12-step programs are available, these would be used by the reality therapist to facilitate a healthy recovering personality. Consequently, the use of reality therapy requires not only knowledge but what some call "artistic skill," that is, skill that goes beyond the blind application of the procedures. Similarly, knowledge of community resources is useful and even necessary.

More Effective Life Direction

Just as the personality can be characterized by ineffective behaviors, an ineffective or destructive life direction, and out-of-control behaviors, the healthy personality develops in the opposite direction. This individual possesses a willingness to meet, as well as a repertoire of skills for meeting, the five needs in positive ways. Such people have chosen a set of inner wants radically different from the one described above. They also choose more effective behaviors such as those described now. Wubbolding (1988) has designated two styles of effective behaviors as being parallel to the less effective stages.

Stage 1. "I Want to Change and I Want to Grow." The desire to fulfill human needs effectively without infringing on the rights of others represents the first stage in the development of a more effective life direction. Such a desire is usually quite implicit, but should be made explicit in practicing reality therapy with clients whose commitment is the opposite of "I give up," and even those who have progressed further. Operationally, this is related to eliciting a level of commitment and is a central component of the W in the WDEP system.

Such a desire to turn around is evidenced by clients who genuinely intend to change and who express their commitment. "Yes, I want to change"; "I want to improve"; "I am going to solve the problem." Shelby might say, "I am going to solve the problem," or "I am going to raise my grade and work at getting along with my parents. And I will try to find someone I can call 'friend.'"

A mistake made by neophyte users of reality therapy is to see the lack of change or follow-through as pure failure. A better way to see the lack of formulation or implementation of plans is not as resistance or a low level of commitment, but rather as a suitcase of behavior that does not include such skills. The lack of follow-through to the "I want to change" stage can also be reframed from negative to positive. At least the client wants to change. Now it is a matter of inserting into the behavioral suitcase new behaviors that result in reaching the second stage of effective behaviors.

Shelby would be questioned about whether he wants to discard some pain and misery. Would he like to rid himself of some hassles? A "yes" answer is the first step toward an appropriate outcome of therapy with Shelby. Further, the level of commitment, as described in chapter 9, is determined at this stage.

Stage 2. Effective Behaviors. The second stage in the development and an effectively in-control life direction is, again, the mirror image of ineffective behaviors (Wubbolding, 1988).

Assertive and Altruistic Actions. The healthy person is characterized by actions indicating the person's skill in defining and pursuing effective want- and need-satisfaction. Formulating goals and seeking their fulfillment is a major part of reality therapy because these skills are characteristics of people who have an effective life direction. Moreover, contributing to society through work, philanthropy, church or synagogue, volunteerism, and family are added indications of effective behavior. The therapist would not avoid a discussion of self-destructive behaviors with Shelby, but in therapy the emphasis is placed on alternatives: When did he succeed in school? When did he contribute to someone's life in a positive way, such as helping at home even in a minor way? When did he have fun with someone without getting in trouble? The therapist helps Shelby choose positive actions no matter how apparently trivial at first glance. Following the dictum, "A journey of a thousand miles is begun with one step," the therapist begins by helping Shelby make minute, effective, and altruistic choices to take action that is the reverse of past harmful choices. The emphasis in such choices is on actions that will enhance human relationships (Glasser, 1998a).

Positive and Effective Thinking Behaviors. The mirror image of ineffective self-talk (IST) such as "I can't," "I'm no good," "They made me do it," is effective self-talk (EST). Underlying and accompanying effective actions are such statements as, "I will," "I have control of my behavior,." "I am a valuable person," "I am responsible for my behavior," and most especially, "I will choose what is helpful and effective."

EST related to choice theory is characteristic of effective behavior. After having Shelby evaluate the helpfulness of his IST, he would then be assisted to tell himself on an occasional basis the opposite: "I am responsible for my current choices," "I can change what I'm doing," "I have more control than I thought I had." These effective statements or affirmations are at times general, but most often are specific formulations geared to the exact situation and individual person.

Positive Feeling Behaviors. Just as anger, rage, depression, self-pity, and a multitude of other emotions are characteristic of out-of-control and less effective behavior, the more effective personality is also characterized by feelings. Thus another goal in Shelby's therapy is to help him develop such emotions as patience, trust, self-acceptance, hope, self-confidence, self-reliance, a sense of idealism, enthusiasm, persistence, determination, resilience, and involvement with others. These "feelings," of course, extend beyond what are traditionally seen as pure emotions. Their inclusion as feeling behaviors is somewhat arbitrary. As with all behaviors, both positive and negative, they are "total behaviors" and thus embrace all four aspects of behavior.

In order to help Shelby develop emotions that are characteristic of a more effective life direction, the reality therapist would assist him to discuss them as desired goals that are more satisfying than their opposites. These counselors know that endless discussion of these feelings would not necessarily result in productive change. These feelings would come into the discussion only as part of the action symptom, which is the most directly changeable component of so-called personality formation.

Effective Physiological Behaviors. Characteristic of the effective person is physiology, which contributes to personal growth. Clients are encouraged to choose behaviors that are life-giving rather than life-diminishing. Appropriate eating habits, moderate use of alcohol and nicotine or even total abstinence, as well as regular physical exercise will all add to a positive life direction. Because of the healthful effects of exercise, aerobic exercise is often part of the treatment plan. Brisk walking on a regular basis has enhancing effects on all levels of behavior, and in relationship counseling such activity serves to provide quality time on the condition it is need-satisfying and enjoyable (Wubbolding, 1988).

Some therapists have a tendency to underestimate the value of positive plan making in the above categories, especially regarding the value of exercise. Yet the salutary effects of a regular program of aerobic activity have been shown to help lessen stress and overcome depression. In reality therapy, such activities are seen as choices that satisfy belonging, power, freedom, and fun. They include all four levels of behavior. Brisk walking, for instance, is a positive action resulting in an enhanced sense of belonging if done with another person. It also results in a feeling of being in control of one's life, at least for a few minutes. People who continue such actions often say they enjoy it and that their minds are free to create strategies and solutions for their other decisions and problems. The self-talk can be positive during this time, and clients report that they find it hard to worry or depress themselves while walking briskly.

Thus even with a psychotic, delusional, compulsive, or harmfully addicted person, the reality therapist emphasizes the sane and congruent part of the personality. No one's life is completely characterized by giving up or ineffective behaviors; even the negatively addicted person has some positive behaviors. In the process of reality therapy, these strengths are identified and expanded. Similarly, even an effective life direction sometimes has pockets of give-up and negative, ineffective behaviors. Consequently, reality therapy is a system not only for remediating deficits but also for facilitating the growth of a healthy person.

Stage 3. Positive Addictions. Relatively few people are able to reach a state of "positive addiction." This condition—the opposite of the negative addiction described above—is the result of explicit, life-enhancing choices. Although other activities can create mental states that approach the positive addiction state, Glasser (1976) found two activities especially helpful in achieving the conditions necessary for positive addiction: meditation and running. These two behaviors involve all the necessary conditions of a positively addicting activity.

- The behavior is chosen on an almost daily basis for a limited amount of time. A person who runs for hours every day and whose relationships, career, or health are destroyed is not *positively* addicted. Persons with a reasonable balance in their behaviors report that 45 to 60 minutes a day is the maximum time for the positive addiction.
- Positive addiction does not occur quickly. It results when the activity is chosen for a protracted period of time. Six to eighteen months seems to be the usual amount of time required to achieve a positive addiction.
- An altered state of consciousness accompanies the activity. After fulfilling the above two requirements, many persons report that they experience a "high" for short periods of time. Such rewards might last only minutes per week, but they make the effort worthwhile and help the person sustain the activity.
- The activity requires little concentration. On the contrary, the mind is freed from the responsibility of attending to procedures, rules, and even ideas. Positively addicted people report that their mind is allowed to float and that they frequently complete the activity with solutions to problems and creative behaviors that result from allowing their mind to wander rather than from effortful thinking.
- Cessation of the activity is painful. So important and need-satisfying is the activity that to be unable to perform it is at least uncomfortable. Runners report that if they take up a sedentary life, they feel guilty, restless, and apathetic. The cessation of such an intensely need-satisfying behavior results in withdrawal pains.

Even though few people reach the positively addicted state, many enhance their personal growth by activities that have some of the qualities of pure positive addiction. All such endeavors can be goals of therapy. Travel, reading, walking and thousands of habitual enjoyment-related behaviors can serve as alternatives to an ineffective life direction. These life-enriching activities are not seen as superficial diversions from therapy. Provided the person sees them as such, they are intensely need-satisfying. Moreover, because the three stages of effective life direction represent the mirror image of ineffective choices, they are dealt with in the practice of reality therapy.

In my view, some of the activities that lead to therapeutic ineffectiveness are endless discussions of diagnosis, past history, and external, uncontrollable people and events. While such discussions are interesting to the therapist or to anyone who listens empathically to another person, and even necessary at times, they precede the *most* effective use of reality therapy. These useful methods consist of building on already existing effective behaviors, eliciting a commitment to change, defining what is realistically attainable, helping a client conduct a searching and detailed self-evaluation, and making specific plans for enriching one's life. A healthy personality develops when the client moves closer to other people by forming positive relationships.

CHAPTER

More Specifics: What Other Ideas Do I Need to Know?

Reality therapy is a logical system and appears to be common sense, not requiring of the therapist a sense of direction or a knowledge of the components of a healthy personality. Still, it is not a hydraulic system by which change occurs automatically if the therapist pulls a lever by labeling the problem, helping the client gain insight, or analyzing the past. Nor is it like number painting, in which the therapist paints with the WDEP formulation and automatically creates a work of art. Rather, it is similar to the work of artists who, following some basic principles, use their creativity to produce a unique work of art. The product is the result of the application of the principles. The clients still retain their choices. The logic of reality therapy and the artistic creativity of the therapist are thus applied to the current choices of clients.

☐ Psychopathology

Reality therapy recognizes the importance and usefulness of diagnosis but sees psychopathology in terms of behaviors rather than static conditions. Thus, persons do not exist in an immutable *place* when depressed. Rather, clients are said to be "depress-ing," "anxiety-ing," "guilt-ing," "phobic-ing," "compuls-ing," headach-ing," and "sick-ing" on their own. To reframe such phenomena from conditions (nouns) to behaviors (verbs) is to see them as more controllable. Alternatives can be sought. Similarly, clients are not victims of these oppressive problems. They are generators of behaviors. Yet, they are not blamed or criticized for their behavior, as they generate only the behaviors that are available to them. The reality therapist, using the WDEP system, assists them to develop better, more need-satisfying behaviors.

☐ Multicultural Applications

Most psychotherapies originated in the Western Hemisphere, many in North America. Reality therapy began as an American theory applied to the many cultures of the

United States and Canada, but is now taught, studied, or practiced in varying degrees around the world.

In light of this universality, the practice and teaching of reality therapy need to be adjusted to many people whose values, wants, and manner of expressions are quite different, often more "indirect" than in North America. On the surface, reality therapy is a very direct method, yet therapists must apply the method more indirectly in some cultures, especially the "indirect cultures" in the Far East and Middle East where people communicate more indirectly. In these cultures, asking directly about wants is often seen as intrusive or even vulgar. Consequently, explorations of wants are more indirect and, by North American standards, quite subtle. Hal Roach, the Irish comedian, once described how an Irish lad proposes to a girlfriend. The lad is not so direct as to say, "Will you marry me?" He's a bit more subtle: "Would you like to be buried with my people?" Assertiveness is not always seen as a positive trait, but is viewed as rudeness. The word "fun" is sometimes defined not as enjoyment, but as silliness. And so the language and the application needs to be applied in ways that are subtle and indirect.

Moreover, psychotherapists are often seen not as partners on a journey, but as authority figures, as are teachers in schools. Thus maintaining a delicate balance between practicing and teaching the theory accurately and authentically on one hand, and adapting it to "other" cultures requires sensitivity to the culture as well as knowledge of its social, economic, historical, political, and psychological processes. In helping an American student evaluate her own behavior, the therapist, for example, would emphasize questions such as, "Is what you are doing helping or hurting *you*?" "Do your current actions have a reasonable chance of getting you what you want?" In counseling a Chinese Singapore youth it would be appropriate to ask similar questions, but much more emphasis would be placed on such questions as, "What does your family think about your actions?" "Do they approve or disapprove?" "Do your actions bring shame or honor to your parents?"

It is clear that reality therapy is a system that requires specific skills and procedures as summarized in the WDEP formulation. Nevertheless, these should be seen as flexible and adaptable to the style and personality of the user as well as to the experience, manner of expression, thought patterns (total behavior), and specific wants of various cultures. The multicultural dimensions are explored in detail in chapter 11.

☐ An Open System

Reality therapy is best viewed as a system that makes its own, unique contributions, as outlined in this book, to the field of mental health. Still, it is an open system. It is in agreement with Lazarus's suggestion of "technical eclecticism." Empathy and positive regard are important in the establishment of the therapeutic alliance. Paradoxical techniques are a perfect fit for reality therapy and their use is central to the effective use of the principles (Wubbolding, 1988). Disputing irrational thinking is also useful. Mental statements such as, "Even though what I'm doing is not helping me, I will continue to do it," accompany but do not cause actions. Furthermore, disputation is less useful than helping the clients evaluate the effectiveness of telling themselves they are victims, have no control, or cannot change. Body language can be read by the reality therapist, and resistance, openness, or avoidance noted. But the reality therapist gives only passing attention to those phenomena to which Gestalt and other act-ing out therapies attach greater significance.

☐ Trauma

It is often asked how reality therapists deal with past trauma and the aftermath, post-traumatic stress. Some therapists ask the client to relive the experience but to picture a different result. The attacker is visualized as approaching the client. Instead of suc-ceeding in the rape or abuse, the perpetrator is repulsed and defeated in his attempt to humiliate, subjugate, or dominate the victim.

Clients experiencing this therapy feel much relief . . . for a while. However, they now have incorporated warring fantasies. According to Landis (1995), the effect of this method is transitory, fading in about 3 months. The client feels good because he or she has *talked* about the disturbing event. This, in fact, is the danger of many talk therapies. People delude themselves into thinking that they have dealt with the issue because they have talked about it.

The effective reality therapist, on the other hand, believes that while the trauma has resulted in a wound, it need not cause a perpetual and painfully excruciating scar. When the client learns how to fulfill the five needs effectively (survival, belonging, power, freedom, and fun) *now* in his or her life, the scar will be less painful. Moreover, the current stress is most effectively handled by helping the client develop or deepen current relationships. When current relationships are not satisfying, clients turn to ineffective behaviors such as stress-ing, flashback-ing, and a myriad of other behav-iors that are less than adequate.

In counseling an adult woman abused as a child, it is useful for her to discuss the abuse briefly, especially if she has never previously brought it into the open. The emphasis in the counseling, however, is placed on helping her examine current rela-tionships: how to form, maintain, develop, and enhance her skills in connecting with other people, thereby satisfying her current need for belonging. Such changes in her behavioral direction (actions, thinking, and feeling) help her gain an added sense of self-esteem, self-worth, inner peace, self-confidence (power), and overall well being.

☐ Behavior

Based on the principle that we are born with at least five generic needs that we seek to fulfill with even the minutest behavior, reality therapy provides a structure for helping people gain more effective perceptions of survival, belonging, power or achievement, freedom or independence, and fun or enjoyment. Thus, the overall goal of the practi-tioner is the more effective need-satisfaction of clients as well as the fulfillment of their quality world wants. Because behavior is most evident to the rest of the world, it is useful to observe it in the following context.

Purposeful

Behavior is the mechanism used to fulfill the human needs. Marcus Aurelius, perhaps the world's first choice theorist, stated, "Nature has an aim in everything" (Wubbolding,

1994). We act as sculptors molding the clay of our behaviors in an attempt to shape the world around us to match the image of what we want. The vaudeville joke describes a universal truth: The chicken crossed the road for a purpose. The human behaviors of acting, thinking, feeling, and even "physiologic-ing" are teleological, that is, they serve a purpose and have an aim. Their purpose is to fulfill human needs and meet quality world wants.

It is useful for the helper to see behaviors, such as depress-ing, having two interconnected goals: an outcome purpose and a communication purpose. The outcome purpose is the desired impact on the external world, for example, to control the family or even, if ineffectively, to gain more control of one's own life. The process purpose is the signal or message that is sent. Thus the practical question to ask depressed clients is not only, "What is the purpose of your behavior?" A process-centered question is, "What are you telling your family or yourself by your depress-ing actions and feelings? What message do you want them to get?" "What message do you think they are actually getting?"

The process purpose is useful in the therapy relationship itself. Client resistance is often a signal that the therapist is not dealing with issues important to the client. Sometimes clients resist the pace of the therapy. Brief therapists often state, "There are no resistant clients, only unimaginative therapists." Teachers can ask the explicit question, "What are you trying to tell me when you act uninterested?" "When you argue with me, miss class, or make a half-hearted effort, what message are you trying to send? I really want to know."

While influenced and limited by environment, culture, past personal experience, family, and peers, human behavior is not determined by past internal influences nor current external pressures. Still, to the outside observer, a behavior might *seem* to be purposeless, aimless, and senseless. But to the agent of the behavior, it represents his or her best attempt at that moment to satisfy a need and a related specific want by impacting the external world with the twofold hope of getting something from it and of sending a message. Because many people have conflicting images of what is desirable, their behavior appears to be confused and senseless. Others have clear images of what they want, which are helpful to themselves and to others. Some wants can also be destructive, with the resulting behavior of effectively fulfilling the harmful want, for example, injecting heroin or taking crack cocaine. On the other hand, wanting the legitimate goal of victory in a game or in an election could be achieved by purposeful yet socially or personally destructive behaviors. A Faustian bargain equals short-term gain and long-term pain.

Chosen

Behavior is seen as a choice. One of the most empowering aspects of reality therapy is experienced by people when the practitioner repeatedly speaks of "choice" when talking with them. While the word is not used with the identical meaning for all behaviors, it is useful to discuss with clients, students, and others the degree of choice that they perceive they currently have. And while they might not be able, instantly or directly, to choose to make radical changes in their feelings or thoughts, they can make, at least, small incremental changes in their actions. Over a period of time these modifications carry along a change and even a transformation in feeling, thinking, and, at times, physiological and health-related behaviors. People depress-ing them-selves are encouraged to choose actions similar to those of cheerful people, with the injunction that "motion creates emotion." *Changing* the most *changeable* component in the suitcase of behaviors brings about a *change* in the remaining components.

Consequently, reality therapy totally rejects the notion that human beings are vic-tims of external stimuli or conditioning which allows little or no choice. Even in life-threatening situations there is still the possibility of a choice. This choice is, of course, related to what is seen as need- and want-satisfying. For example, while most people would select panic as the only accessible behavior when their survival is threatened on a crashing airliner, a person who intended to commit suicide might opt for a sense of relief. Even in such dire circumstances, human beings retain at least some choice. This choice is unalterably linked to the fundamental motivators: needs and wants.

Focus on the Present

Since choice is a "here and now" phenomenon, the therapist emphasizes current and recent lifestyle behaviors. It is true that our personal history is important and interest-ing. Our current life and direction for the future is the sum of all that we have experi-enced. Still, as Glasser frequently points out in his lectures, we do not need to find the pothole that ambushed the car in order to realign the front end. Past behavior should be discussed only as it impacts or predicts future choices. If someone has repeatedly attempted suicide, the therapist needs to know. Regarding the discussion of past be-haviors, reality therapists suggest, "Look but don't stare." The continual uncovering of forgotten events and experiences is of little value to the reality therapist. True in-sight is the realization, "I am responsible at this moment not for past failures, but for my current choices and my future direction, and I can change."

☐ Therapist's Attitude

The responsibility for leading or following the client is an individual decision and varies according to the setting. Private practice is different from a prison or correc-tional setting or from a classroom. The use of reality therapy with an emotionally upset and grieving person is vastly different from its use with an alcoholic who firmly denies the condition and blames others for the accompanying problems. In the former case the therapist listens supportively and gently helps the client take better charge of need-satisfying actions. In the second case, the therapist is somewhat confrontive by feeding back specific behaviors and asking for dozens of self-evaluations. Questions would include, "Did drinking a fifth of liquor and passing out at the party help or hurt your relationships?" "Is missing work and shouting at the kids a behavior you would like to increase or decrease in the next few months?"

But no matter what the setting is, the practitioner creates a firm and friendly envi-ronment, that is, a safe atmosphere conducive to change. Sometimes this is accom-plished quickly, but more often it is the result of *continued* effort by the user of reality therapy to avoid the pitfalls and to listen empathically.

Treatment: Is It Used Individually, In Groups, or In Family Therapy?

Reality therapy has been used in virtually every kind of setting from private practice to prisons. In private practice it is usually short term but in institutions where residents live on a long-term basis it is used as long as clients are required to be in the program or until their rehabilitation is sufficient to allow them to return to society. Moreover, the method is applied to individual, group, and family therapy.

As the case of Fay will demonstrate, it is helpful to view clients in the context of their relationships with other people. Therapists using reality therapy are always advised to focus on their relationships first.

☐ Individual Therapy

Many clients who experience reality therapy receive treatment on a one-to-one basis. As in any therapy the therapist discusses professional details including the procedures used in treatment. Clients generally are then asked to tell their story. They often describe their upset feelings and that they are stressed about something that has happened to them, how society is unfair, or how they want their external worlds to change. Some already have a sense of inner control and wish to change their own behavior. They admit they are depressed, angry, shamed, or guilty and wish to find better choices. Involuntary clients, on the other hand, are sometimes resistant, hostile, withdrawn, or passive; most often, they are quick to make excuses about their predicament or to blame outside people or factors for their frustration.

The therapist attempts to make psychological contact using skills that are fundamental to most theories: active listening, reflection, clarification, and many others useful in establishing the therapeutic environment. Allowing clients to tell their story as they see it helps the therapist determine the perceived locus of control of the client, that is, how much responsibility the client has taken for past behavior and can realistically take for immediate future choices. Having determined the perceived locus of control by patiently listening to the client's perception of his or her story, the therapist helps the client set goals for the therapy by asking what he or she wants to have happen as a result of the relationship with the therapist. More specifically, it is useful to ask what the person wants to gain from the session today. The impact of this question can hardly be overestimated. The implicit message is that some change can be made immediately and that there is hope. For the upset depressed person living in psychological darkness, even a glimmer of daylight is greeted with astonishment.

Focusing on the current behavior of the clients rather than on past history or on the onslaughts from their external worlds helps them become aware of their routine actions, the component of their behavior over which they have most control. Depending on the style of the therapist, they are asked intermittently or cumulatively to make judgments on their wants. Are they realistic? Are their wants beneficial, or would having their wants met be harmful to them? Are their overall behavior and their specific actions helping them? The therapist then asks the clients to make plans that fulfill the characteristics of effective planning, frequently using simple and uncomplicated planning sheets. In private practice optimal termination occurs through a joint decision by therapist and client based on whether the client has been able to insert more effective need-fulfilling behaviors into the behavioral suitcase.

☐ Group Therapy

Reality therapy is especially applicable to groups. After ice-breaking activities during which people psychologically connect with the therapist and with each other, genuine reality therapy begins.

Wubbolding (1991b) has shown how reality therapy is integrated into the stages of groups (Corey, 2000b). At every stage of group development the needs of the clients should be addressed, though it is not possible for all needs to be consistently met to the same degree. The need for belonging is met in the initial stage in that everyone feels included in the group. The therapist asks what people want from the group. Total behavior is also explored: life direction, specific actions, ineffective and effective self-talk, feelings, and even physiological behaviors.

In the transitional stage of group development the power need is addressed when anxiety, conflict, and resistance surface. The therapist listens, assures, and reframes conflict and resistance from negative to positive, pointing out that they are evidence of group maturity.

In the third stage, the working phase of group development, belonging is addressed when the group members come to believe that others in the group can be of some help to them. Power or achievement is evident when participants begin to want to change. The leader helps them determine their level of commitment and raise it, if necessary, by asking such questions as, "How hard do you want to work?" or "How much energy do you want to put into figuring out more helpful plans and into following through on them?" The central importance of this phase is illustrated by the emphasis given by the therapist to helping group members evaluate the various aspects of their own control systems: wants, levels of commitment, and total behavior. Through the persistent use of the E (evaluation) of the WDEP formulation, the members genuinely evaluate their success at gaining what they want, restructure their thinking, and eventually make plans for change. This "E work" makes planning (P) for changes in thinking and action easier. At this stage therapists ask group members to assist each other in making self-evaluations. One member or even the entire group is asked about the effectiveness of the other group members' choices. The counselor might say, "Fran and Lou, when Sam did such and such, do you think it was helpful for him or for the relationship he is searching for?" Such questioning helps at least three people learn the principle of self-evaluation. Follow-through or lack of it is discussed, and persistent involvement and empathic confrontation (not criticism) are used when the leader and members, who have by now learned the process, help one another self-evaluate.

In the consolidation and termination stage, further planning helps address the fun and belonging needs. Touching on the need for freedom or autonomy, discussion of progress is emphasized. Final closure of the group is brought about in many ways depending on the decision of the group members.

The specific techniques used to facilitate the stages of group development vary depending on the setting. Self-selected groups in private practice have a different character than prison inmates or juveniles in a detention center. But because reality therapy is based on universal principles of motivation and behavior, it is applicable and adjustable to any population in which group therapy is used.

☐ Marriage and Family Therapy

Reality therapy is a preeminent tool for marriage and family therapists (Altamura, 1996; Wubbolding, 2000a). The method can also be integrated into systems theory by adding a practical structure and delivery system. It is important to communicate to the family that it is helpful for them to discard the perception "It's you against me." Rather, "It is you and I against the problem." This mind-set reduces guilt and hostility and also leads to a "We will work it out" attitude.

Premises Underlying Reality Therapy and Family Counseling

The practice of reality therapy flows from principles implicit in choice theory.

1. As in the experiential family therapy of Whitaker and the communications theory of Satir, one of the principles of reality therapy used in family therapy is that families are composed of both individuals and structures. If family members are to change their operating systems or substructures, they first need to *want* to change and follow through on behavioral plans for altering the way they interact or deal with one another. This means changing their attitudes, actions, and perceptions of their roles in relation to one another. Gladding (1998) states, "For family systems to change, those who are part of them must alter their behaviors" (p. 170).
2. In counseling families or couples the counselor focuses on relationships. Family members are asked to examine whether they are moving closer together or putting distance between one another.
3. Family therapists using reality therapy do not see the counseling experience as a long-term process. They attempt to elicit a commitment from the family to work on their problems and to expect early progress and success, but not magical quick fixes. When couples or families take quick action and see even a modicum of change they feel hopeful, confident, and motivated to continue to change.
4. Reality therapy, a directive method, appeals to therapists who tend to be more

active rather than reflective in their interventions. But it needs to be adapted to the perceptions and cultures of the clients. Some families are patriarchally structured, others are based on the principle that the mother "rules the roost." Whether the sex roles are traditional, postmodern, Western, Eastern, African, Middle Eastern, European, Indian, or "good ole American" (as one family described itself to me), the therapist needs to respect the family's culture and adjust the use of reality therapy to it.

Goals for Family Reality Therapy

The desired outcomes are based on the family's quality worlds, perceptions, and total behaviors.

1. A target for family therapists using reality therapy is that family members gain at least a modicum of need-fulfillment and quality world satisfaction. As in all applications the therapist helps family members fulfill their five psychological needs as expressed in their specific wants without infringing on the rights of other family members. Realistic goals or wants are determined with the help of the therapist.
2. Members often change their levels of perception. Family members learn to lower their levels of perception from putting a value on behavior to merely recognizing it and suspending judgment about it. They are helped to change their communication and treatment of each other if demeaning and dysfunctional. Instead of putting an intense negative value on the actions of others, they are encouraged to see them at a less emotional level.
3. Family members are taught to understand the importance of how to use "quality time" (Wubbolding, 1999a). Time spent together in a noncritical way, doing activities that are enjoyable, builds a storehouse of positive perceptions that serve as a basis for healthy interactions required for future problem solving and for negotiating decisions.
4. The therapist helps family members change behavior. The most visible goal is to help family members change how they interact, both in the therapy session and in the ongoing life of the family. When they change how they interact, they change the quality of their relationships.
5. Family members learn various aspects of choice theory, such as the five motivators of all human behavior and the fact that individuals can control only their own behavior and not the behavior of other people. They can also be taught the WDEP formula for making decisions, for solving problems, and for communicating more effectively.

Process Used in Family Reality Therapy

The use of the WDEP formulation of reality therapy flows better if a counselor conceptualizes the process under three overlapping categories:

1. *Assessment of Goals.* Family members define what they want from the therapy, how they see themselves in the family, and how they see one another. This phase also includes a description of current total behavior; that is, they sort through recent problems as well as successes in the life of the family. The therapist notes the various alliances among family members and the strength of relationships.

2. *Self-Evaluation Intervention.* Overlapping with the first phase, but with its own distinguishable features, is the more directive intervention by the therapist. Family members are encouraged to make self-evaluations of their own behaviors, the overall direction of their family life, the helpfulness of alliances identified in phase 1, and the realistic attainability of keeping the family together, solving problems, and progressing more harmoniously. The amount of quality time spent together is reviewed and its characteristics are taught. They are asked to evaluate whether their own specific actions bring them closer together as a family or set the stage for growing further apart.
3. *Action.* The third phase, which overlaps with earlier interventions, is the planning and implementation segment. Family members make SAMIC (simple, attainable, measurable, immediate, and consistent or repetitive) plans. Their actions outside the counseling session, designed for more effective need-fulfillment, should be SAMIC. Plans for strengthening relationships are emphasized.

Because human beings function as creatures who choose behaviors to satisfy their needs, it is crucial not only to use reality therapy with the family as a whole, that is, as a system, but to examine, with each member of the family, individual and collective goals, their attempt to function as a family, the effectiveness of their individual total behaviors, as well as their perceptions of the family's total behavior. Only when these preliminary components are present can action planning be successful.

☐ Case Example: Relationship Therapy or Counseling

Fay, 28, is single, has had two years of college, and works as a buyer for a large department store. Fay has a history of transitory relationships with men who become interested in her to the point of proposing marriage. She says she finds them attractive but when "they get too close," she turns away from them. Although she claims she wants to get married, her friends tell her she is too demanding in personal relationships as well as fearful of intimacy. Approximately 1 year ago she was attacked on a street while on an out-of-town business trip. Though not raped, a male stranger aggressively grabbed her, jostled her, knocked her to the ground, yanked her purse, and roughly seized her jewelry from her. Since the assault she has been experiencing an increased fear of journeying out at night, even to shopping malls, and has turned down numerous dates from attractive and eligible men. Her parents, who live in another city, and her friends have urged her to seek psychological therapy.

The therapist reviews the professional details regarding informed consent, the rights and responsibilities of both client and therapist, professional credentials, the nature and limitations of confidentiality, possible benefits of therapy, and fees. A summary of reality therapy is presented, and both client and therapist sign two written statements indicating that the client understands the issues. She receives a copy and the original goes into her file. The following transcript picks up Fay's therapy after this initial stage is completed.

T (Therapist): *Fay, now that we've discussed the professional details, including the fact that I'll be asking you a lot of questions, I'd like to begin by asking you a very important one. Is there anything that you don't want me to ask you about? Anything I should stay away from?*

F (Fay): *No, I don't think so. I'm a little nervous, but I'll let you know if you ask about such topics.*

T: *OK. Tell me what your parents and friends said when they urged you to come here.*

F: *They said that because of the mugging a year ago, I am acting strange, keeping to myself, not wanting to be around them. Kind of withdrawing.*

T: *What message are you sending them by this kind of action?*

F: *They're getting the idea that I'm gripped by fear.*

T: *Are they accurate in their opinions?*

F: *They're right. What they say is true, but they don't know the whole story. I'm much more afraid than I let on to them. When I have to be out at night, I'm afraid of every shadow. They also don't know something that haunts me even now after about 18 years.*

T: *Do you want to tell me?*

F: *I've been wanting to get rid of this burden for a long time. But it's hard to say it out loud.*

T: *Do you want to get it out suddenly or gradually?*

F: *I might as well say it right now. When I was 10 years old, I was abused by a friend of a neighbor. He was visiting his friend and I went into the neighbor's house, which I did regularly, but this time he was there alone and he touched me sexually, rubbing my genital area.*

T: *Did he rape you?*

F: *No, it wasn't that bad, but the thoughts have remained with me all these years.*

T: *In other words, this is not a past event, it is still very present in your mind and you even have some of the same creepy feelings about it?*

F: *Yes. I still feel guilty and ashamed.*

T: *I'm not sure you will believe this just yet, but I'd like to assure you, that absolutely, positively, without doubt you were not to blame.*

F: *I know that, but I'm not yet convinced as much as I need to be. I've read a lot about this problem and it could be that I'm having trouble with men because of it.*

T: *Is that what you tell yourself? "I can't relate to men because of this past experience"?*

F: *Yes. When I drop some guy that thought goes through my mind.*

T: *Does it help you to indulge that kind of thinking?*

F: *What do you mean?*

T: *Does it really help you to tell yourself that you can't relate to men as you want to because of events that are past and therefore beyond your control?*

F: *No, but I can't help it.*

T: *Until today you can't. I would like to help you rid yourself of this pain—if you want to work on it. But first, I have another question. What signal do you send him even before you tell him "goodbye"?*

F: *That I'm afraid of the relationship, maybe even afraid of him.*

T: *Do you want to change that message?*

F: *That's why I'm here. I want so much to get rid of this pain. It's like carrying around a weight on my shoulders.*

T: *I like how you describe it. Maybe you could leave part of the weight here.*

F: *I'd like to leave it all here today!!*

T: *How realistic is it to drop this weight all at once?*

F: *Well, I guess not very realistic.*

T: *How do you feel at this very moment now that you've talked about it?*

F: *Oh, I feel relieved that I said it out loud.*

T: *So, already you've tasted relief, dropped part of the weight. Maybe you can work hard so as to drop the rest of it. After all, you have taken two major steps to turn your life around.*

F: *I have? What are they?*

T: *You came here. That's a major step. How long have you been thinking about getting help?*

F: *Years. Maybe 3 or 4.*

T: *So you took the big step. Congratulations! You also have talked about this. And you've disclosed the details to me so quickly. That's very unusual. You have a lot of motivation to achieve your goals.*

F: *Well, it's on my mind. And I learned that many people have had even worse experiences.*

T: *I just thought of a third strength.*

F: *What is that?*

T: *You seem to be willing to work at feeling better.*

F: *Yes, I am, indeed.*

T: *OK. We'll come back to that point. But I'd like to ask you some other questions. Besides leaving behind some or all of the weight on your back, what else do you want to accomplish through this therapy?*

F: *I'm afraid to go out at night and I'm having problems with relationships.*

T: *Are these goals you would like to work on—feeling comfortable wherever you are and having more satisfying relationships with men?*

F: *Yes, I'd like that.*

T: *Now, could you be more specific about these goals? What would you be doing differently if you achieved these goals?*

F: *I'd be happy if I could go to the shopping center and other places without being so fearful. And I'd like to date a man regularly without dropping him quickly.*

T: *How many times would that be? A specific number would be helpful.*

F: *I'd say 10 times. That's more than I usually see someone.*

T: *Let's work on that. You could drop him after 10 times.*

F: *Yes, it would be good if I could hold on to him a while.*

T: *So you've stated what you want from this counseling in positive terms, not merely in terms of what you want to overcome?*

F: *I think we both said it that way. Even more, I really want to feel free of a weighty burden, go out at night, and get married.*

T: *Get married! You've gone beyond what I expected as a goal. That's terrific!*

F: *I might as well aim high.*

T: *OK, we have three goals and you've stated that you have actually already felt better about the abuse, at least for a few minutes. You know, the thought just occurred to me that when you did something about the situation, you had some slight relief. That's so interesting.*

F: *Why does that seem so intriguing to you?*

T: *Because there's a lesson in there.*

F: *I think I know it. When I take action, things get better.* [Smiling broadly.]

T: *Right. When you take action about the other two goals you will feel better.*

F: *I read your summary of reality therapy and it did indicate that you would focus on my choices and that this would lead to happier feelings.*

T: [Smiling.] *You're absolutely right. Action leads to change in how you think, what you think, how you feel, and even your physiology.* Motion creates emotion. *By the way, do you have any chronic aches and pains?*

F: *No, but I have nights when I don't sleep very much.*

T: *That doesn't surprise me in the least. All these things go together. And when you change what you're doing, your thoughts will change. Your feelings will be more pleasant and I believe you'll sleep more soundly. Now how do you want to proceed? There are two roads. One involves spending a lot of time rehashing the past. Or we could move to the part of your life over which you have control.*

F: *Well, I guess I better emphasize what's going on now.*

T: *That sounds good to me. If you feel the need, you can talk about past events any time. Talking might provide momentary relief.*

F: *That's good to know.*

T: *Now before we end, I have one more question. How hard do you want to work at turning things around?*

F: *I'd sure like to turn things around.*

T: *Does that mean you'll give it a try or will you really do it?*

F: *I'll do my best. Do you think there's hope?*

T: *Absolutely. On one condition . . .*

F: *What is that?*

T: *That you are willing to work at it.*

F: *I said I would.*

T: *And you said you would do your best. But let me ask you this. If you were on a plane and the pilot announced over the loudspeaker, "I'll do my best to land the plane," would you feel confident?*

F: *I see what you mean. I need to say that I'll give it my all.*

T: *I think you are truly motivated to make some changes.*

In this initial session the therapist helped the client to decide what she wanted from the therapy and to express it in action terms. He helped her reframe the problems as positive wants, helped her briefly examine her current thinking, and helped her self-evaluate its effectiveness. The level of commitment was also identified. Throughout the dialogue, he put responsibility on her to decide direction and topics for discussion while suggesting that he can best help her if she is willing to talk about behaviors that are controllable. He helped her feel free to discuss the past trauma, but wants to proceed on the premise that she will feel better in the long run if she takes action, not if she merely talks about the trauma. Finally, he helped her determine her level of commitment to working at the problem. At the end, he intentionally avoided pushing for a plan, as it seemed necessary to spend more time on the D and E aspects of the WDEP system.

Fay's "Problem"

The problem is not what appears obvious at first glance. Although the problem is indeed connected to the traumatic events of Fay's past, the underlying problem is the unmet need for belonging and a gradual lessening of her ability to fulfill the power need. In the absence of free and easy social connectedness, she is not enjoying her life and feels trapped. Even her physiological (survival) need is frustrated, as evidenced in her lack of sleep and perhaps by other symptoms not yet brought to the surface. In order to help her fulfill her needs it is necessary to define precisely her wants and the degree of energy she expects to exert to satisfy them. Moreover, she is directing her life toward even less effective behaviors when she avoids desirable relationships with men and when she chooses "fearing" behaviors such as staying indoors. The message she sends is that she is afraid. The therapist will help her evaluate these signals and choose other actions that signal confidence and hope.

Further Treatment

Reality therapy within a friendly, empathic, and hopeful environment was used to help Fay take more control of her life. The therapist helped her identify attainable wants: letting go of pain, closer relationships, even marriage, and freedom from fear.

In future sessions, Fay examined her specific behaviors relative to dating relationships and going out of her home in the evening and at other times. She was continually asked to make self-evaluations as to the effectiveness of specific actions. Even though she was already uncomfortable and pained by her present choices, she was asked, "Did it help?" "Did it hurt?" "What was the relationship between what you did and your want for a close relationship with a man?"

Her enthusiastic commitment to change remained, but at times, she chose to put off total success. Paradoxical techniques were used, which helped her shift her energy from resistance and move toward a change in her perceptions. Resistance is always an attempt to control.

The following exchange took place 1 month into the weekly appointments.

T: *Fay, I'd like to ask you about something you mentioned last week. You said that you could not follow through on the plan about looking men in the eye for a few seconds when you pass them on the street or at work or when you walk through a store. You said that it was not something you felt comfortable doing.* [The therapist and Fay had formulated an action plan aimed at helping her feel more inner control and less fear. She would look briefly at the eyes of several men as she walked past them. She agreed to this, stating that a brief glance, not lingering eye contact, would be appropriate. Both therapist and Fay understood that too much eye contact might communicate an undesired message to strangers. Moreover, this behavior was not in violation of her cultural practices.]

F: *It was not easy. I didn't really want to do it.*

T: *What impact will not taking these steps have on you?*

F: *I know, I know. It won't help. But it's more uncomfortable than I thought.*

T: *Well, maybe we rushed into that plan too soon. It seems you're not ready for that. But it is still a step forward because we both know that we need to work on other things first. Could I make another suggestion?*

F: *Yes, I'll try anything!*

T: *This week, will you make a definite effort to avoid men's eyes, even men you feel comfortable around, such as the friends who encouraged you to come here or your colleagues at work?*

F: *Yes, I could do that. It's sounds stupid, but fairly easy.*

T: *I'd like to ask you what will seem like a strange question. What are other choices you could make to worsen your situation? How could you really make your life miserable?*

F: *That's a weird question.*

T: *Yes, I have a lot of them. Could you answer it, just for fun?*

F: *Well, I could quit my job. I could refuse to date* any *guy. I could sit around my condo even when I feel like going out.*

T: *You could turn your back when you talk to men, especially your boss at work or a date you sort of like.*

F: *Yes, that would really mess me up* [laughs heartily.]*!*

T: *It's good you can laugh.*

F: *I'll just avoid looking strangers in the eye because it's a bit silly not to look at any men.*

T: *It's the best you can do now and what's the difference if you look away?*

F: *It's just a quirk.*

T: *What's wrong with quirks? Could you indulge your quirk for a week or so?*

F: *It might be hard to do that for a week.*

T: *Well, give it your best shot.*

F: *OK, no eye contact with strangers.*

The therapist used the paradoxical techniques of prescription and restraining, and the client rebelled, saying the tasks are hard to do. Whether she follows through on this plan or not, she wins. She gains control of the symptom by explicitly choosing it. This follows the evaluation of the previous plan as inadequate. She did continue to rebel in her real world behaviors by looking at strangers and reported that to force herself to avoid their eyes took too much effort and thought.

Resolution

Fay increasingly gained better control of her life and was seen by the therapist for about 6 months. More effective need-satisfaction was judged by her own self-evaluation. She said that she felt better and was able to have long periods when she was not bothered by the abusive incident. When she did experience mild guilt and shame she simply told herself that this is part of her experience and that it will be less of a weight in the future. This self-acceptance paradoxically lessened the intensity of the flashbacks.

Looking at men quickly became no problem and soon she was able to sustain satisfying social relationships with men. The counselor insisted that after she gets to know a man fairly well, one whom she had dated for a while, she should share her fears with him. In other words, she should bring into the open with him her hesitancy to relate to men and the reasons for it. If he is a man she really wants to put into her quality world, he would understand and accept her even more. She still dated several men at the time of closure in the counseling, and she had shared her fears with most of them. It turned out that for various reasons she was not interested in marrying any of them. Though she still felt appropriate fear at times when away from home, she took necessary precautions. Even though her excessive fears overtook her occasionally, they did not stop her on an habitual basis from performing the tasks necessary to function as an independent professional woman.

Follow-Up

A telephone call a year later revealed that she continued to progress and had become seriously interested in a man. She was mildly hesitant about the prospects of commitment and so was delaying her decision, but she was considering marrying him. She noted that this new experience indicated immense progress. She stated that occasionally she "gave in to the fear" of not going out, but that she was functioning as a "normal human being."

In retrospect, the therapist thought of an idea that might have been useful earlier. By suggesting that she decide to stay home, say, one out of three times when she wanted to go out, she might come to change her view of staying home alone. Instead of seeing her decision to remain in her condo as a sign of fear, she could begin labelling this choice as self-protection, setting her own comfort levels, and controlling her own life more effectively.

Her parents were quite pleased that she was not permanently scarred by the street attack. Fay stated that she had summoned the courage to tell them about the child abuse and that they were furious. Telling them was a good idea she said, as she thought it unwise to keep such a secret from them any longer. They felt assured that she was now past the event in her mind. Fay told them to talk over their feelings with a reality therapist.

This chapter presents an overview of several general principles helpful in understanding choice theory. It also serves as a backdrop for the detailed explanation of the environment and procedures used in reality therapy, that is, the WDEP system or the "how to" of reality therapy. These components are the thoroughfares in the journey to behavioral change. The subsequent chapters describe specific interventions that counselors and therapists use in reality therapy. You are invited to think of ways to use the principles in the management of employees and students, in parenting, and in all your relationships.

CHAPTER

Getting Even More Specific:
The Atmosphere and Composing
the Proper Therapeutic Music

Anyone practicing reality therapy first establishes an environment in which the clients can trust. In the language of choice theory, the client inserts the therapist into his or her quality world as a need-fulfilling person. This process depends primarily on the skill of the therapist who deals with such barriers as age, gender, race, and ethnicity.

Upon this foundation is built the system of therapeutic interventions described below and expressed as the procedures leading to change, i.e., the WDEP formulation. These comprise the essence of the practice of reality therapy (The William Glasser Institute, 1999; Wubbolding, 1988, 1991a, 1996b).

But before using any of these procedures, a counselor first establishes a relationship. Like practitioners of other theories a reality therapist attempts to enter the perceptual world of the client, and so empathy is a central part of the delivery system of reality therapy. Expressing empathy simply means seeing the world as a client might. The ideas below are specific suggestions for helping therapists catch an accurate glimpse of their clients' quality worlds so that they can view the world from the perspective of the clients. The *don'ts* that follow describe impediments to empathy. Empathy is not a new concept. It was described in the 19th century as *Einfeeling* and was seen as an awareness of another person's affect for sharing feelings (Hill, 1996). Still, in the context of choice theory and reality therapy, empathy takes on an added meaning: seeing the clients' point of view and accepting them as they are, but even more, *visioning what they can become and accepting them as they can be if they are willing to choose to make different choices.*

☐ Environment

Developing a friendly, mutually involving relationship is common to many counseling theories and methods, even those very different from reality therapy. Patalano

(1997) emphasizes the importance of the "working alliance" for successful marital therapy in the psychodynamic approach. The psychoanalyst must demonstrate "humanness, compassion, concern, and a sense of rapport" (p. 498). Thus the roles of all those involved can be clarified. Then the therapist can help clients ponder their situations more effectively and strengthen the alliance.

The atmosphere in the reality therapy relationship in any setting is one of firmness and friendliness. Because reality therapy practitioners come from many disciplines other than psychotherapy, such as corrections and education, they remain resolute in establishing boundaries and reviewing consequences with clients. On the other hand, the relationship is a partnership in which both client and therapist struggle to find more effective behavioral patterns for the client. Specifically, therapists use many of the following skills, some of which are common to other therapeutic methods concretizing their openness, receptiveness, and empathy.

Using Attending Behaviors

Ivey (1980, 1999), and Ivey, Ivey, and Simek-Morgan (1999) have described many aspects of body language of which reality therapists are cognizant, such as eye contact, posture, verbal following, and nonverbal behavior. Such actions are not interpreted in their every detail, nor is a specific meaning given to each motion of the client, as is the case with some gestalt therapists, but the reality therapist attempts to connect with the clients' thinking and feelings by displaying empathic listening skills by actions as well as by words.

Still it is important to attend to the nonverbal behavior of the client or student. Books and videotapes abound with suggestions about the meaning of posture, eye contact, silence, etc. Tone of voice can indicate the opposite of what was explicitly stated. Asking, "What do you want?" can be accusatory if not asked in a friendly tone. In some cultures, this question is seen as at least somewhat intrusive. The famous movie scene in *Taxi Driver*, where Robert DeNiro  is standing in front of the mirror practicing to be a tough guy is illustrative of the various meanings which tone of voice can give to a single question:

"*Are* you talking to me?"
"Are *you* talking to me?"
"Are you *talking* to me?"
"Are you talking to *me*?"

Similarly, on a warm summer day my wife, Sandie, and I were driving through a suburb near our home looking for a park where we could take a walk. We found a picturesque unmarked park with a large grassy area and a soccer field manicured like the green of a golf course. It appeared to have never been used. And indeed, on this comfortable warm day, much to our surprise, we saw only one person in the entire park. A woman about 20 years old was sunning herself. Next to the near-perfect soccer field was a sign boldly proclaiming, "Stay off the Playing Field." It did appear that no one had ever walked on the virginal unbent grass. We both thought of Robert DeNiro and how many ways the prohibition could be stated aloud. To realize the various meanings that can be conveyed, the reader is invited to say out loud the command emphasizing each word:

"*Stay* off the Playing Field."
"Stay *off* the Playing Field."
"Stay off *the* Playing Field."
"Stay off the *Playing* Field."
"Stay off the Playing *Field*."

Each rendition of this simple command carries a slightly different message. The basic message was, of course, unambiguous. The intent was that this playing field was not a tool for satisfying the fun need.

Practicing AB-CDE

A guideline for establishing the desired relationship is "always be" one thing or another. Therapists in private practice start with "always be courteous" and they easily see the merit in this guideline—so much so that to them it often appears unworthy of mention. Still, it is neither evident nor easy to implement in many settings where the relationship is more managerial than counseling, that is, when the client is "involuntary" or in a school classroom. Moreover, courtesy does not rule out firmness. Courtesy implies respect for the client or valuing the client or student as an independent, self-sustaining human being. In some settings, maintaining this quality requires consultation as well as the self-evaluation of the therapist.

AB–D. "Always be determined" implies the effort on the part of the therapist to communicate a sense of hope, especially in the first session. Clients often feel powerless and depressed, and at the prospect of facing life's challenges they are tempted to surrender to forces beyond their control. The therapist, imitating their behavior and often exhibiting too much empathy or sympathy, fails to see outside the pit of despair. Still, the effective user of reality therapy remains determined and gently communicates a well-grounded optimism to clients.

AB–E. "Always be enthusiastic" means looking for strengths or positive, effective, need-satisfying behaviors. When faced with multiple problems and clusters of behaviors that fit many diagnostic categories, it is imperative that the therapist surmount such barricades. Enthusiasm is linked with determination and involves more than sloganeering, cheerleading, and encouragement in a vacuum. Enthusiasm can take the form of discussing only sane behaviors with a psychotic person. A student who has no friends is asked to describe even the slightest successful contact he or she has had with another person. Parents whose child is seen as a bundle of problems are asked to describe a recent time when they felt good about a conversation with their child. And yet enthusiasm does not mean ignoring the negative. All users of reality therapy face the negative side head-on, but spend most of the time looking for a positive side and remembering that night is darkest just before dawn. Thomas Edison once remarked that if we left our children nothing but enthusiasm, the legacy would be incalculable. Frequently, reframing can help clients change their perceptions and discover that they already have within them the seeds of success and untapped potential for better mental health.

Using Self-Disclosure

Reality therapists are not distant, impersonal analyzers or interpreters. Rather, they form a "real" relationship in which they feel free to disclose pertinent information about themselves. Such appropriate self-disclosure has nothing to do with Freud's classic concepts of transference or countertransference. A reality therapy context is less psychiatric and more pleasantly relational. Two people encounter each other in a professional but friendly relationship. When therapists share a bit of themselves, they facilitate the deepening of the relationship and thus enhance the counseling environment by creating a climate that makes client self-disclosure an easier choice.

Listening for Metaphors

Creating an atmosphere of mutual understanding is advanced even further when the therapist listens for, reflects on, and extends the figures of speech used by clients. Rather than discarding the graphic language used by clients, it is useful to refer to it. "I feel like a floor mat" can be met not with, "You feel depressed," but, "What are you doing to keep yourself on the floor?" or, "What is your plan for standing up?" or even, "What the heck is wrong with feeling like a floor mat?" The use of such metaphors is not the essence of reality therapy and need not be used to symbolize the person's entire lifestyle. Their utilization, however, serves to help clients laugh at themselves and ultimately take better control of their current choices (Wubbolding, 1991a).

Listening for Themes

The most fundamental skill common to all methods of behavioral change is that of listening. A therapist using reality therapy listens and reflects less on unconnected feelings than on piecing together ideas that form a theme. The therapist, for example, might feed back to the client everything that the latter said regarding his or her wants or everything that has been tried that has helped or has hurt. The themes are related to the client's control system: needs and wants, behavior, perception, as well as the procedures to be described in chapter 9. In chapter 7, for example, the therapist helped Fay identify the theme of moving closer to other people.

Staying Ethical

In order to communicate that the relationship has boundaries, informed consent is part of the therapeutic environment. This means discussing professional credentials and qualifications and laying out the limitations of confidentiality. In addition, the reality therapist brings to the surface other professional disclosure issues, explains the theory and practice of reality therapy, and emphasizes the underlying philosophy and the general procedures to be used. These include self-evaluation and action planning but do not include hypnosis, psychoanalysis, or behavioral reinforcers.

Using Consequences Judiciously

The use of consequences has long been associated with reality therapy. The limitation of consequences is that they can be confused with punishment and vindictiveness.

Their importance as an effective tool can also be overinflated. When these conditions prevail the imposer of consequences can unintentionally backslide to external control psychology, which is the antithesis of the WDEP system.

With this caveat in mind it is important to recognize that William and Carleen Glasser (1999) incorporated consequences in 8 of 52 (15%) scenarios describing how to use choice theory. For example, they suggested that an employer tell an alcoholic employee, "The only way I can save your job is if you go into treatment today" (p. 94). To the child who watches TV late at night they would state, "As long as you are quiet and don't disturb anyone, you can go to bed when you get sleepy" (p. 8). The adolescent who wants to purchase a car should first gather information about cost, insurance, cleaning, maintenance, and repairs. *Then* the parent would listen to the plea for the privilege of owning a car. In other words, when people make choices, they are advised to be aware that there are outcomes, feedback, payoffs, and inconveniences which follow.

Similarly, in discussing school discipline, W. Glasser (1999) stated that students in school should not be threatened or punished, but if they continually disrupt and cannot get their work done in the classroom, "They will be removed to a special help room where they can do their work without disturbing others" (p. 23). He adds that when they can commit to effective classroom behavior through their own choice, they can return to the classroom.

A story told to me by a workshop participant about his uncle who was a beekeeper illustrates the connection between choices and outcomes. The uncle was called to a nursery to remove a swarm of bees that were huddling there, preventing the customers from entering that part of the store.

The beekeeper told the owner it would cost $75 to deal with the problem. The owner readily agreed. The beekeeper immediately removed the queen, took it outside, and placed it in the bed of his truck. The bees immediately followed peacefully. The owner was then asked to pay the agreed-upon fee of $75. The owner appeared to be astonished that the project was completed effortlessly and in only a few minutes. He said that because it was such a brief and easy job he didn't think it was worth $75, and so he refused to pay, offering $25 instead.

The beekeeper thought a moment, reminded the store owner of the verbal contract, and asked if he thought such a refusal was reasonable. The owner adamantly insisted that the work was not worth $75, asserting, "Take it or leave it." The beekeeper said, "I'll leave it." He then went to his truck, recovered the queen bee and replaced her in her previous home. Functioning as a tightly organized team, the swarm of bees quickly returned to their home of first choice in the nursery. The beekeeper returned to the owner's office and said, "The bees decided they really like your nursery and no amount of money can induce them to move." After viewing the swarm back in his nursery, the owner sheepishly said, "Maybe it is worth $75."

The principles of reality therapy are based on the importance of people evaluating their own behavior and the attainability of their wants. Genuine change can occur only when a person makes an inner decision to change.

A second example is that of Phil, a high school teacher who said he wanted to use consequences with his son, whom he had caught using snuff. Phil disapproved of this behavior, so he required that his son sleep in the garage for a night. The boy became angry, unrepentant, and cold toward Phil for several days. On the other hand, Phil lay awake feeling guilty. Sometimes it is the punisher who feels more pain than the punishee. The distinction between consequences and punishment can be elusive.

A more effective parental relationship is illustrated by the behavior of Megan. Her two teenage daughters, who were approximately the same age, developed the habit of bickering. After taking a 4-day workshop in reality therapy, Megan decided to use the entire system to resolve ongoing disputes. She helped her daughters explore what they wanted from each other, evaluate their respective behaviors, and make plans. By mutual consent they negotiated an agreement to go shopping together and buy each other a small gift when they had an irritating argument. Having learned the WDEP formulation, they had a system for resolving conflicts as well as inconvenient but prearranged consequences if they did not resolve them. With this structure in place, Megan could withdraw from altercations and put the responsibility on the girls, where it belonged.

Questions

- What do the above examples demonstrate regarding inner self-evaluation and choices?
- How do the above situations relate to inner control vs. external control thinking?
- What is the difference between (a) punishment and rewards, and (b) consequences?

These examples of techniques, while not exhausting all possibilities, serve to illustrate how relationships can be enhanced. Setting the atmosphere is an ongoing process that continues throughout the relationship. Even utilizing the procedures seems to enhance the environment, and so the distinction between environment and procedures is not absolute. In the appendix, a further description of "The Cycle of Managing, Supervising, Counseling and Coaching," a chart used for teaching reality therapy, contains more suggestions.

The above positive behaviors not only facilitate a firm but friendly counseling, teaching, or managing relationship, but help the practitioner avoid contrary behaviors. Wubbolding (1999b) (cf. the Appendix) has described environmentally toxic behaviors as ABCDEFG. Avoid *a*rguing about perceptions such as the fairness of rules, who is to blame for a problem, or whether the clients' wants are realistic. Avoid *b*laming and *b*elittling efforts. Even a feeble effort can be used by the therapist to lead the client to a higher level of effective behaviors. *B*oss managing is the opposite of lead managing. The boss's motto is "It's my way or the highway," a style of managing that is opposed to reality therapy. Do not *c*riticize or *d*emean when clients fail or make mistakes. It is useful to emphasize this "don't" when counseling families. It can be taught and suggested that even "constructive criticism" is an oxymoron. In his lectures, Sid Simon, EdD, a founder of the Values Realization Institute, known for his work in values clarification, refers to it as "constrictive crudicism." Most importantly, it is crucial to avoid asking for and getting embroiled in *e*xcuses. When clients, whose perceived locus of control is external, are asked why they are in trouble regarding their actions or emotions, that is, why they broke the law or why they are depressed, they will usually attribute the causality of their actions and feelings to external forces. They are depressed because someone rejected them. They got into a brawl because someone else started it. To encourage excuses is to make it more difficult for the client to take responsibility. The French axiom applies: *Qui s'excuse, s'accuse,* or "One who excuses oneself, accuses oneself." The practitioner need not slip into the trap of finding *fault*, especially about past failures. It is useless "to water last year's crops." Finally, the therapist avoids giving up on the client or on the WDEP system. Change can be laborious and the practice of reality therapy involves a willingness to have the confidence that through repeated self-evaluation by clients and their positive planning, they will take better charge of their lives.

These methods for establishing a healthy, firm, and friendly therapeutic environment are useful not only to therapists, but to classroom teachers, managers, parents, and others who wish to be more effective in their interpersonal behavior. These tactics have been found to be practical and usable by consultants, trainers, and family therapists who wish to be active in teaching clients, students, and others how to set a high-quality atmosphere in their office, classroom, business, or home, where the importance of interpersonal relationships is paramount.

☐ Case Example

The powerful impact of setting an example and modeling successful, achieving, and mentally healthy behaviors is illustrated in the case of Richard Ruffalo, a New Jersey schoolteacher. He received the award of top teacher at the American Teacher Awards for 1995, a program sponsored by the Walt Disney and McDonald's corporations. Twenty years ago he was diagnosed with retinitis pigmentosa, an incurable disease that leaves victims blind. Phillip Pina (1995) stated, "Those times were tough for Ruffalo. He considered quitting teaching. But the examples of his own teachers, urging of his bosses and faith in his God, Ruffalo persisted."

This story might seem to be a tribute to one man's determination and strength. Indeed it is, but it is also a reflection of the importance of the environment. Faith in God is more easily translated into action if leaders provide a supportive, no-excuses, friendly, and firm atmosphere. Managers in companies, coaches of teams, classroom teachers, parents of children, that is, administrators at any level, can have a measurable outcome through the atmosphere they establish.

CHAPTER

The Procedures: What Are
the Interventions I Need to Use?

While the skills used in establishing an environment conducive to change spill over to those used in the delivery of procedures, still there are clearly identifiable interventions that constitute the essence of reality therapy. Glasser frequently remarks that the art of counseling is to weave these components together in ways that lead clients to evaluate their lives and to decide to move in more effective directions. Wubbolding (1996b, 1999b) has expressed these in a way that makes them easy to remember. The WDEP formulation is a pedagogical tool useful for understanding and teaching the concepts to students and clients. Each letter represents not an isolated procedure but a cluster of possible skills and techniques for assisting clients to take better control of their own lives and thereby fulfill their needs in ways that are satisfying to them and to society.

☐ W

Ask Clients What They Want

In this procedure, the therapist assists clients to formulate, clarify, delineate, and prioritize the elements (desires) contained in their quality world or mental picture album. The exploration of wants includes but is not limited to the three essential elements contained in the quality world: relationships, treasured possessions, and core beliefs (W. Glasser, 1998a). The importance of thoroughly exploring what clients want related to their needs can hardly be overemphasized. Emerson said, "Beware of what you want. In all likelihood you will get it." All human beings have wants related to each need. Some are clear and nonnegotiable, such as the desire for air. Others are weak whims, such as selecting a specific pair of socks from a drawer. All are related to the five sources of human motivation, the needs.

And so, by means of skillful questioning, therapists assist clients to describe what they want from:

- themselves;
- the world around them;
- the therapy process itself;
- parents, children, teachers, school;
- spouse, partner;
- job, manager, supervisor, or coworkers;
- friends, relatives;
- associates or acquaintances;
- religion/spirituality/higher power;
- any institution that impinges upon their lives.

Not only is the quality world explored, but the clients also identify their out-of-balance scales. (The technical word for out-of-balance scales is "frustration.") Clients describe what they *are* getting and what they are *not* getting from each of the above 10 categories. There are many possible areas for discussion related to specific wants of clients, for example, a general exploration of each of the 10 categories or discussion of the fulfilled or unfulfilled wants in each category. Of course, not every category is relevant for each client. Both client and therapist determine the current relevance and importance of the many components of the quality world and of both the in-balance and the out-of-balance scales.

During the course of therapy it is useful to teach the nature of the quality world. Practitioners of reality therapy explain the procedures to their clients and students. By reading appropriate books and listening to tapes they can progress faster and further in their effort to gain more effective control of their behavior.

Ask What They Want For . . .

Important relationships, treasured possessions, and core beliefs are the content of the quality world and can be viewed in a more active way by asking clients about their goals regarding them. The question could be rephrased, What do you want for:

- your family and the individual members of it?
- your own personal growth?
- your career?
- your financial status?
- your intellectual life?
- your recreational time?
- your spiritual development?

As with any lists or series of questions, making them specific and unique to individual clients, students, or employees constitutes the *art* of practicing reality therapy. The reader is invited to formulate questions to be used on yourself and with your clients.

Ask How Hard They Want to Work

The W of the WDEP system of procedures also includes a discussion of the clients' level of commitment or the question, "How hard do you want to work at solving the problem or gaining a better sense of control for yourself?" Wubbolding (1988, 1996b) has identified five levels of commitment related to the intensity of motivation. These are expressed in language often used by clients or students.

1. "I don't want to be here. Leave me alone. Get off my back." This level is, in fact, no commitment at all. Still, it is sometimes expressed by clients who are required to attend therapy sessions.
2. "I want the outcome, but I don't want to make the effort." This level of commitment is slightly higher but represents a reluctance to take action. Such a person wants to lose weight, wants other people to "leave me alone," wants a better relationship, wants to be more assertive, wants a job . . . , but fails to formulate effective strategies for taking action. Sometimes, this level is more of a wish than an intense desire.
3. "I'll try." "I might." "I could." "Maybe." "Probably." The middle level of commitment indicates a willingness to make a change, to take action, to begin to turn toward a more effective style of living. On the other hand, it is not an earmark of effective change. "To try" is to allow room for excuses and failure. If an airline pilot were to announce, "We will now try to land the plane," the passengers would feel at least worried, and would expect a higher level of commitment from the flight deck. Similarly, this level of commitment is often expressed with the statement, "I'll do enough to get by."
4. "I will do my best." This statement indicates a higher level of commitment and usually signals the beginning of action planning. Yet, it still contains an escape hatch to failure. To do one's best to land the plane does not automatically mean 100% follow-through. A hospital patient's family would experience a moment of fright if the surgeon told them, "We did our best."
5. "I will do whatever it takes." The highest level of commitment implies that the person is willing to make choices that are efficacious and that will produce the desired result. Such a person consistently follows through on plans without making excuses for less-than-desirable results.

It is important to recognize that wants exist at various levels of desirability. There are many individuals who have a difficult time determining their priorities. People raised in a home characterized by turmoil and inconsistency often insert contrary data in their minds. Chemically dependent families, environments characterized by attention deficit disorder, and other dysfunctional families lack a structure with predictable and consistent rules and expectations. Anyone praised one day and demeaned the next for the same behavior has difficulty establishing a definite set of priorities, that is, what is more important and what is less important.

> *"I will now*
> *TRY*
> *to land the plane"*
> *–Airline Pilot to frightened*
> *passengers*

Similar to the idea that wants exist in priority is the intensity of the want. If someone intensely desires something, that is, if the want is a very high priority, the person is more likely to follow through on a plan to fulfill it. Renna (1996) refers to the high-level intense want as *will*. Asking people what they want or really want or even what needs to be done regardless of whether they want to do it is a valuable technique. Still, clients or students often do not follow through on genuinely need-satisfying plans. The reason is that they didn't have the will to do it. Renna states, "teaching them how to cultivate their will and strengthen their resolve will give them 'perceptual intensity'." (p. 20). Time and solitude are thus necessary for some clients to gain the will to make a change. This intensity of perception, or lack of it, leads some people to be viewed as "strong willed, high spirited, intense, focused, determined, driven, even stubborn" and others as "weak, lazy, excusers, procrastinators, hysterics, laid back, etc." (p. 22).

Another way of viewing this phenomenon is to realize that if making plans is not working, one should try another approach. If clients repeatedly *say* they will do something but fail to do it, clearly they don't want to do it. The following alternative routes can be helpful in creating the high-level intense want or will.

Using Affirmations

Statements about oneself are common to many self-help programs and are ways to assist clients, students, or employees to enrich their creative behavioral systems. Affirmations are most effective when they are stated in the present tense, are positive, and are repeated. Some favorites are:

- "If it is to be, it is up to me."
- "Yes, indeed, I succeed."
- "I am lovable and capable."
- "I weigh [desired weight] pounds."

Downing (1996) has adapted this technique to elementary school children. With the encouragement of adults, even children under 9 can use such affirmations as:

- "I try hard in my math work."
- "I do my work on time."
- "I am responsible for everything I do."

Downing (1996) states that affirmations "can address issues of interpersonal relationships, performance concerns, basic skills or virtually anything" (p. 176). It is important for clients to understand that affirmations are often future goals, not current conditions of their lives.

Bibliotherapy.   Using books, tapes, and magazine articles can help people evaluate their own lives and can provide models for imitation as well as motivation for change. But most importantly, clients learn to clarify what they want from the world around them.

As a young man I was heavily influenced by Viktor Frankl's *Man's Search for Meaning*, Hemingway's *The Old Man and the Sea*, *The Fairy Tales of Oscar Wilde*, especially "The Selfish Giant," Rudyard Kipling's poem "*If*," and Francis Thompson's (1947) *The Hound of Heaven*. The latter still exerts a haunting influence.

Exercise.   Kierkegaard, the Danish philosopher and theologian, once remarked that there is no problem so great that it cannot be solved by walking. The mental and physical benefits of exercise need not be documented here. It is sufficient to say that some activities allow the mind to wander and solutions to emerge (W. Glasser, 1976).

Positive Symptoms.   Choosing behaviors that seem to have little to do with the problem can, in fact, help solve it or provide an avenue to Renna's (1996) "perceptual intensity" or will. I once conducted a 4-day training session in the United States for 12 people, all of whom had received therapy from one individual therapist. They had all been diagnosably disturbed in varying degrees. An absolute condition of their therapy and an integral part of their treatment plans had been their involvement in a volunteer activity that was altruistic and ongoing, as well as time consuming. A few hours a week would not suffice.

I was astounded to learn of their previous conditions, for they were eager learners, assertive, generous, and free of negative symptoms. Victor Frankl spoke of the importance of finding meaning in one's life. These individuals had a sense of purpose and were able to relinquish their diagnoses. They had the will to make plans for their own effective need-satisfaction.

Renna (1996) put it another way: "The act of reaching out and doing a good deed need not be of heroic proportions, but done daily with interest and enthusiasm. The pure pleasure from this activity will further increase the frequency and intensity of . . . self-evaluation (and strengthen) the human will" (p. 26).

Relaxation and Meditation.   Jacobson's (1938) relaxation activities are still widely used. These can be used in dealing with anxiety and fear along with many other strategies, such as facing the fear head on. In these exercises, often done with the help of audiotapes, the person alternately tenses and relaxes arm muscles, leg muscles, torso muscles, and on through the rest of the body. Thus the person explicitly chooses to relax. Meditation takes many forms. Some prefer visualization activities (Omar, 1994), while others suggest an activity similar to that taught to me by Len Rand, a close friend and confidant. Sitting in a comfortable chair the person repeats a nonsense word, such as "Schrang" over and over again, allowing thoughts to bubble up and dissipate. Eventually the mind is cleared of distractions and allowed to "float" in a manner described by W. Glasser (1976).

Visualization.   Imagining the attainment of a goal or activity can be a first step in its attainment, even for a person too shy to try or lacking confidence to begin. It is reported that Jack Nicklaus played every hole of the golf course in his mind before even entering the locker room.

Boyd (1990) described how George Hall played 18 holes of golf every day for several years. He then shot a 76 in the National Open. His years of practice, however, were mental—they occurred in a prison camp in Vietnam. His visualization not only helped him preserve his sanity but made him a superb golfer in the real world.

Another characteristic of wants or pictures is that some can blur or at least become more general than others, as Figure 2 illustrates. When wants are unclear, it is likely that behavior seems to be random. Some people have nervous habits that seem to serve no purpose even to themselves. Still there is a pervasive purpose: to fulfill wants. But when the wants are unclear, the behavior is ineffective. Thus the interaction of the behavioral system is confused and its effectiveness lessened.

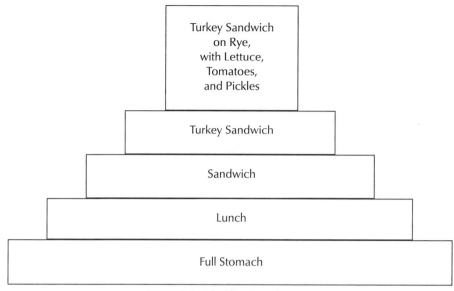

FIGURE 2. Clarification of wants.

When speaking about organizations, W. Edwards Deming (1986), the famous prophet of quality, frequently said, "Without an aim there is no system." In reality therapy we say, "Without a clear want, behavior is ineffective." Figure 2 illustrates the fact that in our daily lives we continually clarify our wants as we interact with the world around us. In the late morning we often have a rather general want. As we approach the noon hour we define the want more precisely, and eventually we settle on an attainable, concrete want that is understandable to others.

Ask What They Want to Avoid

Some clients and students have a difficult time clarifying what they want. Therefore, it is sometimes useful to explore what they don't want, what they want to avoid, and what they dislike. The user of reality therapy can translate a negative to its opposite, from a "don't want" to a positive want. "I don't want hassles" becomes "I want more independence." "I don't want to work around people" becomes "I prefer to work on my own on a job." "I don't want to hear voices" becomes "I want internal freedom and peace."

Such a discussion facilitates a higher degree of trust in the helper. Some clients demonstrate resistance and put a counselor to a test by insisting that "I don't know what I want." When they come to trust the helper, to put him or her into their quality worlds, they feel less defensive and are willing to describe their positive wants.

Ask What They Want Regarding Needs

An essential part of practicing reality therapy is teaching choice theory to clients. After explaining the difference between internal and external control as well as the five needs as motivators, it is often productive to explore what they want regarding their needs:

- Survival: Health, self-preservation, risk taking;
- Belonging: Acquaintances, friends, intimacy, altruism;
- Power: Security and safety, skills, achievements, sense of pride and self-esteem, sense of transcendence and spirituality;
- Freedom: Independence, autonomy;
- Fun: Activities that are tolerable, enjoyable, exciting, and creative.

Assisting clients and students to clarify desirable characteristics of friendships can be effective as a prerequisite to plan making. They can also clarify their idea or picture of security and accomplishment. The person nearing retirement can delineate exactly what a secure retirement lifestyle and income looks like. In career counseling it is helpful to consider whether the person wants to depend on a large company or be an independent, self-starting entrepreneur. Depress-ing clients are often led to better feelings when they decide exactly what they can barely tolerate and what provides them with laughter and mirth as well as specific sources of fun. Do they prefer more active fun such as skydiving, or more passive fun such as watching television, or something between these extremes? Determining this can provide a wealth of material for therapy and education. Exploring the quality world includes a consideration of the various levels of intensity or desirability in wants connected with each need.

Ask What They Want to Be

Another aspect of quality world exploration is what clients want to be. Inquiring about total behavior makes this question more definite. Questions include:

- What would you like to *do* relative to your needs?
- What would you like to think? What kinds of thoughts would you like to have? What core beliefs and self-talk do you admire in other people?
- How would you like to feel? (Clients can be taught the difference between a thought and a feeling. A thought is a sentence with a subject and predicate; a feeling is a word, such as fearful, guilty, hopeful, patient.)
- What do you want to be like physically? What physical characteristics do you admire? What are some physical activities that you would like to be good at, such as sports or exercise?

This line of questioning interfaces with the D of the WDEP formulation in that it leads to a discussion of behavior, especially action. A key question is, "What would you be doing if you would be doing what you want, getting what you want, and having your needs met?"

Ask How They See (Perceive) Their Control, Themselves, and Others

W refers not only to the wants, but also to perceptions. More specifically, the perceived locus of control is discussed. The therapist helps clients ascertain how much control they think they have. The reality therapist accepts a high correlation between a perceived external locus of control and ineffective behaviors. To put it another way, persons depress-ing themselves feel at the mercy of outside circumstances. Nonassertive people see themselves as victimized. Many people seeking therapy believe they are held powerless because of past experience, or the damage other people have caused them, or events that create a deprivation within them. Burnett (1995) states that society in general is "tired of people claiming to be a victim every time someone confronts them for an antisocial behavior" (p. i). He cites the classic statements of Bart Simpson as examples: "I didn't do it." "Nobody saw me do it." "You can't prove anything. . . . " One of the goals of therapy is to help clients perceive that they have inner control, which they can increase by changing their behavior. In this way they can begin to resolve past issues and relinquish the condition of victimhood.

To accomplish this it is sometimes useful to help clients externalize the problems and to reshape their relationships to their problems. They *are not* their problems, thus we use the technique of externalizing and personalizing the problem. Some therapists help clients see themselves not as angry or depressed or guilty, but rather as strong individuals held hostage by a tiger. The feeling is abandoned if they see it as a mask that they are free to wear or to discard. These metaphors do not contradict the theoretical principle that behavior is chosen. Choice theory—in fact, any theory—is best applied and made concrete through techniques. The use of rich metaphors is a technique designed to assist clients in gaining more inner control of their behavior. The fact is that if they perceived their painful behavior as a choice, they would have already chosen another behavior. Seeing it as a choice initially might be ineffective. Thus the paradoxical truth is that they can cut loose the ineffective behavior if they see it as an "unchoice" and are indirectly led by a skillful counselor to the perception of choice.

Under the W, the counselor explores wants, levels of commitment, and perceptions. Figure 3 indicates many aspects of the quality world, wants, and the perceptual system that can be discussed. The figure's grid contains 132 possible questions or areas for exploration, such as, "What do I want that I'm getting from my family?" (A-1); "What will I settle for from my job?" (E-5); "What do I think I need to do relative to the organization even if I don't really want to do it or would prefer to avoid it?" (H-11).

☐ D

Ask Clients About Their Overall Direction

"Where is the accumulation of your current choices taking you?" "Are you headed in a direction where you want to be in a month, a year, two years?" "Describe the direction without making a judgment about it." These questions are global and are an attempt to help clients increase their awareness of what their choices look like from a distance. By describing their overall destination, they are then ready to present the most controllable part of their behavioral system. W. Glasser (1990a) stated, "Ask clients . . . about the directions they would like to take their lives. If they say they do not know, continue to focus on what they are doing now to make sure that they realize they are choosing their present directions."

Fundamental generic question: "What do you want?"	1. What do I want that I am getting?	2. What do I want that I'm not getting?	3. How much do I want it?	4. How much effort or energy am I willing to exert to get what I want?	5. What will I settle for?	6. What am I getting that I don't want?	7. What am I getting that I want?	8. What is my level of commitment to categories A to L?	9. How do I perceive categories A to L?	10. What do I have to give up to get what I want?	11. What needs to be done regardless of whether I want to do it?
A. From my family											
B. From my spouse											
C. From my children											
D. From my friends											
E. From my job											
F. From my manager											
G. From my subordinates											
H. From the organization: Religious, civic, etc.											
I. From my coworkers											
J. From my recreational activities											
K. From myself											
L. From my counselor/ teacher											

FIGURE 3. W questions: 132 questions for exploring quality world and perception.

Ask What They Are Doing

The D also signifies doing. Doing encompasses action, thinking, feelings, and even physiology. The components of the behavioral system over which we have the most control are actions and thinking. Extensive and detailed therapeutic discussions, therefore, focus more on action and thinking than on feelings and physiology. Wubbolding (2000b) suggests that each word of the all-important question, "What are you doing?" is crucial to this procedure.

"What" connotes specificity. A therapist helps the client describe exactly what happened at a definite time. If there was a family argument, the client describes exactly who said what, how it was said, where the argument took place, and other relevant details. The description could also be an exposition of what went well. "What were you doing the last time you felt really well?" and "When was the last time the family did something together that was enjoyable to everyone?" are frequently asked questions.

"Are" means accentuating current or recent behavior. Past successes provide useful data as a basis for future effective choices, but endless discussion of past misery is less fruitful. Rehashing past, out-of-control behaviors serves only to increase the clients' perception of the importance of problems over which they have no current control. During the first certification week in reality therapy held in Kuwait in May 1998, Siddiqa N. M. Hussain put it succinctly: "The past is a springboard not a hammock. You don't drown by falling in the water. You drown by staying in it."

The value of stressing current efforts to satisfy needs is not the result of mere speculation. Feinauer, Mitchel, Harper, and Dane (1996), studied female survivors of abuse and found that "hardiness" was a significant factor in their adult adjustment. Hardiness was seen as a high level of commitment, control, and challenge. In the language of choice theory this means pursuing a clearly defined want, a sense of power or achievement, and in general, the ability to satisfy *current* wants and needs.

"You" implies focusing on *controllables* rather than *uncontrollables*, that is, the client's own behavior rather than on forces over which they have no control. Persons whose victimization is real, imagined, or exaggerated tend to talk about "them." To encourage the discussion of uncontrollables only delays the choice of alternative controllable behaviors.

It is helpful to ask clients to describe each component of their total behavior. Thus, "doing" implies not only a discussion of direction and specific action, as emphasized earlier. Drawing from Ellis's work and making the necessary adaptations to align with choice theory, I have added to the basic practice of reality therapy the concept of IST and EST based on choice theory. This self-talk accompanies actions. IST includes the following statements:

- "No one is going to tell me what to do."
- "I'm powerless to do anything to change."
- "I can control other people."
- "Even though my present behavior is not getting me what I want, I will continue to choose it."

Self-talk also accompanies effective action. EST includes the following inner discourse:

- "I am happy when I live within reasonable boundaries."
- "I am in control of my actions. I choose my behavior. I can change. I am in charge of my life."
- "I cannot control other people's behavior."
- "If what I'm doing is not helping me, I'll stop doing it and try another course of action."

> *You can act your way to a new way of thinking easier than you can think your way to a new way of acting*

Unlike rational emotive behavioral thinking described by Ellis, this self-talk is based on choice theory and accompanies rather than causes ineffective actions.

Emotions such as guilt, depression, shame, resentment, rage, anger, loneliness, fear, sullenness, and shyness are often the most prominent component of the person's presenting behavior. Identifying, labelling, and even allowing for some elaboration of these most obvious behaviors in the clients' presentation can be necessary and useful. The therapist can demonstrate empathy, diagnose the degree of pain, and connect more effectively with the client. But in contrast to person-centered therapy, W. Glasser (1990a) stated, "Avoid discussing clients' feelings or physiology as though they were separate from their total behaviors. Always relate them to their concurrent actions and thoughts over which clients have more direct control." Emotions do not cause actions and cannot be changed by mere conversation. Like self-talk, they accompany actions and should be discussed as behaviors, which are inexorably tied to actions. Wubbolding (2000b) described "total behavior" as the "suitcase of behavior." It is as though a person has a range of behaviors layered in a suitcase with a handle attached to the *action* component. Beneath are *thinking, feeling,* and *physiology*. Grabbing the suitcase by the handle is the best way to move it from one place to another. When a person changes the actions in the behavioral suitcase, the entire suitcase changes position. However, changing our thinking and feelings, the result of changing our actions, is not immediate. There is often a time lag between choosing a new action and experiencing a new feeling.

W. Glasser's (1990a) analogy of the car illustrates that behavior functions as a unit, a system. When the car moves along the road, it moves as a whole. Carrying the analogy further, the front wheels represent the action and thinking components of behavior. The driver has more direct control over the front wheels. When they turn, the car changes direction. The rear wheels symbolize feelings and physiology. They are important to a well-functioning behavioral system, but the driver has less direct control over them. The user of reality therapy emphasizes the front wheels in conversation. When clients gain clear, more effective, and explicit control of actions and thinking, all components of the car work more harmoniously.

Case Example: Connecting Feelings With Actions and Thinking.   The case below illustrates how a counselor or therapist helps a client link together the various components of the behavioral system. We pick up the interchange between counselor and client in the midst of such a discussion. (CN = counselor; CL = client.)

CN: *You started to talk about how you feel . . .*

CL: *Yes, I'm always down about something.*

CN: *Does the word* depressed *or* down-in-the-dumps *describe it?*

CL: *Yeah, that's it.*

CN: *Talk more about it.*

CL: *I always have the blues, feel rotten.*

CN: *I have a very important question for you.*

CL: *What is it?*

CN: *This is central to the counseling. It's extremely important.* How do you know you're depressed?

CL: *Well, I uh . . . I just feel bad all the time.*

CN: *But how do you know you feel bad?*

CL: *I'm always down.*

CN: *I know I'm pressing you a little, but how do you know you feel down?*

CL: *Everything looks bleak, dark, and hopeless.*

CN: *OK, Now you've said something extremely important.*

CL: *I did?*

CN: *Yes, you seem to view the world around you in a negative way. You always see the dark side. Is that accurate?*

CL: *Yes, that's for sure.*

CN: *So you not only feel bad, you think or see the worst.*

CL: *Yes.*

CN: *How else do you know you're depressed?*

CL: *Well, I don't feel like doing anything.*

CN: *Oh, I see. You are kind of immobilized, can't do what you want to do?*

CL: *Yes, I just do what I have to and then mope around.*

CN: *So you aren't taking the actions you want to take?*

CL: *Right.*

CN: *What do people who seem to be happy do that you don't do?*

CL: *They are involved with friends, take care of their homes, have fun. They do the things I once did.*

CN: *So you used to do what others do now—happy things.*

CL: *Right.*

CN: *If you felt better, how would you know it or what would be better? How would other people know? What would lead someone to say, "There is an upbeat person who has an optimistic outlook on life?"*

CL: *I'd be happy.*

CN: *That's how you would feel. But what would you be doing?*

CL: *I'd be joking, active, outgoing, have friends.*

CN: *What would you be doing today if you would be outgoing?*

CL: *I guess I'd be talking to my neighbors and walking around the neighborhood for a while.*

CN: *So you know you're unhappy by looking at what you're doing. Let's talk about how you spend your time.*

CL: *OK.*

In the above dialogue there is a key question— the pivotal question—which is a transitional question. Reread the interaction and see if you can find it. The axiom on the right is central to understanding the concept of total behavior. From an internal point of view behavior is an attempt to put scales in balance, fulfill a quality world picture, and meet one or more needs.

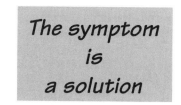

The symptom is a solution

From the point of view of the external observer such as a counselor, therapist, teacher, parent, or manager, behavior is the symptom of an underlying problem. Both perceptions are, in fact, accurate. If the behavior is effective there is no problem. If the behavior helps the person meet his or her needs and meets the standards of a civilized society, there is little reason for concern from the standpoint of mental health. On the other hand, if the behavior is ineffective in the ways described above, it is a symptom of a problem. In either case the symptom (behavior) is the person's solution to an out-of-balance scale, unfulfilled want, or unmet need.

It follows, then, that helping clients substitute ineffective, unhealthy or harmful behaviors with effective, healthy, and altruistic behaviors helps them balance their scales and satisfy wants as well as needs.

It could even be argued that therapists need not identify individual needs in order to help clients discover more useful behaviors. If behaviors are harmful to relationship building, the therapist can help clients move expeditiously and effectively by recognizing that "the symptom is the solution." In other words, clients' choice of behaviors is in their own minds their attempt to fulfill their wants and needs, and therefore they perceive their choices, that is, behaviors as their best efforts at a given moment. Their "symptoms" are indeed their perceived "solutions."

In summary, behavior composed of action, thinking, feelings, and physiology is an attempt to meet needs and fulfill wants. We have most direct control over the action component. In transporting the suitcase, or changing behavior, it is more effective to focus on the actions when counseling clients. According to a well-known axiom, "You can act your way to a new way of thinking easier than you can think your way to a new way of acting."

The goal of reality therapy is behavioral change, personal growth, improvement, enhanced lifestyle, better decision making, remediation of personal deficits, and, in the language of choice theory, the more effective satisfaction of the psychological human needs: belonging, power, freedom, and fun. It is categorically impossible for human beings to make changes until they first decide that a change would be more advantageous. Thus, the users of reality therapy are relentless in their efforts to help clients conduct explicit self-evaluations of each component of their control systems.

Because we attempt to deal with the whole person in reality therapy, even the physiological condition can be described. This is often done to facilitate a referral to a physician, and no attempt is made by a psychotherapist to treat a medical condition. Still, when clients gain better control, make better choices to enhance their relationships, gain a sense of power, freedom, and fun, they relinquish some of their aches and pains.

Thus D refers to a cluster of interventions related to direction, specific actions, ineffective and effective self-talk, relating feelings to actions, and determining the physiological impact of out-of-control and in-control behaviors. No one changes behavior unless a judgment is first made that current behaviors are not helpful.

☐ E

Ask Clients to Conduct a Searching Inner Self-Evaluation

It is important to establish rapport with the client or client system, in family therapy. As stated earlier, empathy implies seeing the clients' points of view, but it means more in the context of reality therapy. Empathy means perceiving the client not as a problem nor even seeing and feeling the clients' problems exclusively. It also includes viewing clients as people who have tried solutions, that is, have attempted to get their scales in balance, but have not been successful. Their behavior, categorized in the *Diagnostic and Statistical Manual* (American Psychiatric Association, 1994), has been their best attempt to gain control and fulfill their needs. Therefore, they are not "people with problems." Rather, they are people who have tried solutions but found them lacking. Their ineffective behaviors have not helped them. Thus the therapist assists them to self-evaluate, to conduct a searching inner inventory of their own actions, cognition, and feelings.

Glasser (1990, 1990a) described self-evaluation as the core of reality therapy. Wubbolding (1990, 1991a) viewed it as the keystone in the arch of procedures. It holds the others together, and if it is removed, the arch crumbles. It is indeed the heart, the essence, the most important component, the quintessential segment of the delivery system.

Reality therapists ask clients to do more than merely describe their behavior, their wants, their perceptions, their levels of commitment, or their plans. They ask clients to make *judgments* about them. It is as if they are asked to look in a mirror and to determine, with the help of another person, whether their lives are the way they want them to be, whether what they want is realistic and helpful to them, whether their behaviors work for them or get them what they want, and many other forms of evaluation delineated below.

> *If the horse is dead, get off*

The reason that this procedure is so important is that many people repeat behaviors that are not helpful and sometimes even harmful. Wubbolding (1998a) stated, "As human beings we have inside of us a characteristic I have called an undying belief in behaviors that do not work'" (p. 196). Most people have had the experience of misplacing a set of keys or important papers. They then look for them in the same places dozens of times with the futile hope that they will find them eventually. It is far more helpful to stop the fruitless search, to sit down, and reflect, "Is this really helping me?" If the answer is "no," then an alternative choice can be considered and the ineffective behavior relinquished.

Below are listed various words and phrases that can be used in helping others make precise evaluations. Please note that only the outer ends of the continuum are listed. You are invited to identify a range of differences between the two extremes.

Help	Hurt
Easy	Difficult
Important	Unimportant
Satisfying	Unsatisfying
Significant	Trivial
Pleasurable	Painful
Useful	Not useful
Meaningful	Meaningless
Results centered	Futile
To your advantage	Not to your advantage

```
Helpful to people  . . . . . . . . . . . . . . . . . . . . . . . . . . . . Not helpful to people
High quality  . . . . . . . . . . . . . . . . . . . . . . . . . . . . . . . . . . . . Low quality
Best effort  . . . . . . . . . . . . . . . . . . . . . . . . . . . . . . . . . . . . Least effort
Excellent performance  . . . . . . . . . . . . . . . . . . . . . Minimal performance
Success  . . . . . . . . . . . . . . . . . . . . . . . . . . . . . . . . . . . . . . . . . Failure
Close to you . . . . . . . . . . . . . . . . . . . . . . . . . . . . . . . . Not close to you
Worth it . . . . . . . . . . . . . . . . . . . . . . . . . . . . . . . . . . . . . Not worth it
Willing to sacrifice  . . . . . . . . . . . . . . . . . . . . . . . Not willing to sacrifice
Desirable consequences  . . . . . . . . . . . . . . . . . Undesirable consequences
Plus  . . . . . . . . . . . . . . . . . . . . . . . . . . . . . . . . . . . . . . . . . . . . . Minus
Realistic . . . . . . . . . . . . . . . . . . . . . . . . . . . . . . . . . . . . . . Unrealistic
Attainable  . . . . . . . . . . . . . . . . . . . . . . . . . . . . . . . . . . Unattainable
Within reach  . . . . . . . . . . . . . . . . . . . . . . . . . . . . . . . . . Out of reach
Possible  . . . . . . . . . . . . . . . . . . . . . . . . . . . . . . . . . . . . . . Impossible
Doable . . . . . . . . . . . . . . . . . . . . . . . . . . . . . . . . . . . . . . Not doable
Practicable . . . . . . . . . . . . . . . . . . . . . . . . . . . . . . . . . Not practicable
Workable . . . . . . . . . . . . . . . . . . . . . . . . . . . . . . . . . . . Not workable
Compatible  . . . . . . . . . . . . . . . . . . . . . . . . . . . . . . . . . Incompatible
```

It is evident that evaluation is a way to help clients restructure their thinking: to make judgments they have not previously made; to perceive their behaviors and wants differently than in the past; to take more need-satisfying actions. Using this component of the WDEP system, the therapist assists clients to identify their values as they relate to their choice. The essential component of evaluation is the client's internal judgment.

More Than an Observation.   Thus, evaluation is more than a statement of factual information. A conclusion is reached and action follows. Furthermore, not only does the client do something, as in D, but also, this action is *judged* to be helpful or hurtful, useful or useless, significant or meaningless, etc. And so evaluation looks both at current actions, wants, perceptions, and commitments as well as at future plans.

Self-evaluation contains a wide range of tools for counselors, teachers, supervisors, and managers to use as they help another person become more effective. It is important to recognize that the practitioner selects what is relevant at a given moment without feeling the necessity to utilize every aspect of self-evaluation in every session with a client, student, or employee.

Types of Self-Evaluation

The following 22 forms of inner self-evaluation are described and illustrated in this chapter. Each aspect of the control system or choice system can be evaluated.

1. Overall behavioral direction and purpose.
2. Choices.
3. Specific behaviors: effective or ineffective.
4. Specific actions related to rules.
5. Specific actions: acceptable or unacceptable.

6. Thinking behaviors: ineffective or effective self-talk.
7. Belief system.
8. Feeling behaviors: helpful or harmful emotions.
9. Clients' best interests: Specific actions and thoughts that enhance or diminish their long-range interests.
10. High-quality or low-quality behavior: Quality is the standard.
11. Life enhancement: Life is improved whether or not the behavior or want initially appears to be personally satisfying.
12. Behavior as measured by goals of the organization.
13. Wants: Realistic or attainable.
14. Wants: Beneficial or harmful to self, others, or the organization.
15. Wants: Definite and clearly enough defined to cause consistent action.
16. Wants as nonnegotiable, highly desirable, or mere wishes.
17. Perceptions: Viewpoint, plus or minus.
18. Perceptions: Locus of control.
19. Values and behavior: Congruence or lack of it.
20. Level of commitment: High enough to get desired results.
21. Evaluation of the plan of action: $SAMI^2C^3$.
22. Professional self-evaluation.

Self-evaluation is the heart, the essence, the most important component, the quintessential segment of the delivery system. It has long been the centerpiece in the process of reality therapy. W. Glasser (1972) described evaluation as the "basis for change." He added, "If there is a specific time in reality therapy when people begin to change, it is when the client evaluates what he or she is doing and then begins to answer the question, 'Is it helping?' People do not change until they decide that what they are doing does not help them accomplish what they want" (N. Glasser, 1980). Self-evaluation, the core of reality therapy (W. Glasser, 1990a, 1990c), is enshrined as one of the essential components of the quality school (W. Glasser, 1990c). This component of the process holds the other procedures together, and if it is removed, the arch crumbles. *This chapter contains a significant extension of these ideas and a comprehensive discussion of the client's self-evaluation as well as several ways that I have formulated for practitioners to evaluate their own behavior from an ethical point of view.*

The 22 Forms of Self-Evaluation

I will now describe in more detail the types of self-evaluation that clients and others can make as well as questions illustrating each type. Self-evaluation questions are applied to each aspect of the human choice system: behavior, quality world, and perception. Not all of these applications are used with each person. The evaluations made by the client are illustrated by a series of hypothetical dialogues. The skilled practitioner selects the relevant components and fits them to the clients' therapeutic issues.

Even though self-evaluation is the heart of reality therapy and even though it appears simple, it is often skipped by practitioners of reality therapy. It is, like the totality of reality therapy, easy to understand but difficult to practice (Wubbolding, 1985b).

Each form of evaluation is detailed below. Some useable questions are presented first. This is followed by a hypothetical dialogue illustrating each kind of self-evaluation. As with all transcripts, I have distilled longer conversations, omitting the extraneous "give and take" that occurs in all human conversations. Only the essence of each form of self-evaluation is presented. Also, many clients are more resistant and show more avoidance than is evidenced in these transcripts. The purpose of the dialogue is not to show every aspect of counseling but to illustrate the evaluative questions in their essence.

Overall Behavioral Direction and Purpose. It is axiomatic for the reality therapist that behavior has a purpose. Because the purpose can be both outcome centered and process centered these behaviors are rich in self-evaluation potential. After the clients define and clarify their precise wants and purposes, a searching evaluation of the effectiveness of current overall behavior is appropriate. They are asked to examine whether their life journey is headed toward a desirable destination. A person who consistently overeats is asked where he or she will be in 5 years, 10 years: "Where is your overall journey taking you? Is your destination a place where you want to be?" This form of evaluation need not be lengthy. If the therapist asks a few well-targeted questions, clients can generally make this evaluation. As with all interventions in reality therapy the use of metaphors is useful. "Closeness," "distance," "near," "far away," "up," "down," "plus," "minus," and many others can be used to help the client conduct inner self-evaluations. The following questions can be tailored to specific persons to lock their perceptions onto their behavior and to intensify and internalize more deeply their judgments regarding the helpfulness of their behavioral direction. The theme is the enhancement of relationships. The basic issue/question underlying self-evaluation is whether people move toward each other or away from each other.

> *If you find yourself*
> *in a hole,*
> *the first thing*
> *to do*
> *is stop diggin'*

Questions

- Is the overall direction of your life in your own best interest?
- Is your direction taking you to a more or a less desirable destination?
- Is the overall direction of your life taking you closer or farther away from your goal or from what you want for yourself?
- Is your overall direction getting you more or less involved with the people you care about?
- What impact did you expect to have when you chose that behavior?
- Looking back, what impact did you actually have?
- What message were you trying to give by your actions or words? Did they have the hoped-for effect?
- How did the receiver of the communication perceive your message?
- What is the difference between the actual impact, the intended communication, and the message received?
- Describe in detail.

The following case illustrates the skillful asking of self-evaluation questions related to direction and the purpose of behavior, both the outcome purpose and the process purpose. Kelly, a parent, speaks to a counselor about a child, Terry, who is bright, obstinate, and unwilling to obey the parent. Subsequent examples in other cases include a married couple as well as a parent and teenager. (K = Kelly; CN = counselor.)

CN: *Kelly, you said very clearly that you want Terry to come in after school by 5:00 and to study each night for an hour and a half. You also want Terry to be cooperative and to go to school each day without a fight about whether he'll go.*

K: *That's right. It seems reasonable to me. I don't think that is asking too much even from an 8-year-old.*

CN: *Tell me about last night. What happened?*

K: *Terry came home at 6:00 p.m., ate, and watched TV, refusing to study.*

CN: *What did you say to Terry?*

K: *I said, "You'd better study or you're grounded."*

CN: *What was your tone of voice like?*

K: *I was furious. Very upset.*

CN: *What message did you intend to give?*

K: *That it is important to be in on time.*

CN: *What message do you think Terry got?*

K: *Probably the same one I've been sending?*

CN: *And that is . . .*

K: *That I want Terry in at 5:00 and I want Terry to study. The same one I sent for a long, long time, and that I'm the boss.*

CN: *What other message was present in your tone of voice?*

K: *That I was very, very upset.*

CN: *Kelly, this is an important question. Did the repetition of the threat and the intensity of your tone help you or help Terry? Did it help you get closer to your son?*

K: *Probably not, but I'm getting tired of his lack of cooperation and Terry's unwillingness to listen to me.*

CN: *Let's put it another way: You have stated unequivocally what you want Terry to do. Now, when you said what you said last night in the way you said it, do you think you got closer to or farther away from achieving your goal?*

K: *I don't know. I don't know.*

CN: *Think about it for a moment . . . closer . . . or farther away from your goal?*

K: *But I don't know what to do!*

CN: *Closer or farther? Please answer the question.*

K: *You want me to say "farther."*

CN: *I want you to say exactly what you think—exactly what you believe about what you are doing.*

K: *To be honest, I guess it took me farther away from my goal.*

CN: *The ultimate goal, and in fact the means to other goals, is a close relationship with Terry. Which way are you heading?*

K: *Away from the kid. I guess I'm moving farther away as I said before. Terry just got a message that I'm upset.*

CN: *Are you willing to look at a better way to handle this situation?*

K: *I'll try anything.*

It is at this point that the client appears to be ready to at least examine the possibility of choosing alternate ways to talk to and interact with Terry. This case illustrates that such evaluation can take more time than perhaps was previously thought. Self-evaluation, like the practice of reality therapy, is "deceptively simple."

Evaluation of Choices. Behavioral choice occupies a place of paramount importance in the practice of reality therapy. Human beings make hundreds, even thousands, of choices each day, most of which have some connection with the external world. Each decision impacts the agent of the choice, other people, or the environment around them. Consequently, choices can be evaluated globally or specifically.

Questions

- You will not remain in a fixed position. You will always be moving forward or backward by means of your choices. What choices can you make, and will they help or hurt the situation?
- Will your choices bring you closer to or farther away from people around you?
- You mentioned several possible choices. Which is most effective? Helpful? Realistic? Acceptable to you and others?
- Whose choices can you control? Your own? Your spouse's? Your children's? Your boss's? Your teacher's?

The continued dialogue between Kelly and the counselor below illustrates this form of self-evaluation.

CN: *Kelly, you've made many choices about how to fix the problem.*

K: *I sure have. I've tried and tried and tried to straighten out that kid but he just can't see things right.*

CN: *So your choice to change him has not gotten any results?*

K: *Right.*

CN: *This situation is similar to something else. It's like the company that has a product to sell to the public. Through their advertising they continually tell the public how good the product is and how they can benefit from it. But after relentless efforts the public just can't see the light. What would you do if you were the president of the company?*

K: *I'd dump the product, drop the advertising effort, and forget the whole thing. But I can't do that with my kid.*

CN: *No, but maybe as in the case of the product there are other choices. You could redesign and repackage the product.*

K: *How can I do that?*

CN: *Well, let's look at your choices up to now. You've tried the choice to get him to change.*

K: *Right.*

CN: *Has your choice to get him to change gotten the results you wanted?*

K: *No, nothing has changed.*

CN: *So working on* his *behavior is a dead end. This points out a basic principle that is crucial in human relations.*

K: *What is that?*

CN: *Actually it's a twofold principle. You can only change your own behavior and you can't force other people to do what you want them to do. You can't force the public to buy the product.*

K: *So I guess I'd better think about the first part of that idea.*

CN: *I couldn't say it any better. Do you want to work on your own actions?*

K: *Yes, I better try some different things.*

CN: *Make some other choices about your own actions?*

K: *I think it's time to take a radically different tack.*

CN: *Let's talk about how to work on your own behavior rather than on his.*

K: *Sounds good.*

In this session Kelly sees the futility of his coercive attempts to change Terry. Such choices are doomed to failure. We have control only over our own actions. Kelly and the counselor can now begin to deal with more effective choices.

Specific Behaviors: Effective or Ineffective.   The most commonly used form of self-evaluation is a judgment made about the effectiveness of *specific* actions. In this segment, the helper asks the client about *specific* evaluations regarding *specific* actions. The counselor asks the client to become a TV camera recording and reporting exactly what happened at a specific time and place.

Questions

- Is your present specific behavior helping or hurting you?
- Is it helping or hurting the people around you?
- How is it helping you get what you want?
- When you did such and such yesterday, what impact did it have on you or on others?
- Does each of your behaviors help you *enough*? In the long run as well as in the short run? How, specifically?
- (To a student) Did it help you to procrastinate studying for the test?
- (To a parent) What impact did lecturing your child about school three times a day have on him? Did it help? What did it do to you and your family? Are you a closer family or are you more divided as a result of your actions?
- (To a husband and wife) If you don't talk to each other, or if you avoid each other as you did yesterday, will you get what you said you want, a happier marriage? A happier relationship?
- What's keeping you from being worse off?

In fact, it is useful to ask all clients if their specific actions bring them closer to other people or if these choices drive them apart. Once again, relationships underlie much of the work of the reality therapist.

The second case is that of a parent of a teenager. JL comes to you for help with his son, who is flunking in school. The son is sullen, does not talk to the family, and refuses to do his household chores. JL has "tried everything" and is very frustrated about the situation.

CN: *I'm glad you came today. How can I help you?*

JL: *My son has created a lot of pain for me lately.*

CN: *What's been happening?*

JL: *He's flunking in school, won't talk at home, refuses to do any work at home, quit his job, and ignores whatever I tell him.*

CN: *How have you been talking to him?*

JL: *I really get mad at him.*

CN: *What is your tone of voice when you talk to him?*

JL: *Constantly shouting.*

CN: *What do you say to him when you talk about school or his job?*

JL: *I usually tell him he's got to pass and ought to keep his job.*

CN: *You usually get pretty upset with him? This probably bothers you a lot and is on your mind.*

JL: *I can't get away from it.*

CN: *I have a very important question about your overall direction, the entire range of behaviors toward him. Are they helpful to him, to you, and to your relationship with your son?*

JL: *I guess not. I seem to be more upset.*

CN: *What about yesterday when he came home? What did you both say and do?*

JL: *He came in late. I asked him where he'd been. He told me it's none of my business. I proceeded to lecture him about school and about respect.*

CN: *Did the lecture get you the result you hoped for?*

JL: *No, not even close. He just went to his room and closed the door and didn't come out the rest of the night.*

CN: *So it is clear that you're going in a direction that is not helping, and we know that yelling at him doesn't get you what you want. Correct?*

JL: *I don't like to admit it, but that's it exactly.*

CN: *When was the last time you spent some time with him doing something enjoyable to both of you?*

JL: *I don't even remember.*

CN: *OK. We'll come back to this later.*

In this dialogue, the counselor helped JL, the parent, evaluate his overall behavior. But the counselor carried the evaluation further by asking about what happened "yesterday when he came home." It is essential that the counselor help the clients examine specific actions. We can change specific actions, the accumulation of which comprises the behavioral direction and a need-satisfying or a need-attacking lifestyle.

Case Discussion. Because of the importance of helping clients and students evaluate specific actions and because of the widespread use of this form of self-evaluation, I've included two brief summaries of situations in which this form of self-evaluation proved useful.

The first example is a 17-year-old boy brought to a counselor by his mother because the boy refused to brush his teeth. The therapist conferred first with the mother and asked her if she had ever told him to brush his teeth. She replied that she tells him about five times per day. The counselor helped her calculate that if she told him five times per day and five days a week the total would be 25 times a week, 100 times a month, and 600 times in a period of 6 months. The counselor then said, "If you tell him one more time, would he gain any new information?" She, of course, provided the obvious answer. They went on to discuss the futility of repeating behaviors that have not been helpful. She then made a plan to focus her conversation on topics that would bring them together rather than bring both of them pain.

I told this story at a workshop in February several years ago. In November of that same year I conducted a training session in Ann Arbor, Michigan. Kim, a teacher who had attended the previous session, approached me and reminded me of this use of self-evaluation. She related how she had hassled her own son for 5 years about homework. But then she stopped talking about homework, putting the responsibility on him. Six months later, he was an honor roll student. He now tells her how good it feels to complete his homework early. He can then celebrate his freedom in the evenings.

These cases are described here not to illustrate happy endings. We have no guarantee of outcomes. It is unethical for an author, therapist, or helper to make such shameless guarantees. The anecdotes are presented to demonstrate the process of self-evaluation and the power of asking clients, "Is what you are currently doing helping or hurting?"

Specific Actions Related to Rules and Specific Actions: Acceptable or Unacceptable.   These two forms of self-evaluation are used especially with involuntary clients or in any situation that can be called disciplinary. Despite even heroic efforts of therapists, some persons insist that antisocial behavior has helped them. Prisoners often insist that robbery, violence, and other destructive actions have been beneficial to them. They learned some things *not* to do so as to avoid getting caught again. Students sometimes feel proud that they won a fight and announce that the fight proved their superiority.

These two forms of self-evaluation involve the clients' judgments about their behavior as measured against others' expectations. They are asked to decide if their actions are appropriate vis-à-vis the rules of an institution and the unwritten norms of the group or family impinging upon them. These external standards are quite different from the internal standards implicit in the question, "Are your current actions helping you?" Relevant questions are therefore derived from external norms.

Questions

- Is what you are doing (e.g., fighting), against the rules?
- Is what you did yesterday acceptable to your family, to your friends? If you don't know for certain, take a guess.
- Is what you're doing acceptable to the society in which you are living?
- Will such behavior get you in trouble or keep you free of hassles?
- Is acting against reasonable rules or norms to your best advantage? Will such actions get you in trouble with others or with the law?
- How? Describe in detail.

There are many other artful ways to ask questions. "Was your action against the written or *unwritten* rules of the institution?" "Take a guess as to what your parents might think about this." "Did the judge think it was a good idea for you to hold up the gas station or, as you claim, to merely drive the get-away car?" As with all forms of client self-evaluation, the therapist can play an active role, while restraining the urge to criticize, condemn, or belittle, even if the clients' judgment seems outlandish.

Many people can make such judgments based on external standards when they are indifferent to the harm inflicted on others or to the self-sabotaging effect on their own best interests.

In the narrative below we pick up the dialogue between the counselor and Hal, the son of JL. (H= Hal; CN = counselor.)

CN: *Hello, Hal, how are you today?*

H: *OK.*

CN: *I talked to your father and he told me there is a big problem in your house.*

H: *Yeah, he's the problem. I don't have any problem.*

CN: *He says you come in late at night and talk back to him, and don't study.*

H: *Well, he starts shouting at me before I can even say anything.*

CN: *Is there a rule in your house about what time you have to come in and about how you address your father?*

H: *It's a stupid rule.*

CN: *What is the "stupid" rule?*

H: *I'm supposed to come home and study for an hour right after school.*

CN: *When was the last time you did that?*

H: *I don't remember.*

CN: *Is not coming home as you're supposed to against the house rules?*

H: *It's stupid!*

CN: *But is it against the "stupid" rule?*

H: *Sure, it is.*

CN: *I'd like to ask you about school, too. What do you do in your classes?*

H: *They're so dumb I sleep.*

CN: *Is sleeping OK? Do they allow you to sleep if you feel like it?*

H: *No, you're not supposed to sleep.*

CN: *What about getting along with the teachers?*

H: *They're always on my back, too.*

CN: *How do you talk to them?*

H: *I think they're jerks.*

CN: *But, how to do you talk to them? Give me an example like yesterday.*

H: *I told one of them off.*

CN: *Is that acceptable in the school?*

H: *No, I got sent to the office.*

CN: *So you're breaking the rules at home and at school and doing some things that are going to get you in trouble?*

H: *Yes, I am.*

This dialogue illustrates that part of self-evaluation includes asking the person to evaluate whether a behavior is against the rules or is acceptable at home or at school. The behavior is measured against a standard. The reality therapist does not try to persuade the person that rules are fair or beneficial. The use of such logic is a waste of time for many people, especially for Hal, our adolescent client. Clearly people, unable or unwilling to evaluate their behavior on the basis of internal standards, require external norms and consequences for making judgments.

By applying internal and external standards, managers use the above forms of self-evaluation to help employees evaluate their effort and work. Posing these questions and using the entire WDEP system makes coaching employees to perform at a high level of quality more effective (Wubbolding, 1996a, 1998c).

Thinking Behaviors: Ineffective and Effective Self-Talk. Users of reality therapy help clients evaluate their action as well as the other wheels of the behavioral car or the other layers of behavior in the behavioral suitcase. Previously I described IST as the ineffective self-talk accompanying the unhelpful action choices of clients. Among such IST, or inner language, are such statements as:

"I can't."
"I've always been that way."
"No one is going to tell me what to do."
"I have no control over what I do . . . no choices."
"I want what I want when I want it, and I want it now."

Therapists ask clients to determine, judge, and evaluate whether such cognitive statements help them. Worth reflecting on is the adage, "Whether you think you can, or whether you think you can't, you're right." The goal of this component of self-evaluation is assisting clients to examine their thinking. Because we control first our actions, second our thinking, and only third our feelings, the cognitive self-evaluation component is used less frequently than the self-evaluation of actions and more frequently than the direct evaluation of feelings.

In the dialogue below the therapist helps JL, Hal's father, self-evaluate the thinking segment of his behavioral suitcase.

CN: *I'm wondering about another aspect of this situation.*

JL: *What's that?*

CN: *We've talked about whether your own efforts have been paying off. I got the idea that you didn't believe your efforts were effective. But sometimes you didn't seem convinced that you could try something different.*

JL: *Yeah. I don't know if I really want to change.*

CN: *I have a question, but I want to explain something first. Whenever we make choices to do something there are always thoughts that accompany and underlie them. They don't really cause our actions, and we are not always aware of them, at least in the form that I'll discuss with you now. I would like to ask you, what are you telling yourself about your son's behavior?*

JL: *I keep thinking he needs to change.*

CN: *That's what you think about* his *actions. I'm asking you about what you're telling yourself about* your own *actions.*

JL: *I keep thinking that I can get him to change . . .*

CN: *. . . that you can force him to change?*

JL: *I don't use the word "force."*

CN: *But I hear you saying that at least you can control him . . . that you can motivate him in some way. You're not saying that explicitly, but it seems to underlie what you're doing.*

JL: *Yes, I don't say that explicitly but now that you mention it, I suppose I think that way.*

CN: *The statement I hear is: "I can control my son." When you think this way, you are dooming yourself to feelings of frustration.*

JL: *But in the past I could control him.*

CN: *Could you really control him if he didn't want to do what you wanted him to do?*

JL: *No, I guess not. He did whatever he did because he wanted to do it.*

CN: *In other words, can you force him to do something if he truly doesn't want to do it?*

JL: *I guess not.*

CN: *So telling yourself "I can control my son" is not helping.*

JL: *You're right. It's not helping me and it's not helping him. It only gets me upset.*

CN: *So I'd like to help you tell yourself something different and act differently toward him.*

JL: *Sounds good.*

The counselor helped JL look at his own cognitive or thinking behaviors. This form of self-evaluation springs from the fact that reality therapy is not only action centered, but is quite cognitive in its approach to clients.

And though it appears simple, this form of self-evaluation is often overlooked, even by experienced practitioners of reality therapy. It is, like the totality of reality therapy, easy to understand but difficult to practice. The dialogue below illustrates the self-evaluation of the son Hal related to the thinking segment of the behavioral suitcase.

CN: *You said you were sleeping in class and coming home late after school.*

H: *Yeah, I guess that's what I've been doing.*

CN: *I'd like to talk about not only what you've been doing but what you've been thinking when you make these choices.*

H: *What do you mean?*

CN: *What goes through your mind when you come home? Or better, let's try to identify the unspoken but underlying thought you have when you come home.*

H: *How do you mean?*

CN: *Well, you arrive late because you don't feel like coming home on time.*

H: *Right.*

CN: *What were you thinking when you came home late? What went through your mind?*

H: *I guess I was thinking that I felt like staying away.*

CN: *But there is a rule that says, "Come home on time." So what was underlying the choice regarding the rule?*

H: *I see what you mean. I guess I said, "I don't care about the rule!"*

CN: *Can I put it another way, more dramatically?*

H: *OK.*

CN: *"Nobody is going to tell me what to do." It's a more generalized kind of thought. But I wonder if you haven't justified a lot of what you do by telling yourself such things.*

H: *Well, I sure don't like people telling me what to do.*

CN: *Sounds like that could be the thought that accompanies your choice. We call it "self-talk" because that's what you tell yourself.*

H: *I hate to admit it, but I think you're right.*

CN: *What is the result of telling yourself things on a regular basis?*

H: *It sounds a little silly when I hear it out loud.*

CN: *But it's what you think and it does serve a purpose. I have two questions for you: How realistic are these demands, and does this kind of thinking help you?*

H: *It's brought me only grief up to now.*

CN: *Another point: You said you told off the teacher when he asked you to do something.*

H: *Yeah. I don't feel like doing much in school sometimes. I'd like to do other things.*

CN: *Could there be some thinking accompanying these kinds of choices, choices to do what you feel like doing?*

H: *Could be.*

CN: *Maybe it's another version of the same kind of self-talk.*

H: *Like what?*

CN: *Well, you said you wanted to do something other than what the teacher wanted. And you really wanted to make your own choice. Right?*

H: *Right.*

CN: *How about "I want what I want when I want it, and I want it now"?*

H: *That's similar to the other one.*

CN: *Yes it is. Maybe there's a theme here.*

H: *You mean that I'm telling myself that no one has a right to tell me what to do?*

CN: *I like how you said it. My most important question is, "Is this self-talk a plus or a minus for you in the long run?"*

H: *It's a minus because I'm getting a lot of grief at home and at school.*

This conversation shows how the counselor helped the client identify the IST and then evaluate it. At this point, there is no attempt to illustrate how to help Hal replace the IST with EST.

Global Evaluation of Belief System.   The evaluation of inner self-talk includes a more fundamental judgment. It is certainly helpful to ask clients to evaluate their inner self-talk statements about specific situations, but it can also be useful to help clients examine their core beliefs in an evaluative way.

CN: *I wanted to ask you an even more fundamental question. Have you thought about what you want your family to be like in the future?*

JL: *Well, not all that much. But I'd like us to live as a unit with some degree of harmony and yet independence for each person.*

CN: *OK. The important question is, Does your present belief system, that is, what you* *think about your role, your ability to control, or the amount of freedom you allow people to have support the way you are living and the way you want to live in the future?*

JL: *That's a powerful and very basic question.*

CN: *Yes, it is. And it's very important.*

JL: *As I think about it now, somehow my underlying beliefs are standing in the way of progress.*

CN: *It's very important to realize that you're not going to make major changes quickly. It will be important to look at these beliefs in some detail and their relationship to a harmonious family life.*

JL: *Sounds interesting to me.*

The counselor then helped JL examine his basic belief system. His beliefs about freedom, independence, and his own role as a communicator and father as well as his impact on Hal were the center of his global self-evaluation of his belief system. Questions revolved around whether these core beliefs about family roles facilitated or impeded harmony in family relations. This particular dialogue can easily be added to or integrated into other forms of self-evaluation.

Feeling Behaviors: Helpful or Harmful Emotions.   Though evaluation of feelings is not done in isolation from other more frequently used forms of self-evaluation, the reality therapist helps clients assess their own feelings. To help clients abandon destructive emotions the therapist asks evaluation questions as a prelude to effective change. A discussion of negative and positive feelings often provides an impetus and major source of motivation for making the needed changes in actions. Such changes in actions lead to changes in feelings. The behavioral car functions as a unit. The entire suitcase is controlled by the handle, which is attached to the action level. Such questions about feelings might include:

- Is feeling anger, resentment, guilt, self-pity, or loneliness helping or hurting you?
- What is to your advantage: To nurse the negative feelings of self-pity, depression, and resentment, or to let them go?
- Have you endured feelings of powerlessness and victimhood long enough?
- What impact do positive feelings of trust, hope, self-confidence, self-esteem, and positive mental attitude have on your physiology?
- Do the positive and negative feelings draw people toward you or push them away?
- Do the positive and negative feelings help you get what you want? How? Or do they prevent you from getting what you want? How?
- What effect does your anger have on your body? Describe in detail.
- Do other people or situations really have the power to *make* you upset?

A conversation between JL and the therapist might be as follows:

CN: *JL, is this problem on your mind pretty much?*

JL: *Yes, I think about it all the time.*

CN: *How do you feel inside?*

JL: *I'm always in a state of turmoil, always upset.*

CN: *Do you ever get angry?*

JL: *You bet.*

CN: *I'll bet you are really upset at times?*

JL: *I boil inside.*

CN: *How has it affected you physically?*

JL: *Sometimes I can't sleep if we have an argument at night.*

CN: *How about appetite?*

JL: *I can't eat if we have an argument around mealtime.*

CN: *So this anger is not helping you to solve the problem?*

JL: *No, it's not.*

CN: *Getting upset is preventing you from enjoying life?*

JL: *It sure is.*

CN: *You said that when you argue you get upset, can't eat, can't sleep. How do you feel after one of these blow-ups?*

JL: *I feel like I made a fool of myself.*

CN: *Are you saying you feel . . . ?*

JL: *Guilty!!!*

CN: *So guilt and anger are feelings you have, and they impact your health to some extent.*

JL: *Yes, they sure do.*

CN: *You definitely have good reason to try something different. You said that you have these feelings around arguments?*

JL: *Right.*

CN: *Your feelings are connected with arguments. That means your feelings are connected with what you do. I can help you change how you deal with Hal, and that change will impact how you feel. This change in how you feel will not be immediate. It will take time but eventually you will notice the difference*

JL: *Are you telling me that I need to stop arguing?*

CN: *I think it would help. What do you think?*

JL: *Could be.*

In helping clients evaluate their feelings the reality therapist connects them with actions. Discussing how a person feels separate from their actions provides only momentary relief. Goleman's (1995) research shows that ventilation of anger worsens it rather than lessens it.

We now return to the earlier case of the parent (K, for Kelly) and the 8-year old.

CN: *You said you were furious with Terry.*

K: *I was out of my mind with rage.*

CN: *Did it help to feel this rage?*

K: *I had no control over how I felt.*

CN: *Yes, I understand. But did the fury and rage accomplish anything?*

K: *No, but I couldn't help it.*

CN: *This might be true in the past, but what impact will it have on Terry if you indulge the anger, nurse it or feed it?*

K: *Well, I guess it won't get a very good result.*

CN: *I think you're right.*

K: *Are you saying I should not feel annoyed?*

CN: *No, I'm only asking at this point if giving vent to the annoyance you feel is helping you get what you want.*

K: *No. It certainly is not.*

CN: *I'm also asking what impact this rage has on you physically.*

K: *It seems to make me feel upset.*

CN: *How?*

K: *I lose my appetite.*

CN: *Does your face turn colors? Do you sweat or get an upset stomach? Does your head pound?*

K: *Yes. How did you know?*

CN: *Sounds familiar!!*

K: *I see.*

CN: *So the feelings are not helping?*

K: *Not the ones we've talked about.*

CN: *What single feeling would be more useful?*

K: *Patience.*

CN: *What impact would that have on Terry and on you physically? And how would it impact your relationship?*

K: *It might be better for our relationship, and certainly I would not blow a gasket.*

CN: *Let's talk about what you could do differently to develop such feelings.*

K: *I'd like that.*

In this section the client makes specific evaluations about feelings. It is important to state, once again, that the feelings are not discussed as causes of actions, nor are they discussed in isolation from actions. Kelly's feelings will change as a direct result of a change in actions. By changing action choices Kelly will come to believe that there is "no one behind our cognitive and psychological behaviors, orchestrating their events" (Barbieri, 1997, p. 20). Still, emotions are often the most prominent element in the minds of clients. They are also one of the wheels of the car as well as a very important level in the behavioral suitcase. Following the above dialogue, the counselor will help Kelly connect even more explicitly the actions and feelings.

Clients' Best Interests: Specific Actions and Thoughts that Enhance or Diminish Their Long-Range Interests.
Clients, employees, or students are asked to examine whether a short-term payoff for a decision is really in their best interest. They evaluate their behaviors on the basis of the question, "Does short-term gain equal long-term gain?"

In the employee assistance program (EAP) at the XYZ company, an employee, Lisa, angered by the way she has been treated by her supervisor, relates her story. After listening patiently, the therapist asks the client to self-evaluate. (L = Lisa; TH = therapist.)

TH: *Lisa, tell me more about what happened.*

L: *Today was the straw that broke not the camel's back but my back, and the straw was my manager.*

TH: *What did she say?*

L: *I worked hard on the project and had a low error rate, stayed late, and got it finished on time. She then criticized me and chewed me out in front of other people.*

TH: *We've talked about this before. It's been an ongoing problem for you.*

L: *It sure has. Actually, she's jealous of me because I do such a good job and she nitpicks because she has to let everyone know she's in charge. I very nearly told her where to go in front of everyone.*

TH: *I'll bet you were really angry.*

L: *I still am. I'm going back in there and tell her off in her office. The office is glass and people will see that I'm not going to be treated like that. I don't care if the big bosses know. I don't even care if I get fired. Screw this whole company!*

TH: *If you do that, is there a possibility of getting sacked?*

L: *Definitely. The bosses could not tolerate me telling off a manager even if I am right. But I don't care.*

TH: *OK. OK. Lisa, I know you are upset. But stop and think for a moment. If you tell off your manager with as much rage as you obviously feel, will you feel better at that moment?*

L: *You're damn right!*

TH: *And then you will get fired?*

L: *Yeah, it could happen.*

TH: *So, for a short-term good feeling you are willing to sacrifice the long-term satisfaction of having a job here?*

L: *Well . . .*

TH: *You know the expression, "short-term gain, long-term pain?"*

L: *That pretty well describes it.*

TH: *So the key question for you to answer is whether you are willing to trade long-term pleasure and satisfaction in exchange for a fleeting sense of vindication at having given vent to your anger?*

L: *I see what you mean.*

TH: *In other words, Lisa, which choice is in your best interest?*

L: *Probably to cool off.*

TH: *You know, your situation reminds me of something that happened to me when I took my first full-time job. It's not exactly the same but it's similar.*

L: *What was that?*

TH: *Well, I thought I had been shafted by the supervisor, really taken for granted after I had done some extra things and never asked for more pay. There were a lot of things involved, but I was fuming. I came in breathing fire and smoke. Could hardly sleep. I didn't say anything, fortunately. But after a couple of days I was ready to lay into the boss, tell him off but good! I was over at a friend's house and his mother asked how things were going at my new job. I'd been there about 9 months. I was so glad she asked. I told her the whole story. She said that I'd be looking for another job with a bad reference and that I might feel good for the moment* *but I'd feel like crap later. She said, "I have two pieces of advice. Do you want to hear them?" I thought I'd pass them along to you, Lisa, if you want me to.*

L: *Sure, go ahead.*

TH: *She said, "Don't do anything when you're mad, and don't do anything to hurt yourself." I've let that guide me ever since, and I pass it along occasionally. I don't know why but that story just popped into my mind. I haven't thought about it for quite a while.*

L: *Well, it makes sense. What was that again?*

TH: *Don't do anything when you're mad and don't do anything to hurt yourself. You know, sometimes it is best to do nothing when you're upset and angry. Wait till the anger subsides. Then think about a strategy that will be best in the long run.*

L: *That's what I do when I drive. If I get upset with another driver I don't do anything. It's dangerous to act when I'm mad. Road rage is not my thing.*

TH: *You know, Lisa, that's interesting that you say that. Our behavior is like a car. [Therapist explains the metaphor of the behavioral car.] If we act quickly and impulsively on our feelings, our car can go off the road and we can get hurt.*

L: *I see what you mean.*

TH: *So what is in your best interest?*

L: *To wait a while.*

TH: *How about coming back and talking before you do anything?*

L: *Great idea.*

The EAP therapist helped the employee decide to weigh the pros and cons of a decision that might have an immediate payoff but that would almost inevitably have disastrous long-term effects. The focus is not on actions in this discussion, but on thinking. The EAP counselor asks her to ponder and carefully consider which action choices are in her long-term best interests.

High-Quality or Low-Quality Behavior: Quality Is the Standard.   Besides counselors and therapists, educators make extensive use of the WDEP system. Sullo (1997) stated, "The only time you can be reasonably assured that someone will put forth the effort and energy required to do quality work is when they have had a chance to self-evaluate and have determined that behaving in a particular way will add quality to their lives" (p. 100). Managers in agencies and companies also find the system beneficial, efficient, and practical. The following generic questions need to be fitted to each specific situation (Wubbolding, 1996a).

- Are you functioning at the highest level possible?
- What effect does your behavior have on the quality of work?
- How does your contribution add to the quality of the organization?
- How much are you inwardly satisfied by the quality of your work?

What follows is an example of a manager helping an employee self-evaluate. Pat, ordinarily a conscientious middle manager for a large company, has been exhibiting several unacceptable behaviors. The senior manager asks to have a talk with Pat.

Mgr: *Pat, how are things going?*

Pat: *I've worked here 6 months and I would like a promotion.*

Mgr: *We haven't promoted anyone before they've worked here 9 months. How realistic is it for you to expect a promotion 3 months early?*

Pat: *I guess I'll have to wait.*

Mgr: *That's right. There are some other things I wanted to talk to you about, Pat. I've noticed that you've been leaving early, and it's also been quite noticeable to people under you.*

Pat: *Yeah, I guess I have. But I also worked overtime last month.*

Mgr: *If you continue to leave early, what effect will it have on the distribution of the work?*

Pat: *Some people have to do more work than others.*

Mgr: *How about the effect on the length of time to get the work done?*

Pat: *It probably takes longer.*

Mgr: *Aside from the amount of time, what effect does it have on the people under you when they see you leave early?*

Pat: *I guess they aren't too impressed when their supervisor sets a bad example for them.*

Mgr: *I've also noticed you've been complaining in front of your people. What effect does griping and leaving early have on the promotion you are shooting for?*

Pat: *I guess it won't help.*

Mgr: *What would help you get what you want?*

Pat: *I need to get back to my old self.*

Mgr: *I agree. Also, what about the rules?*

Pat: *It's pretty clear we're supposed to be here until 4:45; salaried people are not exceptions.*

Mgr: *You know, there's no rule about complaining, but how does it impact other people?*

Pat: *It hurts their morale too.*

Mgr: *What about the overall quality of a leader's action; what impact does it have on others?*

Pat: *They'll perform at a lower level if I lower my level of quality.*

Mgr: *So what about the future?*

Pat: *I guess I need to turn around.*

Mgr: *In other words, a higher level of quality would be a worthwhile goal?*

Pat: *Of course.*

Mgr: *Could you make a plan?*

Pat: *I guess so.*

Mgr: *A firm plan?*

Pat: *All right. All right. I'll stay till 4:45 from now on.*

Mgr: *"From now on" is too long. What would be more realistic?*

Pat: *I'll do it for 2 weeks.*

Mgr: *What about complaints?*

Pat: *Yeah, I'll stop.*

Mgr: *Maybe just bite your tongue for a few days. Let's talk again in a week or so.*

Pat: *We've said it before, in fact, quite a bit around here. Quality is a moving target.*

Clearly choice theory and the WDEP system are applicable to the workplace. It is the responsibility of management to create an atmosphere that is physically and psychologically safe and congenial. In this environment managers more effectively use the WDEP system in a friendly, firm, and fair manner.

Life Enhancement: Life Is Improved Whether or Not the Behavior or the Want Initially Appears to Be Personally Satisfying.   All behaviors are chosen and all wants are desirable, because at first they appear to satisfy the basic human motivators: belonging, power, freedom, or fun. But some people choose behaviors harmful to themselves or others. They also have wants that might be equally hurtful. The skillful practitioner asks them to conduct a deeper and broader evaluation of these choices and wants besides merely asking the generic question, "Does it help or hurt?"

For example, the question about life enhancement is relevant to a person who overeats. The dialogue below is an inner conversation between "I" and "Me" conducted by someone who seeks to lose weight. The inner debate and self-evaluation might be the following. It is Saturday at 8:00 a.m.

I: *Today is Saturday. I'm off work and I've gotten exercise twice this week and pushed away from the table all week. The doctor gave me a detailed plan. My family said that they would like me to follow it.*

Me: *But I'm tired and hungry. Besides, I've been "good" all week. So I deserve to lie around and eat while I watch TV all day.*

I: *It might feel good, but how does such a series of decisions enhance your life?*

Me: *It's only one trip to the bakery!*

I: *The least you could do would be to walk to the bakery.*

Me: *Four miles? No way!*

I: *Driving and eating and sitting would not help me live longer. And exercising would be a good example to my family.*

Me: *So what! Who cares?*

I: *The question still remains: What improves your life and what threatens it?*

Me: *OK, OK. Even though I want to take the line of least resistance, it's more to my advantage to stick to my low-sugar, fruit-eating, no-fat, 1-hour-of-exercise Saturday.*

The self-evaluation component had many nuances. It even transcends judgments based on the immediate gratification of unevaluated wants and behaviors.

Evaluation of Wants

Because of the importance of the quality world and the wants as the proximate triggers for all behavior, they are self-evaluated very carefully in the process of counseling or therapy using reality therapy. In speaking about self-evaluation W. Glasser (1996) made the point that all effective self-evaluation is based on measuring the external or real world against the internal world or quality world. The specific wants contained in the quality world are each connected to one or more of the generic needs. When needs are fulfilled the person is happy. Consequently, all people seek to be happy. Happiness, however, is an elusive and highly nuanced concept. Some changes in the external world appear to make us happy, but in the long run result in pain and sadness. A woman wishing her husband dead kills him and experiences momentary relief, only to discover that the result is a life prison term and long-range loss of free-dom, deep depression, and an uncomfortable life of danger and violence characteris-tic of incarceration. A similar distinction can be made with drugs, cheating in school, procrastination, arguing, antisocial behavior, and any choices that bring a momen-tary sense of relief followed by pain or unhappiness.

Whether the pleasurable internal payoff is short range or long range, we all seek happiness. There was a song in the 1950s that said, "Happiness, happiness, we all run round in a race, everybody's looking in a different place." A norm often used in self-evaluation is our happiness; whether we are fulfilling wants and needs and whether we have the quality of relationships that we want.

Behavior as Measured by Goals of the Organization.   At a faculty workshop of The William Glasser Institute in November 1997, Kaye Mentley, principal of the first Glasserian quality school in the United States, provided an additional insight into self-evaluation.

Managers and administrators seeking organizational harmony ask employees to self-evaluate on bases broader than individualistic satisfaction of the employees' qual-ity worlds. In a school, individual teachers might choose behaviors that are personally need-satisfying or even helpful to their classrooms. Workers in companies often self-evaluate that their behavior helps their departments. Still, there is a broader basis for effective judgments. Individuals, teams, and even departments need to evaluate whether their behavioral choices take the *entire* organization closer or further away from the basic mission and goal of the company, school, or agency as a whole. They are asked to examine whether their choices, behavior, or attitudes are congruent with the overall direction and goals of the institution.

Choice theory legitimizes the individual satisfaction of needs, which can lead to a naive and even inconsiderate style of behavior. The person who practices choice theory and reality therapy to the fullest is able to be independent while recognizing the im-portance of interdependence. Thus, once again, the value of relationships emerges as central to the high-quality functioning of an organization.

Wants: Realistic or Attainable.   The quality world comprises intensely desirable wants that each of us has developed beginning with infancy. In this component of self-evaluation, clients are asked to evaluate the attainability of their wants. Adoles-cents often want "to be left alone." They are asked to evaluate how realistic it is for parents to give them free reign to do as they please. Spouses who have tried to force their partners to change evaluate if such a change can truly occur through continued coercion. Part of this evaluation is helping clients distinguish between what is most desirable to them and what they are willing to settle for as minimally satisfying their wants. Several evaluative questions are pertinent to the attainability of wants.

- Is what you want attainable or realistic for you?
- Is there a reasonable chance of getting what you want in the near or distant future?
- How likely is it that the world around you will change to meet your desires?
- How possible is it for you to make the changes in your own behavior that you've said you want to make?
- Is there anyone around you to whom you want to be closer than you are at the present time?

In the dialogues that follow, the counselor speaks with the father, JL, and then with the son, Hal.

CN: *When we were talking about what you expect from your son, you said you wanted him to study, to pass his courses at school, to come in on time, to do his chores, to get along with the family. That would be quite a turnaround for him.*

JL: *It's really very reasonable. After all, he does live in my house and he is my son.*

CN: *From your point of view and from mine, it's not asking too much. But how realistic is it that you will get everything you want? How possible is it for him to make a dramatic change?*

JL: *Well, he hasn't done it yet, in spite of my efforts.*

CN: *You've done a lot to bring about the change you wanted and you said it hasn't worked. So how likely is a radical change on his part?*

JL: *I guess not very likely.*

CN: *Well, what are you willing to settle for, in view of the fact that you probably won't get everything you've been hoping for?*

JL: *I guess I'd be happy if he'd make* some *effort in school and at home. This would be OK with him, too.*

CN: *Then getting part of what you want and allowing him to have part of what he wants will be good for the relationship?*

JL: *Yes.*

The counselor in this dialogue helped the father evaluate whether he could make the internal concession to settle for an approximation of his ideal want. The point to keep in mind is not what a father, an adolescent, or *any* client would really say to these questions. For the purpose of understanding the principles it is enough to attend especially to the questions asked by the counselor.

Wants: Beneficial or Harmful to Self, Others, or the Organization.   All wants are related to needs and thus *appear* to be need-satisfying and genuinely helpful to the client. Still, many people have desires which, upon further examination, might not be truly advantageous. Consequently, clients evaluate their wants regarding the short- and long-range impact on themselves, on others, and on their environment. The person who wants to injure himself or another person is asked if reaching such a goal is truly beneficial. He might feel better for a short while after the attack, but will going to jail really be helpful to him? The less dramatic example of Hal illustrates several questions that might be asked.

- Are your wants truly in your own best interest?
- Would getting what you want help you? How? Would others be helped? How?
- Is getting closer to another person whom you know realistic for you?

In the next portion of the dialogue, the counselor helps Hal examine whether his wants are genuinely helpful to him or whether they are hurting him in any way.

H: *Well I'm back again.*

CN: *It's good to see you, and I have some more questions for you.*

H: *Fire away.*

CN: *What do you want from your father and from the teachers at school?*

H: *More than anything I want them off my back so that I can drop out of school.*

CN: *So you'd really like to drop out of school?*

H: *That's it. I want to be on my own, free of people telling me what to do, and free to get a job.*

CN: *Let me get this straight. You want to say goodbye to your education permanently?*

H: *That's it.*

CN: *I want to ask you if that will truly be to your best advantage.*

H: *What do you mean?*

CN: *Let's put it this way. Would you like to make $25.00 a day more than you're making now?*

H: *That'd be OK.*

CN: *That's $125 a week or $500 per month or $6000 per year.*

H: *That's a pretty good deal. I'd buy a car.*

CN: *That's how much more a person makes* a day *who has a high school diploma over what someone makes who does not have a diploma.*

H: *I see . . .*

CN: *You can probably triple that for a college degree. Of course, I'm speaking about* legal *income.*

H: *That's a lot of money.*

CN: *So my question again is, Is it helpful to you, in the long run, to want to quit school.*

H: *No, but I still hate school.*

In the above dialogue the counselor asked very pointed questions in order to quickly help Hal consider the long-range and legitimate advantage or disadvantage of his wants.

Wants: Definite and Clearly Enough Defined to Cause Consistent Actions.
Besides the clearly defined and intensely desirable wants, the treasured possessions, and the cherished beliefs in the quality world, human beings also have wants that are ill defined, vague, and blurred. Any parent with a teenager has had the experience of hearing the answer "I dunno" to such questions as, "What do you want to do this weekend?" "What do you want to do when you graduate?" "What kind of summer job will you look for?"

Questions

- If you had a clear picture of what you want, what would you be doing differently from what you're doing now?
- Describe in outline form what you want.
- Even though you're not clear on what you want, just take a guess about what it *might* be.
- What are some things you *don't* want? What do you want to avoid?
- Do you want to be around people, things, data, or ideas in your career?

Unlike the other types of self-evaluation, this one lacks a sample dialogue. An exercise recommended to the reader is to create a conversation between a parent and a 16-year-old high school student, "Hazy."

Wants as Nonnegotiable, Highly Desirable, or Mere Wishes.   Human beings have wants that are necessary for life itself. No one trades the desire for oxygen. It is indispensable for all people. Rare is the person who trades physical health, such as eyesight, for any amount of money.

On the other hand, some wants are less than nonnegotiable but are intensely desired. For example, the retention of prized possessions, an antique car, a family heirloom, a favorite piece of clothing, a monthly check, might be intensely desirable but could, under certain circumstances, be negotiable.

Moreover, some wants are mere wishes and are not supported with relentless and determined pursuit. Winning a lottery, wearing a particular suit on a given day, and being precisely on time for all social events are, for some, whimsical at best, in the sense that they do not involve a high level of commitment.

Discerning that there are appropriate degrees of desirability, that is, levels of wants, is at times difficult. Part of recovery from addictions and codependency is learning that some wants are more important than others. Wanting a child to come in from play at 5:00 p.m. rather than 5:05 p.m. might not be as important as the relationship between parent and child, which is damaged when a parent lacks the understanding that a child's concept of time is different than the adult's. "I want what I want when I want it and I want it now. And if I don't get it now I'll kick butt" is often a theme of the rigid thinking of an alcoholic and a codependent and is the content for serious self-evaluation.

A major effort of the person using reality therapy is assisting clients in their self-evaluation of the relative importance of their wants. This task becomes more crucial when dealing with persons living in environments characterized by turmoil or inconsistency. In such an atmosphere defining wants can be a task of olympian proportion.

Evaluation of Perceptions

Because we only know the world through our perceptions, exploring and evaluating them is integral to the reality therapy process. We can only know and deal with the information gleaned from the world around us.

When clients conduct self-evaluations of their self-perceptions and their perceptions of the world around them, they are not evaluating the effectiveness of their behaviors or the attainability of their wants. Rather, they question whether their perceptions of themselves or their world views are accurate. Sometimes they are asked if a negative view of themselves is accurate or even if their view of themselves as "the greatest" or as omnipotent represents their *total* self.

Many people feel inferior to others and fail to achieve their full potential because they see themselves as unworthy, inept, or even impostors. Frequently, they compare their inner sense of inadequacy with the external ways in which others present themselves. Such comparisons are unfair and result in perceptions of the self as less competent than others.

Reality therapists help clients determine whether their viewpoints are accurate and helpful to themselves or others and if they are in line with the viewpoints of important people in their environment: family, teachers, spouse, judge, probation officer, employer, or the entire organization in which they live or work. In short, they examine the connection between their perceptions and their wants, and whether their viewpoints or perceptions add to or subtract from their interpersonal relationships. Some generic questions include:

- When you compare your internal sense of limitations with the external ways in which others present themselves, are you being fair to yourself? Why? Why not?
- Is it realistic to see yourself as totally incompetent, inept, or worthless?
- How is it helping or hurting you to see yourself in this way?
- Is your self-criticism based on your self-perception taking you "up" or "down"?
- Even if you have inferior skills in one area, where is it getting you if you see yourself as pandemically inferior?

Perceptions: Viewpoint, Plus or Minus.   After therapists assist clients in describing their perceptions of the current situation, especially their perceived locus of control, clients decide if the way they see the world is genuinely best for them. A parent who only sees the negative side of his or her children is asked to evaluate this viewpoint. Persons seeing the future as dismal are asked if focusing on the uncontrollable future to the exclusion of the controllable present is helping or hurting them in the short run and in the long run. More often, with the help of the reality therapist, clients evaluate whether their perceived place of control is accurate, as demonstrated in "Perceptions: Locus of Control," below.

In evaluating perceptions it is useful to ask clients how they perceive the world, family, school, job, etc. This differs from asking what they want from these elements and what they are doing about them. Reality therapists ask directly if the way clients see the world and what they choose to see in their world is helping them and helping their situations. Relevant questioning incorporates the following:

- Does it help to look at the situation the way you currently see it?
- Is your perception a plus or a minus for you?
- Do you feel better or worse when you nurse or intensify your current viewpoint?
- How does it help if you see the situation or person from a high level of perception? From a low level of perception?

In what follows, the counselor helps the father, JL, evaluate how he sees Hal, his son.

CN: *We've talked about what you want from Hal and what you can realistically expect to achieve. I'd like to ask you now about what you see when you see your son. What do you make judgments about, both favorable and unfavorable? What do you like and dislike?*

JL: *There are some things that I see that I like. He's really a nice kid in so many ways. In some ways he's very considerate. When my mother lived with us until she died last year, he was very good to her. They were very close to each other. I can't help thinking that some of his problems are that he misses her.*

CN: *Anything else?*

JL: *He's really smart and can fix things around the house. But lately I haven't gotten any help from him.*

CN: *If you could see more of this, would it help you to feel better?*

JL: *It sure would. I'd love to see this more often.*

CN: *What else do you see?*

JL: *It's hard to see the good. There's so much negative, like what we've talked about before—his schoolwork, his surly attitude, his late hours, his defiance, etc., etc., etc.!!*

CN: *There is a lot to see that is harmful to him, to you, and to the family. But I want to ask you a very important question. What are the consequences for you and for him if you only see the negative, if the only things you talk about and think about are the problem behaviors? What impact do these viewpoints have on your family connectedness?*

In this session the counselor helps JL examine his perceptions. The implication is that even how we look at the world around us either serves to engage us more closely with each other or adversely expedites the unraveling of our relationships.

Perceptions: Locus of Control.   People feeling victimized and powerless believe their control is outside of themselves. Convinced that they do not choose their behavior, they cling to the idea that the origin of their actions, thinking, and feelings is external.

From the point of view of choice theory and the delivery system, reality therapy, behavior is always generated from within us. The locus or place of control is always inside the person. Many people believe that their control does not originate from within them and demonstrate this belief with the language of external control (Glasser, 1998a):

> "They made me do it."
> "I don't drink too much. My family has a problem."
> "She upsets me."
> "You make me angry."
> "A fit of depression came over me."
> "I had an anxiety attack."
> "This weather gets me down."
> "There's not enough time."
> "The teacher's always picking on me."
> "I hit him because he hit me first."

The questioning of the client about perceived locus of control includes such questions as:

- Given your circumstances, what choices do you have?
- How much of all your trouble do you think you yourself are causing?
- What can you control and what is out of your control?
- In spite of your environment, family, and current external pressures, what decisions could you follow through on today, even for a limited time?
- Is it true that you really have no control, that you are completely incapable of making the situation better?
- If you haven't caused any of the trouble you've experienced, is there any way you could make the situation worse? [A paradoxical question to be used only within ethical guidelines.]

- When you compare your internal sense of limitations with the external strengths of others, are you being fair to yourself? Why? Why not?
- Is it realistic to see yourself as totally incompetent, inept, or worthless?
- How is it helping or hurting you to see yourself in this way?
- Is your self-criticism resulting from this self-perception taking you "up" or "down"?
- Even if you have inferior skills in one area, where is it getting you if you see yourself as pandemically inferior?

The counselor again talks to Hal:

CN: *Hal, we've talked about school hassles, trouble at home, etc. Where do you see yourself in this situation?*

H: *What do you mean?*

CN: *How much trouble are you bringing onto yourself?*

H: *They're doing it to me.*

CN: *I understand. Do you think you've brought any of it on by your choices?*

H: *No!*

CN: *You haven't done anything at all. You're totally at the mercy of everyone else?*

H: *No, I'm not at their mercy.*

CN: *So how much have you brought on? Give me a percentage.*

H: *I've caused no more than 20%.*

CN: *That much! You'll take responsibility for 20%?*

H: *Yeah.*

CN: *So you have made some choices that have not been too cool. I'd like to help you make some better ones.*

H: *I'd like that.*

CN: *OK. Let's talk about what you have control of, not what you don't have control of. Can you really control the teachers, your parents, etc.?*

H: *No.*

CN: *That leaves one person.*

H: *OK. OK. I know. I can only control my own choices.*

CN: *I think you've got it.*

H: *It's all my fault.*

CN: *I never said that, and I don't believe it. You made the choices that you thought were best. I'm thinking more about what could be better for you.*

H: *In other words, I should think about the future.*

CN: *And what choices you can control.*

H: *My own.*

CN: *Exactly.*

In this segment the counselor helps Hal evaluate the place of his control. He has no control over others, and he has more inner control over his own behavioral choices than he thought previously.

Values and Behavior: Congruence or Lack of It.

Because values exist in degrees, some are more important than others. Thrift might be a cherished value for a person, but not as significant as a relationship. While saving money is valued, spending it on travel to be with a friend or relative in crisis could have greater value.

On the other hand, it is possible to espouse a value and to act contrary to it. The thrifty person, on occasion, could spend a considerable amount of money frivolously. An infrequent indulgence is rarely presented to a therapist. This form of self-evaluation, however, applies to clients when values and behavior are so incongruent as to interfere with the person's life or the lives of others.

Questions

- How are you helped or hurt when you do violate a principle that you say is important to you?
- How does shouting, arguing, and preaching at your child, spouse, or employee fit with your belief that patience, acceptance, and listening are important to you?
- If someone were to watch you carefully for a day, what would they say is important to you? What would they say your core values are?
- How do your actions match or fail to match your words?

The counseling with Hal about this form of self-evaluation could be as follows:

CN: *Hal, you said that you thought having a peaceful house was good for you. Is that still right?*

H: *Yeah. I'd like to be left alone. If they would leave me alone, things would be better at home.*

CN: *So you want things to be better. You really value the family living like a team where the players work together, at least to some extent?*

H: *Yes, that describes it.*

CN: *If you really value the team idea, how does that fit with what you're doing when you are home?*

H: *If they would just leave me alone . . .*

CN: *[Interrupts] I know, but I'm asking you about team work, which you said is important, and how that fits with your actions.*

H: *I don't understand.*

CN: *Does telling off your father and refusing to do your chores fit with your idea of teamwork? I said your idea of teamwork, not their idea or what they do.*

H: *I'd have to think about that.*

CN: *Well, as you sit here now, what is your first thought?*

H: *If they would just . . .*

CN: *[Interrupts] Hal, what do you think?*

H: *Well, I guess my actions and what I believe are different from each other.*

CN: *Do you want to bring them closer together?*

H: *It would make sense.*

In this session, the therapist used a very subtle kind of self-evaluation. As with many clients, Hal had a hard time connecting the two ideas. This advanced form of self-evaluation, used less frequently than others, involves teaching clients the nature of values and behavior as well as differences between the two concepts. It also fits with the recent development of teaching choice theory and reality therapy to clients (Glasser, 1998b).

Often, in exploring the overall direction and specific wants, the user of reality therapy helps clients uncover the incongruity between what they want and their present direction. When such an incongruity is identified, it is useful to help clients determine if they wish to work on bringing their behavior into line with their value. They are asked to evaluate whether their stated value is really as important as they at first thought. They can then be helped to deepen the value so that there is a more appropriate relationship between their stated value and their behavior. This is an extension of the evaluation of self-perception.

Also, in dealing with the perceptions of the client, it is useful to explore all three levels of perception. Through the low-level filter the client recognizes the external world and labels the input. By means of the middle-level filter the client understands the interrelationships of experience. And in the high-level filter the client puts a value on the experience. Exploring whether specific behaviors are reflective of the values claimed by the client helps him or her understand the high-level filter or value system. At first glance, the interconnections in this form of evaluation are rather subtle. As a change of pace an exercise chart is provided in Figure 4 to help you practice using this aspect of evaluation and clarify the interconnection between values and behavior.

Questions that relate to this subtle form of self-evaluation are derived from the following generic questions:

- Is your behavior congruent with what you say is important to you?
- Which of the following outweighs the other, the satisfaction of getting what you want or the dissatisfaction of not getting what you want? Which of these moves you to action?

This form of evaluation is especially useful with a person who wants to take action on a decision or a problem (i.e., a scale out of balance) but whose search for an effective choice in the suitcase of behavior is futile. The following case illustrates this type of evaluation.

Freddie has been married for 23 years; he and his wife have no children. The couple has drifted apart and Freddie finds the sparse communication inconsequential. Freddie describes the marriage as one of "convenience." Freddie clearly wants neither the pain nor the loneliness of a divorce, nor the coolness of the present unsatisfying relationship. (F = Freddie; CN = Counselor.)

CN: *Freddie, we've talked now several times about the fact that you seem to be stuck between the undesirable choice of divorce and the unattractive fact of a cool marriage relationship.*

F: *That is a good summary. I don't want to be alone. The marriage is not so bad that I'm ready for the lawyer, but I'm not very happy either.*

CN: *You also said that you wanted to make it better.*

F: *Yes, I have said I want to do that. But I can't seem to do a lot to bring that about. I'm just not trying to improve the situation.*

CN: *I'd like to ask you about how afraid you are of a divorce?*

Describe congruent and incongruent behaviors for numbers 4 through 10.

Value, i.e., something perceived and described as important	Specific behavior that is incongruent with the value.	Specific behavior that is congruent with the value.
1. Patience with children	1. Shouting at a child	1. Asking child, "Did it help you to do that?"
2. Communicating frankly with spouse	2. "Clamming up," the silent treatment	2. Saying what you want, etc.
3. Involving others in decision making	3. When under pressure, acting like a dictator	3. Asking others for input.
4. Being prompt		
5. Saving money even to the point of giving up something		
6. Being an active member of a civic or church group		
7. Using short periods of time efficiently		
8. Respecting others without putting them down		
9. Being honest with the customer		
10. Helping others		

FIGURE 4. Congruence between values and behavior.

F: *I am very much afraid of divorce. The insecurity of living alone is fearsome, not to mention the financial burden.*

CN: *And so you have a sense of safety and security in the marriage?*

F: *Yes, I do.*

CN: *So in many ways this marriage is satisfying you.*

F: *Oh, it's not all bad. My spouse is a good person; we're just not as close as we could be.*

CN: *Do you believe that it is possible to make it more satisfying?*

F: *Yes, I still think so. But if I come on too strong, my spouse will become uncomfortable and might want a divorce.*

CN: *So do you want to take action to improve the situation?*

F: *I do. Because we might be heading in the divorce direction, which might be the case now anyway.*

CN: *Which of these ideas is more likely to get you to make more plans: the* possible *pain of a possible* divorce *or the* possible *pleasure of a* possibly *improved marriage?*

F: *Well, I think I'm more afraid of the divorce than hopeful that things will improve.*

CN: *So being on your own, having to start over by yourself, spending long hours without someone to talk to, having to budget, shop, and take care of every detail without anyone to rely on is a strong motivator—stronger than the remote possibility that you and your spouse can be close.*

F: *Right. I think you singled out the one push I have inside of me that might lead me to take some action.*

CN: *So, I think it would be wise to refer to what a divorce is like whenever you hesitate to follow through on your plans.*

F: *In other words, concentrate on the big "D" every time I feel like not reaching out to my spouse?*

CN: *Would it help you to take action to think about it, at least once in a while?*

F: *I suppose it would.*

CN: *Then I'd say, use it as a motivator. Maybe later we'll come up with another one, who knows? Meanwhile the word you use, "concentrate," is significant. It means more than just mulling over the D word. It means letting the meaning and consequences of a divorce really sink in.*

F: *Yes, I need to let it sink in, but I hope to develop more positive motivation.*

This dialogue illustrates helping a client (male or female) identify an efficient, practical motive to immediate action. The counselor hopes that the motivation will change and feels confident that after some movement on the part of the client, a more efficacious motive can replace the negative one. Perhaps Freddie will later be motivated not to avoid the undesirable, but to achieve a more attractive, positive, and direct sense of satisfaction by enhancing the marriage relationship.

We revisit Hal in the next case, which again illustrates self-evaluation regarding the congruence of values and behavior.

CN: *You said you'd like to make the $15 per day more than you will make if you drop out of school. Is money important to you?*

H: *Sure, it is.*

CN: *How about a car, nice clothes? Are these important to you?*

H: *Of course. I'd like to have a job where I can make a lot of money.*

CN: *And yet you want to do something that will not get it for you! A very curious situation!*

H: *Yeah!*

CN: *How about getting along with your father? Is that important to you?*

H: *Yeah, he is my father and he does a lot for me.*

CN: *So harmony at home is important to you? How about a clean house, where the chores get done?*

H: *Sure, we all have to live there.*

CN: *What have you been doing that reflects your opinion that the place should be liveable?*

H: *I guess I don't do much any more.*

CN: *Would you like to make life more satisfying and enjoyable for yourself, and make the situation at home better for yourself?*

H: *Sounds like a good idea.*

This evaluation, subtly different from the other forms, connects Hal's behavioral system with his high perceptual level on topics such as money, school, and home. Connecting money, school, and home with other more basic values such as harmony and happiness often precedes action planning. Hal values being happy, feeling good, and having a sense of satisfaction at home and school. Linking specific behaviors to these values leads to the insight of their incongruity.

Level of Commitment: High Enough to Get Desired Results.

Identifying the seriousness and intensity of clients', students', and employees' willingness to make changes, that is, how hard they want to work at the task of improving their lives and fulfilling their needs in more satisfying ways, pertains to their level of commitment. Where they see themselves on the scale of the five levels of commitment reflects the current depth of their motivation to change. Reality therapists question them about the effectiveness of their current level of commitment, that is, whether it is the highest they are capable of. The five levels of commitment from the least to the highest are:

1. "I don't want to be here. You can't help me."
2. "I want the outcome. But I don't want to exert any effort."
3. "I'll try. I might. I could."
4. "I'll do my best."
5. "I will do whatever it takes."

There is no need to be overly precise and exacting when helping clients identify their level of commitment. But it is quite helpful to ask them to evaluate if their current level of commitment is their highest realistic choice. They also evaluate and formulate specific action behaviors which, if chosen, would demonstrate an even higher commitment.

Below are questions pertaining to this form of evaluation.

- Is your present level of commitment the highest you are willing to make?
- If you work as hard as you are now working, will you be able to get what you want as quickly or as fully as you want to get it?
- Is your present level of commitment the highest quality you can aim at?
- Is "I'll try" enough to accomplish your goals?
- If you qualify your commitment with "probably," "I could," "maybe," or "I might," will you be where you want to be within the time frame you have selected?

To illustrate the evaluation of the level of commitment, we rejoin JL, Hal's father, who is now ready to make a plan. But before the therapist allows this to occur, he or she attempts to help JL define and evaluate his level of commitment.

CN: *You asked me what you could do to change the way you look at your son. I'd like to ask you how hard you'd like to work at this situation.*

JL: *I've been working very hard at it.*

CN: *I mean, how committed are you now to try some different strategies?*

JL: *I want to do it. For sure.*

CN: *Is that a "maybe" or an "I'll work hard"?*

JL: *I'll try my best.*

CN: *Is "trying" the most firm commitment you can make?*

JL: *What do you mean?*

CN: *Let's put it this way. If you're on a plane and the pilot says, "I'll now try to land the plane," you are going to be nervous because you would like a higher commitment.*

JL: *I sure would and I see what you mean. I need to be more committed to doing my part.*

CN: *So an "I'll try" is not as much as you can do?*

JL: *I can do better than that. I'm firmly committed.*

CN: *Sounds good.*

The dialogue illustrates the evaluation of levels of commitment to change. The levels are developmental, and so "I'll try" could be a major step up for Hal, who came to counseling under some coercion. He lacked motivation to change and it is unrealistic to expect that he is capable of the highest level of commitment. JL, however, came highly motivated and is capable, with the help of a counselor, of raising his level.

Evaluation of the Plan of Action: SAMI²C³. A hoped-for outcome of using reality therapy is the formulation and follow-through of action plans. One of the many determinations made by the client is the answer to such questions as:

- If you follow through on your plans, how will your life be better?
- How will you be living a more need-satisfying life?
- What specifically will you have, in terms of inner need-satisfaction, that you don't have now?
- Does the plan fulfill the characteristics of an effective plan? Is the plan a SAMI²C³ plan?
  S = Simple: clear and uncomplicated.
  A = Attainable: realistically doable, possible to carry out.
  M = Measurable: answers such questions as, "When?" "How many times?" "Where?" "With whom?" "How, specifically?"
  I = Involved: performed sometimes with the assistance of the counselor but only if necessary.
  I = Immediate: followed through soon, not put off.
  C = Controlled by the planner: not a plan dependent on what others do.
  C = Consistent: done repetitively.
  C = Committed to: firm.

Now listen to a counseling session with Hal. He wants life to be more pleasant and rewarding and has decided that some of his behaviors are not working.

CN: *Hal, you were saying that you wanted life to be better for yourself and you wanted your situation to be better at home and at school.*

H: *Yeah, I guess things could be better.*

CN: *How about making an effort to make things better?*

H: *I could try.*

CN: *What do you have to lose from trying?*

H: *Well, nothing really.*

CN: *What could you do differently at home?*

H: *I could do some of my chores. It really bugs my father when I don't help out.*

CN: *What will you do that is different from what you did in the past?*

H: *I could pick up after myself before he comes home from work.*

CN: *What if you did that for a few days?*

H: *I could do it.*

CN: *Will you do it?*

H: *Yes.*

CN: *When will you start?*

H: *Today.*

CN: *What time? Be exact in setting a time.*

H: *Ok. I'll pick up today at 4:00 p.m.*

CN: *How long will it take?*

H: *About 20 minutes.*

CN: *So your plan is to clean up the house, pick up your clothes and other things for 20 minutes starting at 4:00 p.m. today. How many days will you do this?*

H: *I'll do it every day for 5 days.*

CN: *Sounds good. One more question. What impact will this have on your relationship with your father?*

H: *It can only help.*

In this final dialogue, Hal formulated a plan of action with the help of the counselor. The plan is then evaluated on whether it contains at least some of the characteristics described by the acronym $SAMI^2C^3$.

I have attempted to summarize and briefly illustrate 21 types of self-evaluation that clients, students, and others find beneficial. These judgments precede changes in behaviors or more need-satisfying choices. The inner evaluation by the client is the core of reality therapy. W. Glasser (1992) described two types of people: those who are not doing very well because their energy is spent on evaluating others' behavior, and those who are doing well because they are skilled at evaluating their own behavior. I have broadened this self-evaluation to include judgments made on all components of the human choice system as well as the interrelationships between the various components.

Essential as the self-evaluation by the client is, the user of reality therapy need not be overwhelmed by the description of 21 kinds of evaluation. Not every interaction with clients or students realistically contains all 21 kinds of self-evaluation. The practitioner selects whatever is relevant to the situation. With the help of a counselor's skillful questioning, the client evaluates the functioning of each part of his or her choice or control system.

Additionally, in many cases, counselors, therapists, educators, or supervisors *ap-*

pear to make the judgment for the client in that they describe their own perception of what, for example, works, helps, or is realistic. This is necessary at times because many clients do not have easily accessible experiences required to make independent evaluations. Chemically dependent families, ADD families, or people raised in environments where there are inconsistencies often have major difficulties in their self-evaluations. A child praised on Monday for a behavior and criticized on Tuesday for the same behavior puts contradictory judgments into his or her mind about the effectiveness of such a choice. Also, some cannot distinguish between neutral or threatening events around them. Frazer (1996) suggested that family preservation programs would do well to look at the cognitive processes used by aggressive children in social situations. He stated that aggressive children have not learned to solve problems without the use of force. They often misinterpret neutral social interactions as threatening. Such families and individuals require the explicit teaching of choice theory and the WDEP system. Eventually, clients "buy into" and accept this evaluation as their own when they see the ineffectiveness of their past evaluations and when they perceive the helper as a need-fulfilling person. Thus the relationship—the warm, firm, but friendly and safe atmosphere—is the basis for the use of the WDEP system.

Self-Evaluation in the Classroom. The many applications of self-evaluation are central to effective counseling. Its use, however, extends to education at all levels including the classroom. Students evaluate not only their behavior (actions regarding conduct), they also evaluate their effort and their work. Sandy Dunaway, teacher at Columbus Alternative High School, reports that 90% of the student self-evaluations agree with her assessments. The rest evaluate their work and effort at a level lower than the teacher's judgment. Only on rare occasions does a student self-evaluate at a higher level than the teacher's evaluation.

This example could easily be misinterpreted. Continual self-evaluation by students can be successful only if it is built on the foundation of a student-centered and need-satisfying classroom atmosphere. Attempts to initiate and maintain a program of student self-evaluation in any way other than by lead management (Glasser, 1990c, 1993, 1994) results in creative avoidance, shoddy work, and overinflated student self-evaluation.

The goal of reality therapy is behavioral change, personal growth, improvement, enhanced lifestyle, better decision making, remediation of personal deficits, and, in the language of choice theory, the more effective satisfaction of the psychological human needs: belonging, power, freedom, and fun. It is categorically impossible for human beings to make changes until they first decide that a change would be more advantageous. Users of reality therapy are, therefore, relentless in their efforts to help clients and students conduct explicit self-evaluations of each component of their control systems.

Professional Self-Evaluation. Mickel (1996b) suggests that professionals utilize a self-evaluation model for determining the effectiveness of their work, beginning with a baseline for behavior. The dependent variable is thus measured and then remeasured when the independent variable is manipulated. The effectiveness of treatment is determined in a scientific way rather than in a speculative and hit or miss manner. This is especially useful in the age of managed care, when counselors and therapists are asked to justify their skills. Thus accountability as determined by client progress can be measured and demonstrated.

Part of effective evaluation is the inner self-evaluation of the therapist. Wubbolding (2000b) has described how practitioners of reality therapy, and perhaps other therapists, can ask questions about their own performance:

- How am I facilitating my own professional growth?
- Do I have a plan for continuing education?
- Do I work within the boundaries of my limitations? How do I know this?
- How committed am I to my profession and to this particular client?
- How am I using a supervisory or consultative relationship for professional growth?
- Am I aware of the special ethical applications of reality therapy?
- Do I understand the multicultural applications of the theory?
- Do I understand how to adapt the practice of reality therapy in a cross-cultural setting?
- Does my therapeutic practice measure favorably against the ethical principles established by my profession?
- Is the quality of my service to the public the highest it can be? What is my system for evaluating my service? How can I improve my service and my self-evaluation system?

Ksenija Napan (1996) applied choice theory and reality therapy to social work instruction at the university level in Zagreb, Croatia. The model for instruction, called "The Contact-Challenge Method," consists of theory, lab work, contact with clients, and supervision. Students examine how their own needs are met and whether there have been changes in their own quality worlds during the experiences. While the components of the organizational structure do not appear to be new, the infusion of choice theory as a system of student self-assessment is rare in social work education. The author has stated that the method is "radical, extraordinary, provocative, striving for quality, constantly changing and correcting itself, and valuing feedback from all participants" (p. 41).

The therapist's continual self-inspection is a cornerstone of the effective use of reality therapy. If therapists are to be skilled in helping others confront their own wants, actions, thoughts, feelings, and motivational level, it follows that they must be willing to engage in the same process.

Self-Evaluation: Implicit and Explicit

In a sense, we are always evaluating the various aspects of our control or choice systems. When we take a chance on a lottery we evaluate that we can win even though the odds might be millions to one. When adolescents want total freedom from parental restraint, they believe that such independence is possible. When a new driver attempts to park a 16-foot car in a 15-foot space, he or she believes that it can be done. Often a parent lectures, preaches, and shouts at the adolescent, then adds to the harangue a tirade followed by consequences, punishments, and other repercussions. After trying this approach for weeks, months, and even years, the parent increases more of the same behavior. Even though the parents have evaluated that these behaviors are not helping, the appropriate course of action appears to be to repeat them and to escalate their intensity.

On the other hand, many people have dozens of wants that are fulfilled every day: in relationships, successes at work, winning a game, or improving a skill. When we fulfill our wants we come to an implicit judgment that the behaviors that satisfied our wants were helpful and effective. We then repeat these behaviors.

Whether the wants are realistically attainable or not, and whether the action behaviors do or do not bring about the desired result, we tend to repeat them, evaluating that they are all realistic or effective. And so we are continuously evaluating our wants and behaviors in a silent, implicit manner. The value of the E—the self-evaluation component of reality therapy—is that we make explicit the inner self-evaluation component. We help clients, students, in fact, anyone, stand back from their wants and behaviors and look at them from a different perspective. We help them hold their wants and behaviors in their hands and examine them not only from the front but from the top, bottom, and both sides.

In short we ask parents who want their 15-year-old child to have a 35-year-old head, "How realistic is it to have your adolescent do all that you want him or her to do?" "If yelling, grounding and other punishments have not worked up to now, will they work tomorrow?" The adolescent is asked, "How realistic is it for your parents to allow you to come and go as you please while they are paying for your room, board, entertainment, school, clothes, etc.?"

Similarly, we can ask about realistically attainable wants and effective behavior. "When you planned the project, developed a time line, secured the necessary resources, and followed through, was your effort successful?" The specific variations of self-evaluation are described below. But before proceeding, I suggest you pause to give some thought to your own self-evaluation by discussing the following questions:

- In my life, overall, am I going in a direction that is best for me?
- What do I want to accomplish in the next few years intellectually, emotionally, professionally, financially, spiritually, physically, and regarding family relationships?
- Under what circumstances do I display the "dirty laundry" (negative behaviors) in my behavioral suitcase?
- How am I trying to insert "clean laundry" (positive behaviors) in my suitcase?
- Have I developed an SIP (self-improvement plan)?
- What relationships do I wish to intensify?

The first step in using this component of reality therapy with clients or students is to use it with oneself. An ongoing debate in the helping professions centers on the willingness of helpers to do what they expect others to do. Teachers need continuing education, physicians need personal health enhancement programs, and therapists are advised, but not required, to undergo counseling (Corey, 2000a). I do not take the position of requiring therapists to receive therapy, but I do stand firmly on the belief that it is *almost* necessary. The *very least* an effective user of any psychological theory and method, including reality therapy, can do is to be willing to apply the ideas in his or her own life.

Question: Is Self-Evaluation Sufficient?

Seeing self-evaluation as the only component in the delivery system or exaggerating its role reduces the panoramic picture of reality therapy to a miniature. Self-evaluation is the cornerstone requiring a foundation and the keystone requiring pillars for support. Few patients wish a surgeon to operate on them unless there is some "external" corroboration that the doctor is qualified. Similarly, as Glasser has pointed out in his lectures, it is congruent with the principles of reality therapy for someone to tell the blind person that he or she cannot become an airline pilot. Likewise, in buying a house, the consumer rarely fails to inspect the quality and "check it out" before closing the deal, even if the builders have evaluated their own work and presented it to the buyer as the best possible product. In other words, self-evaluation can involve more than even a very enlightened judgment of one person. Self-reports have more credibility when verified.

Levels of Self-Evaluation

Self-evaluation does not occur in a vacuum. Many people deny information that would help them evaluate in a more self-actualizing manner. A substance abuser minimizes destructive behavior. Some students project blame on others to cover their own lack of commitment.

The best kind of self-evaluation occurs when a person incorporates information from the external world, serving as a basis for assessing the effectiveness of behavior or the attainability of wants. Thus there are levels of effective self-evaluation.

The levels demonstrate that self-evaluation is developmental rather than static. These levels are derived from experience as well as from the work of W. Edwards Deming (1986, 1993), a major figure in the quality movement.

Level I: Self-Evaluation With Little or No Information.
It would make little sense to award a driver's license to a person whose sole "test" of quality driving skill was his or her own self-evaluation. Anyone teaching driver's education in high school has encountered 16-year-old students who boast that they are skillful drivers and can handle any car, only to discover that some of them can't put the gearshift into reverse. Similarly, many instructors of choice theory and reality therapy meet participants in training sessions who assert that "I've used reality therapy for many years. I get people in touch with the real world so as to adjust their attitudes."

Finally, even a neophyte marriage counselor has met the spouse who provides very convincing evidence that he is thrifty, uses foresight, is patient, is helpful, and spends quality time with the family. Such a person's self-evaluation is precise and sincere. He is a very good spouse, but the other person is overly demanding.

These self-evaluations might be incomplete or one-sided and in need of further exploration. Without knowledge, information, input from others, and standards, such self-evaluators learn nothing from experience. They continue to make the same mistakes, and after 30 years do not have 30 years of experience but 1 year repeated 30 times. The American system of governmental checks and balances, admired by many countries, is based on the principle that self-evaluation is insufficient when it stands alone.

Level II: Self-Evaluation With Knowledge and Information.
A more sophisticated level of self-evaluation results when a person increases his or her information and knowledge about the behavior to be evaluated; the more information, the higher the likelihood of a better self-evaluation. When driver education students see a

movie, hear a lecture, or watch an expert driver behind the wheel, they are in a better position to self-evaluate. The person hearing a lecture, watching a training tape, or reading a book about reality therapy more readily sees the importance of dealing with perceptions, asking questions, and recognizing the gap between what he or she is doing and what happens when using reality therapy effectively.

Similarly, a husband as well as the marriage counselor can come to quite different conclusions when, for the first time, the wife describes in detail how she sees the husband's behavior: miserly not thrifty, passive and uninterested, impatient and unhelpful—and the so-called "quality time" means telling the family what they will watch on TV.

This second level of self-evaluation represents a higher level of insight into the quality of a person's behavior. The added informational input helps the driver, the participant, and the spouse alter their perceptions of their previous actions, and weigh the benefits of change. However, if knowledge were enough to insure change in actions, then training seminars, treatment programs, or support groups would be superfluous. Information is more than abundant in libraries, through the media, and on the internet. To ensure the effective use of self-evaluation, it is necessary to proceed to the next level.

Level III: Self-Evaluation Based on Feedback and a Standard.   The highest level of self-evaluation, based on feedback and a standard, helps the self-evaluator achieve the highest level of quality. The student in the driver education class practices driving, gets "corrective feedback" from an instructor, then moves to a higher level of skill achievement. The instructor concomitantly evaluates the performance level of the driver and verifies that the student has achieved a level of driving skill acceptable to society or is at least prepared for the driver's test conducted by persons empowered to make such a codetermination.

In like manner, the workshop participant chooses to practice the skills of reality therapy and gets "corrective feedback" from an instructor, supervisor, or peer. He or she then moves to a higher level of performance. Of course, this process is not linear: practice, receive feedback, make correction. Rather, in most cases it is cyclical: practice, feedback, practice, feedback, practice, feedback, etc., while achieving appropriate levels of performance and integrating behavioral corrections along the way.

Setting the Standard

The above model allows for and recognizes the validity of external standards as benchmarks of quality. And though concomitant self-evaluation and instructor evaluation converge, the norm for excellence is often set by an external agent.

Training and certification in reality therapy serve as an example. The William Glasser Institute has defined standards and criteria against which performance and knowledge are measured. Do participants have a grasp of choice theory? Do they see the connection between each component of the theory? Do they practice the environmental and procedural components in an identifiable manner? Do they genuinely grasp and make operational the overriding principle of building relationships? As in many quality organizations, much work remains and will always remain to be done in setting standards in such areas as the degree of specificity regarding skill level, performance, and knowledge.

In the teaching and helping professions, educators and therapists help students and clients identify the expectations and standards set by society, family, school, and employer. The individual's subjective self-evaluation is essential, but it does not exist in isolation from external standards established by agents in the outside world.

The three levels of self-evaluation demonstrate a developmental process based on levels of knowledge having many applications. Enlightened self-evaluation transcends a whimsical, uninformed, and naive feeling of quality. It includes informational input and feedback from peers or mentors in the context of standards of performance.

The component most easily identified with reality therapy is planning. The one most characteristic and central to the successful use of reality therapy, however, is self-evaluation. Clients, students, employees and professional people function more efficiently when they conduct ongoing, fearless, and searching self-assessments of their lives and then decide how to add genuine quality to them.

☐ P

Ask Clients to Make Plans to More Effectively Fulfill Their Wants and Needs Without Infringing on the Rights of Others to Do the Same

When clients make plans and follow through, they are taking charge of their lives by redirecting their energy and making action choices. Using reality therapy facilitates plan formulation and teaches clients several characteristics of successful planning, that is, SAMI^{2}C^3.

- Simple or understandable, not complicated.
- Attainable or realistically doable, not grandiose or overly difficult.
- Measurable or exact, not vague. Answers the all-important question, "When?"
- Immediate or soon, not delayed longer than necessary.
- Involved or assisted by the helper. The helper expedites plan making but only to the degree judged necessary.
- Controlled by the client, student, or employee, not an "if" plan or one depending on, for example, "if someone else changes."
- Committed to or firm, not characterized by "I might" or "maybe."
- Consistent or repetitive; the ideal plan is one that is repeated and becomes habitual.

The most effective plans originate within clients, students, or employees (Figure 5). Answering the question, "What is your plan for change?" with a detailed strategy proclaims that they are clearly taking better charge of their life directions. Often, especially in the initial stages of counseling, many clients do not or cannot formulate such plans. Consequently, a second level of planning, plans made jointly by therapist and client, is needed.

A third level of planning, suggestions initiated by the therapist, is quite acceptable in reality therapy, but the effectiveness of these suggestions depends on the client's perception of the therapist as someone who is helpful. Though not sufficient for change, a friendly, empathic atmosphere is a prerequisite for successful therapist-initiated plans. Such an atmosphere communicates to the client that he or she has some inner control

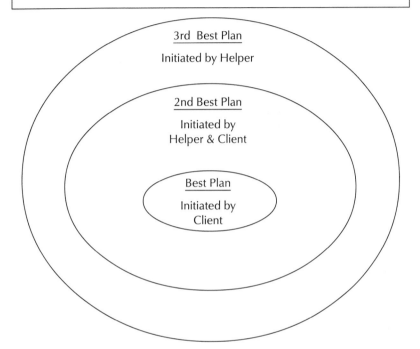

FIGURE 5. Effective plans.

and is capable of more effective actions. While less desirable than the previous two levels, counselors' suggestions can be very useful and effective. Moreover, the effectiveness of counselor-initiated plans hinges on an unflagging adherence to the prior use of client self-evaluation. If clients have made the assessment that they want change, that their behavior is not helping them enough, they are then often willing to listen to suggestions. The mistake made by neophyte and even, at times, experienced practitioners of reality therapy, is to impose a plan too quickly on an unwilling or resistant person or to indulge in paternalistic (or maternalistic) advice giving.

The procedures used in the effective practice of reality therapy have wide application to virtually every type of person. Their use is only limited by the creativity of the practitioner. Because behavior is seen more as a series of ineffective choices rather than static pathological conditions, therapists spend a maximum amount of time exploring better choices for fulfilling needs and a minimal amount of time reexamining past problems. Even psychotic persons have some effective behaviors in their suitcases; these should receive much attention and interest from the therapist. Every attempt is made to build on and expand successes, while helping clients self-evaluate both less effective and more helpful behaviors.

The same reasoning is predicated on other ineffective behaviors. Drug abuse, depression, low self-esteem, acting out behaviors, and the entire catalogue of out-of-control behaviors are discussed to some degree. But the most helpful and efficient use of the procedures involves a relentless search for a positive lifestyle characterized by a wide range of habitual choices. Standards for acceptable choices include not only the inner satisfaction of clients but the perceptions of their families and employers and the expectations of society at large.

Case Example.   Below is a summarized dialogue of part of a typical first session of therapy. Prior to this, ethical issues have been discussed: therapist's credentials, informed consent, confidentiality and its limitations, rights and responsibilities of both client and therapist, and other professional details common to any therapy. Omitted from this excerpt are the getting acquainted and rapport building stages. In this abridgement, only the components of reality therapy are presented.

Louis, 39, unemployed for 8 months, has looked unsuccessfully for a job at the middle managerial level. His wife is employed and they have two children, a boy, 12, and a girl, 10. On the telephone, Louis described his ongoing feelings of anger toward his previous employer. He adds that at times he is depressed about not finding work. Family problems include long-standing tension between him and his wife, Sally. (L = Louis; T = therapist.)

T: *Louis, we've talked about the professional details and you said you understand them. You also gave me a summary of your situation on the phone. What do you want to accomplish as a result of this therapy?*

L: *I think if I found a job everything would be fine.*

T: *You indicated on the phone that the "no job" situation is a major factor. What else is bothering you?*

L: *I'm still angry at the company for letting me go. It absolutely wasn't justified.*

T: *What else is going on with you?*

L: *I've searched for a job, and gone to the out-placement firm. But not finding a job is getting me down. This just adds to the other problems.*

T: *You hinted at other problems on the phone. Do you want to describe them?*

L: *My wife and I haven't gotten along for a long time, probably 3 or 4 years. And it's had an effect on the children. They seem to be nervous, have low grades, and bicker more than most kids.*

T: *So you have a number of goals: job, feeling better, and happier family life?*

L: *You describe them a little differently than I did.*

T: *Oh, how?*

L: *I'm not sure.*

T: *Like framing them as goals to reach rather than merely as problems to overcome?*

L: *Yes, that's it.*

T: *As you hear them described in this new way, what thoughts go through your mind?*

L: *I've never thought of these problems as goals. I've thought of them as standing in the way of reaching my goals.*

T: *From working with people, I've found that if they can think of their problems in a differ-*

ent way, they become more manageable.

L: *It's hard to think that way.*

T: *Yes it is, and it won't happen merely because we agree that it is a good idea. But let me ask you this, Has thinking about your situation the way you've thought about it been helping you or holding you back?*

L: *It's definitely held me back. I've been shackled by these problems.*

T: *I like how you said that, "shackled." Let me try to understand that more. "Shackled." What does that mean?*

L: *I've been imprisoned by this mess.*

T: *Wait, that's a new idea. "Shackled" and in "prison." Even if you broke the bonds you would still have a wall to climb. Is that accurate?*

L: *Right! I'm feeling trapped, cornered.*

T: *So, if you chose to see your situation differently, would it help or hurt?*

L: *It couldn't hurt.*

T: *And it might help?*

L: *Yes. But that's not the main problem. The problem is no job, wife, and kids.*

T: *Yet, for an instant, when you thought about your problem differently, how did you feel? Better or worse?*

L: *I guess just a tiny bit better, maybe slightly encouraged.*

T: *The shackles felt a little looser for a minute?*

L: *Yeah, could be.*

T: *That's interesting. Would you like to take that microsecond of change and extend it to minutes, hours, days, weeks, and even a lifetime?*

L: *That's why I'm here.*

T: *And that's why I'm here. To help you make it happen.*

L: *Do you think it can happen?*

T: *I believe it can. And I'm saying that, not as a wishful thought, but as evidenced by the microsecond we spoke of. There is already some solid data. What do you think this data tells you about the "shackles" and "prison?"*

L: *That I can get rid of the mess I'm in.*

T: *Exactly. I agree. Now I want to ask you about something else. How hard is it to simply say, "I'll change how I think about my situation?"*

L: *Well, I don't think it is very easy.*

T: *I agree. It will be necessary to change more abstract or even concrete thoughts. You can sit around and think about a job all day, and I doubt if a job will find you. Thinking about it is good and helpful, but not enough. You need more specific choices.*

L: *I'm an action sort of person, so I'm not averse to doing something.*

T: *So, tell me what you chose to do yesterday about these issues, or as you used to call them, your "problems," "shackles," "prison cell," "swamp," "quagmire," and "solitary confinement?" In other words, what did you do, which if you kept doing it, would get you outside the walls?*

L: *Did I say all that? The situation is not really that bad.*

T: *Oh, so there's more hope than it seemed at first?*

L: *Do you think there is hope? Can I live outside the walls?*

T: *No doubt about it in my mind. I suppose I was exaggerating when I used all those labels. But I do believe you could live outside and far away from the walls, in the sunshine of freedom.*

L: *[Smiling wryly.] I got your point.*

T: *It's good you can smile, even for a moment. So we've had two bits of data showing that you can feel better!*

L: *You do look for even the slightest success!*

T: *Yes, any successful choice is a step in the right direction. What's the saying? "A journey of a thousand miles is begun with one step."*

L: *I've taken two steps.*

T: *Actually, you've taken more. You also came here. That is a major step. You took action.*

L: *Yeah!*

T: *Now, let's talk about what happened yesterday. Describe your actions , starting in the morning.*

L: *I got up about 10:00 a.m., looked through the paper, ate breakfast, watched TV, and loafed most of the day.*

T: *Could you be more specific by describing in detail exactly what you chose to do? What precisely did you do?*

L: [Client elaborates on how he spent his time from 10:00 a.m. until bedtime at 10:00 p.m. He was passive, accomplishing none of his goals.]

T: *Now, I'm going to ask you what might, at first, seem to be a simple and obvious series of questions. Are you ready?*

L: *Yes.*

T: *Did the way you spent your day yesterday help you or hurt you? Did it help you achieve your goals or get you closer to your family?*

L: *It hurt. But in the afternoon I did do some things around the house that had to be done.*

T: *And so what impact did the entire day have on your overall direction?*

L: *My wife was glad I did a few things.*

T: *So, doing things for her helps? And you didn't loaf all day. You were quite active for a good part of the day?*

L: *Yes. I didn't think of it that way till now.*

T: *So, that part was slightly helpful regarding the relationship with Sally?*

L: *Yes.*

T: *Did the rest of the day take you where you wanted to go?*

L: *No, it was a waste.*

T: *And if you continue to go in this direction, where will you be in 6 months or a year?*

L: *Nowhere.*

T: *Will you feel better or worse?*

L: *Worse.*

T: *What effect will it have on your marriage and on how you feel?*

L: *Everything will be worse.*

T: *But if you do more of the positive things for your wife, or other actions relative to getting a job, what will happen?*

L. *Things might turn around for me.*

T. *We'll get very specific about that later. But what do you want to come away with from this session, today?*

L: *A way to get out of this swamp.*

T. *I believe you can. But one more question. How hard do you want to work at turning your life around and getting on the right track?*

L: *I would like to do it!*

T: *Is that a "maybe" or an "I will?"*

L: *"I will."*

T: *So what will you do differently tonight? What will you choose to do that is different from what you would have done if we had not had this conversation?*

L: [Client formulates a realistically attainable plan that helps him to move in a positive direction.]

The above dialogue illustrates various components of reality therapy: asking what the client wants, the client's summary description of actions, thinking, and feelings with emphasis on actions, the client's self-evaluation and a minor plan. However, the main goal of the first session rests on a deeper level. If the procedures are used properly, the client gains a sense of hope. By using the WDEP system the client learns, as a side effect, that his life can improve and that he need not be locked in prison permanently. This underlying message is one of hope—the primary goal of the first therapy session.

But important as hope is, it will sustain a person only for a short time if substantial help is not available. The real value of the WDEP system of reality therapy is that change can happen and can be accomplished quickly. In fact, reality therapy was once criticized for its short-term nature. It can now be said that this brief therapy is based on a solid theory of brain functioning and is substantiated by research studies. Some of these are summarized in chapter 12.

Realistic Plans.   Plans often do not and need not achieve 100% need-satisfaction. Because of external restraints and limitations, reaching a level of total love and belonging, complete inner control, total freedom, or hilarious fun is not always possible. But sometimes the person can attain at least part of what is desired. For example, Nien Cheng (1986) described her 6 years in solitary confinement in China in the 1960s and her interrogations by the Maoists. After being passive and depressed for a time, she realized that if she took action against her interrogators and chose anger and shouting as behaviors, she would gain a sense of anticipated and imagined belonging and power. Even though she could not speak to the other prisoners she knew they would approve. The choice helped her overcome her depress-ing and gave her a sense of power.

The English writer G. K. Chesterton once said that trifles make perfection and perfection is *no* trifle. There is a danger of minimizing the value of small changes, of seeing them as insignificant. Yet any change begins with one step. There is no second step without the first. Have you ever turned the steering wheel of your car a quarter of an inch while driving 60 miles per hour? Of course you have. You noticed that a major change was brought about very quickly. If you raise your body temperature 5% you would feel a major change. You would be flat on your back in bed. But your employer could say, "What's the big deal? It's only a trifle! Such a tiny change should not make a difference." In fact, this "tiny change" is a major change, which we all recognize. The same is true in counseling. Even if the therapist helps clients make "insignificant" changes, these changes serve as a foundation for more plans and more successes.

Sometimes the question arises, "What if the client insists on a plan that in the mind of the helper is unrealistic and clearly doomed to failure?" Rather than push one's own agenda and try to convince clients of the futility of a particular strategy, it is often advisable to agree or even encourage the ineffective path. (Of course, this must be done within ethical boundaries. No harmful behaviors are encouraged.)

Watzlawick (1988) stated that sometimes it is necessary to proceed on the wrong path in order to know it is the wrong path. Stated another way, a mirage must be approached before it can be seen as a mirage.

The skilled reality therapist in the dialogue that follows utilizes the slogan "experience is the best teacher" with the person who is recently sober and has accepted that he is a recovering alcoholic. In the very early stage of recovery the following session takes place. (CL = client; TH = therapist.)

CL: *I really want to make a 180-degree turnaround: get up early, work a full day, go on a sugar-free and fat-free diet, lose 30 pounds in 2 months, spend time with the kids, take care of the yard, . . .* [He names several more tasks.]

TH: *How about selecting one or two to start with?*

CL: *No, I need to go all the way. Getting sober is the best thing I ever did and I know I need to keep at it. But I have a lot of work to do and I've got a lot to make up for. I can do these things "one day at a time."*

TH: *Can you realistically work on all of these at the same time, even one day at a time?*

CL: *The theme is "one day at a time." I can do it if I "turn it over." But you don't seem to think I can do all of this?*

TH: *I think these are all necessary to work on. But I want to help you examine whether you can work on so many fronts at the same time.*

CL: *I can and I will.*

TH: *In that case why not try it for a week and see how it works. We can talk about it, reevaluate it next time. Okay?*

CL: *Sure.*

TH: *We'll have the experience of a week and we can see what happens.*

CL: *Sounds good.*

Questions

- How did the therapist reframe apparently unrealistic plans?
- How did the therapist use the axiom "experience is the best teacher"?
- How would you handle the next session if the client succeeded in all the plans?
- How will you handle the next session if the client fails in all or in several of the plans?

Accepting clients as they are and helping them evaluate their plans represents both environment and the procedures of reality therapy, respectively. In the above dialogue the counselor accepted the sober grandiosity of the client who is clearly in an early stage of recovery. And so, if clients insist on attempting the impossible, even a failure can be reframed as a success, a necessary step to help them conduct a searching and more realistic self-assessment.

Sabotaging Success.   Therapists, counseling staffs, and teachers of persons with more severe problems frequently describe a phenomenon in which clients, students, or residents make lengthy and visible progress which is clearly documented. Then, just before therapy is terminated, or a scheduled release to a less restrictive placement occurs, they seriously mess up.

The following examples illustrate such situations. You are asked to speculate about them by answering these questions:

- Based on your knowledge of choice theory how could these people make such choices?
- How would you counsel these individuals to prevent such incidents?
- How would you work with them *after* the incident?

Case 1: Jamal, a Student.   Jamal has been in a special school for "behaviorally disturbed" students for 2½ years. After many false starts Jamal became a serious and trouble-free student. Just before being sent to the "regular" high school, Jamal openly and flauntingly distributes cigarettes to other students in the hallway—blatantly violating a major rule.

Case 2: Jamie, a Probationer.   For 2 years Jamie has done very well on probation. He's been drug free and employed, choosing to live within the boundaries of the probationary rules. The very night before he was to be released, he steals a car and drives it downtown in front of the police station, breaking two or three traffic laws and insuring that he would be caught. His probation officer interviews him and says that Jamie is upset because he believes that everyone is leaving *him*.

Indirect Paradoxical Planning.   *Case 3: Geneen, a Teacher, and Edgar, a Student.*   Geneen, a teacher, related the story about a student who insisted on walking around the classroom and then "needed" to go outside and smoke. In this class for emotionally disturbed high school students, accommodation is made for students with limited impulse control. While smoking on school grounds is forbidden, the students indulge their apparent nicotine addiction without punishment. The faculty believe it is wise to help students choose to relinquish smoking rather than try to coerce them into giving it up.

Edgar, 14, insists on avoiding his school work by pacing around the classroom when an assignment is given. He then exits the room for a cigarette outside the building. The teacher repeatedly uses the WDEP system, asking what Edgar wants, what he is doing, and whether it is against the rules. This mechanical use of this system only results in Edgar's anger escalating.

The teacher realizes that linear plans are ineffective at times and looks for a more creative application of the system. She makes a point to teach the student that "pacing" is different from walking. "Pacing" means "nervous energy." Walking is chosen when a person wants to go somewhere. This brief enigmatic explanation serves to arouse Edgar's curiosity.

Then, instead of attempting to stop him from pacing she approaches him *before* the assignment is given and *before* he begins to pace. She asks him to get out of his seat and pace around the room. She then gives the assignment encouraging him to pace *before* smoking.

The teacher reported that the problem did not completely vanish, but the result of this indirect intervention was more school work, less pacing, and fewer cigarettes.

Follow-Through.   In teaching reality therapy I am frequently asked what to do when students, clients, or employees fail to follow through on plans. There are several choices and considerations for the therapist, teacher, parent, supervisor, or anyone using the WDEP system of reality therapy.

The first choice involves remembering that plans are often not implemented because self-evaluation was weak. The person has not truly judged that current behavior is ineffective. The neophyte user of reality therapy often skips this important component. Many clients want a change in their lives and to be free of pain, and, in effect, they say, "I want the outcome but not the effort" (Level II commitment). Helpers often assist clients in identifying what they want and prematurely ask what they will do to get what they want. Sometimes clients, wishing to please the helper, meekly or even insincerely agree to a plan. Then when they go out the door the plan goes out of their quality worlds. Effective therapists help clients conduct searching, relentless, and unflinching self-evaluations of their current behavior, the attainability of their wants, and their level of commitment. Helpers using reality therapy revisit the E of the WDEP system by asking, "If you don't follow through, will anything change? Will you feel better? Will you get what you want?" As a result, clients interconnect their quality worlds with their behavioral systems, perceptual systems, and levels of commitment.

Another technique is asking clients to experiment with a plan. Explain that they are simply "trying" or "testing" a technique. It might not work, and so they can quickly discard it if it proves to be useless. Oftentimes, feeling that the plan is not permanent, clients paradoxically adopt it and insert it into their behavioral suitcase evaluating it as helpful. An effective question is, "If you tried this plan for a week, what would you lose?"

A third suggestion is to ask them to do something to feel better or get along better, etc., for a very limited amount of time, for example, 30 seconds or a minute. Subsequently the therapist asks whether they can do it for a longer period of time. After all, they don't need to change their behavior permanently. They can make temporary changes and then determine whether it is worth the effort to continue.

When I counsel someone who feels hopeless, depressed, alienated, or upset in any way (in choice theory terms, someone who is hopeless-ing, alienated-ing, upset-ing), I can almost always get a fleeting smile or a brief laugh from them. I watch their nonverbal behavior carefully and when I see a change, I ask them about it. The dialogue usually is something like the following. (CL = client;   TH = therapist.)

TH: *I noticed that you changed your expression for just a moment.*

CL: *What do you mean?*

TH: *Your face kind of lit up. You smiled, almost even laughed.*

CL: *Well, it was funny.*

TH: *How did you feel inside when you smiled? Did you feel a slight bit of enjoyment?*

CL: *Yeah, I felt a little better.*

TH: *So it is possible for you to feel better?*

CL: *Well, I did feel better for a few seconds.*

TH: *So if you can feel better even for a few seconds, maybe, just maybe, it is possible to lengthen those seconds into minutes.*

CL: *How can that happen?*

TH: *When you felt better even for a few seconds, you did something. You took action. You were in charge of your decision at that instant. So if you are willing to extend that kind of choice and decision making, you will more than likely feel better. It will take time, but it can happen with a sustained effort.*

CL: *Makes sense.*

TH: *So let's talk about what you will do today that is different from previous days. What will you do even for a few minutes this afternoon—something which would give you the feeling of being in charge of your own actions? Keep in mind that a change in the feelings will follow.*

In this session the therapist builds on an immediate success utilizing an important technique emphasized by W. Glasser (1998, 2000).

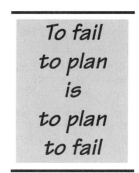

The unadorned teaching of the various concepts contained in choice theory and reality therapy in an abstract or schoolish manner diminishes its impact on clients. Timing is pivotal. The concepts are best taught when a client has experienced them. In this case, the plan is immediately successful and the client is more highly motivated to further implement it because of both the experience of success and the intellectual understanding of choice theory and reality therapy. The client learns the axiom "changing actions = changes feelings" (CA = CF). The reality therapist acknowledges the eminent role of planning. While rapport, therapeutic alliance, involvement with the clients, and empathy are the foundation of effective counseling, the superstructure of reality therapy is WDE and the culmination is P–SAMI^{2}C^3 planning. Individual and organizational change happens when people evaluate their own unique and systemic behaviors and follow up with the formulation and implementation of specific plans. This mapping out of their journey positions their behavioral cars on a promising new highway. The destination is need- and want-satisfaction, a higher quality of life, and a measurable contribution to the lives of others.

10

CHAPTER

Style, Language, Communication, and User Qualities: What Do I Need to Do and Have in Order to Use Reality Therapy?

Individual uses of reality therapy reflect the unique personality, style, and cultural characteristics of each practitioner. One therapist is directive, another more laid back. Some use mostly a questioning technique. Others are more reflective. Some communicate in a direct manner, others are more indirect. Some are puristic in using the language of internal controls. Others utilize the basic philosophy but gradually lead clients to use words like "choice." Some begin by assertively asking about the clients' relationships. Others spend more time establishing a safe, friendly atmosphere.

The principles of the theory and practice are universal. They apply to all human beings, and their use reflects the uniqueness, the skill, the experience, and the creativity of people who practice them. The delivery system, rooted in the bedrock of choice theory, lends itself to an unlimited number of personal enunciations.

☐ Deficit or Strength? Two Approaches to Reality Therapy

A more fundamental difference in the application of the WDEP system is the direct emphasis on client deficits, which need remediation, or the emphasis on strengths, which can be enhanced. The two approaches are illustrated below.

Case Example

Lana, 44, is referred to a therapist by her physician. She has discovered she has abdominal cancer, which adds to her already existing problems. Previously, her husband of 21 years told her he wanted to separate from her. She was also permanently laid off from her job in retailing when the company downsized by closing several stores. Because she had devoted herself to her career and to her children, she has little social life and virtually no friends. She reports that she spends hours crying and remains in bed for much of the day. Her husband has been staying with her out of pity but is hoping to follow through on the separation. (L = Lana; TH = therapist.)

TH: *Lana, you told me on the phone that you had many things you'd like to talk about. Where do you want to start?*

[Lana tells the entire story, describing the above problems and how she is extremely upset about how her life is going. The therapist listens at length with empathy and understanding, reflecting on her plight and attempting to become part of her quality world.]

TH: *Lana, I have a very important question. Of all the things you told me which of these would you like to work on?*

L: *I would like to be healed . . . healed in every way. I feel so powerless. I'm so upset I don't know what to do. I'm so down I can hardly move.*

TH: *It is clear to me that you do feel powerless and down. I'd like to ask you about how you spend your time. Tell me what you did yesterday.*

L: *I got up about 10:30 and ate breakfast.*

TH: *What did you have for breakfast?*

L: *Donuts and coffee.*

TH: *How many donuts?*

L: *Three.*

TH: *What did you do then?*

L: *I turned on the TV and stared at it.*

TH: *Do you remember what you watched?*

L: *No.*

TH: *Do you remember anything else, like what you did in the morning?*

L: *I just cried.*

TH: *Kinda felt sorry for yourself?*

L: *Yeah, I guess so.*

TH: *You sound tentative about that. You're not sure how you felt?*

L: *Well, I guess you're right. I felt like everything is going against me and no one is there to help.*

TH: *Tell me what you did then.*

L: *I went back to bed and stayed there until almost suppertime.*

TH: *You didn't go out and look for a job?*

L: *That's the farthest thing from my mind. I'm not capable of that, can't even think about it. I'm so upset I can't begin to keep a job and act cheerful.*

TH: *Sometimes it helps people if they just get exercise. Have you been doing anything like that?*

L: *No, I told you on the phone I used to jog and play tennis and racquetball. But I gave that up about 8 months ago.*

TH: *If you got back into shape what would that do for you?*

L: *I suppose I'd feel proud of myself.*

TH: *Lana, I want to ask you a few questions about what you've told me so far.*

L: *Go ahead.*

TH: *Is staying in bed from 10:30 till suppertime with only a few hours out of bed going to help you to feel better? Is it going to get you involved with people?*

L: *Probably not, but I just can't face the day.*

TH: *If you don't face the day, where will you be in 6 months?*

L: *Right where I am.*

TH: *That's a possibility. How about eating donuts and skipping lunch? Is that helping?*

L: *No. But I can't do anything else!*

TH: *What about staying at home, rather than looking for a job?*

L: *I guess that's hurting me too.*

TH: *And how about no exercise?*

L: *I feel terrible about that. But I just don't have any energy. I just don't feel like doing anything.*

TH: *You came here to turn things around. Where do you want to start?*

L: *It seems so hard and so impossible.*

TH: *Are you willing to try?*

L: *I guess so.*

TH: *Let's talk about what you can do today.*

L: *Well, OK.*

The therapist has done a credible job of using the procedures, especially the E of the WDEP formulation. The client was asked to evaluate each component of her behavior and to consider a specific plan. Had the session continued, the therapist would have helped the client make a specific, attainable plan to do something different *today*. A discussion of her physical condition and her cancer would certainly be included.

Please compare the above dialogue with that below. It starts exactly as did the previous one.

TH: *Lana, you told me on the phone that you had many things you'd like to talk about. Where do you want to start?*

[Lana describes the background and the therapist listens carefully, as above, establishing an empathic environment.]

TH: *Lana, you've told me all the things that are troubling you. I think there is a difference between your upsetness and the way you are handling it.*

L: *What do you mean?*

TH: *You lost your job and maybe your husband and you've been told you have cancer. The way you're handling it is by staying in bed.*

L: *Yeah, sad way to handle it.*

TH: *Not at all. Tell me, with the trouble you've had why wouldn't you stay in bed?*

L: *What do you mean?*

TH: *Those are your ways of coping. Everyone has ways of coping with the assaults from the world around us. And you have more than your share.*

L: *But these aren't very good ways to deal with these "assaults."*

TH: *Who says? How can anyone say that he would do better than you're doing?*

L: *You mean this mess is not unusual?*

TH: *Not at all. You know, in a way, I'm surprised you are doing as well as you are.*

L: *What do you mean?*

TH: *In spite of this enormous onslaught you are able to come here today and are willing to work on your problems! It's amazing!!*

L: *Oh, come on! It's not that hard to do.*

TH: *Really?*

L: *Yes, I can get up to come here.*

TH: *And you did it. You made it here. Before I forget, I want to ask you about coming here. When you came it must have taken some kind of major effort.*

L: *Yes, it did. You scheduled me at 9:00 a.m. I'm not used to getting up early enough to be somewhere at 9:00.*

TH: *But no one dragged you out of bed. You chose to get up and come here. You got cleaned up, wore your good clothes, transported yourself over here, walked in, talked in detail about this with someone who is almost a stranger.*

L: *Well, I guess you're right.*

TH: *Lana, tell me, what did you feel when you went through this different schedule today?*

L: *Come to think of it, even though it was an effort, I felt like I was doing something worthwhile and maybe I would get some help from someone.*

TH: *A sense of accomplishment and even a slight bit of hope or comfort?*

L: *Yes.*

TH: *So even when you choose to do a so-called "small thing," there's an internal payoff.*

L: *Yes, I felt better.*

TH: *And you know, it was not a "small thing." It was a major project, and you succeeded.*

L: *I never thought of it like that.*

TH: *Well, what do you think now?*

L: *You're right. It is a success.*

TH: *And right now as you sit here, what do you feel?*

L: *Better.*

TH: *Give me a percentage. What percentage do you feel better?*

L: *Not really very much. Maybe 15%.*

TH: *No kidding! You feel* that *much better from getting up and taking action? That's quite a major change from the way you felt before. Think of that! A 15% change from choosing a different way of spending your time this morning.*

L: *You have a way of turning things around.*

TH: *That's what I do. But let me try to understand this. Stop me if I'm wrong. Let's see if I've got it. When you take action you feel better. When you do things differently from the way you've been doing them, you feel better. Is that right?*

L: *That's it exactly.*

TH: *I see.*

If the session were to continue, the therapist would help Lana make specific plans to turn her life around. Questions would be posed such as, "What were you doing when your life was more satisfying as far as friends, children, job, hobbies, etc.?" The counselor would add on a thorough discussion of Lana's relationships: which ones are strong and which ones need to be improved. As in the other scenario, it would be appropriate, at some point, to focus on her perceptions of her illness and how it has impacted her life.

What Is the Difference Between These Two Sessions?

In the first session the therapist uses the principles of reality therapy, the WDEP system, accurately. Helping the client make self-evaluations about behaviors that are holding her back, the therapist employs a deficit model. The first positive, strength-inducing discussion appears at the plan-making stage. Because of the emphasis on her current ineffective behaviors the plan will be less likely to succeed and will need to be smaller in scope. After all, her best efforts to cope are seen by her as less than helpful, if not simply harmful.

In the second scenario the therapist communicates indirectly that staying in bed is Lana's best effort. The question, "Why wouldn't you stay in bed?" indirectly helps the client to change her perception that she is powerless and that her efforts are humiliating. In short, the second therapist works from a strength model, seeing the client's behaviors as not totally worthless but rather as her best effort to cope. They are solutions that have not worked. Both styles are legitimate and necessary at times. The question is, when should one be emphasized over the other? While there is no easy or scientific way to determine this, in practice the two can be used simultaneouly or separately.

> *People don't choose problems*
> *They choose solutions which do not solve problems*

☐ The Language of Reality Therapy

We are all verbal animals. At least this is one way both Eastern and Western philosophers describe human beings. This means we can think and speak and are sentient, that is, we have emotions. When we speak we use words and language. Communicating through language is the primary tool at the disposal of the therapist, teacher, parent, manager, salesperson, etc. The use of language and verbal techniques, an outgrowth of these philosophical assumptions, is embraced by reality therapy. Moreover, the language of reality therapy reflects the principles that behavior is chosen, that we frequently have more control than we think we have, and that human motivation is internal not external.

Understandable Language

W. Glasser and Wubbolding (1995) stated,

> In formulating the principles of reality therapy, a conscious decision was made to use easily understood words. The use of simple words, such as *belonging, power, fun, freedom, choices, wants,* and *plans,* is not an accident. The happy result of this effort has been to introduce basic concepts of mental health to new audiences. Yet this demystification and relative understandability of the concepts is a two-edged sword, and the principles of reality therapy are more difficult to practice than to understand. (p. 302)

The nonesoteric vocabulary can lead to the false conclusion that reality therapy is easy to practice. But experience has shown that an 18-month training program for certification is needed to provide a solid groundwork of experience, knowledge, and skill. And so, to see the world through the lenses of choice theory and reality therapy requires time, effort, and the unlearning of previously learned skills which often interfere with the effective use of reality therapy.

The system is a dynamic one with clear stages of growth. It existed in a seminal way at the Ventura School for Girls. The eight steps were an expression of the delivery system. WDEP is a current language used to teach and understand how to implement choice theory. "Control theory" became "choice theory" in order to emphasize the internal origin of human behavior and because the word "control" has too many negative meanings and is easily misunderstood.

Using language readily grasped by both professionals and the public has been a purposeful theme. Down-to-earth language offers a partial explanation for the popularity of this system with the public, as well as its neglect by psychology and psychiatry. In recent years this inattention has turned to at least curiosity and even positive regard, as reality therapy is now represented in many counseling and psychotherapy textbooks.

Language of Inner Control

Teaching clients and students the language of inner control includes recognizing the value of phrases such as "I chose to do it" rather than "He made me do it," or "I'm depress-ing," instead of "I got depressed." Depending on their readiness to hear such ideas, clients and students learn this advanced form of reframing from a therapist, case worker, teacher, or anyone using reality therapy effectively.

In choice theory emotions are seen not as static conditions but as behaviors that we generate from within. Anxiety becomes "anxiety-ing," depression becomes "depress-ing," and anger becomes "anger-ing." On the other hand, as with any theory, there is a temptation to develop cultic and politically correct language. Persons not using the appropriate language can be labelled and even corrected in their speech, especially in training programs. I reject this inelegant, rigid, and puristic adherence to a "correct" form for describing internal controls. Language is important and the vocabulary of choice theory and the WDEP system is important, but correct language need not replace substance.

With the above caveat, I suggest you practice the transition from external control thinking to internal control thinking by using the reframing activity in Figure 6. The word "choice" as in statement 1 provides an initial way to make this transition.

Using the language of choice theory, reframe the language of external control and powerlessness on the left into that of inner control and choice on the right.

1. "I can't."	"I choose not to" or "I won't."
2. "You didn't tell me."	
3. "He made me do it."	
4. "That kid drives me up the wall."	
5. "My parents won't let me . . . "	
6. "A fit of depression came over me."	
7. "I had an anxiety attack."	
8. "I can't stand it."	
9. "He makes me sick."	
10. "That situation upsets me."	
11. "This weather gets me down."	
12. "She really gets to me."	
13. "My job is stressful."	
14. "My child is such a worry to me."	
15. "You don't give me any choice."	

FIGURE 6. Language of inner control.

☐ Questioning Clients

Posing questions based on the concepts underlying the WDEP formulation characterizes the practice of reality therapy. Therapists often ask dozens of questions during a session. To the trained eye, the therapist is helping clients search inside themselves to uncover insights, understandings, and possible solutions. Wubbolding (1996b) has identified four purposes for the use of questions to move the process far beyond reflective listening, interpretation, and advice giving.

1. *To enter the world of the clients.* By asking clients what they want, what they think they need, and the range of possible areas for exploration in the WDEP formulation, the therapist can become part of the client's quality world. Skillfully timed questions help establish the relationship, a prerequisite for change. Reality therapists respect what clients want and do without presuming to know what is good for them, except that good human relationships alleviate much human suffering.
2. *To gather information.* The reality therapist needs information to assist clients in their self-evaluation and planning. Gathering data about exactly how a depressed person spends time is a prerequisite for asking, "Is the way you used your time

yesterday morning helping you relinquish your depression ("depress-ing") or making it easy for you to depress yourself?" Or, more specifically, "Did staying in bed yesterday until 11:00 a.m. add to your energy or lessen it?" Therefore, collecting data is not the ultimate goal of questioning. It is only the beginning and leads to the more important purposes below.

> *Question:*
> *Why do you always answer a question with a question?*
>
> *Answer:*
> *Why not?*
> *Doesn't everybody?*

3. *To give information.* The implicit, unspoken message, often not consciously intended by the therapist, is recognized by the client as important and interpreted at a high level of perception as meaningful information. Wubbolding (1988) stated, "paradoxically, this purpose is served best by de-emphasizing it as a purpose" (p. 163). Clients receive an implicit message when asked, "What will you do tonight to turn your life toward a more desirable direction?" It is as though they catch an unintended message, not explicitly taught or discussed in any detail: *"Even though you've been upset for years, a better life is possible. You have more control than you think you have. Choices are available that you never dreamed you had."* Such messages are significant and do not appear to clients as clichés or slogans.

4. *To help clients take more effective control and make better choices.* Appropriate and empathic questioning helps clients take better charge of their lives by providing opportunities for them to identify their motivation, that is, their wants and needs. They can then focus their perceptions on their doing behaviors and on their actions. Most importantly, they evaluate all aspects of their control or choice systems, the attainability of their wants, and the effectiveness of their actions and thinking.

The D and E of WDEP formulation is referred to as the "mirror technique." It is as though clients look in a mirror and examine their specific action (D) as well as their overall life-direction (D) in order to evaluate (E) their effectiveness.

The basis for skillful questioning is the fundamental principle that human motivation originates from within. Thus external stimuli such as lecturing, arguing, and coercing are worthless unless the person is receptive to change. Weinberg (1985) describes the "buffalo bridle." It is neither an object nor an action. It is a very significant piece of knowledge. "You can get a buffalo to do whatever you want it to do . . . if it wants to do it." Higher on the scale of intellectual life, human beings are assisted in exploring their inner motivation by skillful, artistic, and targeted questions.

☐ Metacommunication

Metacommunication is the message under the message. Nearly every form of human interchange contains several levels of communication. Even the simple question, "How are you doing today?" contains several implicit messages such as, "I am interested in you" and "Today is important, perhaps more important than the past or the future." Anyone who has spent time in a singles club knows that besides the enormous amount of communication transferred through body language, an equal amount occurs through implicit verbal messages. The single mingle constitutes a topic for many sociological studies. Because my focus here is on the implicit message of reality therapy in a professional setting, the dialogue below centers on a very different and sober topic.

In the following dialogue the client has discussed a death of a loved one:

TH: *You were talking about the death of your brother, James. Tell me more about this.*

CL: *Yes, we were very close. We worked on cars together, had a business, and recently negotiated the sale of this business.*

TH: *You must miss him very much.*

CL: *We were very close.*

TH: *And now that he's gone you are even more conscious that you really valued your relationship. At a time like this you probably want it to continue even more.*

CL: *I really wish he was still here.*

TH: *And you can no longer have the closeness. You want it so much and can't have it. This is plenty reason to be upset!*

CL: *Yes, I think that's it.*

In the above dialogue the metamessage based on choice theory is that behavior, including actions, thinking, and even feelings such as loss and grief, originate in the gap or difference between what a person wants and what one receives from the world. It would be tasteless, cruel, tactless, inappropriate, and even outrageous to state such a principle in its bold truthfulness to James. The art of counseling requires graceful timing. Presented as an empathic reflective statement emphasizing the pain of loss, the metamessage is received by the client and incorporated into his perceived world. The client might even be unaware of incorporating the message, but the skillful user of reality therapy builds on this aspect of the client's perceived world.

Reality therapy, an open system, accommodates techniques adapted from other theories. The use of metaphor (Kopp, 1995), narrative (Freedman & Combs, 1996), and even some Ericksonian techniques (Haley, 1996; Zeig, 1985) are quite compatible with choice theory and reality therapy.

Both a directive and a nondirective therapist style can be effective. Students learning reality therapy need to adapt the system to their own styles and use it in a manner comfortable to them. In this way communication occurs on many levels.

In summary, reality therapy is best seen as an open system, one that has its own identity different from other methods but at the same time is flexible and nondogmatic. It accommodates techniques that come from many directions.

☐ Qualities of the Reality Therapist[1]

This book clearly delineates the methodology followed by the effective user of reality therapy. Thus I have described what a person *does*. However, the question is often asked, "What are the personal or professional qualities of the reality therapist?" It is

---

[1]Adapted from Wubbolding and Brickell (1998).

my belief that someone using this system attempts to show or aspires to, the following personal and professional characteristics.

Personal Qualities

The qualities described below are not intended to answer the above question with any degree of finality. Rather, these descriptions pave the way for further discussion about a dimension of mental health and educational practice, a topic of conversation for decades, as well as to prepare researchers to investigate further.

Empathy, Congruence and Positive Regard. The practice of reality therapy embraces what Rogers (1957) referred to as "the necessary and sufficient conditions for change." Empathy is the ability to see the world from a client's point of view. It does not imply agreement. Rogers spoke of the "as if" quality, that is, even though helpers enter the perceptual world of the client, they are able to keep some distance, thereby avoiding the pitfall of sympathy, which is an overidentification with the plight of clients or students. In speaking of teacher attributes, Moore (1943) said, "He has discipline, but he never hurts a child's feelings or frightens him into obedience by a formalistic recountal of the dire consequences of his behavior" (p. 216). Congruence is not a single quality, but a construct or an aggregate of characteristics. In general, it implies that the helper has at least some degree of mental health. Such people are able to take responsibility for their actions, see their control as internal, and can relate to others in healthy and direct ways. Positive regard means that the helper values the consumer of services. There is a clear distinction between the person's ineffective and even harmful behavior on one hand and the valued person on the other.

In reality therapy, empathy and positive regard take on an added dimension. Students, clients, and employees are accepted for what they are. The helper attempts to see the world through their eyes. But additionally, they are accepted for what they can be and will be. The person who stays in bed most of the day is accepted as she is: a client choosing depress-ing behaviors. But it is most empowering to see her and accept her as someone who can have healthy relationships, who can become employed, and who can live a full life. Abused people need empathy about their current plight, but they need the conviction and foresight that they have choices. It is disempowering to demonstrate sympathy or excessive empathy for the current situation of people who are emotionally wounded. The victim of racism needs only a small amount of empathy. What is needed is an open door, an extended hand that pulls—not one that pats the person on the back in bleeding heart fashion. Reality therapy allows for the helper to gently nudge clients, students, employees to achieve their fuller potential.

Another aspect of empathy is whether clients put the user of reality therapy into their quality worlds. Do they see us as more than warm and friendly? Rather, do they see us as people who can help them? From a more action-centered point of view the helper needs to check with clients to insure that we are working on their agenda, not merely ours. Consequently, empathy is more than a warm feeling, more than a friendly environment. It looks to the future.

Energy. The effective user of reality therapy possesses qualities similar to those asserted for Ericksonian therapists by Haley (1996), such as going the extra mile. A teacher in the Cincinnati Public Schools, not satisfied with the ramshackle desks in his classroom, encouraged the students to discuss the problem and approach the principal and then the downtown central office. He helped them formulate a request for desks without holes that did not present a threat to their safety when sat upon. He helped them in ways beyond the minimum expected of him. Counselors, too, get more involved in the lives of their clients than many office-bound therapists. When William Glasser was a young psychiatrist, he occasionally made house calls to clients unable to come to his office. Remaining within ethical boundaries is a major principle at the basis of all such professional relationships.

Ability to See Everything as an Advantage. "Anything I do differently will be a step in the right direction," was a comment made by a new school principal who took a job in a school with the worst teacher morale in the district and in a building equally dilapidated.

In counseling an ex-offender who had gotten fired from nine jobs in 10 months, the counselor remarked that the client had an amazing talent for getting a job. Some clients believe they have hit bottom because they must involve an "outsider" in their problems. The skill of seeing advantages is valuable in these circumstances and can be expressed by congratulating clients for taking a positive giant step in the right direction toward self-improvement. Coming for help is a big plus.

Positive but not Naive View of Human Nature. Clients and students are seen as wanting what is best for themselves and generally aiming their lives in a positive direction. Still, many are victimized by external circumstances such as abuse, violence, drugs, and other dysfunctional environments.

Recognizing human nature as it is implies the realization that human progress is like going up a "down escalator" or rowing a canoe upstream. It is only with continuous effort that individual or societal progress is made. People can be beguiled, bedeviled, and bewildered. We are often illogical, ill-prepared, and irresponsible. Our actions can be hesitant, halting, and horrifying to others. We can be disgruntled, disturbed, disillusioned and disgusting. We can be selfish, self-absorbed, self-indulgent, and self-aggrandizing.

On the other hand, human beings can be persevering, parental, protective, and philanthropic. We are capable of giving our lives and living our lives for others, donating bone marrow, kidney, and eyes. We initiate Marshall plans, disaster relief, scholarships, foundations, donations, and salvation armies. We cherish charity, children, crosses, and crescents that are red. We can forgive and forget. We can even bury the hatchet without marking the spot. In short, the reality therapist recognizes that behavior can be helpful or harmful.

A way out of this human wheel spinning is using choice theory and reality therapy on a society-wide basis and using lead management in schools, businesses, and agencies. Extending realistic and developmentally appropriate choices to students, clients, workers, and families helps them fulfill their needs without threatening the ability of others to do the same (Glasser, 1998a).

Professional Characteristics

Functioning as a professional person in the 21st century requires more than an integrated personality, a sound mind, and personal responsibility. Specific skills are necessary. Many people predict, for instance, that in the very near future, insurance companies will limit their reimbursement for specific psychological problems such as depression (i.e., "depress-ing") to therapists who use empirically validated cognitive-behavioral protocols.

Listed below are several professional skills useful in practicing reality therapy. Additionally, many credentialing and licensing boards such as government teacher certification departments require that the person be of "good moral character" and have such a recommendation from a colleague.

A Sense of Paradox. Wubbolding (1988, 2000b) described paradox as a centerpiece of reality therapy. Moreover, in the classic training tape, "Woman With Psychosomatic Problems," W. Glasser (1975) repeatedly employed reframing and directives or prescriptives and encouraged the client, "Edna," to enumerate her symptoms, adding, "You're sick. There's not a part of you that's well." Similarly, in another training tape he encouraged a cantankerous couple to continue to bicker (Glasser, 1988) and later described the usefulness of paradoxical counseling (1998a).

Seeing problems as opportunities to teach choice theory and reality therapy is a reframing skill needed by lead managers in schools and agencies which seek to achieve a higher level of quality. For the reality therapist, laziness means great potential, resistance implies deep convictions, and manipulation suggests creativity. Redefining problems as opportunities provides abundant possibilities for productive, positive choices in teaching and counseling.

Ability to Communicate Hope. Part of entering the clients' and students' quality worlds is helping them realize that no matter how difficult the situation, they are best served if they retain hope in the future. This hope springs from the simple fact that they have choices. The options are sometimes quite limited, as in the case of terminal illness, but the user of reality therapy communicates a realistic, not false, sense of anticipation and expectation. Moore (1943) remarked, "It is very important . . . that we realize that the strings of our destiny are in our own hands, and that no blind fate cuts through the strands of our mental health with the shears of a fatal heredity or the steel of the mechanics of the unconscious" (p. 309).

Ability to Define a Problem in Solvable Terms. This quality described by Haley (1996) for Ericksonian therapists, especially useful in an age of brief therapy, corresponds with the need to document quick results in schools and agencies. It also harmonizes with the WDEP formulation of reality therapy.

Reality therapy is, of its nature, specific in how it addresses issues. Conversely, global or ungrounded strategies are not effective. As long as human beings are alive they generate behaviors. These behaviors are specific and measurable. Consequently, users of reality therapy are concrete and specific when they discuss behavior and when they help clients formulate action plans.

Ability to Use Metaphors. In an early and anonymous training tape an alcoholic told Glasser that he got drunk each day after work at a bar called the "Open Door." Glasser referred him to Alcoholics Anonymous, telling him the first choice must be "to close the open door." The metaphorical meaning of changing his life direction was evident.

Another client told a therapist, "When I took the job, I was the new kid on the block, kind of green, but I learned the ropes and found my way around. Then things heated up. I got knifed in the back and now I'm back on the street." Even an unskilled user of metaphors can find several similes to "jump on" here.

Instead of paraphrasing the client's statement, "I'm down in the dumps," as "you're upset," the metaphorist could say, "What does it look like in the dumps? What would being out of the dumps in the sunlight look like?" "What can you do today to climb out of the dumps?" Using the metaphor by extending it further than its originally intended meaning keeps the counseling process moving at a steady pace.

Willingness to Work Within the Boundaries of Professional Guidelines, Standards, and Ethics. Knowledge of and adherence to standard practice is the mark of a genuinely professional person. The possession of degrees, certificates, and licenses are necessary conditions for acceptance and functioning in the current professional world and will be more important in the 21st century. These credentials imply a commitment to standards of behavior that transcend those of The William Glasser Institute (Wubbolding, 1998b). Professional therapists, counselors, social workers, correctional workers, prevention specialists, halfway house employees, case managers, and all those with a professional identity need to know how to deal with suicide threats, to avoid dual relationships, to know the limits of confidentiality, to work within their limitations, to recognize conflict of interest, to provide informed consent to client systems, to disclose openly their own professional credentials, and to represent the theories of others accurately.

Cultural Sensitivity. Because the world has been shrinking for at least half a century, we are becoming an increasingly multicultural worldwide society. In his book *The Lexus and the Olive Tree* (1999) Thomas Friedman argued that "globalization" has replaced the cold war. He stated that the segmentation of expertise is diminishing and that the "boundaries between domestic, international, political and technological affairs are collapsing" (p. 19).

Theories of human behavior are often criticized as being "Euro-American," a term that is often intended to be less than complimentary. Skilled users of reality therapy appreciate their own culture and recognize that what is appropriate in one part of the world might miss the target elsewhere. The ability to adapt the principles of reality therapy to cultures other than that in which they originated takes study, flexibility, consultation, and a willingness to adjust the ideas. For example, teaching choice theory and reality therapy in the Middle East is rendered virtually ineffective without allowing for the incorporation of, or at least referring to, religion, and more specifically Allah and the Koran.

In summary, consumers in the 21st century expect an increased amount of skill and knowledge. Users of reality therapy need to maintain a thorough and updated knowledge of the principles of reality therapy. But the qualities enumerated above surpass the minimal skill and knowledge levels learned in training specifically limited to a single counseling theory or method.

CHAPTER

Multicultural Dimensions of Reality Therapy: Can Reality Therapy Be Used Cross-Culturally?

Helping professionals dealing with an increasingly multicultural society is a theme in education and in the helping professions. This chapter presents ideas about using reality therapy in cultures other than that of North America. In speaking of cultural differences, it is first necessary to define "cultures." Does the "West" constitute a culture? Does the "East" comprise another culture? This differentiation hardly seems adequate. There are eastern Europeans who are quite different from northern Europeans. In Asia, Africa, the Middle East, South America, and Australia, there are hundreds of distinct cultures.

Within North America itself there are French speakers, English speakers, Polish Americans, Hispanics, African Americans, North American Indians (Native Americans), Euro-Americans, and many others. No matter how the concept of "culture" is circumscribed, further subcultures and class distinctions can be made. Hence, a clear and unambiguous definition of "culture" and "cultural difference" is difficult. Nevertheless, I have accepted the sixth meaning of the word as provided by *Webster's New World Dictionary* (1980) as a working definition of "culture" even though I believe it is significantly less than perfect: "The ideas, customs, skills, arts, etc., of a given people in a given period: civilization" (p. 345).

Because culture is so much a part of our lives and penetrates all our behaviors, it is evident that nearly everything we say or do in our communication is "ethnocentric." In a sense we are all, as Wrenn (1962) said, "culturally encapsulated." A person born into the Chinese culture of Shanghai adopts the ways of the Chinese civilization. Someone from southern Italy will act "Italian" in customs, skills, or the arts. And a person from Minnesota pronounces some words in a slightly different way than a native of southwestern Ohio. It is next to impossible for many adults to lose their accents when moving to another part of the same country. (An "accent " is the way someone speaks who is from a part of the country other than my own!)

☐ Religious and Cultural Adjustments

Throughout history, nations and cultures have borrowed and adapted ideas and values from other cultures. Christianity has often been seen as a Western religion, but many leaders see the need to unencumber theology and make it less culturally encapsulated.

Taiwan Cardinal Paul Shan Kuo-Hsi suggested that the Roman Catholic church will not be intelligible to the people of Asia if it is a carbon copy of the Western church. He stated that Asia is home to the great religions of the world: Hinduism, Buddhism, Judaism, Christianity, and Islam. Quoted in Wooden (1998), Cardinal Kuo-Hsi said that Christianity must adapt to the important cultural and spiritual elements of other religions:

> The centrality of the will of God with Islam; with Hindus, the practice of meditation, contemplation, renunciation of one's will, and the spirit of nonviolence; with Buddhists, detachment and compassion; with Confucianism, filial piety and humanitarianism; with Taoists, simplicity and humility; and with traditional religion, reverence and respect for nature. (p. 5)

He encouraged missionaries to be aware of the cultural context, where intellectual expositions and doctrinal formulations are less important than the personal experience of the divine (Wooden, 1998).

☐ Pitfalls

Even when some superficial adaptation is possible it remains very difficult to enter another culture and see the world as a member of that culture. If refining empathy skills for others within the same culture takes years, it is even more difficult to see the point of view of a person from another culture.

Imposing the values of one culture on another culture is a major form of cultural imperialism. For example, to describe certain Oriental values or Middle Eastern customs as "sexist" is to denigrate cultural behaviors and impose one's own ideas of equality. Such issues present an ethical dilemma to the cross-cultural counselor: to work within the boundaries of that culture, thereby putting in the background one's own ideas about equality, or to impose ones values on the culture as though they were better than the values of the other culture. Some cultures have a "keep it in the family" attitude toward family problems and do not regard self-disclosing as helpful. In the Western way of thought, self-disclosure is encouraged as a path to better mental health and is one of the goals of counseling.

Allen Ivey has spent a lifetime teaching attending skills and intervening techniques. In applying what he calls "intentional intervening," he emphasizes that Western techniques need to be adjusted when used in many "other" cultures (Ivey, 1994; Ivey, Bradford-Ivey, & Simek-Morgan, 1999). Direct eye contact is valued in one culture but seen as rude in another one. One of his observations is especially relevant to the novice practitioner of reality therapy: "Some groups find the rapid-fire questioning techniques of many North Americans offensive" (Ivey, 1994, p. 11). Softening the questioning techniques and making them more reflective constitutes a major adaptation of reality therapy to indirect cultures.

Additionally, Ivey (1999) extends the definition of culture to include *subcultures,* which is "any group that differs from the 'mainstream' of society" (p. 12). The user of reality therapy attempts to adapt the WDEP system to the obvious racial, ethnic, and minority groups, but also to the young and the aging, the sick and the dying. Similarly, White (1990) even delineates a "drug culture," peopled by those who use drugs. Dealing with this culture requires further adjustment—often a very confrontive style and method.

☐ Worldwide Instruction in Reality Therapy

Besides teaching reality therapy workshops in North America, I have taught in Germany, the United Kingdom, Slovenia, Croatia, Italy, India, Korea, Japan, Taiwan, Hong Kong, Singapore, and Kuwait. Other instructors in reality therapy have traveled to Russia, Spain, France, Israel, New Zealand, Australia, Scandinavian countries, and South America. Renna (1998) utilized the principles of choice theory and reality therapy in teaching students, both Jews and Arabs, from Israel. He described how they discussed the Jewish–Arab conflict in the context of choice theory, enabling the students to move their relationships to a deeper level. Moreover, indigenous reality therapy instructors are teaching the ideas in most of the above countries.

Both the widespread instruction in reality therapy and my own experience confirm that making generalizations about another group of people is dubious and hazardous. The content of teaching and the art of practicing reality therapy differ (or should differ) even within a short drive from my home in a large Ohio city. For example, a drive of 10 miles takes me to an area populated with Appalachian migrants, a culture rich in tradition, yet very different from my own. Even more, differences should be considered when applying the principles to clients from distant lands or to clients who are racially, ethnically, or culturally different from the therapist or teacher. So it is with this understanding that I wish to emphasize that reality therapy must be adapted and adjusted if it is to be taught to persons from cultures both within and outside North America. How different is the presentation to audiences in Los Angeles versus audiences in eastern Russia (Bogolepov, 1998)!

Democratic or lead management is, for the most part, a Western or, more specifically, an American phenomenon. In some Chinese cultures, on the other hand, the manager of a company is definitely in charge of the operation. Teachers are so highly regarded in Japan that even their title, "Sensai," is highly revered. In many cultures worldwide, parents rarely ask children about their wants or quality worlds.

The need to adjust the teaching of reality therapy was brought home to me by an incident during one of my workshops. In Hong Kong, the sponsor of the workshop, who was not a participant, wanted to sit in the small group experience for a few hours. I had no objection to this, but wanting to model a management by involvement style, I asked the group to consider the request. An embarrassed silence was the answer. Consequently, I made the decision to grant the request. Later I was able to "smoke out" the issue. Being a person of higher rank than the participants, it was inappropriate for me to seek their acquiescence. Because the request had come from a person of rank higher than that of the participants, it was my responsibility, as leader, to make the decision.

It is clear that the principles of lead management, or reality therapy applied to

> *"We are more alike than we are different"*
>
> -Maya Angelou

management, need to be fitted to the contours of various cultural values and behaviors.

No attempt is made here to resolve the dispute described by Pedersen (1988): "Should the therapist emphasize the culturally unique (emic) or the humanly universal (etic)?" He adds, "If the cultural element is underemphasized, the counselor will be insensitive to the client's values; if it is overemphasized, the counselor will stereotype clients" (p. 167). But whether uniqueness or universality is stressed, the principles of fairness and respect are central.

The code of ethics of the American Counseling Association (Corey & Herlihy, 1996) not only states that counselors must not engage in discrimination (A.2.a.), it also insists that differences be respected:

> Counselors will actively attempt to understand the diverse cultural backgrounds of the clients with whom they work. This includes, but is not limited to, learning how the counselor's own cultural/ethnic/racial identity impacts her or his values and beliefs about the process. (A.2.b.)

Moreover, the Association for Assessment in Counseling has suggested that individuals recognize that cultural patterns and backgrounds must be considered when selecting, administering, and interpreting assessment and testing instruments. For example, the populations used in norming the instrument might be quite different from the person or groups being assessed (Prediger, 1993).

The data about cultural differences and their relationship to counseling practice are increasing but there is still much that needs to be done. A shortage of information about ethnic and minority therapy still exists. Bean and Crane (1996) postulate that many more studies on the needs of minorities could be undertaken.

☐ Meeting the Needs of Minorities

Because minorities underutilize mental health services in the United States, the multicultural movement aims at making mental health services more accessible. Yamashiro and Matsuoka (1997) found that Asian and Pacific Americans, including Chinese, Japanese, Korean, Vietnamese, Hawaiians, Samoans, Guamanians, and others underutilize mental health services. They attribute this to the tendency to deny self, focus on pleasing others, and a community orientation. Sometimes suffering is seen as part of life and *karma*. Family secrets should not be disclosed to outsiders, as this tends to bring shame to the whole family. This hesitancy, they said, is less for persons who are acculturated than for those who are immigrants.

In studying the underutilizations of a college campus counseling center, Brinson and Kottler (1995) stated that most of the counselors represented the majority culture, while their minority clients' needs were quite diverse. Latin-American students often required help securing financial aid, while African-American students felt victimized by racial discrimination. Sometimes racial identity and cultural barriers created a reluctance on the part of minorities to remain in counseling.

☐ Updating Helper Knowledge and Skills

To help counselors and therapists become more skilled, Arredondo et al. (1996) further developed and operationalized multicultural competencies, including the formulation of three dimensions for seeing people "more completely." They stated, "the model highlights our different identity-based affiliations, memberships and sub-cultures and, therefore, complements the discussion of multiculturalism" (p. 3). There are three Dimensions of Personal Identity. The A Dimension is a profile of people based on characteristics. Some are fixed, such as age, gender, and ethnicity, and some are more changeable, such as social class. The C Dimension implies that all individuals must be viewed in a context. History, politics, economic status, etc., are important influences. The impact of local conditions and family history impinges on a person's cultural development, behavior, and values. Counselors are advised to learn as much as possible about these influences so as to be able to assist clients more effectively.

The B Dimension is listed last because it includes the consequences of the above two dimensions. For example, Arredondo et al. (1996) observed that many more women of color are able to attend institutions of higher education because of the increasing number of opportunities in the last 25 years. Understanding the all-encompassing nature of multicultural competencies can help counselors provide better services to clients. Interventions and advocacy can be more informed when based on the Dimensions of Personal Identity model.

Corey (et al., 1998; 2000a) has provided a comprehensive description of beliefs and attitudes, knowledge, as well as skills needed for effective multicultural counseling.

- Beliefs and attitudes include awareness of our own values, appreciation of diverse cultures, and a willingness to refer the client to a minority therapist.
- Knowledge includes an understanding of various sociopolitical systems, an awareness of institutional barriers that prevent some minorities from getting help, and an understanding of the value systems of various groups, especially the group one is working with.
- Skills include those consistent with the life experience of various groups, the ability to modify and adapt counseling approaches, and recognizing one's own limitations and their impact on people who are culturally different from the helper.

In summary, the user of reality therapy cannot function with all clients in an identical manner. While the qualities of the helper, common to all effective work, are empathy, congruence, and positive regard, also important for the user of reality therapy is a willingness and skill in adapting the methodology to each particular person. Based on Ho (1985), Corey, Corey, and Callanan (1998) provided a summarized comparison of "direct" and "indirect" cultures (Figure 7).

☐ Culture and World View

Understanding the diversity of world views provides another aspect of the indispensable adaptation of reality therapy to a pluralistic and globalized society. Cottone (1991) distinguished between the psychological and systemic world views. The psychological world view is described in four propositions.

West	**East**

Values

West	East
Primacy of individual	Primacy of relationship
Democratic orientation	Authoritarian orientation
Nuclear family structure	Extended family structure
Emphasis on youth	Emphasis on maturity
Independence	Interdependence
Assertiveness	Compliance
Nonconformity	Conformity
Competition	Cooperation
Conflict	Harmony
Freedom	Security

Guiding Principles for Action

West	East
Expression of feelings	Achievement of collective goals
Uniqueness of individual	Uniformity
Self-actualization	Collective actualization

Time Orientation

West	East
Future orientation	Traditionalism
Innovation	Conservatism

Ethical Orientation

West	East
Morality anchored in person	Morality linked to relationship

FIGURE 7. A comparison of the Western and Eastern systems. From *Issues and Ethics in the Helping Professions, 5th edition,* by G. Corey, M. S. Corey, and P. Callanan. ©1998. Reprinted with permission of Wadsworth, a division of Thomson Learning. Fax 800 730-2215.

1. The focus of study is on the individual.
2. It is assumed that individuals possess characteristics and traits, learned or unlearned, that endure and that represent predispositions to act (e.g., self-concepts, disorders, maladaptions, interests, attitudes, values). These characteristics or traits can be isolated and influenced in a counseling context.
3. Causes can be directly defined. Symptoms (e.g., inappropriate behavior) and conditions (e.g., incongruence) can be treated directly through a therapeutic relationship.
4. One person can affect change in a second person only to the degree that the first person influences the characteristics, traits, or psychological conditions (internal or external) of the second person.

The systemic world view, on the other hand, is summarized as follows:

1. The focus of study is on relationships.
2. Relationships can be isolated for study and defined, but only with the understand-

ing that the acts of isolation and definition are relative to the observer and his or her system (relationships) of reference.

3. Cause is nonlinear or circular within the confines of the defined relationships.
4. Therapeutic change occurs through social relationships.

Reality therapy has evolved over the years to the point where it incorporates a systemic world view. Lead management (W. Glasser, 1990c, 1994, 1998a) is based on the principle that when relationships change, the behaviors of the student and the worker change. Wubbolding (1996a) advises managers "to look fearlessly at your own behavior with a view to changing it for the better" (p. 3). It is through better coaching that the famous "chain reaction" of W. Edwards Deming takes place. Productivity increases because workers feel the joy of work. Deming (1986, 1993) perfected his ideas in Japan, but they are equally applicable in any culture because all people have a need for belonging and possess the capability to make choices.

Similarly, relationships between spouses or partners improve when their interaction changes. Rather than looking for cause and effect in the relationship, each person examines his or her own behavior, quality world and especially how this interfaces with that of the other person (W. Glasser, 1995; Cockrum & Cockrum, 1994).

Danger of Stereotyping

The purpose of this chapter is to demonstrate and illustrate how reality therapy is adapted to persons from a variety of cultures. However, I cannot emphasize too much that reality therapy is used effectively when each person is treated as an individual with a unique quality world and unique behaviors. Such treatment means adapting it to each individual person. For example, the expectation that because a person has Asian roots, his or her behavior will always be "indirect" is outside the boundaries of effective reality therapy. The same is true when dealing with *anyone* of *any* race, sexual preference, social class, geographical area, gender, religious affiliation, or age group. General cultural characteristics, though important, do not supersede the individual quality worlds and the wide range of chosen behaviors. Clients should be considered individuals, not representatives of a culture. Vontress (1999) states, "Labeling the help seeker a cross-cultural client does not relieve the help-provider of this responsibility" (p. 18).

In any list describing cultural differences there is a danger of oversimplification, leading the reader to impose expectations on clients. Users of reality therapy are advised to review such lists, but recognize that each individual is unique and no one fits any preconceived mental stereotype. With the above caveat in mind, it is useful to illustrate ways that reality therapy applies in various cultures.

☐ Japan

The Culture of Japan

In speaking of the Japanese culture, Goshi (1984) stated, "Our history shows us to be both a very special, unique culture, but also a culture that has a long tradition of learning from others. Sometimes in our history we have stressed our uniqueness, and sometimes we have stressed the value of learning from other cultures, East and West.

Right now we are at a special time where we have a kind of balance between the two values" (p. 9).

It is not my purpose to present an exhaustive discussion about the differences between the Japanese and Western cultures. But I do wish to describe *some* differences in thought patterns and language illustrating the importance of learning about other cultures as well as adapting the principles contained in choice theory and reality therapy. A special debt of gratitude is owed to Masaki Kakitani of The William Glasser Institute Japan, who has helped me over a period of 12 years to relate these principles to the Japanese culture. But the final interpretation is my own, that of a westerner and an outsider to Japan.

Because of the efforts of Masaki and Sumiye Kakitani, reality therapy has blossomed in what is perhaps the most indirect of Asian cultures. In reviewing Alfie Kohn's book, *Punished by Rewards* (1993), Kakitani (1999) stated that personal responsibility and inner motivation are quite compatible with Japanese culture. These concepts are also central to choice theory and the practice of reality therapy.

Purpose of Language

One of the basic differences between Western and Japanese cultures is purpose of language. In Western civilization the goal of communication is to "get across" ideas to another person, to become one with them in thought. We are taught to say what we mean, assert ourselves, and ask clearly for what we want. The purpose of the language in Japan includes, possibly even as a primary purpose, to express politeness. When we say "hello" in English, we wish to greet someone, give recognition to another person. In Japan, frequently "hello" requires a paragraph in order to show proper politeness and recognize the status of the other person. Assertive communication is not appropriate, especially between a child and parent or between an employee and supervisor. Because of the importance of authority and the desire to show respect, the purpose of language takes on a different cultural value than in the West.

Inference, Intuition, and Authority

In Japan communication is often referred to as *shoji and fusuma. Shoji* is the paper screen between rooms, the thickness of one sheet of paper. *Fusuma* is the thickness of two sheets. In the Japanese home there is both oneness and separateness. One senses, guesses, and intuits the events in the next room and is one with them. So, too, in communicating, it is not always necessary to ask every detail. Intuiting, inferring, and sensing a deeper level of meaning is part of Japanese communication. This is especially relevant to the role of authority.

The relationship between client and therapist in the United States is often somewhat democratic. In Japan the helper is seen to be more of an authority figure. Anyone who is in a position of authority is revered in most Eastern cultures, and thus the counselor of the Japanese client recognizes that what might seem as off-hand statements to an American could be taken quite seriously by the Japanese client. Goshi (1984) emphasized that for communication and cooperation to be long lasting, mutual respect is necessary.

Because the helper is someone to be respected, he or she readily becomes a need-fulfilling person to clients. In fact, respect and reverence are cultural expressions by which the helper enters the quality world of clients.

Procedures Applied to Counseling Japanese

When communication is indirect, the utilization of the WDEP system is quite different than when used in cultures where communication is more linear.

Wants. It is not necessary to ask clients to articulate their precise wants or to encourage them to express their goals. Indirect questioning and a more circuitous route taken by client and counselor achieves the same result as direct questioning. Such questions are illustrated in the next dialogue.

Evaluation. To ask if behavior "helps" is meaningless since "help" implies superiority. A parent helps a child. A person in authority helps a subordinate. But to ask if behavior "helps" is to ask a question that is not translatable. The dialogue below illustrates how this question can be presented to the Japanese client.

Moreover, in helping clients evaluate their own behavior it can be a mistake to use the Western, direct, individualistic questions built around whether specific behaviors meet the clients' needs. Rather, its impact on the family and, conversely, the influence of family on the clients' behavior occupy a place of paramount importance. For example, several Japanese sailors refused to participate in the war in the Persian Gulf (known to Middle Easterners as the Arabian Gulf). Their reasons were not that the war was wrong or unnecessary, nor that they were of a nonviolent nature, nor that they believed Saddam Hussein was right. They said that their families objected.

Planning. There is no exact Japanese translation for the word "plan," just as there is no exact word for "accountability." It is ironic that such Western concepts do not have parallels in Japanese.

Recent history provides ample evidence that if any nation can plan and is accountable, is known for high quality in products, and even safety on city streets, it is Japan. The dialogue below indicates that the principles can be adapted and the WDEP system used quite effectively. (H = Hanako, female client; T = Taro, male counselor.)

T: *It's so good to see you today. I hope you did not have difficulty finding my office.*

H: *No, it is near the bus stop.*

T: *Please have a seat in this chair. I believe it is comfortable.*

H: *Thank you very much. It is quite comfortable.*

T: *What can I do for you today?*

H: *I am very much ashamed to tell you what is wrong.*

T: *Try your best to tell me. Maybe I can be of some assistance to you.*

H: *It's all my fault. I'm very embarrassed by this problem.*

T: *I'd like to hear about it. I doubt if it is so hopeless that nothing better could happen in your life.*

H: *That's encouraging. My husband is not interested in me or in the family anymore.*

T: *That's too bad. You must be very saddened by this.*

H: *Yes. I am very humiliated. Sometimes the children blame me.*

T: *That must make the situation worse for you.*

H: *It does. It's terrible. I don't know what to do.*

T: *Could you describe what he does that you are upset about?*

H: *It's very hard but I'll do my best. He comes home after work. He's very tired. I serve him dinner. After dinner, he sits at the computer by himself for hours every night.*

T: *He pays no attention to you?*

H: *That's right. That's not all.*

T: *What else is troubling you?*

H: *He plays computer games or browses the Internet when he comes home early from work. Some nights he comes home late and he's drunk. I think there is another woman.*

T: *This shames you very much?*

H: *Yes. I can't face him or the children.*

T: *Have you talked to him about this?*

H: *No. I've not said anything to anyone.*

T: *So, today is the first time you said anything out loud to anyone about the situation?*

H: *Yes.*

T: *Does it make the situation better if you keep this inside of you?*

H: *I don't know. I'm not sure.*

T: *Do you have a thought or an opinion about it that you could share now?*

H: *Well, I guess keeping it inside of me doesn't make it any better.*

T: *What did you have in mind when you came here?*

H: *To get help from you.*

T: *So sharing the family problem with me might lead to a solution?*

H: *I guess that is what I had in mind.*

T: *I can't say for sure that the situation will get better but I'd like to see if together we can look for a solution for you, at least something that would be an improvement.*

H: *Yes, I'd like to find an improvement somewhere.*

T: *OK. Could I ask you some more questions?*

H: *Yes, I'll try to answer.*

T: *My first question is this: What are you looking for in this marriage?*

H: *I would like my husband back. He seems to be going away from his family.*

T: *So you are hoping to make it the way it was.*

H: *Yes. What can I do to get him to change?*

T: *That's a very good question. And we'll have to work on it. I'd like to come back to it in a few minutes. First, I have another question. Tell me what happened last night when he came home.*

H: *He came home about 6:00 p.m., ate, and played the computer game until 11:00 p.m.*

T: *What did you do?*

H: *I served him supper and cued up the computer game for him.*

T: *What else?*

H: *I waited on him while he played the game, browsed the net, and entered the chat room.*

T: *Are you looking for a different way to spend your own evening?*

H: *Yes. I would like to talk to him.*

T: *But if he continues to refuse to socialize with you, are you interested in finding something enjoyable to do once in a while in the evening?*

H: *I'm a member of a women's social club.*

T: *When was the last time you went to a meeting?*

H: *A few months ago.*

T: *Do you miss your friends there?*

H: *Yes, but I'm ashamed to go.*

T: *Could you tell me more about the shame?*

H: *There must be something wrong with me to cause him to do this.*

T: *Hanako, do you really and truly think you forced him into this?*

H: *Well, I guess not.*

T: *If you didn't "force" him into it, do you believe you can "force" him to change again?*

H: *No, but there must be something I can co.*

T: *Let's try to find something you can do to feel better. Would that be worth searching for?*

H: *Yes. For sure.*

T: *You said you miss your friends at the social club.*

H: *Yes, I do.*

T: *It must be painful to be alone—no husband for you and no friends either!*

H: *Yes.*

T: *Would you be interested in finding a way to get back to the social club for an evening or two?*

H: *Well, that would be OK.*

T: *Would it be a plus or a minus for you to go to the social club?*

H: *It would be a plus to see my friends again.*

T: *How could this be a partial solution for the problem?*

H: *It would make me feel better for a while.*

T: *Would it be worth the effort?*

H: *Yes, it would.*

T: *Will you go to one meeting at the social club?*

H: *I'll try.*

T: *Let's talk for a moment about the relationship with your husband. You said you haven't said anything to him about how you feel?*

H: *That's right.*

T: *What would happen if you told him you are upset and came to see me?*

H: *I don't know what he'd say.*

T: *No matter what he says, would it add to or subtract from your effort to find a solution if you told him you are upset and that you came here?*

H: *I'm not sure.*

T: *Let me put it this way. If you search for a solution by trying to do some different things, will you feel better or worse?*

H: *That is why I came here.*

T: *Do you think you are willing to try to do this?*

H: *Yes. I'll try.*

T: *Are you looking for even more ways to deal with this situation?*

H: *Yes. I'd like to search for more solutions.*

T: *What would be enjoyable to do in the evenings with your husband?*

H: *It would be nice to go to the park and look at the flowers like we used to.*

T: *When was the last time you asked him to do this with you?*

H: *I don't remember.*

T: *Does it sound like a good idea or a bad idea to ask him?*

H: *It sounds good to me.*

T: *You have several ideas that you'll try?*

H: *Yes; go to social club, tell him I'm upset and that I'm coming here, and finally ask him to go to the park.*

T: *How do they sound to you?*

H: *They seem to be pluses.*

T: *I think this will take a while to solve. We need to talk more. For instance, we need to talk about how the children are doing.*

H: *I agree. I feel like I have more to tell you. But I'll try these ideas first.*

T: *Can you come back in a week?*

H: *Yes, I'll see you then.*

T: *In one week.*

Commentary. In this session the counselor applied the components of the WDEP system in a more indirect way than would a counselor who practiced the Western, direct style of reality therapy. He accepts the realistic fact that Hanako probably will not assert herself like a "liberated" American wife might. Rather, the counselor helps her share her upset feelings, describe her husband's behaviors and their impact on her, and fulfill her needs by getting involved with her husband through nonconfrontive choices. Rather than establishing goals and wants that are explicitly stated in Western style, the counselor helps Hanako decide what she "is looking for." The evaluation is in terms of "making it better," "plus or minus," rather than "help or hurt." And finally, rather than pressing for a firm commitment which is undermined by "I'll try," Taro recognizes that in Japan "I'll try" is often a firm commitment. Figure 8 summarizes these differences in communication.

☐ Korean

Hal Roach, the Irish comedian referred to in chapter 6, described an Irish lad's marriage proposal, which illustrates that indirect communication characterizes some people in the West as well as in the East. Similarly, in one episode of *Inspector Morse*, the TV sleuth from Oxford, England, a Mr. Boynton who is smoking a cigar asks Morse, "You smoke cigars. Do you want one?" Morse replies, "I wouldn't say no." Nevertheless, it is safe to say that Western communication is more direct, sometimes even harsh, to

Japanese	Western
Deal indirectly with husband.	Confront husband. Assert self. Stop waiting on husband.
Ask what client "is looking for."	Determine "wants" of wife. Set clear goal for counseling.
Evaluation is indirect: "plus or minus."	Evaluate directly: "help or hurt"?
Accept "I'll try" as a firm commitment.	Does not settle for "I'll try." Pursues explicit firm commitment.

FIGURE 8. Differences in communication.

the Asian ear. Dr. In-Za Kim, professor emeritus at Sogang University and director of the Korean Association for Reality Therapy, facetiously describes Koreans as "the Irish of the Orient." The message contained in the words is often unheard by the Western ear. The following example illustrates this point.

Case Discussion: Man in the Hospital

A man in the hospital suffers from a serious disease. It is the custom for Korean doctors to tell the family members of the condition but not to speak directly to the patient about it. The man's wife is hesitant and fearful about calling the doctor to ask about her husband's condition.

Western-style questioning might include, "You're afraid to call your doctor?" and "It must be hard to take such a step." Korean style of questioning would be more like, "What do you think about a phone call to your husband's doctor?" and "What will happen if your husband knows about the situation?"

The Western-oriented helper, asking directly about the fear of calling, acts appropriately. The Korean helper seems to be asking about how the wife is evaluating a decision and about the consequences of the decision. Actually, such questioning is a form of acknowledging the person's fear.

One intervention is direct and one is indirect. Both are appropriate and would be heard differently by clients with varying cultural backgrounds. A special thank you to Kim Young Are of Seoul, Korea for this example.

Questions Inherent in the WDEP System

In Korea and Japan, "What do you want?" can be an intrusive question. While everyone has a quality world containing specific pictures or strong desires, it is useful to develop ways to ask questions indirectly and in ways that sound softer to non-Western ears.

"What are you looking for?" might sound like a mere rephrasing of "What do you want?' to the Western ear; it is actually a more gentle way of inquiring when translated into Korean and Japanese. "What dō you want from me, your therapist?" might be better stated, "What would you like to have happen today that is different from what has happened before?" "How hard do you want to work at solving the problem?" becomes "What would happen to your life if you decided to do things differently?"

These excellent questions can be adapted to the assertive and direct Western culture. The WDEP system of reality therapy, begun in America, applied to Europe, altered in the Middle East and Asia, and reinterpreted to Americans is greatly enriched by being filtered through many cultures.

☐ Chinese Culture

Sister Elizabeth Tham, Kwee Hiong Ong, Rhon Carleton (instructors with The William Glasser Institute), and I have introduced reality therapy to Singapore, a culturally diverse and densely populated country with Chinese, East Indians, Malaysians, Caucasians, and other peoples. "The response from teachers has been enthusiastic" (Abu Bakar, 1994). They find the ideas of reality therapy very useful because they can assist students in taking responsibility, a very important value in Singaporian culture.

Case Discussion (from Diane Koh, Singapore)

A married couple approaches you for counseling. Having recently moved, they are now experiencing a major strain in their relationship. Prior to the move, their relationship seemed to be quite harmonious.

His family now treats her, as she says, "very badly." They call her a whore and think she should be a maid. The husband doesn't want any physical contact with her anymore and shows her no affection even though she is an amiable person and quite attractive. She says that she is by nature very demonstrative and he is now both distant and cold.

Questions

- How would you counsel this couple? Make an outline for a treatment plan.
- In making a treatment plan are you presupposing they are a White couple?
- Would your approach be different if they were not a White couple? How?

You are probably saying it is difficult to answer the questions because of sketchy factual information. The following information might be useful.

- She is Filipina. He is Indonesian.
- They were married and lived in the Philippines.
- The "move" was to Singapore, where his family lives.
- Many maids in Singapore are Filipinas.

Questions

- If you now make a treatment plan, how would it be different from the previous one?
- How would you balance respect for their cultures and respect for them as individuals?
- Is such a balance possible?

- Is such a balance desirable?
- Do your own cultural values clash with theirs? How?

Exercise. Write your own dialogue for counseling this family, keeping in mind your own values and biases, as well as your sensitivity to the cultures represented. On which issues would you focus?

Case History: Karen, Chinese age 15

The following case is a challenge to the multicultural counselor in several ways. You are asked to consider the various dilemmas and to untangle the strings of this Gordian knot. As a therapist how would you deal with your own values?

Karen, a 15-year-old Chinese girl, is sent to a counselor. She attends a convent school in an Asian country which has a strict code of social conduct and forbids any public display of affection by the students, such as fondling, kissing, and sexual touching. Society in general frowns on such behavior much more than in the United States. Karen and her close friend Matilda are suspected by the faculty of having a lesbian relationship. The general practice is for one girl to be the "active" partner and the other "passive." Karen is thought to be "active" because of the way she dresses. The active girls in such relationships in this school are referred to as "Tommies." Karen is doing poorly in her classes: She fails to complete assignments, falls asleep in class, shuns social interaction with faculty and students, is indifferent to being called "Tommie" by other students, and appears to be depressed. Her only relationship seems to be with Matilda, as is evident by their closeness. Several times they have been caught hugging, kissing, and fondling on school grounds. The parents and teachers are pressuring her to abandon the relationship and cease the lesbian behavior, as they believe it is a form of rebellion for her. (K = Karen; CN = counselor.)

CN: *Karen, how are you today?*

K: *I'm OK.*

CN: *You walked in sort of slowly. Are you tired?*

K: *Yeah, but so what?*

CN: *Well, you were sent to me by the principal (head teacher) who said she wanted me to talk to you. What did she say to you about coming here?*

K: *She thinks I'm messed up.*

CN: *What did she say?*

K: *The teachers are tired of scolding me all the time. They just don't like me.*

CN: *They're always after you about something?*

K: *I don't like it here.*

CN: *So she sent you to me. I'm supposed to do something?*

K: *Yeah, I guess so.*

CN: *How about home? How are things going there?*

K: *All they do is yell at me. They're like the teachers here. I want to move out and be on my own.*

CN: *Do you think that is going to happen?*

K: *Probably not, but I want to be on my own.*

CN: *Be independent? Make your own decisions? Be free of restrictions?*

K: *Yes.*

CN: *But it sounds like you also believe that such a thing won't happen.*

K: *Probably not.*

CN: *So I guess you're stuck at home for a while?*

K: *I guess so.*

CN: *Like I said before, you don't seem happy; you sound like you're down in the dumps. Are these things bothering you?*

K: *None of these problems can be solved.*

CN: *Are you saying that absolutely none of these things can be worked out?*

K: *Right.*

CN: *Are you really in a hopeless situation?*

K: *It seems like it. Nothing can help.*

CN: *I'd like to ask you an important question. Of all the problems that cannot be solved, which is the most difficult to solve?*

K: *Matilda.*

CN: *Are you happy with that situation or do you want to change something about it?*

K: *Everyone is against it. Nobody wants me to be around her.*

CN: *So that seems hard to resolve. You want her, and everyone else says to break it off. That's the hardest problem to deal with?*

K: *Right.*

CN: *Now, on the other hand, which is the easiest to solve?*

K: *I want to live alone.*

CN: *Will your parents let you?*

K: *No.*

CN: *So that one is really painful too, isn't it?*

K: *I guess. There's nothing that can be done to solve it.*

CN: *No solution to it, at least right now?*

K: *Yes. I want to live alone. If only I could live alone.*

CN: *Then you could have Matilda over to your place?*

K: *Not exactly.*

CN: *At any rate you have described two really tough problems. Maybe we could talk about some things that are easier to work on, something that is not so severe.*

K: *What will that do?*

CN: *Sometimes it can really be helpful to work on something that is solvable. Who knows? You might feel better—not perfectly happy, just better. What would you lose by talking about it?*

K: *Nothing, I guess.*

CN: *Describe something that is bothering you. But be sure this time it is an issue you can do something about.*

K: *Maybe school work. My grades are real bad. I'll never catch up!*

CN: *Sounds like you have a lot of pressures. Maybe none of these can be solved. Do you think you will just be miserable the rest of your life, faced with problems that are overwhelming?*

K: *Maybe. It's hopeless.*

CN: *Really? It's that bad?*

K: *Well, probably not hopeless.*

CN: *Karen, do you really have to be down in the dumps when people won't let you do what you want to do?*

K: *I don't know.*

CN: *It sounds to me like you have a lot of reasons for doing something about this frustration that you feel. Let me ask you a very important question. We touched on it before. How is the school work situation different from the other two?*

K: *Well, I'm the one who can't catch up and who is falling behind.*

CN: *That's the idea. That one depends more on you than on other people. What about your school work?*

K: *I fall asleep in class. Just can't keep my eyes open.*

CN: *What time do you go to bed at night?*

K: *I like to stay up late.*

CN: *What time did you go to bed last night?*

K: *About 1:30 a.m.*

CN: *So you're really exhausted in class.*

K: *The classes are so boring and when I read, I fall asleep.*

CN: *You know, I've noticed over the years that when people don't get enough sleep, they are almost always unhappy. In fact, I don't know anyone who is happy without enough sleep. I'm not sure why, but it seems to be true.*

K: *I'd like to solve these problems. They're so bad! But I can't solve them.*

CN: *That's why I say, let's focus on the school work for a while.*

K: *I want to study. But I can't.*

CN: *I'll bet you think about all this stuff day and night? Kind of replay the frustrations over and over again like a tape recorder.*

K: *Yes, I think about this all the time.*

CN: *Karen, how has thinking helped?*

K: *What do you mean?*

CN: *Has turning it over and over in your mind gotten you anywhere? Has this internal tape recorder solved any problems?*

K: *I still have the problems. They won't go away.*

CN: *So has it been a plus or a minus for you?*

K: *It's been a minus.*

CN: *Let's take the Matilda problem and your parents' refusal to let you live alone and set them over here on the side in a box for a while* [motions that these problems are now to the side of the desk].

Commentary. At this point the therapist is helping Karen explore her perceived world, especially where she sees her control. She describes two problems that she believes are caused by external forces: her relationship with Matilda and her inability to live on her own. The therapist asks if she ruminates about these and then asks a crucial question, "Has constantly thinking about this changed anything?" This self-evaluation, central to the use of reality therapy, is the keystone in the WDEP arch.

The therapist then helps her focus on school work, an issue for which she takes some responsibility. To communicate a sense of hope to those who feel overwhelmed or powerless, the counselor helps them focus on what is controllable. Thereby, clients learn that they can fulfill their need for power, gain a sense of control, and, in general, act in more appropriate ways.

The session resumes:

CN: *You said you have big difficulties: at school, sleeping, moving out, and parents. Which of these things are inside of you? Remember your parents are outside of you.*

K: *They all seem too hard! Everyone keeps talking about them.*

CN: *It's like you're under pressure?*

K: *Yes.*

CN: *I get the idea that you are in pain about these things. You have a lot of motivation to solve them or at least make them less painful.*

K: *Do you think I can do something about them?*

CN: *I have no doubt about it. But these things are on your mind constantly. People are putting pressure on you.*

K: *If only they would leave me alone!*

CN: *Life would be perfect! But how easy or hard is it to get other people to make changes?*

K: *I don't know.*

CN: *Let's put it this way. They've tried to force you to change?*

K: *Yes.*

CN: *How hard is it for them to get you to change?*

K: *They have failed so far.*

CN: *How hard will you have to work to get them to change?*

K: *Real hard* [jokingly].

CN: *I see from your smile that you realize that if they cannot get you to change or convince you that you are wrong, then you probably can't force them to do anything differently either.*

K: *I see what you mean.*

CN: *But you still want to have a better life?*

K: *Yeah.*

CN: *I agree with you that if the situation is to improve, it won't come from others! So what do you think about trying something different?*

K: *But they're always keeping an eye on me.*

CN: *I have a hunch they are going to keep doing that. Do you know anyone in the class whose parents don't keep an eye on them?*

K: *Yeah.*

CN: *Who?*

K: *Friends.*

CN: *Name one.*

K: *Jessica.*

CN: *What's she like in school?*

K: *She does her work.*

CN: *Do you hang out with her?*

K: *Not really. I just know her.*

CN: *But this is really fascinating. The kinds of kids who work hard at their studies don't have their parents on their backs telling them what to do.*

K: *But I look at the books in class and I fall asleep.*

CN: *One of the things I'd like to do is to help you get more sleep. In school, you say when you read your texts you fall asleep. Is that right?*

K: *Yes.*

CN: *And you stay awake late at night, which makes you tired in the daytime?*

K: *Yeah!*

CN: *You know what? I'll bet there is a connection.*

K: *What do you mean?*

CN: *You stay awake at night and sleep in the day, and reading books puts you to sleep.*

K: *I get it! I get it!*

CN: *Get what? Explain it to me.*

K: *If I read the book at night, maybe I'll fall asleep early.*

CN: *You know what? I think you're onto something here!*

K: *But I like to stay up.*

CN: *Do you like all these people criticizing you?*

K: *NO!!!*

CN: *So what time will you study your book tonight?*

K: *How about 9:00?*

CN: *Sounds good to me. Which book would you want to read?*

K: *Math.*

CN: *You know, I've heard of students doing similar things and they say it helps.*

K: *Really?*

CN: *Yes. Oh, one more thing. I almost forgot. When you read, you might limit your time to about 15 minutes and try hard to stay awake.*

K: *Sounds weird.*

CN: *It is, but what's the harm? Will you do it?*

K: *Sure.*

CN: *One more question. How do you feel now as you sit here?*

K: *I don't know.*

CN: *Better or worse than when you came in?*

K: *A little better.*

CN: *That is very interesting to me.*

K: *Why?*

CN: *Well, when you try to solve a problem, the result is you feel better. And when you just stew about it, you don't feel any better. And here we are trying to solve it, trying to figure out how to take action. So which is better, to stew about it or to make a plan to solve something?*

K: *Make a plan.*

CN: *OK. I'll talk to you tomorrow. Maybe we can have a 10-second talk when you come to school?*

K: *Sounds OK.*

CN: *See you then.*

Commentary. I attempted to be somewhat indirect with the student when exploring her quality world. Instead of directly asking, "What do you want?" the therapist reflected on her motivation for changing what she saw as the encroachment of others on her rights. Instead of asking, "Is your current behavior helping or hurting you?", the therapist asked her to describe the behavior of someone who is happy and how that behavior differs from hers. These questions, more subtle than they appear, helped her come up with the idea that sleeping in class and staying up late are connected and that if she read the texts at night she might fall asleep earlier, get more rest, and feel better during the day. The therapist suggested she limit her time and try to stay awake with the idea that she almost certainly will have a winning experience. If she stays awake and reads longer, she gains knowledge. If she falls asleep, she gains rest. The paradox is that whether she follows through or not, she wins. She cannot lose.

Still, the therapist did not deal with every conflict. The rationale here is that in helping her gain some control she will more effectively tolerate other pressures. In fact, more than likely, she will formulate realistic plans for meeting her own needs without aggravating her parents and school officials. Please notice I said, "more than likely." I often tell clients: no guarantee. If you want a guarantee, buy a toaster.

Indirect questioning, a multicultural adjustment of reality therapy, and indirect reflection and paraphrasing, are appropriate and applicable to all cultures.

Case Discussion: An Older Chinese Woman

Mrs. O, an older Chinese woman living in America, reluctantly seeks help from a counselor at the urging of her son who was born and educated in the United States and who has traveled widely. She, herself, is an immigrant and is embarrassed because her "child" rather than her husband prevailed upon her and persuaded her to discuss her situation with a therapist. Her hesitancy is also manifest as the session opens.

TH: *Mrs. O, I'm so glad you came to see me. Was your trip to the office pleasurable?*

Mrs. O: *It was fine.*

TH: *Do you like how we've decorated the walls? I understand you're very good at decorating your home.*

Mrs. O: *Yes, the office is very nice.*

TH: *I'm glad you like it. It's important for you to feel comfortable here. How can I help you?*

Mrs. O: *I don't think anything is wrong. I simply need to respect my husband's wishes.*

TH: *How do you mean?*

Mrs. O: *He wants me to be a traditional Chinese wife and that really is my place.*

TH: *And what do you want?*

Mrs. O: [States shyly and unconvincingly] *I just need to do what he wants me to do as I always did.*

TH: *But what do you want for yourself which might be different from what he wants for you?*

Mrs. O: *It's OK. I need to stop going to the meetings that my daughter has been taking me to.*

TH: *Oh, what kinds of meetings?*

Mrs. O: *It's a group of 300 to 400 women who meet at a town hall to listen to speeches.*

TH: *And what do they talk about?*

Mrs. O: *It's nothing. I need to stop going.*

TH: *If I guess would you tell me?*

Mrs. O: *I suppose so.*

TH: *Do they talk about business?*

Mrs. O: *That's not it.*

TH: *Do they talk about children?*

Mrs. O: *Once in a while.*

TH: *But they emphasize what the mothers teach their children?*

Mrs. O: *Sort of.*

TH: *I wonder if they ever talk about the role of the mother and her relationship to her husband.*

Mrs. O: [Registering surprise and pleasure.] *Yes, that's it!*

TH: *And you liked what they said.*

Mrs. O: *At first I did not. But my daughter said to keep going.*

TH: *So you went to please her?*

Mrs. O: [No answer. Just a shrug of her shoulders.]

TH: *Well, at any rate, you heard some new ideas?*

Mrs. O: *Yes, they were really new. I have read about them but never heard anyone except my daughter talk about them.*

TH: *How did the ideas sound to you?*

Mrs. O: *Some of them were OK.* [She then talked about the content of the lectures, the meetings, and what the other women thought about the ideas.]

TH: *Mrs. O, we've talked about what the others thought and what they felt about their family situations. Tell me, what do you want from your husband?*

Mrs. O: *It's OK. I'm happy.*

TH: *But are you getting what you want from him as far as help around the house, a feeling of independence, respect, treatment as an equal, etc.?*

Mrs. O: *Yes, everything is OK.*

TH: *What is the problem, then? What would you like to get from our visits?*

Mrs. O: *I think everything is OK.*

Questions

- Were the questions of the therapist appropriate or inappropriate? Which ones? Why or why not?
- Were the questions about the wants of the client clear and direct? What was the impact of these questions on the client's willingness to self-disclose?
- How would you have proceeded differently? What would be a more indirect way to explore the client's quality world?

Commentary. The therapist was entirely too intrusive in the questioning about the client's quality world. Mrs. O reflected a cultural value in behavior in her reluctance to avoid an explicit expression of her wants. In this case inquiries of an older Chinese woman about her wants regarding her husband resulted in what a Western therapist might inappropriately label as evasiveness or resistance. But what was inappropriate was the failure to adapt the questioning to the client. The questions appear to the client to be intrusive, assertive, and impolite.

The therapist was more effective in the questioning about the meeting, i.e., building up to the pivotal question about the husband–wife relationship issues presented at the meetings. But it is difficult for *some* people in *some* cultures to unequivocally and directly state what they want. Direct questions, which to the therapist seem to be simply assertive, often feel aggressive and intrusive to clients.

The case above, and all the cases, illustrate how reality therapy is adapted when used cross-culturally or multiculturally. The clients' behaviors are not intended to represent generalities that could always be expected of everyone in their respective cultures.

Exercise. Rewrite the above case using a more indirect line of questioning, as well as more reflective listening.

☐ A Cultural Comparison

Among the resources for becoming conversant with the field of multiculturalism is the work of Bette Bao Lord (1990). Other authors include Schlesinger (1998), Sowell (1994, 1996, 1998), Thernstrom & Thernstrom (1997), Storti (1991), and Augsberger (1986).

Lord speaks eloquently as a bicultural person. Born in Shanghai and raised in the United States by parents, one of whom was Chinese and one of whom was American, she later lived in China and married a former U.S. Ambassador to the Peoples Republic of China. She says she is doubly blessed with two cultures and converses in English and in Chinese. When she speaks from her American side, she says that the conversation is like playing tennis. There is no reason to converse unless score is kept. On the other hand, conversing in Chinese is like going fishing. "There is ample pleasure in drifting hour after hour along the lake." From her Chinese perspective, a vacation is sitting and talking and drinking tea. But her American influence prompts her to be active and to accomplish something.

She also philosophizes from both sides. Her Chinese side wonders why Americans busy themselves with unceasing activity: changing jobs, moving from town to town, changing relationships, encouraging their children to move away, and moving away from their own parents. Why Americans plunge into waters and go down icy slopes is something that is unknown to her Chinese side. She observes that Americans are programmed to be active and don't stay put long enough to discover who they are.

Conversely, her American side wonders why the Chinese sit on their seats and why they are lacking in get-up-and-go. They cling to ancient ways and refuse to pull up stakes and move. They live under the same roof with a mob of relations and put their own desires in the background. They are such a homogenous group restrained by their genes from doing things on their own. They never act on what they want, but they wait to be told what to do.

As an American person she has a definite individual strength but lacks the strength of her kinsmen. As a Chinese person she has a sense of connectedness but her individuality is submerged.

Lord's poignant book (1990) describes multiculturalism not from the point of view of racism, rejection, or lack of appreciation by the many, but from the internal locus of perception of a truly multicultural person.

In making a case for the modification of reality therapy, it would be foolish to conclude that there is only one kind of adaptation to a Korean, Japanese, or Chinese person. The goal of this discussion is to motivate persons learning reality therapy to learn about "other" cultures and also to make a sincere attempt to connect with the cultural perceptions and values of individual clients and students.

The vast majority of clients and students that practitioners of reality therapy relate to are not living in Japan, Korea, Singapore or Hong Kong. Rather, practitioners need to apply the principles to persons from these cultures and many others living in their immediate communities, such as those alluded to below.

☐ Ireland

Brian Lennon has shepherded the reality therapy movement in Ireland. He reports that as early as 1994, one in every 5,000 people in Ireland has taken a basic intensive training workshop in reality therapy. Among those trained are guidance counselors, teachers, nurses, addictions workers, and employment workers. Though I have taught there a few times, Suzy Hallock-Bannigan, senior instructor and liaison to The William Glasser Institute, along with Dick Pulk (now deceased), initiated the movement and provided the indispensable leadership for this transcultural and very successful adaptation of reality therapy (Lennon, 1994).

Irish Americans

Writing about the Irish in America, McGoldrick and Pearce (1981) summarized various cultural influences. Their paradigm includes the impact of the potato famine of 1845–1846 and the influence of the Roman Catholic Church as a primary cultural factor, with its repressive influence on sexuality, etc. They cite even the Irish jig as a paradoxical caricature of "Irish repression of bodily experience": "The skilled dancer agilely moves only his or her feet, while keeping the rest of the body as motionless as possible" (p. 226). The Irish are seen to be articulate but yet unable to express their inner feelings.

These descriptions appear to be an interpretation of behavior based on American psychology. Behavior that is acceptable in one culture might be less than healthy in another. An example of indirect questioning was made clear during one of my training sessions. The counselor was an unmarried priest. The client spoke of her relationship with her husband, stating, rather hesitantly, that there was no sexual contact between them. The priest's question was, "You wouldn't want to talk about it, would you?" The reader is invited to ask yourself whether this is a repressive question or one that is a multicultural invitation. Is it a door opener or a door closer?

☐ African Americans

African-American clients experience multicultural counseling in the United States when their therapists ethnically differ from them. Wilson and Stith (1991) provide many useful principles for working with the largest minority in the United States. They state counselors need to be aware of five critical issues:

1. *Historical perspectives,* such as the impact of racism: This phenomenon has resulted in segregation, a systemic form of oppression.
2. *Social support systems:* Because of the psychological scars resulting from segregation, many people struggle for survival, struggle to overcome negative stereotypes, and struggle to express anger, distress, and pain appropriately.
   On the other hand, this group struggle has elicited many strengths that therapists need to be aware of, such as the importance of church and family, spirituality, the values of sharing and affiliation, and the importance of the extended family.
3. *Differences in values:* Because of the need to adapt to rejection by major elements in society, many values developed as a result of victimization. Referring to Pinderhughes (1982), Wilson and Stith (1991) stated, "White Americans place greater emphasis on independence, achievement, material assets, planning, youth, and power; Black Americans put greater emphasis on sharing, obedience to authority, spirituality, and respect for elders and heritage." They add: "the experience of oppression and racism (i.e., victimization) may discourage a strong sense of self-esteem" (p. 106). This leads to discouragement and stress for some.
4. *Overcoming communication barriers:* Clients are not always being resistant, sullen, or uncooperative when they are silent. A problem might be an inability to speak as the counselor speaks. On the other hand, many clients have a keen ability to detect lack of genuineness on the part of the therapist.
5. *Strategies for effective treatment:* Some African-American clients are suspicious of therapists, the institutions they represent, and the therapy process itself. Therefore, the helper needs to pass the test of sincerity and genuineness. The specific strategies cited by Wilson and Stith (1991) are quite similar to those described by Corey (2000a) and Corey, Corey, and Callanan (1998).

In researching the expectations of African-American students about counseling, Kemp (1994) suggested that professionals need to attend to environmental factors as well as to helping students feel welcome in order to freely express themselves. In applying this principle to counseling and education as well as to other fields, I believe the therapist is an advocate and a consultant encouraging educators, employers, and others to create a classroom or work place atmosphere conducive to the satisfaction of belonging, power, freedom, and fun. When this occurs students and workers are quite likely to increase their productivity and inner control of their lives.

Progress and Hope

Recent history provides ample evidence that immense progress has been made in Black–White relations in the United States. The Thernstroms (1997) have provided extensive documentation on the decline of racism and the progress of African Americans. More specifically, Sowell (1998) has described the rapid increase in literacy since emancipation as an event unparalleled in history.

It is my contention that if majority counselors use only an "oppression" model as the basis of their perceptions, they will, in effect, oppress their minority clients. For they will communicate to clients that their achievement will depend on the moral about-face of the majority. In other words, their fate remains in the hands of others, a very disempowering prospect indeed.

Reality therapy is a method of counseling and education that presumes a willingness to enter the world view of the client or student with empathy skills, listening skills, attending skills, and inquiry skills. However, above all, it emphasizes action. For decades Black Americans have been listened to and sympathized with. Still, many continue to underutilize mental health services. When the principles of reality therapy are understood and used they become a liberating force.

In describing how reality therapy applies to African-American families, Mickel and Liddie (1998) discussed the importance of appreciating the struggle for empowerment. They stated, "Those who would promote hopelessness and failure are not in tune with the principles that uplift" (p. 32).

Without being specific, Mickel and Liddie (1998) added that the traditional values of the African-American family need to be incorporated into therapy. Another element in the therapist's repertoire of skills is the timing of interventions coupled with client readiness. Change occurs when the family judges it is ready to make better choices.

Michel and Liddie (1998) concluded by presenting a preeminent quality of the therapist: the expectation of change. "Recommitment to our highest ideals, the human personality, and the African-centered matrix provide the foundation for a self-fulfilling prophecy. The self-fulfilling prophecy posits that African-centered prevention and intervention under reality therapy/choice theory is a viable alternative for those who wish to consider a different way to work with families" (p. 32).

Okonji et al. (1996), even more decidedly, found that African-American males preferred more directive approaches to counseling rather than person-centered ones. Not only does the counselor's ethnicity play an important role, but the counselor's style is crucial. The authors concluded, "If agencies or counseling programs need to train people to serve ethnic minority clients, they need to consider various treatment modalities, especially directive approaches such as reality therapy" (p. 337).

☐ Native Americans

Many persons who find reality therapy especially useful are Western Hemisphere Indians. I use the latter term because it is a general term and easily understood. But in an effort to use words economically there is a danger of superficially generalizing and "lumping together." Sowell (1998) states, "the various indigenous peoples of the Western Hemisphere have been no more alike in their economic, cultural, military, or other achievements than the various peoples of Europe, Asia, or Africa have been" (p. 249).

In order to fully understand any culture it is crucial to realize that cultures borrow and adapt customs from other groups. Europeans could cross the ocean because they could steer with rudders, which the Chinese invented. They could navigate and calculate because of an invention from Egypt, trigonometry. Their numbers, and ours, were developed in India. North American Indians, that is, Native Americans and First Nation, in turn, used the pack and draft animals introduced to them by Europeans to transport grain. The exchange of diseases with Europeans and the relegation through conquest to a vast system of segregation have also impacted North American Indian culture. In spite of many adversities the North American Indians have retained a deep sense of the spiritual, a respect for nature, a high valuing of relationships, and a sense of personal responsibility to each other. In training workshops they relate that choice theory and reality therapy fit with their cultural values.

As with most counseling theories, much remains to be done in determining the best ways to create reciprocity between the cultural values and the principles of reality therapy. Nevertheless, some suggestions can be presented.

Baca (1996) emphasized the importance of incorporating the native folklore in working with Navajos. He stated, "It appears as though folklore may be helpful in educating young people. As professionals, we must consider incorporating these legends with our current curricula *to break through cultural barriers*" (p. 44).

Furthermore, Matthews (1996) asserted that the use of reality therapy is enriched by incorporating other techniques used by Native Americans, such as medicine cards depicting animals that are ascribed medicinal powers. The medicine cards were developed from the legends of several tribes. Matthews believes these can be used to help clients identify their needs and clarify their wants. She stated, "The cards can be used to help establish goals in therapy by asking clients to select a card that depicts their current total behavior and one that represents how they would like to behave after therapy" (p. 48).

It is my belief that it is not possible for teachers, therapists, or helpers to enter their clients' worlds completely. Learning about their clients' history, values, and behaviors, however, enables them to use choice theory and the WDEP system of reality therapy more empathically and effectively. This is accomplished by study, listening, consultation, and supervision.

☐ Puerto Ricans

Miguel Arrieta Morales (1995) described how reality therapy is an exceptionally workable and effective model for use with Puerto Ricans. He stated that when using any psychotherapy model three considerations are crucial:

1. Knowing the theory and practice of the selected theory.
2. Preferring to use the specific model over other models.
3. Understanding the cultural context in which the model is used.

The above suggestions can be generalized for use with any culture—as is seen in this chapter, reality therapy can be adapted for use in virtually any culture.

Highlights of Puerto Rican Culture

As with any discussion of culture and as emphasized here, it is helpful to outline several characteristics of the culture. Still, this description should not be interpreted to mean that every person can be expected to fit perfectly under these generalizations. Each individual is unique and is treated as such in using reality therapy effectively. In his description of the "outstanding characteristics which allow a better idea about our frame of reference" (p. 12), Morales (1995) included the following.

- *Responsibility in obligation to others.* Duty is an important value in Puerto Rican culture. It implies a relationship between two people. A person carries a sense of obligation toward children, supervisors, relatives, parents, and spouse. When these obligations are not fulfilled, a person is seen as acting against an ethical code and thus often feels guilt. Unlike the prevalent view in North America that guilt is unhealthy, Puerto Ricans often see it as an indication that a person possesses an ethical code. Pride and a sense of dignity are consequences of keeping an ethical code.
- *Expectation that problems will be solved quickly.* There is an urgency to resolve painful situations and move onward. Morales (1995) stated, "Our accomplishments as a people consists in obtaining results as soon as possible" (p. 13).
- *Identification with the disadvantaged.* Words like *bendito* (blessed) are used to imply compassion for the less fortunate. Gratitude is a related characteristic and leads to altruism, especially when there are emergencies or disasters. People forget about barriers and embrace a common cause. Connected with this generosity is a self-effacement or reluctance to brag about contributing to the welfare of others.
- *Conservativism in decision making.* According to Morales (1995) taking risks is a matter for serious consideration. He noted that a commonly used phrase is, "It is better to have a known evil than an evil to be known." This approach to life has served the people of Puerto Rico very well. He stated, "There has been dramatic development in the arts, culture, economy, literature and education" (p. 14). Forty years ago malnutrition, poverty, and illiteracy were widespread. Today much progress has been made to address these issues because of a deliberate decision-making process. The attitudes accompanying this hesitancy to take risks have provided stability and a steady social structure.
- *Loyalty.* Letting people down is a source of guilt and shame. The opposite, loyalty and hospitality, are positive expressions of healthy interpersonal relationships. This characteristic has been weakened to some extent with increased urbanization, but it is still strong. While there is some personal payoff that is desired, still, "loyalty goes far beyond self-benefit. Loyalty at work, with family and with others is of such importance that it can entail the sacrifice of individual aspirations. In a matter of loyalty, the individual interests are put aside, many times not even to be considered later" (Morales, 1995, p. 14).

These characteristics of Puerto Rican culture provide a backdrop crucial to the effective adaptation of reality therapy.

Negative Side of Culture

Unlike much of the multicultural literature, Morales (1995) has the audacity (i.e., courage) to point out the limitations of his own culture. In my opinion, such willingness elevates him as a person as well as a professional. Moreover, the culture of the people of Puerto Rico is so strong that it can endure and even welcome an exposition of its limitations.

- *Seeing duties as absolute.* Some clients act like slaves or prisoners to their roles when, in fact, they are able to make choices. Wives, sometimes blindly loyal to their husbands when they are irresponsible and even abusive, feel obligated to fulfill the duties of a wife. They even ask the counselor what they can do to help their dictatorial husband. Similarly, parents are sometimes overly protective of their children. Employees are overly faithful to their employers and are often hesitant to offer opinions even when asked.
- *Quick decision making based on insufficient evaluation.* While rapid decision making is sometimes necessary, as in times of natural disaster, "working as if there were emergencies all the time tends not to produce optimal decisions" (Morales, 1995, p. 16). Some clients make their lives worse by what can be described as impetuous and hasty decisions.
- *Overidentification with others.* While empathy is a strength, especially for therapists, too much of it can lead to a failure to work on one's own identity. Excessive solidarity with others leads to blind loyalty and loss of one's own autonomy.
- *Missed opportunities.* Because of an excessive conservatism in making decisions, possible achievements are not seen. Self-evaluation is the cornerstone of reality therapy. With this in mind, Morales (1995) stated, "sometimes we are so mindful of what we have that we miss the opportunity to have better things. Avoiding the risk of losing what we have, we pay the cost in opportunities lost." (p. 17.)

In general, people sometimes feel responsible for others to an excessive degree and believe that assertiveness can hurt another person. But persons asserting themselves need not feel responsible for the hurt feelings of others. A child leaving home to study need not feel guilty for the intense pain felt by parents.

Responsibility is a strong characteristic of the Puerto Rican culture and worthy of imitation. But like many cultural characteristics, it has a down side to it. Similarly, individual responsibility, a characteristic of the Euro-American civilization and a genuine contribution, can be carried to the extreme of rugged selfishness, which ignores the rights of others as well as social responsibility. Clearly, every culture has its strengths and limitations as seen through the perceptual lens of another culture.

Characteristics of Reality Therapy

Several aspects of reality therapy render it appealing to Puerto Ricans: it is short term and results driven, respectful of clients' dignity, clear and precise in problem definition, and appropriate in the placement of responsibility, that is, effective in dealing with excuses.

- *Brevity.* Clients prefer to solve problems quickly. In fact if they do not see results in the first several sessions they are inclined to terminate counseling. Reality therapy, formerly criticized for being a short-term therapy, is quite in the mainstream not only in Puerto Rico but also in mainland North America. If practiced properly, each session contains specific plans geared to the individual client.

- *Dignity of client.* Working in harmony with client goals and helping them gain what they want has always been a cornerstone of reality therapy. Assisting clients to define their own problems and evaluate *their own* behavior is an implicit and often explicit way to demonstrate respect for clients and for their ability to determine a better life direction.
- *Inner responsibility.* One aspect of the Puerto Rican culture, according to Morales (1995), is a deep sense of responsibility. The refusal of the practitioner to encourage excuses leads to increased pride in clients' successes. Morales stated, "When people see themselves as responsible for their actions . . . they stop paying attention to the casual opinions of others and evaluate what has been wrong (ineffective) about their own actions" (p. 6).

    Another cultural characteristic related to inner responsibility is the tendency to identify with the afflictions of others. This can even result in the hesitancy to discuss one's own accomplishments, which might be seen as bragging. Consequently, the user of reality therapy is well advised to be careful in discussing the positive attributes of clients.

In summary, as Morales (1995) noted, "All the elements found in reality therapy make it very adequate for work in Puerto Rico" (p. 6).

☐ Ethical Considerations

The use of reality therapy in a cross-cultural setting is subject to the principles of ethics that are standard practice and that are described in the codes of ethics of professional organizations. Users of reality therapy are cognizant of issues involved with informed consent, conflict of interest, dual relationships, respect for diversity, confidentiality, duty to warn, record keeping, and others. Still, there are ethical issues that pertain specifically to reality therapy. These are outlined in an article by authors from 10 countries (Wubbolding et al., 1998), which I will quote here:

1. The practice of reality therapy is used most effectively and ethically in a multicultural setting when it is *adapted* to the client or student.
2. Because of this need for adaptation, reality therapy should not be seen as a monolithic system that is applied in the same way to everyone or to every culture.
3. The skill in adaptation requires sensitivity on the part of the helper, i.e. understanding of *more* than choice theory and the practice of reality therapy. It requires understanding and appreciation of the client's world view.
4. Teachers and users of choice theory and reality therapy are advised to examine their own attitudes, knowledge and skills with a view to learning more about how other cultures impact the quality worlds, perceptions and behaviors of individuals.
5. Commentators on the application of reality therapy need to understand that the theory is adaptable and flexible. They need to know enough about the theory to understand the openness of the system as well as the universality of its applications." (p. 6)

Based on human nature itself, choice theory explains all human behavior. It is therefore not culture specific. All human beings have five inner motivators. They have an inner quality world of specific desires, core beliefs, and mental images of what is important. They choose behaviors and seek perceptions or informational input from the world. The theory thus can be used by peoples of all cultures. As Maya Angelou has said many times, "We are more alike than we are unalike." Similarly, in a 1998 program at Cincinnati's Xavier University entitled "Justice and Race," Ilyas S. Nashid (1998), the Imam of the Cincinnati Islamic Center, stated, "Our human identity must become more sacred than our racial or ethnic identities." He said that we are rapidly developing as we were divinely ordained to do. We are "one human community in the beginning and one human community in the end." Along that same line, Jocelyn Elders said, "We're all just people. We all have red blood flowing in our veins" (DeRosa, 1995).

The specifics of content contained in the quality world are determined by a person's interaction with the external world. And the external world is limited by the culture in which a person lives. Consequently, the content of the quality world is circumscribed by the cultural environment in which a person is raised. The chosen behaviors are also limited to what have been found to be effective. Of course, there can be exceptions to this general principle, as when people spontaneously create new behaviors that they have never perceived in their cultural environment. These exceptions are important and can be encouraged, but generally people choose behaviors that are within the boundaries of their culture. The specifics of the quality world, the behavioral choices, and the informational input or perceptions are culture specific.

It is clear that the use of reality therapy, the delivery system for choice theory, is altered when it is used and taught in multicultural settings. The reason the principles can be adapted is that they are universal. Furthermore, if counselors, therapists, educators, trainers, parents, or managers are to be effective, they need to be aware of their own knowledge, skills, and values as well as how to bridge the divide that exists between them and persons who have backgrounds different from their own. They are well advised to familiarize themselves as much as possible with the history, communication styles, sociopolitical influences and customs that make up the intricate fabrics of other cultures.

Reality therapy offers a model based on establishing an environment characterized by empathy and regard. Part of this is to recognize the systemic origin of pathology and maladjustments. Furthermore, the WDEP system of interventions is based on the principle that no matter what the oppression has been, there are still choices available to any client. The past need not determine the future. In the words of Ashley Montague, "Heredity is not predestination." To focus on the negative, whether it is a personal deficit, a systemic limitation, or a psychological assault from the environment, is another subtle way to prevent self-actualization and effective need-satisfaction. Vanquishing the downward pull of such negatives are the strategies of helping clients identify their wants, examine and evaluate their own behaviors, formulate a relentless sense of determination, and learn specific tactics for getting what they want.

Rocketing into the fast moving, computerized, globalized world of the 21st century requires specialized and finely tuned skills to balance the centrifugal forces that tear apart human relationships. And yet, close interactional relationships focusing on enhanced belonging facilitate the need-satisfaction of human beings and the deepest yearnings in the human soul. The mental health professional, the educator, the parent, the manager, the clergy, and the salesperson stand at the helm of the *relation*SHIP carrying us into the 21st century.

Research Studies:
How Do I Know It Works?

In my opinion, there are two kinds of research: cerebral research and fire-in-the-belly research. The former consists of the many scientific studies on any topic or discipline on the premise that the proponents of any theory are accountable to the extent that they can demonstrate and validate their system empirically. This chapter contains a summary of several such studies that validate the effectiveness of reality therapy. One of the criticisms of reality therapy has been the alleged absence of a legitimate research base. This chapter demonstrates how groundless this objection is in the light of the many studies illustrating the effectiveness of reality therapy in a variety of settings. We can never have too many valid and reliable outcome studies documenting the usefulness of reality therapy. No one would deny the usefulness of more such research. Even if we had 1,000 studies, we would work to produce the 1,001st.

Many theories and practices have amassed a solid research base to justify their use. The kind of research that will lead you, the reader, to embrace the principles and techniques of reality therapy is not scientific empiricism. The most persuasive documentation is the fire-in-the-belly research. To give the flavor of the passionate purpose that this kind of research can serve, I have for many years, made the following suggestions to audiences:

> Use these ideas in your own lives first. If these methods do not work for you, don't apply the techniques to other people. If, on the other hand, they favorably impact your own lives and those of your family, you will become convinced that clients, students, employees, and others will benefit in the same way.

As the Director of Training of The William Glasser Institute since 1987, I have had ample opportunities, along with Linda Harshman, the institute administrator, to observe the personal use of reality therapy as demonstrated by trainees in the certification process. However, such an assertion is, of course, unproven and so, to move this discussion past the anecdotal, I present the following summaries of research studies.

In all research related to helping people improve their lives the question remains: What exactly is the object of the investigation, the theory and practice of a particular orientation, the relationship between a helper and a subject, the attention and nurturance a client receives, the placebo effect, or some other target? What role does the halo effect or the Hawthorne effect play?

In this age of accountability, justifying professional behavior and decisions is crucial. A basic principle of ethics is *standard practice*, that is, the common level of service that members of the various professions provide. Each profession also has a code of ethics, which members adhere to if they are to remain in good standing. Moreover, licensing laws are designed to move professional behavior to a higher level of accountability and liability.

For the purpose of accountability, therefore, an indispensable requirement is to follow scientific procedures in validating the delivery system used in a particular therapy. The body of research that points to the efficacy of using cognitive-behavioral protocols with various topics is continually expanding. This chapter, therefore, contains a sampling of research studies conducted on various aspects of reality therapy, for example, applications to schools, addictions, multiculturalism and self-concept, and many other topics.

The need for research in reality therapy is a theme that I have emphasized for a decade. Research is now increasing on the underlying principles of choice theory and the importance and efficacy of the helping relationship. The research citations below show how reality therapy applies to many problems and issues as well as to a variety of settings. A general critique of these studies appears at the end of the chapter.

☐ Relationship Research

At the heart of effective reality therapy is the ability of a therapist to connect with one or more clients and to lead them to self-evaluate and make plans to fulfill their needs through effective, assertive, or altruistic behaviors. Through the eyes of the reality therapy practitioner, most psychological problems have roots in dysfunctional relationships.

The same principle applies to education. When students feel connected to a school and to their teachers, change takes place, as is evident from the results achieved in the first Glasserian quality school in Wyoming, Michigan (Ludwig & Mentley, 1997). Although more research on the quality school movement would be useful, the impact of healthy relationships can hardly be denied.

Relationships and Health

In the health professions the importance of the relationship between provider and patient has emerged in the past 20 years. Cousins (1979) believed that a major part of his recovery from a rare terminal disease was due to his relationship with his physician. Dean Ornish, MD (1998), founder of the Preventive Medicine Research Institute in Sausalito, California stated that "love and intimacy are at the root of what makes us sick and what makes us well, what causes sadness and what bring happiness, what makes us suffer and what leads to healing" (p. 3). He adds:

> That which seems the most soft—love, intimacy, and meaning—is, in reality, the most powerful. . . . There is a deep spiritual hunger in this country as we approach the end of the twentieth century and the beginning of a new millennium. There has been a radical

shift in our society in the past fifty years, and we are only now beginning to appreciate what that really means. (p. 12)

Ornish substantiates his premise that smart nutrition is not enough with an abundance of research studies demonstrating that loving and caring relationships enhance our immune system and help us resist disease. In the "Roseto study," for example, people with a strong sense of involvement with the community had two to five times less risk of premature death than those who were socially isolated! A study at the University of Texas showed that "those who neither had regular group participation nor drew strength and comfort from their religion were more than seven times more likely to die six months after surgery" (p. 51).

Ornish summarized studies related to the harmful effects of hostility, depression, and marital conflict, as well as the salutary effects of support groups, the importance of therapeutic touch, and related experiences that contribute to people's sense of belonging and acceptance.

Showing how universal these findings are, he commented on the multicultural nature of the power of love, stating, "there is a strong scientific basis documenting that these ideas matter across all ages from infants to the most elderly, in all parts of the world in all strata of life" (p. 71).

In summary, Ornish offers a scientific database that points to the pervasive benefit of professional persons connecting with their clients. Even more important than this professional relationship is the significant value of helping clients work first, foremost, and consistently on their relationships with their families, friends, confidants, and community.

☐ Human Needs

Deci (1995) has provided a research base for Glasser's system of needs in choice theory and reality therapy. Deci wrote that all the work that he and his associates have done "indicates that self-motivation, rather than external motivation, is at the heart of creativity, responsibility, healthy behavior, and lasting change" (p. 9). In one of his studies, one group of students worked on puzzles for monetary gain while another did the same work for no extrinsic reward. When the experimenter left the room between segments of assigned work, the students who were working "just for the fun of it" continued to work, while the group going for money was less likely to continue to work. "Stop the pay, stop the play" was Deci's conclusion (pp. 24–25).

More significantly, Deci (1995) highlights the notion of "autonomy support." Teachers and parents are well advised to lessen efforts to manipulate students and children by external rewards and punishments. "Autonomy support means to relate to others— our children, students, and employees—as human beings, as *active* agents who are worthy of support, rather than as *objects* to be manipulated for our own gratification" (p. 100). He furthermore emphasized, "The 'rewards' linked to intrinsic motivation are the feelings of enjoyment and accomplishment that accrue spontaneously as a person engages freely in target activities" (p. 64).

People often ask, "Are the needs complimentary or at odds with one another?" Peterson, Woodward, and Kissko (1991) found that reality therapy trainees judged that a positive correlation existed in need-fulfillment between belonging and fun (r = .29) and freedom and fun (r = .21). On the other hand, they saw a negative correlation between belonging and power ($r = -.09$) and between power and freedom ($r = -.13$).

To some extent the participants in this study reported that fulfilling their power needs meant not fulfilling their other needs. The correlations in these self-reports, however, are weak, and the definition of "needs" might differ slightly from the definition presented in this book.

☐ Addictions

Honeyman (1990) investigated the effects of reality therapy treatment on addicts by inventorying the clients' self-perceptions upon admission to treatment and at the 2nd, 4th, and 6th weeks. Some of the significant changes addicts noted in perceptions of themselves are listed here:

1. Increased sense of self-esteem as a result of what they claimed was a consciousness of their own power.
2. Heightened awareness that they were taking more responsibility for their behavior.
3. Deeper conviction that they were unable to control their drinking if they were to rely on their old thinking and previous choices.
4. Learning to relate to others in altruistic ways rather than exploitive ways.
5. Greater awareness of what being "an addict" means.
6. Realization of the importance of making a "higher power" a reality.

Honeyman (1990) concluded, "As a measure of concurrent validity, the Minnesota Multiphasic Personality Inventory (MMPI) profiles of the 24 clients . . . showed a general reduction in (negative) symptom behavior indicating that clients are in more control of their lives at the time of discharge" (p. 58).

☐ Drug Use in Prison

Chance et al., (1990), studied the effects of using reality therapy with 20 drug-using prison residents. The study sample accurately represented the ethnic mixture of the general prison population. A control group was part of this 30-week investigation.

Results

The overall measure of inmate responses on a Likert-type instrument were significant at the .05 level on one item only, reflecting an added resolve to refrain from drug use and to speak out publicly against drugs. The researchers added, "an analysis of the mean responses indicates incremental and consistent positive change in the inmate self perceptions" (Chance et al., p. 37). Perhaps the most important finding, although not statistically significant, was the fact that 15 inmates remained free of drug abuse "for an extended period of time" (p. 37). The researchers expected that the program would become a model for use with other prisoners.

Conclusion

Although the limited results showed some change in behavior, the need to refine and improve the program and thereby measure results more precisely was evident. Still, the overall direction of the prisoners' self-evaluations and the program evaluations demonstrated that reality therapy can be a powerful tool with prison inmates who have entrenched themselves in a rigid pattern of ineffective behaviors.

☐ Group Therapy: Substance Abusers

In a study covering the very brief time of 1 month, Wesley (1988) found that nine 1-hour sessions of reality therapy with male and female co-therapists made important differences for deinstitutionalized substance abusers labelled chronically mentally ill and commonly known as persons with a dual diagnosis. The significance of the study is the possible interest it carries to communities; a limitation of the study was the 1-month duration.

☐ Juvenile Offenders: Recidivism

Bean (1988) studied the effect of reality therapy on the recidivism rate of 72 juvenile offenders, ages 14 to 17. After examining the technical dispositions of the juvenile court the researcher used a 4×2 chi square analysis and a probability table that showed a significant decrease in the recidivism rate of the reality therapy group compared with the other groups.

☐ Domestic Violence

In evaluating a domestic violence program, Rachor (1995) used self-reports from both men and women. Flawed by inadequate controls as well as participants underreporting their domestic violence, the study still showed notable results. Comparable studies cited by Rachor indicated that treatment programs seldom made any difference in recidivism, while other studies indicated modest decreases in violence.

The Program

Men and women participated in a 21-session program, subdivided into two phases, with each session lasting 2½ hours in length. The first phase dealt with the application of control theory (choice theory) and reality therapy to domestic violence as well as the roots of domestic violence, cycles of violence, and related topics. The second phase consisted in applying the techniques to the family as a unit, to help children, for example, develop an internal locus of control and to encourage all family members to spend quality time in relationships.

Methodology

This survey research included 45 clients (23 females and 22 males), selected randomly, who answered open-ended questions through telephone interviews conducted by trained volunteers. The answers were analyzed and grouped under descriptive headings.

Results

Two-thirds of the males reported they learned better self-control and 40% of the women indicated increased self-confidence and self-esteem and the ability to relinquish attempts to control others. Continued threats of violence were reported by only 17% of females, including 13% indicating multiple acts of violence.

☐ Corrections: Yugoslavia

Lojk (1986) summarized an impressive study conducted while managing a reality therapy program in Visnja Gora, Yugoslavia, when that country was still socialist and nonaligned. Follow-up studies of former residents of the program took place over a 12-year period.

Results

The results showed almost complete resocialization, meaning rehabilitation, for 69% of former prison residents, plus partial success for 15%. The remaining 16% of former residents were either not rehabilitated or could not be contacted by the investigator. Lojk (1986) stated:

> We felt these results were very promising. Unfortunately, some influential people didn't share our opinion. They were very skeptical about the sincerity of the social workers who gathered the data for the follow up study, and about our objectivity. The skeptics acknowledged that the released residents were no longer stealing; they had abandoned promiscuity; they were earning money for themselves and their children; they didn't change jobs more often than usual; they had no trouble with the police; and they didn't need any psychological or psychiatric help. However, the skeptics challenged the results and methodology of our study with the following arguments and questions: "The former residents seem O.K. but who knows?" "Are they internally happy?" "Could it mean that these methods of correction had broken their will for life?" Here you can see major misunderstandings about total behavior. (p. 30)

☐ Humor

Thomson (1990) studied those certified in reality therapy and their perceptions of the role of humor in psychotherapy. Although not designed to assess the effectiveness of reality therapy, this study appears here because the purpose was to measure how people highly trained in reality therapy viewed behaviors related to one of the five innate needs: fun or enjoyment.

Using the delphi method, which is a consensus-building technique with a panel of experts, Thomson (1990) used a group of 56 participants and found the following. The therapeutic relationship is crucial if humor is to be helpful. Humor should be spontaneous by the therapist and comfortable for the client. It also helps clients change their perceptions of their life situations from unmanageable to more manageable.

Alternatively, humor can be inappropriate, such as taking the form of criticism, put downs, ridicule, and humor that exceeds a client's level of understanding.

Thomson (1990) stated that the consensus among the experts on the panel was that therapists should use humor with caution. Therapists should evaluate the appropriateness of humor and not assume that all humor is useful. Finally, discussing the purpose of humor with clients may be fitting at times.

☐ Depression

Another single-subject case study illustrates the effectiveness of reality therapy with a female college student who presented with depression and a failed suicide attempt. Ingram and Hinkle (1990) suggested reality therapy for her because of the emphasis on individual characteristics rather than on group characteristics. Depressed and discouraged about a job hunt as a legal assistant, the client became depressed, felt hopeless, and attempted suicide.

She received treatment weekly for 8 weeks from a counselor certified in reality therapy. The researchers administered the Beck Depression Inventory (BDI) and established a "multiple baseline cross behaviors design" to measure the number of job information interviews she had as well as the number of times she interacted with friends.

The design showed that when she conducted interviews and interacted with her friends she was able to relinquish the depressing behaviors. Additionally, she began reading articles about careers in the legal field and developed new hobbies. Most significantly, her scale on the BDI dropped from a score of 36 on the initial administration to a score of 8 on the final administration. Moreover, her freedom from depression remained consistent, as indicated in follow-up sessions 1 and 2 months after termination.

☐ Arthritis

Maisiak, Austin, and Heck (1995) studied "the effects of treatment counseling or symptom monitoring telephone intervention strategies on the health outcomes of patients with rheumatoid arthritis or osteoarthritis compared with usual care" (p. 1391). The method included a three-group randomized, controlled 9-month trial with 405 patients.

Methodology

Using the Arthritis Impact Measurement Scales (AIMS2), an analysis of covariance (ANCOVA) showed that the total health status of the treatment group improved at a significance level of $P < 0.01$.

Results

Reality therapy was selected as the counseling model because of its priority on changing actions first rather than aiming at changes in emotion or cognition as a starting point.

More specifically, the overall improvement of health was reflected in fewer visits to the physician, less disability, increased ability to cope well with chronic pain, and improved physical functioning.

As an example of highly controlled research, this study is extremely important because it demonstrates both the physiological and psychological impact of the skillful use of reality therapy.

☐ Maintaining Exercise Program

Watson and Fetter (1994) studied the efficacy of reality therapy for initiating exercise and complying with an exercise regimen. Eleven people volunteered to participate in the study and 8 completed the program.

Methodology

After the screening phase, the clients clarified their wants and made their plans for the program. Follow-up sessions occurred once every week for 6 months. During these sessions the clients conducted their own self-evaluation to determine their progress in reaching their goals. At the end of 6 months came a final session during which the clients evaluated the entire program. Another 3-month follow-up showed the degree of continued compliance.

Results

The 8 people completing the study continued to exercise at the end of 6 months. More specifically:

- Five reached their goals very well.
- Two stated that though they did not reach 100% of their goals, they did more than they would have on their own and said that exercise was now a part of their daily routine.
- One person stated that she had reached half of her goals.

Watson and Fetter (1994) stated:

All eight people felt that participating in the study helped them work toward their goals and that meeting and reporting on a weekly basis helped them to comply with their plans. All eight people had made some lifestyle changes. Six stated that they have incorporated exercise as a regular part of their routine. Other changes related to increased energy levels, stopping smoking, getting up earlier, a more balanced life, feeling better in general, improved eating habits, being able to make a plan and carry it through, and having a better attitude toward work. (p. 83)

Three-Month Follow-Up

The follow-up survey showed that the six respondents' level of exercise was adequate but less than the target goal they had originally set. The following statements represent their self-evaluations.

- "Exceeded physiological goals and raised activity level."
- "Never felt better; more energy; lost 10–12 lbs; more to lose to reach goals."
- "I have been successful and now realize if I put my mind to something, I can achieve. Seeing others accomplish their goals encouraged me to succeed."
- "My endurance has increased and I exercise at least 3 times a week."
- "I have done well. Before this study I didn't exercise at all; the study pushed me to work toward goals."
- "I am getting closer to my exercise goals." (p. 84)

Conclusion

Watson and Fetter (1994) concluded that choice theory and reality therapy are useful in helping people develop and maintain a program of exercise. The regular meetings provided support and encouragement as well as facilitating a sense of accountability. Even more, by clarifying their wants and examining and evaluating their behavior, they helped themselves follow through on a program that satisfied their needs for belonging, power, fun, and freedom.

☐ Measuring Instruments

The entire system of choice theory and the method of counseling that flows from this internal control psychology, reality therapy, depends on self-evaluation. Assessing the intensity of one's needs and other aspects of choice theory is fundamentally dependent on subjective self-reporting. Peterson and Parr (1982) developed "Pete's Pathogram" to give clients and students a graphic way to discuss their motivations. Harvey and Retter (1995) developed *The Basic Needs Survey*, "which compares the relative strength of each of the four basic psychological needs" (p. 76). The purpose is to enhance interviews and to lessen the necessity for long psychological assessments for children in grades 4 through 6. In their use of the instrument, the authors found that children almost always misbehave in a failed attempt to gain power or to satisfy their other needs.

Glasser (1995) has described need profiles couples may use to pinpoint areas of mutual compatibility and incompatibility, but offered no empirical data validating the congruence or incongruence of these profiles.

Using Galindo's (1990) psychological needs assessment survey, Miranda (1998) developed and refined a pictures inventory adapted for Spanish people for determining the degree to which each need is satisfied.

Counselors use these various scales in group work with people who are learning reality therapy and to stimulate discussion in counseling.

☐ Self-Concept

Block (1994) investigated the effectiveness of reality therapy in small sessions with fifth- and sixth-grade students. Using a control group, the Piers-Harris Children's Self Concept Scale, and a one-way analysis of variance (ANOVA) to detect differences between pre- and posttests, the researchers found that reality therapy was effective in increasing the overall level of students' self-concepts.

☐ Self-Esteem and Perceived Locus Of Control

Harris (1995) studied the effects of reality therapy on the predictors of responsible behavior in high school students. The experimental group received reality therapy counseling as part of an adolescent pregnancy prevention program, resulting in a significant increase in self-esteem and statistically insignificant increases in their perceived locus of control. Most important to the investigator, the subjects learned to distinguish between responsible and irresponsible behaviors. The participants' subjective self-evaluations revealed that reality therapy had helped them make more effective choices.

☐ Effects of Training in Reality Therapy

Cullinane (1995) investigated the impact of reality therapy training on educators' perceptions of change, relationships, and self-reflection. All subjects, ranging in age from 29 to 54, had completed 1 week of training, with some completing the 18-month certification program.

Using interviews and open-ended questionnaires, the investigator found that they increased their self-confidence, self-reflective skills, ability to communicate satisfactorily, and awareness of their own and others' needs. She added, "Their handling of conflict in their personal and professional relationships was positively influenced by the training" (Cullinane, p. 3546). Of special interest is the fact that the training influenced women more than men.

☐ Minority Groups

Study on Quality School Principles

Edens and Smryl (1994) conducted a significant study over a 6-week block of time on disruptive classroom behaviors. The researchers stated, "The purpose of this study was to assess the effects of Glasser's quality school principles and the use of reality therapy as a means of reducing disruptive behaviors in a middle school physical education class" (p. 40).

Population.   Of special interest in the Edens and Smryl (1994) study is the fact that the population of the school consisted of 583 Blacks (50%), 496 Whites (42%), 61 Hispanics (5%), 30 Asians (2.5%), and 4 Indians (.3%), totalling 1,174 students. The population by gender was almost evenly split, with 568 females (48%) and 606 males (52%). The study's sample was a seventh-grade class of 22 White, 19 Black, and 1 Hispanic students, of whom 26 were female and 16 were male.

Methodology.   Using the Disruptive Classroom Behavior Assessment (DCBI), developed by the researchers, coders recorded the behavioral specifics of students' disruptive incidents. Students responded to a poll of their choices of activities in their physical education curriculum. Notably, 26% of the students stated at the outset that they did not enjoy physical education because the time to get ready for the class and to change clothes again afterwards was too short.

Use of Control (Choice) Theory and Reality Therapy. To encourage the students to start playing and exercising as quickly as possible, they were assured more responsibility by dividing themselves into triads, a more convenient structure for engaging in discussions and carrying out other functions. They also formed teams based on their own choices within a guideline that skill levels should be more or less equal. The rationale for these logistics was that young people who have control over environmental and social conditions meet their needs more effectively, and they are more likely to cooperate and to steer clear of antisocial behaviors.

Additionally, as an integrated part of the physical education curriculum, they were taught the concepts of choice theory. Reality therapy was used to counsel the students whenever they demonstrated misbehavior. They were either counseled immediately or after they sat out an activity until an instructor could speak with them.

Another key element was the opportunity to join in class meetings to discuss choice theory using worksheets containing hypothetical incidents, such as situations they might face in real life and a range of actions and thoughts they might choose under certain conditions.

Results. The recorders noted a total of 61 behavioral incidents during the time frame: Week I: 31; Week II: 11; Week III: 8; Week IV; 7. The authors stated, "The total for the last week was only three until the last day when four more were recorded" (Edens & Smryl, 1994, p. 43), perhaps as one or two practical jokers rushed to get in a last hurrah!

Conclusion. Clearly, teaching choice theory and using reality therapy have salutary effects on students' behavior. As the authors stated, "Using quality school concepts entrusts students to make appropriate behavioral choices. When 'ownership' of one's class is a part of the class structure, middle school students respond favorably. They learn more, have more fun, and disruptive classroom behaviors decline" (Edens & Smryl, 1994, p. 44).

African Americans

Okonji (1995) investigated counseling styles by comparing reality therapy and person-centered therapy, as these two methods relate to African-American male students in a Job Corps setting. Results relevant to reality therapy indicated a statistically significant difference between reality therapy and person-centered therapy. African-American males preferred counselors who used reality therapy.

Asian Students: Locus of Control

Peterson, Chang, and Collins (1997) studied the relationship between reality therapy in groups and the locus of control that Taiwanese college students exhibited.

Methodology. Using a pre- and posttest design, researchers measured the locus of control of 217 undergraduate students from various universities in Taiwan. Subjects received a random assignment to a counseling group, a teaching group, or a control group that received no treatment. The teaching group studied and applied choice theory for 8 weeks, while the counseling group received 2 hours of reality therapy in a group setting once per week for 8 weeks.

Results. Using sophisticated statistical protocols, including ANCOVA, Peterson, Chang, and Collins (1997) found that the control group was significantly higher on perceived external locus of control, while both treatment groups scored significantly lower on scores related to external locus of control. No significant differences emerged between the treatment groups. Additionally, no differences appeared regarding the effect of gender. The authors raised questions for possible future research beginning with the idea of combining teaching choice theory with counseling using reality therapy as possibly the most effective way to increase college students' internal locus of control This study also demonstrates the effectiveness of reality therapy with Asian subjects. But the authors cautioned that further study on this topic was necessary. They stated, "cultural backgrounds and values are also important considerations to be acknowledged when working with college age students" (p. 86).

In my opinion, group size could have been a factor limiting the findings along with the fact that internal locus of control is a relatively stable variable and changes do not occur swiftly, as in IQ and personality test results.

☐ Asian Students: Impact of Choice Theory and Reality Therapy on Need-Satisfaction

Peterson, Chang, and Collins (1998) studied the impact of choice theory and reality therapy on the need-satisfaction of 217 undergraduate college students in four universities in Taiwan.

Methodology

The researchers used Pete's Pathogram, which was originally developed as a clinical tool but has evolved into a highly intricate research instrument. "The pathogram is utilized to compare the profiles in regard to perceived need, time invested, and success achieved for each psychological need" (Peterson, Chang, & Collins, 1998, p. 27). The authors describe a "2 × 3 factorial design with gender (male/female) and treatment (reality therapy counseling group, choice theory teaching group, and a control group) constituting the independent variables" (p. 28). Pre- and posttests were administered and data were analyzed using an ANCOVA and other statistical tools.

Results and Conclusions

The results showed significant increase in need-satisfaction of the four psychological needs by those in the counseling and teaching groups. These group sessions also had a greater impact on females than males regarding the need for belonging. The need for power was more enhanced for males in the teaching group than in the counseling group. Women, on the other hand, gained more than men from the treatment groups in both freedom and fun.

Peterson, Chang, and Collins (1998) concluded that the counseling and the teaching of reality therapy and choice theory is effective with university students in Taiwan seeking to satisfy their needs. They recommended that counseling and teaching choice theory and reality therapy be combined for maximum benefit.

☐ Delinquency: Hong Kong

Miranda Chung (1994), a professor of social work in the Chinese University of Hong Kong, investigated the effect of reality therapy in group counseling with juvenile delinquents in Hong Kong. She selected reality therapy because the method offers a framework for working with a delinquent population that generally demonstrates not only socially unacceptable behaviors but also low self-esteem. Due to these destructive choices and negative behavioral patterns, the delinquent youth are typically impenetrable to counseling.

Chung (1994) studied residents of two correctional institutions, one a local governmental operation and the other a nongovernmental welfare agency. She limited her study to youths on schedule for release within 3 to 6 months. The mean age of the sample participants was 13.5 years. The experimental group had 3 months (12 weekly sessions) of exposure to reality therapy in groups. The goals of the therapy were to

1. enhance self-esteem;
2. develop understanding of self, family, and society;
3. enhance social coping skills.

Instrumentation

The instruments included Hudson's self-esteem index, staff ratings, self-reports, and case records.

Results

The Hudson inventory showed that those receiving reality therapy increased their self-esteem significantly, while the control group showed no significant change. Staff members reported definite improvements in participants' punctuality, problem-solving skills, and communication skills. One anecdote is especially poignant. At one of the institutions a mass runaway incident took place, but two boys from the treatment group refused to join 12 others opting to escape from the same dormitory. They later described how they had considered running but instead chose to act appropriately. They decided to implement choice theory and operate on a more responsible principle that they had learned through reality therapy methods.

Another boy from the experimental group was involved in a bullying incident. Chung (1994) wrote, "Instead of employing his previous evasive and irresponsible attitude, he frankly disclosed the incident to the Home staff and expressed deep regret for his misdemeanors" (p. 76).

Feedback from the staff indicated also that the experimental subjects acted "more respectfully towards them" (a behavior that the traditional Chinese culture values highly) "and also were more ready to discuss their problems with them" as well as to be "more responsive to advice" (p. 76).

Self-reports from participants showed that 65% of them said they improved in their self-understanding, and 60% improved in understanding their families. Also, 55% indicated improvements in social communication while exactly half (50%) reported gains in self-confidence, selection of friends, and problem solving. Finally, a resounding 65% even suggested that the group therapy should extend to 20 sessions.

Conclusions

One would not be overgeneralizing the results to conclude that reality therapy was effective in this short-term counseling application. Among Chung's (1994) recommendations, in fact, is that "in the era of scarcity of welfare resources, time limited and cost effective reality therapy group programs would be worthy of further exploration on extensive use in the correctional field" (p. 70).

☐ Korean Research

Professor In-Za Kim, former dean at Sogang University in Korea, has conducted some of the best examples of research using control groups. Studies have shown a significant increase in self-esteem, planning ability, and sense of internal control of students, both male and female (H. S. Kim, 1997; K. S. Kim, 1997; M. S. Kim, 1998; R.-I. Kim, & M. G. Hwang, 1997; J. F. Song, 1997; A. Woo, 1998).

In commenting on her own 2-year research study, In-Za Kim stated

> Analyzing the results of research from reality therapy applied to groups—one non-delinquent and the other delinquent—we found that the non-delinquent group showed better results than the other group. The reality therapy research in Korea showed the opposite results from that of American juvenile subjects where juvenile delinquents showed better results than non-delinquents. It has come to my attention that the difference may be due to differences in educational systems. We, therefore, believe that parallel research on the education system and reality therapy may be valuable and much needed. For the application and development of research on reality therapy, the research should be congruent with cross cultural psychology. (p. 19)

☐ Schools in the Student's Quality World

A multicultural or widespread process was the topic that Basic, Ticak Balaz, Uzelac, and Vorkapic-Jugovac (1997) studied. The researchers defined the quality world of students as containing both people, such as teachers, advisors, and peers, and activities, such as study, curriculum, rules of conduct, and field trips. Using interviews and their own instruments, they studied 429 students in grades 1 to 8 in Croatia in order to determine whether these students had removed school from their quality worlds, or lessened school's importance in their quality worlds.

Results

Findings showed that school was truly in the students' quality world during the first four grades, but after that time, students gradually removed teachers and schoolwork from their quality worlds.

Significance

Teachers of students in middle school years are wise to relate positively with them and to persuade their students to hold them in their quality worlds. Using curricular tools to help in their efforts at persuasion can work even better.

☐ Deaf Population

Using a single-subject case study approach, Easterbrooks (1995) investigated the effects of using reality therapy on the social language skills of a deaf student. The subject was a profoundly deaf, 25-year-old male college student, who communicated with sign language. He was in his sixth year of college and on a schedule to finish within 2 more years.

Methodology

The subject filled out standard forms in a pre- and posttest format and staff members who did not know that language outcomes were under study completed rating sheets on the student. The staff was certified in reality therapy and worked with the student for one year.

Results

Among the areas of improvement were initiating and continuing conversation, understanding conversation, choosing topics for discussion, and limiting the number of interruptions.

The researchers pointed out the limitations of this study; a small number of subjects (1) and therefore the difficulty of generalizing beyond the deaf population. Their work also points to the need for more research in the use of reality therapy with the deaf population.

☐ Management and Multiculturalism

Rehak (1998), a training manager in a petrochemical plant in Omisalj, Croatia, has applied the union of control (choice) theory and the Deming philosophy of quality management to the petrochemical industry in Croatia. His goal was to meet the standards required by ISO 9000. (ISO 9000 refers to the effort that 90 countries are making to establish international quality standards for goods and services.)

Rehak has further demonstrated the intercultural application of reality therapy and lead management by using the tool developed by Wubbolding (1988). It measures the internal motivation of workers and assists them in examining their own quality worlds, behavior, and perceptions. Rehak (1998) used the instrument to provide data for managers in their effort to increase the quality of goods and services. Conclusions reached by Rehak were that employees perform at a higher level of their capacities when they see the purpose and value in their work and when they see that they can have an impact on improving the product or service provided.

In another study, Rehak (1998) utilized Wubbolding's (1988, 1998c) Job Examination Personal Profile (JEPP) by asking operators, shift leaders, maintenance workers, and foremen ($N = 231$) to self-evaluate, that is, to rate on a scale of 1 to 5 their sense of control in their jobs. Generally, foremen and shift leaders perceived that they have more control of their work than operators and maintenance workers, but researchers found many deficits in the perception of internal control among personnel in all job domains.

The significance of this project is highlighting the requirement that management create an atmosphere where human beings can meet their needs in unique and enjoyable ways. Even more, this international investigation adds a dimension to the growing body of research showing that the principles of choice theory and reality therapy apply in a multicultural context.

☐ Organizational Behavior

Bruce (1985) found reality therapy to be an extremely effective management strategy for keeping a balance between the goals of the organization and the need-satisfaction of the employee. The problem behavior of employees changed dramatically when reality therapy was used in tandem with an employee assistance program.

☐ Quality Education: Quality School Program

Dryden (1994) conducted extensive research on quality schools. Through a qualitative research method that allowed him to examine not the outcomes of the quality school as much as Quality School Consortium principals' perceptions of the impact of the quality school initiatives, he stated:

> Results of this study provide a clearer understanding of a group of schools that are in the early stages of a reform initiative. Results suggest that, even in these early stages, principals of consortium schools report some measure of progress in implementing the principles and practices that are congruent with the Quality Schools literature. Principals and parent representatives in the Quality Schools communities also report a noticeable and positive impact on students. Further study is needed to assess the fit between the views of principals and parent representatives and the perceptions of other participant groups in consortium schools and the wider educational community. The results also add insight into an array of current issues demanding attention if the initiative is to sustain its energy and grow beyond its present membership. (pp. 119–120)

Dryden (1996) also wrote that whether the Quality School Initiative will leave a lasting impact on education in the United States remains to be seen.

Quality Education: Academic Performance and Gender Effectiveness

Holleran (1981) studied the effects of reality therapy in a group setting in which the investigator targeted students' perceived locus of control and their academic performance. The subjects in this research were underachieving junior high school students whose perceived locus of control was external on a normed test instrument. After receiving group counseling twice a week for 15 weeks, the female subjects showed significant gains in their internal perception of control and in their academic achievement.

This study provides evidence that reality therapy is not a male-oriented theory, but is gender neutral and may be equally effective with females if not more effective. The males in this sample, in fact, showed little gain in their perceived internal locus of control. One of Holleran's (1981) conclusions was that "The efficacy of this treatment with underachieving, externally oriented female adolescents is supported" (p. 498).

Elementary School Students' Self-Concept

In a group counseling application, Block (1994) studied the effects of reality therapy on the self-concept levels of fifth- and sixth-grade students. Using two different experimental groups and one control group, Block used a statistical *t*-test and found that reality therapy was significantly effective in increasing participants' self-concept according to the Piers-Harris Children's Self-Concept Scale.

Student Absenteeism

Brandon (1981) studied the effect of reality therapy on students' locus of control and absenteeism. Fourteen high school counselors with *only* two in-service sessions used reality therapy with secondary school students. As one might expect in such a time-limited study, the results showed little change in the subjects' perceived locus of control, but the other finding was noteworthy: the treatment group members showed a significantly greater reduction in absences than did the control group.

What was surprising in this study is that *any* change emerged. As with many research studies, the training of the therapists applying the treatment—in this case, the skills of reality therapy—was minimal. Such studies are useful however, in surfacing speculation about the possible effects of therapists who are highly trained in reality therapy conducting the treatment.

Student Athletes

Martin and Thompson (1995) combined reality therapy with goal attainment scaling and applied the techniques to freshman student athletes. They used a goal attainment guide based on a five-point acceptability range from –2 to +2, combined with *Pete's Pathogram* (Peterson & Parr, 1982) and other instruments. In this way the students assessed their needs, self-evaluated their current behaviors, and made their plans. Martin and Thompson concluded that counselors and coaches need to work together "to provide the student with a chance to learn more about time management, study skill habits, developing peer and social relationships, career opportunities and life transitions, and methods for enhancing one's self-esteem" (p. 53).

☐ Summer School Program

The summer school program at Victor J. Andrews High School in Orland Park, Illinois focuses on incoming students who have had academic difficulties at the junior high level. Program goals mainly address ways of helping students make the transition to high school and maintain as well as enhance the academic skills they need to do quality work.

The program includes concentrated opportunities to learn such traditional subjects as math, science, reading, and English. Athletics and interpersonal skills are a part of the program but do not receive the emphasis given to the academic curriculum. The philosophy behind the program is lead management as described by Glasser. Students learn the inner motivational components of choice theory and reality therapy in detail and practice these methods under guidance from encouraging leaders and teachers.

Results

According to John Hackett (1998), the program organizer, 4 years of data have shown significant gains in vocabulary, comprehension, math, and other areas. Psychosocial gains, as measured by the Rosenberg Test of Self-Esteem scale, the Nowicki Locus of Control Inventory, and other instruments show gains in self-esteem, internal awareness, drive strength, and stress management. The director also reports that the program is highly respected by both parents and educators.

☐ Choice Program

Peterson and Woodward (1993, 1994) investigated the effectiveness of the CHOICE program, a drug education curriculum with a reality therapy thrust. They stated that, "Pete's Pathogram is designed to allow persons to rate the level of their need, amount of time invested, and the level of satisfaction achieved in each of the four basic psychological need areas . . . " (1994, p. 89). They used the above instrument along with the Piers-Harris Self Concept Scale and the Nowicki-Strickland Internal-External Scale for Children.

Methodology

The subjects of the study were 116 sixth-grade students in West Texas. One school took training in the CHOICE program, while another school serving as a control group did not receive the training. Pre- and posttests yielded data that were analyzed with Pearson Product-Moment Correlation Coefficients to measure the direction and size of the relationships among the variables of interest.

Results

Among the findings was one indicating that the CHOICE program was positively associated with improvements in students' self-concept, their perception of their school status, and their self-concept as it relates to physical attributes.

The study also demonstrated that the Pathogram provides an effective way of measuring a child's self-concept, but not locus of control.

☐ Responsibility Room: Sturgis High School

Members of The William Glasser Institute debate the merits of using a responsibility room in school, with some instructors encouraging this structure and some opposing such rooms if choice theory is used throughout the entire school.

My recommendation is that high school facilities utilize such rooms if they judge that their students would benefit. Students who are bereft of healthy relationships and who manifest their out-of-balance scales (frustrations or unfulfilled wants and needs) by acting out in diverse ways are good candidates for a responsibility room. Other names for the room could be "planning room," "possibility place," or a name agreeable to faculty and students.

The results of one such program utilizing a responsibility room are summarized below. A special thank you is due to Carol Griffith (private correspondence, 1999), a teacher at Sturgis High School, in Sturgis, Michigan, who supplied the information that follows.

> The Responsibility Room was initiated in the Fall of 1993 and is staffed by classroom teachers trained in William Glasser's choice theory and reality therapy. The Responsibility Room at Sturgis High School is designed to assist students in evaluating their own behavior and to assist them in planning for success now and in the future.
>
> Students who are having difficulties in the classroom have the opportunity to self-evaluate through a brief discussion and through written plans that they have completed during a brief time-out period. The students learn that they are responsible for their choices and for developing skills to make more effective choices. If a problem persists, however, a student will subsequently be referred to the Responsibility Room and address the issues involved in work habits, tardiness, or behavior.

Results

Prior to launching the responsibility system, the assistant principal at Sturgis met with approximately 30 students per day to discuss such behaviors as tardiness and acting out. After a year, the average number of students referred was down to two or three per week—a 98% drop. In 1 year the percentage of students going to the room dropped from 15% of the student body to 7%. The faculty believes that the improvement in behavior and work habits reflect system improvements that draw not only on the effectiveness of the Responsibility Room, but on the safe and need-satisfying atmosphere of the school.

One administrator commented, "The Responsibility Room has created a major decrease in one-on-one conflicts between teacher and student. We have very few occasions when teachers get angry with students because of students' behaviors. The Responsibility Room provides our school with a valuable classroom management tool. Incidents of classroom misbehavior are few. It also provides a strategy to work with students who are not completing their classroom work."

While not fulfilling the rigors of controlled scientific research, the above comments, the obvious changes in both teacher and student behaviors, as well as better relationships illustrate the efficacy of reality therapy interventions when used for systemic improvements. Allowing for and encouraging a wider range of choices noticeably enriched the atmosphere of the school building. The school personnel have conducted fire-in-the-belly research, which used to go by the label "action research" and is more than mere "feel good" research.

☐ Behavior Management

Applications of reality therapy to school discipline are very widespread. Grimesey (1990) described the result of even minimal training in reality therapy for teachers.

Out-of-class referrals decreased by 11.3% (from 874 to 775) in 1 year. But more importantly, significant changes occurred in the teachers' perceptions. Grimesey stated that "over half of the respondents (to a teacher survey) said they believed that reality therapy and its related functions have helped student rule violators learn to make positive behavioral choices in their lives" (p. 43).

Journal notes revealed many incidences of students taking greater inner responsibility for their behavior. One student, for instance, who had been removed from ritalin for the first time in 7 years, subsequently demonstrated out-of-control behavior. He said, "If they hadn't taken me off the medicine, I wouldn't be doing these things." He added with much emotion, "I can't control what I do" (p. 44). Intensive counseling over a 3-week period resulted in his learning that he can not only control his behavior but can also incorporate choice theory more globally into his life.

Grimesey's conclusion was that the decreased number of administrative referrals reflected the teacher perceptions that students had taken more effective control of their choices and improved their behavior.

☐ School Dropouts

Bonuccelli (1994) attempted to answer the question, "Why does one student out of every four choose to drop out of high school?" She stated, "Although many studies have attempted to answer that question, relatively few have analyzed dropout behavior through the lens of a theory based on internal motivation" (p. 508).

Methodology

This qualitative, phenomenological study of eight female school dropouts used a matrix integrating the five basic needs with four components of total behavior as a basis for interviews.

Results

The major finding of the study was that individuals based their decisions to drop out of school on their personal internal needs.

Conclusion

The small number of subjects and lack of randomization or a conventional control group limits the generalization of the findings, but the study supports my contention that the growing body of research on reality therapy needs even further enhancement.

☐ Quality Education: The Apollo School

The ideas described in *The Quality School* (W. Glasser, 1990c) were first applied on a schoolwide basis at Apollo Continuation School, with at-risk secondary students in Simi Valley, California. Greene and Uroff (1991) described the results the school achieved when the principal and staff expanded their mission to include the components of the quality school, quality environment, quality relationships, and quality work. After attending Apollo for several years the students had a 78% attendance improvement. Weekly drug usage dropped from 80% to 20% of the students. Students on probation dropped from 30% to 5%.

The authors emphasized that the primary purpose of education was not lost at Apollo. They insisted on addressing the affective domain and applying reality therapy in a quality school that would embrace the entire educational experience.

☐ At-Risk High School Students

In a tightly controlled study Comiskey (1993) investigated the impact of reality therapy with at-risk ninth-grade students. She measured the effect of reality therapy on students' self-esteem, locus of control, school achievement, attitude toward school, attendance, and classroom behavior.

Treatment

Researchers set up three groups of students, each receiving a different treatment over 14 sessions. One group received reality therapy counseling alone. The second group received reality therapy counseling combined with a "partial school within a school" program. The third group, a control group, worked on career development.

Results

An ANCOVA and an ANOVA of the pre- and posttests that the students took revealed significant differences in achievement, self-esteem, attitude, and attendance. Reality therapy was most effective when used with students in the school within a school. This suggests that organizational change may be a necessary prelude for at-risk students to fulfill their needs. This group showed notable increases in their English and social science performance.

The researcher concluded that a less coercive environment in which teachers can get close to students helps them fulfill their need for belonging. The results were especially effective because the new reality therapy–based elements changed the system to make it easier for students to insert schoolwork into their quality worlds.

Summary

Reality therapy was shown to be an effective method of counseling even on a short-term basis and was more effective when used as part of even a minimal school reorganization designed to help students meet their need for belonging.

☐ Huntington Woods: Wyoming, Michigan

The first school to proclaim itself a quality school with Glasser's endorsement opened its doors with the quality-centered goals that he had described earlier.

- The daily lives of people in the school will reflect the satisfaction of the five needs.
- Students will do quality work.
- There will be no discipline problems.
- The school will be a joyful place.

Ludwig and Mentley (1997) stated that these goals are approached in the school as a result of continually working to establish a friendly and noncoercive atmosphere, establishing multiage learning families that stay together for 3 years, using cooperative learning and class meetings, lengthening class days from Monday through Thursday, shortening the day on Friday, and extending the school calendar with 6 weeks of intersessions.

Self-directed learning with each teacher functioning as a facilitator is a cornerstone of the process, but the heart of the quality effort is student self-evaluation. Students judge the quality of their own work and figure out how to improve their results within the boundaries they set with their teachers' help. Part of the emphasis on self-responsibility is negotiating solutions to problems and disagreements. Rewards and punishment that lead to distancing in relationships become unnecessary as the students achieve the intrinsic satisfaction of close relationships and quality work.

Hard data are scarce but "achievement scores on the Michigan Education Assessment Program for reading and math consistently exceed averages for our state and district" (Ludwig, private correspondence, 1999). Vandalism and destructive behavior have virtually vanished, and, finally, during the first three years of the transition to quality, the determination to eliminate special education resulted in mainstreaming all but two of 700 students.

☐ Schwab Junior High: Cincinnati, Ohio

This school has received much attention in workshops, presentations at national conferences, lectures, and discussions about the quality school effort because of the intensive quality school training that began in the 1994/1995 academic year. Illustrating the results of saturation training and the need for the entire faculty to demonstrate long-term commitment to the quality school effort, Glasser (1997) stated, "by the end of the year, most of the *regularly attending* students who were *capable* of doing passable school work were doing it. Discipline problems . . . slowly came under control and ceased to be a significant concern by the end of the school year" (p. 600). One hundred and seventy students who failed regularly and who were overage for their grade were put in a school within a school. By the end of summer school, 147 were promoted to high school. They also showed a 20% increase in their math scores.

Louis (1998) studied 28 students selected from the school population to determine attitudinal changes. Pre- and postsurveys showed no significant difference in attitudes, while qualitative data gathered from interviews seemed to indicate improvements in attitude toward school and in-school performance.

More specifically, the official statistics of the Cincinnati Public School system showed that on a schoolwide basis, suspensions decreased from 1,108 the previous year to 749, a decrease of 359 or 32.4%. On the other hand, expulsions increased from 94 during the previous year to 123, an increase of 29 or 23.5%. During the next year, 1995/1996, suspensions decreased to 708, a decrease of 41 or 5.7% (Lewis & Quatman, 1995, 1996).

☐ Chaddock School: Quincy, Illinois

The result of total immersion in reality therapy is represented by the results achieved at Chaddock School (M. Reese, private correspondence, 1994), a residential school for court-referred students ages 13 to 18. In a period of 6 years, several modalities came and went until Gene Simon and Michael Reese introduced reality therapy. In just over 3 years behavioral incidents were reduced to an insignificant level as indicated in Figure 9.

A letter from a student who I'll call Felicia illustrates the most telling result and one that most closely reflects the fire-in-the-belly character of this research review.

> When I first got here at Chaddock, I was manipulative by going and asking another staff a question if I didn't get the answer I wanted from the first staff I asked. I also was very rude and disrespectful towards staff and students by cussing at others and stomping my feet, using inappropriate tones and baby language. I also talked about others behind their backs and acted completely different to their faces. I was rude to my family members, case worker, and friends. I wasn't "I" focused. I blamed all my behavior on others, and all I did was focus on boys all the time. I depended on boys to make me feel good about myself. I didn't self-evaluate. I wouldn't listen to staff when they would try to talk to me. I shut myself out from everyone and depressed a lot and sometimes refused to follow programming. Lots of times I did things that my peers wanted me to do. I involved myself in campuswide negativity. I laughed at students choosing negative behavior and fed it.
>
> Around October I decided to make a change in my life. So I stopped my running behaviors and began to make positive choices for myself. I have changed my manipulative behaviors and started to be patient and take "no" for an answer. I respect my elders and peers and I'm now building strong relationships with others. I go to staff for advice instead of making wrong choices. I ignore negative behavior and am separated from it. I very, very rarely cuss at people. I think probably the last time I cussed at someone was before Thanksgiving. That's very good. I have found more effective ways to handle my frustrations, like taking deep breaths, talking to staff, or I go to my room and write letters. I have grown to respect my case worker and mother. I have built my self-esteem up enough so I don't have to have a boyfriend to make me feel good about myself. I can self-evaluate truthfully instead of denying my behavior. I don't refuse to follow programming and I am doing other things to keep me busy so I don't have time to get uncomfortable, and the extra things help me get ready to move on in life when I leave. I do things like play on the basketball team, I'm on the pom-pom squad, I go to the veteran home, I work

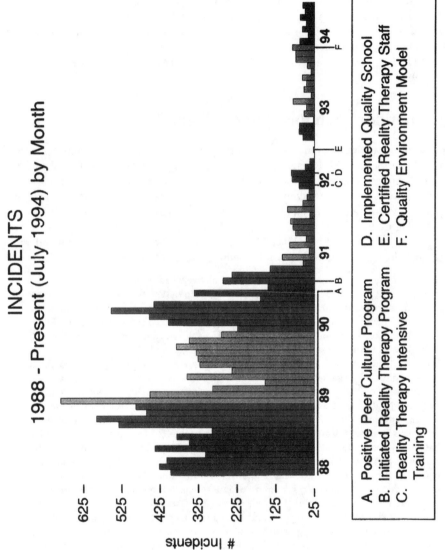

FIGURE 9. Incidents of behavioral problems at Chaddock School.

at a nursing home cleaning, I do things with staff like going and speaking for Chaddock, I'm in the choir and in anything else that I can do to help out. I have built up my self-respect. So I do not fall into peer pressure. I don't strive to get in on all the other cottages' problems and I don't involve myself in any "runaway" conversations or talk about people getting in trouble. I've gotten the picture that being negative is nothing to laugh at or involve myself in.

☐ Benjamin Franklin High School: Palos Heights, Illinois

One of the most significant studies on the effect of reality therapy in schools was conducted at the Benjamin Franklin High School, an alternative school with 138 students in Palos Heights, Illinois (Swenson, 1995). The results are described by Dr. Stuart Swenson (private correspondence, 1999) who provided the following summary of the research.

> The Consolidated High School District 230 research project was a field study. Students in the Benjamin Franklin High School constituted the experimental group (99 of the 138 students in the population), which was compared with a control group of 157 students, a stratified random sample selected from the three home schools in the district. Data showed that the Franklin School population was characteristic of many alternative high schools relative to the performance on the Statements About Schools Inventory, which measured security, social, self-esteem, and self-actualization needs.
>
> Faculty and parents characterized the Benjamin Franklin High School as a "Glasser School." Staff had received advanced training in the technique and the faculty relied on consultants from The William Glasser Institute to assure that they were adopting the Quality School Model. It was important, therefore, to assess the perceptions of the students and the home controls and relationships that had been established in each setting.
>
> Based on Glasser's work, we expected to see Franklin faculty and students emphasizing quality work, self-evaluation and student responsibility on a consistent basis, so that students and parents viewed those characteristics as intrinsic to the Franklin program. The data demonstrated that Franklin students and parents viewed Franklin as emphasizing those characteristics.
>
> Specifically, significantly greater emphasis was perceived by Franklin on quality work than on controls, and significantly more Franklin parents reported teachers emphasizing quality work ($t(339) = 4.72$, $p < .0001$) and encouragement of high aspirations ($t(339) = 4.13$, $p > .0001$). (Significantly more Franklin students vs. 41.5% of the controls reported "almost/always" in this category.) Franklin students viewed their teachers as noncoercive managers who encouraged them to take responsibility for their education. As a consequence, significantly more Franklin students disagreed that it was the teacher's job (a) to evaluate the quality of student work, (b) to manage the class so that students will not be angry or bored, and (c) to make students behave, so learning can take place.
>
> A significant measure of a relationship lies in the expectations that teachers establish in a classroom. When the study was conducted, in March 1995, students had spent many months with their teachers and it was reasonable to assume that they had learned how their teachers would respond to classroom problems that would arise. An exercise was developed in which students were asked to predict the first-hour teacher's behavior in three conditions: In the first condition, a student submits an assignment that the teacher knows is below the quality of work that the student could produce. In the second condition, the student arrives late to class for a third day in a row. In the third condition, after

receiving a classroom assignment, a student remarks, "This is boring and I'm tired." The student then proceeded to assume a sleeping posture, head on the desk and refusing to work.

Students in experimental and control conditions were asked to predict what their first-hour teacher would say under each condition. Responses were judged, using an established rubric, as "Glasser" or "non-Glasser" comments.

In the first condition, which most teachers would handle quickly and objectively, 52% of the Franklin responses and 19% of the control responses were classified as "Glasser responses." In the second condition, in which a student suggests a negative attitude toward the classroom, 49% of the Franklin and 8.8% of the controls provided "Glasser responses." In the final situation, in which a teacher is confronted with an openly negative attitude, 24% of the Franklin responses and 2% of the control students expected the Glasser response. A chi-square analysis was significant at the .0001 level in each condition.

Not only were expectations significantly more consistent among Franklin students, but it was interesting to note a relatively drastic reduction in quality teacher responses among the control students as student behaviors became potentially more personalized and adversarial.

These data demonstrate the impact of environments in which Glasser-oriented interventions occur on a consistent basis. Students expect teachers to confront their behavior in constructive, problem-oriented ways designed to develop more appropriate responses that will serve a productive educational interest. In that setting, all student behavior, including the negative and potentially adversarial behaviors, can be used for the benefit of students. Furthermore, the Glasser responses serve to redefine and clarify teacher–student relationships, removing the power struggles and allowing all interactions in the education program to teach responsible behavior.

☐ The John Dewey Academy: Great Barrington, Massachusetts

Synonymous with reality therapy for many years is The John Dewey Academy, a residential school for alienated and angry adolescents in Great Barrington, Massachusetts (Bratter, Bratter, Maxym, Radda & Steiner, 1993). Its goals are to educate students intellectually and morally and to advocate for them in seeking admission to institutions of higher learning. Bratter, Collabolletta, Gordon, and Kaufman (1999) stated that "before admission 33% of the students had been hospitalized for at least two months, 66% had been treated by psychiatrists, and 66% arrived addicted to potent psychotropics" (p. 9).

Throughout the students' stay, personal choice is a theme along with the opportunity and responsibility to take control of their behavior both in the residence and in school. No heavy psychotropic medication is prescribed.

The program is unconventional from admittance to release. Transcripts, educational records, and test scores, for example, are not used to determine eligibility. Rather, a 4-hour interview is the basis for determining whether a candidate can respond to a confrontative, learning-centered modification of reality therapy.

A study of 313 students showed that 28% graduated, and 75% of those who left received permission from their parents to return home. Bratter et al. (1999) stated that "two crucial statistics are: 100% of the graduates attend colleges of quality and 80% complete their higher education" (p. 11).

Bratter et al. (1999) attributed the success of The John Dewey Academy to the

Attention deficit hyperactivity disorder	54%
Conduct disorder	
Aggressive	12%
Nonaggressive	12%
Opposition defiant	30%
Anxiety disorder	6%
Eating disorder	6%
Substance use disorder	
Alcohol	18%
Cannabis	18%
Cocaine	18%
Heroin	12%
Affective disorder	
Depression	18%
Bipolar	30%
Suicidal	18%
Borderline personality disorder	24%
Sociopathic	12%
Undifferentiated	24%

Diagnoses of students attending The John Dewey Academy.

confrontative therapeutic but nurturing orientation of the school. Students learn the importance of dealing with current issues and making better choices as pathways to effective living (Glasser, 1990d).

☐ Science Curriculum: Parental Involvement

King (1999) investigated the value of involving both parents and teachers in the reform of a middle school science curriculum. The school hoped to engage parents in developing a science curriculum so that they would understand the program and work collaboratively to improve and support it.

Background

Prior to the study, all of the school's staff members and some students took a training course in choice theory and reality therapy. Articles on Quality Schools also appeared in school newsletters. The concept that all behaviors are related to humans' drives to satisfy their basic needs was already part of the culture of the school. Parents had collaborated in many school reform efforts, but none included curriculum development.

Science teachers developed an innovative science program at the school, seeking input from students to refine the curriculum and meet their needs. Rumblings in the community led teachers to realize that parental input had not been a part of the collaboration and that the parents were, in effect, "the missing voice" in the "collaboration for continuous improvement" cycle that was part of the school's culture.

The study was conducted at two levels. Tier I was the work of the parents and teachers on a Project Improvement Team (PIT). This joint team provided a means for authentically involving parents in curriculum development. Tier II examined the process of parent involvement in the science program and provided data related to the research questions.

Methodology (Action Plan)

Questionnaires were mailed to all middle school parents. Follow-up focus groups of parents met to clarify survey data. The PIT analyzed the data and developed an action plan for improving the program to meet parents' needs. The PIT members then published articles in the school's newsletter and conducted workshops to explain the new science program to the rest of the parents. The parents on the PIT listed their names and telephone numbers in the newsletter so that other parents could call them to ask questions about the goals, content, methods, and assessment strategies of the program.

Results

Parents and teachers initially expressed concerns about the propriety of involving parents in curriculum development, but as they became engaged in analyzing data, fear decreased. Follow-up interviews of all PIT members indicated that parental attitudes about both the science program and parent involvement in curriculum development improved dramatically. Parents and teachers demonstrated that they could work together to enhance school programs for the benefit of students. The study supported the basic Quality School principle that human needs drive all human behaviors. Parents and teachers shared the responsibility for the science program and collaborated successfully to enhance it.

☐ LABBB: Lexington, Massachusetts

The second school to become a quality school, the LABBB collaborative program in Lexington, Massachusetts, is a school for students between the ages of 10 and 22 with a variety of cognitive, physical, and social-emotional disabilities. The school "does not chart baselines, shape behavior, schedule reinforcers or do successive approximations" (Renna, Kimball, Brescia, & O'Connor, 1999, p. 1). Rather, teachers measure progress "by determining how effectively they are helped to take control of their lives and achieve independence at the least restrictive level" (p. 1). The program is built entirely around choice theory and the use of reality therapy. To measure the effectiveness of the program, investigators studied 87 graduates from 1992 to 1998. They wore such labels as Pervasive Developmental Disorder, Asperger's Syndrome, Attention Deficit Disorder, and many pathological categories. They had entered the LABBB program with many behavioral issues that impinged on their ability to maintain employment.

Comparisons with the National Longitudinal Transitional Study (NLTS) indicated that LABBB graduates maintained a 63.3% rate of competitive employment compared with 45.7% of the students in the NLTS. LABBB graduates scoring in the average to borderline range of IQ maintained a 75.5% level of employment compared with 60.4% of students with the same classification on the NLTS.

Renna et al. (1999) concluded that "the data indicate [that] a higher percentage of competitive employment than that reported by the NLTS across all domains was attained by students in a program where reality therapy is the psychological framework instead of traditional . . . approaches" (p. 8).

☐ Teacher Education and Related Subjects: Thomas Parish

Dr. Thomas Parish, professor at Kansas State University, is a major researcher in reality therapy applied to higher education. Along with Dr. Arlin Peterson from Texas Technological University, he has added immensely to the credibility of reality therapy as a teaching tool. I am indebted to him for providing abstracts of his research projects, and I have selected several of them as examples of a growing body of research studies.

In one study 35 undergraduate college students learned reality therapy–type strategies for promoting personal commitment and avoiding the use of external pressures, thus fostering greater personal responsibility and an internal locus of control. Consequently, these students demonstrated a higher level of internal control, particularly if they achieved a grade of A in the course. Besides significantly enhancing students' internal locus of control, these students also improved their health ratings and reduced the occurrence of stressful events in their lives, although not beyond the .05 level (Parish, 1988a).

In another study, 76 undergraduate college students were presented with reality therapy–type strategies in order to enhance their personal control over their lives. As predicted, these students subsequently reported that they had adopted more "loving" or positive interpersonal behaviors as well as higher self-concepts. These findings were demonstrated through pre- and postcourse comparisons. The enhanced scores across dependent variables were found to occur regardless of the grade these students had earned in the course (Parish, 1988b).

In another study 36 graduate students learned research methods through the implementation of "Quality School" procedures. Pre- and postcourse comparisons of student enthusiasm and their knowledge of the subject matter revealed that both were significantly enhanced. Such findings provide empirical support for Glasser's "quality school" concepts, that is, that as teachers endeavor to create conditions in which students can more easily fulfill their various needs and interests, they will more enthusiastically learn the subject matter (Parish, 1992a).

Parish (1988a) added that few college courses are feared or hated more than graduate-level statistics courses. In another study on their level of enthusiasm about learning statistics, students responded to surveys (on a 1–10 scale) at the beginning and end of their statistics course. In the interim, the project leaders followed eight steps derived from William Glasser's (1990c) book *The Quality School*. The findings revealed that students moved from an average rating of 3.30 at the outset of the class to a 9.00 at the conclusion of the class. Hence, enthusiasm for doing statistics significantly increased in students who had been taught this subject in accordance with Glasser's "Quality School" model (Parish, 1992b).

Parish (1992b) also attempted to answer the questions of which students are "at-risk," why are they "at-risk," and for what they are "at-risk." This paper examined these questions in addition to students' and teachers' perceptions with an array of psychological instruments that effectively assess self-concept and support system failures, as well as predict the potential of dropping out. Notably, the findings from this study showed that students with low self-concepts and poor support systems demonstrated significantly higher scores on the Potential Dropout Checklist (PDC). These findings support Glasser's (1990c) quality school model, which suggests that when students sense others value them and use no coercion, they do quality work; that is, they do well in school and adopt a positive self-concept (W. Glasser, 1993).

☐ Teacher Education

Wigle (1996) incorporated choice theory and reality therapy into teacher education and studied whether teachers continued to use quality school ideas after their first year. Among the findings were that 65% continued to use the quality school concepts and 78% planned to use them in the future. More specifically, 69% said they were using class meetings and 89% said that using quality school concepts enabled their students to do quality schoolwork.

Wigle (1996) cautiously indicated that the data are only suggestive, but that modeling the concepts on the part of the professors and infusing them into teacher education are excellent ways to prepare new teachers for careers in quality schools.

It may be evident from this sampling of a range of studies that reality therapy works effectively in many settings and applies to many aspects of human interaction. The body of research continues to grow, yet more studies are necessary.

☐ Quality Education: Student Teaching

Babcock (1983) investigated the effects of teaching reality therapy to student teachers. Observations of classroom teaching and test results from a wide range of instruments showed an improvement in the behavior of students taught by student teachers trained in reality therapy theory and practice. The student teachers also felt a greater sense of inner control. Babcock concluded that "reality therapy offers a potential model for student teaching and supervision" (p. 2388).

☐ Research Recommendations

In summarizing six studies on reality therapy in schools, Murphy (1997) recommended the following:

- more conducting of tightly controlled studies to determine the effectiveness of reality therapy in schools;
- gathering empirical evidence; measures should include grades, attendance, test scores, and behavioral checklists;
- "All persons who administer assessments or act as observers should be professionally trained and qualified for their specific tasks" (p. 19).
- "Future research should be longitudinal lasting a full school year" (p. 19).

The need for further research was emphasized by Sansone (1998). In surveying 257 articles from the *Journal of Reality Therapy* he found that only 23, or 9%, were research related. He furthermore cited the ethical codes of four professional organizations that emphasize the importance of conducting research to justify practice. He stated, "We have an ethical *obligation* . . . to seek out co-validating research, to originate and participate in ongoing research that corroborates choice theory and reality therapy principles, and to disseminate this research accordingly" (p. 42).

More specifically, I urge researchers to consider the following recommendations in future studies:

1. Use genuine reality therapy and not spin-offs from it, which represent a diluted or distorted form of the WDEP system that changes that simple framework into an extrinsic tool to manipulate students. Also, the word "control" is used with various meanings, such as social and personal control in the field of corrections. Studies on this type of control are not relevant to the control theory and choice theory that is the basis of reality therapy and that refer to perceptual control.

2. Examine the skill of the practitioner. Many participants in the studies seemed to have minimal training. The William Glasser Institute sponsors an 18-month certification program in reality therapy, requiring training workshops, supervision and a final demonstration of knowledge and skills. A potential limitation in research on the effectiveness of reality therapy is the inadequate skill of the reality therapy practitioner. Therefore, a criterion for including practitioners in a study is that they hold certification in reality therapy. At minimum, the amount of training provided for the participants should be clearly indicated in the presentation of the research.

3. Set an appropriate length of time for treatment. Several studies that show little effect from reality therapy may have included a reality therapy practitioner with insufficient training and a much too abbreviated amount of treatment time provided for the use of reality therapy in counseling or teaching. Sleek (1994) stated that *at least* 16 weeks of cognitive-behavioral therapy are needed in order to see significant results. Reality therapy, a cognitive-behavioral approach, is time limited but not a quick fix. With most conflicts or binds, it takes a protracted period of time for people to make the shift in thinking and acting that will break the longstanding patterns that seem to entrap them.

4. If research on the quality school philosophy and delivery system is to attain a more credible degree of reliability and validity, the training of school staff should become more thorough and always be based on accurate choice theory and reality therapy as developed by William Glasser. In areas such as quality schools, the training of the school staff has been sporadic, irregular, and inconsistent. Some have been trained by instructors who themselves had little experience as professional educators. Others have gotten training in techniques that are antithetical to Glasser's choice theory and reality therapy.

5. Emphasize outcome research. Recidivism in the corrections field is a subject needing research attention. Behavioral incidents and academic achievement in schools need more extensive measurement. The perceptions of those using the system in their building is important but not conclusive in measuring the effectiveness of reality therapy or of the quality school program. When hard data are presented, the effectiveness of the method becomes less disputable and we are propelled beyond subjective "feel good" perceptions common in research studies.

Similarly, independent researchers need to be involved in future studies. Submitting the method to the "white light" of independent evaluation provides further credibility. This would help avoid the criticism of "in-house" evaluation that elicits the charge that "the home team always wins."

☐ A Meta-Analysis of Research Studies

Radtke, Sapp, and Farrell (1997) conducted a meta-analysis of 21 research studies in reality therapy and concluded that, overall, reality therapy had a "medium effect." They emphasized that many of the studies used inexperienced therapists, many clients showed only slight change due to the fact that they were relatively in effective control of their lives at the beginning of treatment, and the dependent variables were not equivalent in the experimental and control groups prior to receiving reality therapy. They concluded that "the variety of applications for reality therapy is virtually unlimited" (p. 9).

Ideally, conducting research studies with therapists and educators who peers rate as having the highest level of knowledge of choice theory, the greatest amount of skills, and the longest experience in their fields would be most valid and useful.

Granello and Granello (1998) emphasized the importance for *students* to address the need for outcome research. With the ever-changing demands of managed healthcare we see greater competition for funding. They stated that students will benefit if they "choose treatments that have research to support them and . . . evaluate their own interventions objectively" (p. 226). They added that the efficacy of treatment interventions needs to be measured in multicultural counseling, career counseling, group counseling, school counseling, and other specialties.

In summary, this chapter presented an overview of research studies on reality therapy. Along with the underlying theory it is used in a wide range of settings. The people using this modality are practitioners in the front lines of the helping professions: case workers, therapists, counselors, educators, and others. Consequently, the research on reality therapy has lagged behind that of other modalities. At the present time, the number of researchers and their output is increasing. Especially noteworthy are the works of Bratter, In-Za Kim, Mickel, Parish, and Peterson. This chapter provided clear and incontrovertible evidence that reality therapy, validated by research findings in many settings, deserves a high-ranking position in current psychological and educational practice.

EPILOGUE

Ayn Rand once remarked that "throughout the centuries there were men who took first steps down new roads armed with nothing but their vision." When William Glasser journeyed along a new road and developed his ideas, he faced the same rejection given to visionaries throughout history. But as is evidenced from his own words in the interview contained in this book, his sustained and often lonely voyage is still in process. Many people now accompany him. I have attempted to show that others have helped contribute to a successful journey. If reality therapy is to flourish in the 21st century, it will not be solely limited to the latest thinking of one brilliant man. It will represent his core psychological and educational principles, but they will *continue* to be expanded and extended by authors who not only understand them but are committed to teaching them.

In these pages I have tried to present reality therapy as a 21st century, useable, expanding, and forward-looking method. It will continue to be used if it is taught as a system with practical tools for therapists, teachers, case managers, supervisors, parents, and anyone who has *any* human relationship. Consequently I have formulated the delivery system as WDEP, an easy-to-remember acronym. At the same time, it is an umbrella concept that embraces many nuances. The user of reality therapy, the WDEP formulation, can scratch the surface of the ideas or dig deeply into them. Perhaps the simple question, "Is it helping you?" is sufficient for some learners. Others find the remaining 21 self-evaluation questions worthy of use. How much you learn about reality therapy is your choice.

Second, the theory and practice of reality therapy have been expanded and will continue to grow. Techniques compatible with choice theory, new ways to help practitioners become part of the quality worlds of their followers or clients or students, as well as new formulations of the E—self-evaluation—have already emerged and will continue to burst forth.

Third, in future decades the system will need to be applied to issues that are as yet unresolved worldwide. If the roots of problems are dysfunctional relationships, a delivery system for improving them can be based on choice theory and the WDEP formulation of reality therapy.

For many centuries the governments of the world have been dealing with local, national, regional, and international crises. The conventional method for resolving conflict has often involved an internecine gladiatorial style of external control psychology. Like many public and private schools, nations often function on the supposition that fear is a source of motivation and can produce international harmony if it is sufficiently exploited.

On the contrary, fear is not a source of motivation. Rather, it is a behavior generated when human needs are threatened. And it is often accompanied by suspicious defensive thinking as well as aggressive actions. If diplomats were to learn choice theory and use the principles of reality therapy, they would have a systematic structure for dealing with each other. They would realize that individuals and nations are motivated to fulfill their needs for belonging, power or achievement, freedom, fun or enjoyment, and survival. When these needs are unfulfilled or even attacked, nations often take hostile, destructive courses of action. But if the community of nations works together to establish an appropriate environment, as therapists and teachers attempt to do, it is more likely that its members will make responsible choices. It is clear that many national leaders operate on a blind carrot-and-stick philosophy, believing the only way to fulfill their needs is to deny others' access to their own need-fulfillment.

Still, it would be naive to say that unjust aggressor nations would change their behavior without action from the outside. And so, defensive or even preventive action might sometimes be required of the more enlightened nations. This unfortunate necessity does not diminish the effectiveness of international choice theory. It merely proves that aggressors do not care to learn and practice the principles described in this book. Hitler or Stalin would never have been deterred from their diabolic goals or behavior. Such tyrants are indeed beyond the logic of choice theory and reality therapy. The real question for nations to ask is how to establish an international atmosphere that is need-satisfying to all. If the answer to this question is continually striven for, the toxic atmosphere that nourishes aggression and the rise of tyrants would be greatly lessened if not completely eliminated. Much work remains for the third millennium.

I have tried to illustrate that reality therapy has universal application. The system can be used in therapy, schools, management, parenting, among friends and family, in church, synagogue, temple, and mosque, as well as on a communitywide basis. It is my conviction that reality therapy is not culture bound. It has been adjusted to and adopted by many cultures. The theory itself embraces universal principles characteristic of all people. All people viewed in the context of choice theory are internally motivated to fulfill their needs and can learn to ask themselves what they want, to evaluate their current behaviors, and to make more effective plans to contribute to the world around them.

The 21st century holds the probability of unimaginable technological and medical progress as well as countless exciting scientific discoveries and advances in artistic expression. Whether these developments uplift humankind or debase it depends essentially on how we manage human relationships. Reality therapy, a practical, down to earth, altruistic, research-based system, addresses this fragile but integral component of human progress.

Oh yes, I almost forgot, . . . about those three questions in the introduction regarding the cause of stress, aggravation, and anxiety. Having read the book, can you now answer the questions as to the origin of these feelings and of all behavior?

ANNOTATED
BIBLIOGRAPHY

Glasser, W. (1998). *Choice theory.* New York: HarperCollins.

Explanation of the necessity for a theory that is based on internal motivation rather than on external stimuli such as punishments or rewards as well as childhood conflicts. Comprehensive and detailed, *Choice Theory* illustrates how relationships, education, and the workplace can be improved when infused with a willingness and commitment to more effective human need satisfaction.

Glasser, W. (2000). *Reality therapy in action.* New York: HarperCollins.

A sequel to his original 1965 book, Glasser demonstrates his personal style of counseling with a variety of clients. The cases are based on role plays conducted during his public workshops. He shows how he has incorporated the direct teaching of choice theory into the use of reality therapy.

Wubbolding, R. (1991). *Understanding reality therapy.* New York: HarperCollins.

One hundred and twenty metaphors, anecdotes, analogies, and similes are presented as concrete ways to understand choice theory and reality therapy. Rather than starting with abstract principles, the author begins with literary examples, scenarios, and stories from everyday life to illustrate central ideas of reality therapy. This book makes the theory of reality therapy come alive.

Wubbolding, R. (1996). *Employee motivation: What to do when what you say isn't working.* Knoxville, TN: SPC Press.

Three types of management are described: authoritarian, laissez-faire, and democratic. The WDEP system, applied to management and supervision, is illustrated with transcripts demonstrating its application to executives, supervisors, and workers. Readers learn how to deal with excuses, apathy, defensiveness, and other issues faced by managers and supervisors on a daily basis.

Palmatier, L. (1998). *Crisis counseling for a quality school community.* Philadelphia, PA: Accelerated Development.

How to use reality therapy in schools. Issues dealt with include foster families, street gangs, death and grief, parental involvement, impulsivity, child abuse, depression, and suicide. This resource provides first-rate practical ideas for transforming schools, as presented by one of the premier instructors of reality therapy.

Richardson, B. (2000). *Working with challenging youth: Lessons learned along the way.* Philadel-
    phia, PA: Accelerated Development.

    A perceptive portrait for dealing with a wide range of youth who share the inability to manage
their emotions or to responsibly meet their needs. This engaging resource integrates reality
therapy with other approaches and offers practical strategies for facilitating positive change.

APPENDIX

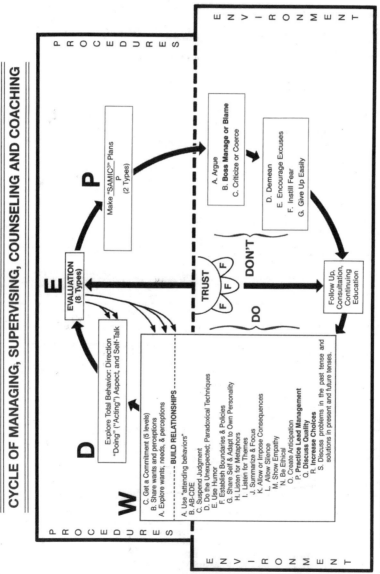

CYCLE OF MANAGING, SUPERVISING, COUNSELING AND COACHING

W D E P

PROCEDURES

ENVIRONMENT

Explore Total Behavior: Direction
"Doing" ("Acting") Aspect, and Self-Talk

EVALUATION
(8 Types)

Make "SAMIC³" Plans
P
(2 Types)

TRUST
F F F
F F
DON'T
DO

- - - - - - - BUILD RELATIONSHIPS - - - - - - -

A. Use "attending behaviors"
B. AB-CDE
 C. Get a Commitment (5 levels)
 B. Share wants and perceptions
 A. Explore wants, needs, & perceptions
C. Suspend Judgment
D. Do the Unexpected; Paradoxical Techniques
E. Use Humor
F. Establish Boundaries & Policies
G. Share Self & Adapt to Own Personality
H. Listen for Metaphors
I. Listen for Themes
J. Summarize & Focus
K. Allow or Impose Consequences
L. Allow Silence
M. Show Empathy
N. Be Ethical
O. Create Anticipation
P. **Practice Lead Management**
Q. **Discuss Quality**
R. **Increase Choices**
S. Discuss problems in the past tense and
 solutions in present and future tenses.

A. Argue
B. **Boss Manage or Blame**
C. Criticize or Coerce

D. Demean
E. Encourage Excuses
F. Instill Fear
G. Give Up Easily

Follow Up,
Consultation,
Continuing
Education

Adapted by **Robert E. Wubbolding, EdD**
from the works of William Glasser, MD

Copyright 1986 Robert E. Wubbolding, EdD
12th Revision 2000

SUMMARY DESCRIPTION OF THE
"CYCLE OF MANAGING, SUPERVISING, COUNSELING AND COACHING"

(The Cycle is explained in detail in books by Robert E. Wubbolding:
Understanding Reality Therapy, Harper Collins, 1991; *Employee Motivation*, SPC Press, 1996)
NEW BOOK: *Reality Therapy for the 21st Century*, Accelerated Development, 2000

Introduction:

The Cycle consists of two general concepts: Environment conducive to change and Procedures more explicitly designed to facilitate change. This chart is intended to be a **brief** summary. The ideas are designed to be used with employees, students, clients as well as in other human relationships.

Relationship between Environment & Procedures:

1. As indicated in the chart, the Environment is the foundation upon which the effective use of Procedures is based.

2. Though it is **usually** necessary to establish a safe, friendly Environment before change can occur, the "Cycle" can be entered at any point. Thus, the use of the cycle does **not** occur in lock step fashion.

3. Building a relationship implies establishing and maintaining a professional relationship. Methods for accomplishing this comprise some efforts on the part of the helper that are Environmental and others that are Procedural.

ENVIRONMENT:

DO: Build Relationship: a close relationship is built on TRUST through friendliness, firmness and fairness.

A. Using Attending Behaviors: Eye contact, posture, effective listening skills.

B. AB = "Always **Be . . .**" **C**onsistent, **C**ourteous & **C**alm, **D**etermined that there is hope for improvement, **E**nthusiastic (Think Positively).

C. Suspend Judgment: View behaviors from a low level of perception, i.e., acceptance is crucial.

D. Do the Unexpected: Use paradoxical techniques as appropriate; Reframing and Prescribing.

E. Use Humor: Help them fulfill need for fun within reasonable boundaries.

F. Establish boundaries: the relationship is professional.

G. Share Self: Self-disclosure within limits is helpful; adapt to own personal style.

H. Listen for Metaphors: Use their figures of speech and provide other ones.

I. Listen to Themes: Listen for behaviors that have helped, value judgements, etc.

J. Summarize & Focus: Tie together what they say and focus on them rather than on "Real World."

K. Allow or Impose Consequences: Within reason, they should be responsible for their own behavior.

L. Allow Silence: This allows them to think, as well as to take responsibility.

M. Show Empathy: Perceive as does the person being helped.

N. Be Ethical: Study Codes of Ethics and their applications, e.g., how to handle suicide threats or violent tendencies.

O. Create anticipation and communicate hope. People should be taught that something good will happen if they are willing to work.

P. **Practice lead management, e.g., democracy in determining rules.**

Q. **Discuss quality.**

R. **Increase choices.**

S. Discuss problems in the past tense, solutions in present and future tenses.

DON'T:

Argue, **Boss Manage,** or Blame, Criticize or Coerce, Demean, Encourage Excuses, Instill Fear, or Give up easily.

Rather, stress what they **can** control, accept them as they are, and keep the confidence that they can develop more effective behaviors. Also, continue to use "WDEP" system without giving up.

Follow Up, Consult, and Continue Education:

Determine a way for them to report back, talk to another professional person when necessary, and maintain ongoing program of professional growth.

PROCEDURES:

Build Relationships:

A. Explore **W**ants, Needs & Perceptions: Discuss picture album or quality world, i.e., set goals, fulfilled & unfulfilled pictures, needs, viewpoints and "locus of control."

B. Share Wants & Perceptions: Tell what you want from them and how you view their situations, behaviors, wants, etc. This procedure is secondary to A above.

C. Get a Commitment: Help them solidify their desire to find more effective behaviors.

Explore Total Behavior:

Help them examine the **D**irection of their lives, as well as specifics of how they spend their time. Discuss ineffective & effective self talk.

Evaluation – The Cornerstone of Procedures:

Help them evaluate their behavioral direction, specific behaviors as well as wants, perceptions and commitments. Evaluate own behavior through follow-up, consultation and continued education.

Make **P**lans: Help them change direction of their lives.

Effective plans are **S**imple, **A**ttainable, **M**easurable, **I**mmediate, **C**onsistent, **C**ontrolled by the planner, and **C**ommitted to. The helper is **P**ersistent. Plans can be linear or paradoxical.

Note: The "Cycle" describes specific guidelines & skills. Effective implementation requires the artful integration of the guidelines & skills contained under Environment & Procedures in a spontaneous & natural manner geared to the personality of the helper. This requires training, practice & supervision. Also, the word "client" is used for anyone receiving help: student, employee, family member, etc.

For more information contact:

Robert E. Wubbolding, EdD, Director

Center for Reality Therapy
7672 Montgomery Road, PMB 383
Cincinnati, Ohio 45236

(513) 561-1911 • FAX (513) 561-3568
E-mail: wubsrt@fuse.net

The Center for Reality Therapy provides counseling, consultation, training and supervision including applications to schools, agencies, hospitals, companies and other institutions. The Center is a provider for many organizations which award continuing education units.

REFERENCES

Abu Bakar, M. (1994, January 12). Therapy focuses on personal responsibility. *The Straits Times*, p. 3.

Adams, R. (1992). *Adult friendship.* New York: Sage.

Akahori, S. (1999). A case of advanced endometrial cancer in a patient who was counseled using reality therapy. *Japanese Journal of Reality Therapy, 5*(1), 25–29.

Altamura, W. (1996). Interfacing reality therapy/choice theory as a method of reducing conflict with families who work together. *Journal of Reality Therapy, 16*(1), 102–105.

American Psychiatric Association. (1994). *Diagnostic and statistical manual of mental disorders* (4th ed.). Washington, DC: Author.

Arredondo, P., Toporek, R., Brown, S. P., Jones, J., Locke, D., Sanchez, J., & Stadler, H. (1996). *Operationalization of the multicultural competencies.* Alexandria, VA: Association for Multicultural Counseling and Development.

Augsberger, D. (1986). *Pastoral counseling across cultures.* Philadelphia: Westminster Press.

Babcock, T. M. (1983). The application of the principles of reality therapy on the student teaching experience: A case study approach. *Dissertation Abstracts, 44-08A,* 2388.

Baca, J. (1996). Alcohol misuse: a traditional Navajo view. *Journal of Reality Therapy, 15*(2), 44–45.

Bandura, A. (1997). *Self-efficacy: The exercise of control.* New York: Freeman.

Barbieri, P. (1997). Habitual desires: The destructive nature of expressing your anger. *International Journal of Reality Therapy, 17*(1), 17–23.

Basic, J., Ticak-Balaz, S., Uzelac, S., & Vorkapic-Jugovac, G. (1997). School in the student's quality world. *International Journal of Reality Therapy, 17*(1), 46–49.

Bean, J. (1988). The effects of individualized reality therapy on the recidivism rates and locus of control orientation of male juvenile offenders. *Dissertation Abstracts, 49-068,* 2370.

Bean, R., & Crane, D. (1996). Marriage and family research with ethnic minorities: Current status. *The American Journal of Family Therapy, 24*(1), 3–7.

Block, M. (1994). A study to investigate the use of reality therapy in small group counseling sessions to enhance self-concept levels of elementary students. *Dissertation Abstracts International, 56-02A,* p. 0460.

Bogolepov, S. (1998). From Russia with love. *International Journal of Reality Therapy, 17*(2), 30.

Bonuccelli, S. (1994). A qualitative analysis of high school dropout behavior through the lens of Glasser's control theory (Glasser, William). *Dissertation Abstracts, A 55/03,* 508.

Boyd, T. (1990). *Skill builder.* Charlotte, NC: Ty Boyd Enterprises.

Brandon, L. (1981). The effects of reality therapy upon students' absenteeism and locus of control of reinforcement. *Dissertation Abstracts. 42-OGA,* 238.

Bratter, T. (1974). Reality therapy: A group psychotherapy approach with adolescent alcoholics. *Annals of the New York Academy of Sciences, 233,* 104–114.

Bratter, B., Bratter, T., Maxym, C., Radda, H., & Steiner, K. (1993). The John Dewey Academy: A residential quality school for self-destructive adolescents who have superior intellectual and intuitive potential. *Journal of Reality Therapy, 12*(2), 42–53.

Bratter, T., Collabolletta, E., Gordon, D., & Kaufman, S. (1999). *The John Dewey Academy: Motivating unconvinced, gifted, self-destructive adolescents to use their superior assets.* Unpublished manuscript.

Brickell, J. (1992, September). The reality of stress and pressure. *Counselling News.*

Brinson, J., & Kottler, J. (1995). Minorities' underutilization of counseling centers' mental health services: A case for outreach and consultation. *Journal of Mental Health Counseling, 17*(4), 371–385.

Bruce, W. (1985). Reality therapy as a management strategy for dealing with the problem employee. *Dissertation Abstracts, 46-09A,* 2433.

Burnett, D. (1995). *Raising responsible kids.* Laguna Niguel, CA: Funagain Press.

Burns, M., Barth, M., Stevens, D., & Burns, L. (1998). Bringing choice theory and reality therapy into the deaf community. *International Journal of Reality Therapy, 17*(2), 24–26.

Carey, T., Farrell-Jones, M., & Rowan, H. (1996). What do you really want? A control theory/reality therapy approach to understanding alcoholism. *Journal of Reality Therapy, 16*(1), 3–18.

Carleton, R. (1994). Reality therapy in the Christian context (Audio cassette). Montgomery, AL: Private Publication.

Chance, E., Bibens, R., Cowley, J., Pouretedal, M., Dolese, P., & Virtue, D. (1990). Lifeline: A drug/alcohol treatment program for negatively addicted inmates. *Journal of Reality Therapy, 9*(2), 33–38.

Chance, E., & Chance, P. (1989). Class meetings: Fulfilling students' pathway to power. *Journal of Reality Therapy, 9*(1), 43–48.

Cheng, N. (1986). *Life and death in Shanghai.* New York: Grafton Books.

Chung, M. (1994). Can reality therapy help juvenile delinquents in Hong Kong? *Journal of Reality Therapy, 14*(1), 68–80.

Cockrum, J. R. (1989). Reality therapy: Interviews with Dr. William Glasser. *Psychology, 26*(1), 13–16.

Cockrum, J. R., & Cockrum, J. (1994). *The relationship questionnaire.* Louisville, KY: Quality Development Seminars.

Comiskey, P. (1993). Using reality therapy group training with at-risk high school freshmen. *Journal of Reality Therapy, 12*(2), 59–64.

Committee on the Elimination of Discrimination Against Women. (1995, September 24). *General recommendations on the articles of the convention on the elimination of all forms of discrimination against women.* New York: United Nations.

Corey, G. (2000a). *Theory and practice of counseling and psychotherapy* (6th ed.). Pacific Grove, CA: Brooks/Cole.

Corey, G. (2000b). *Theory and practice of group counseling* (5th ed.). Pacific Grove, CA: Brooks/Cole.

Corey, G., Corey, M.A., & Callanan, P. (1998). *Issues and ethics in the helping professions* (5th ed.). Pacific Grove, CA: Brooks Cole.

Corey, G., & Herlihy, B. (Eds.). (1996). *ACA ethical standards casebook.* Alexandria, VA: American Counseling Association.

Corsini, R., & Wedding, D. (Eds.). (1995). *Current psychotherapies.* Itasca, IL: Peacock.

Cottone, R. (1991). Counselor roles according to two counseling world views. *Journal of Counseling and Development, 69,* 398–401.

Cousins, N. (1979). *Anatomy of an illness.* New York: Norton.

Crawford, D., Bodine, R., & Hoglund, R. (1993). *The school for quality learning.* Champaign, IL: Research Press.

Cullinane, D. K. (1995). The influence of Glasser's control theory and reality therapy on educators: A case study. *Dissertation Abstracts, 56-09A,* 3546.

Deci, E. (1995). *Why we do what we do.* New York: Penguin Books.

Deming, W. E. (1986). *Out of the crisis.* Cambridge: Massachusetts Institute of Technology.

Deming, W. E. (1993). *The new economics.* Cambridge: Massachusetts Institute of Technology.

DeRosa, R. (1995, November 6). Jocelyn Elders on the airwaves. *USA Today,* p. 21.

Dinkmeyer, D., & Dinkmeyer, D. (1991). Adlerian family therapy. In A. Horne & L. Passmore (Eds.), *Family counseling and therapy* (pp. 384–401) Itasca, IL: Peacock.

Downing, C. (1996). Affirmations: Steps to counter negative, self-fulfilling prophecies. *Elementary School Guidance and Counseling, 20*(3), 174–179.

Dryden, J. (1994). *The quality schools initiative: Analysis of an educational reform as perceived by principals in K-12 consortium schools.* Unpublished doctoral dissertation, University of Pacific, Stockton, CA.

Dryden, J. (1996). The quality school consortium: Insights into defining, measuring and managing for quality in schools. *Journal of Reality Therapy, 16*(1), 47–57.

Easterbrooks, S. (1995). Improving pragmatic language outcomes of a college student with hearing loss: Effects on the individual and staff. *Journal of Reality Therapy, 14*(2), 37–44.

Edens, R., & Smyrl, T. (1994). Reducing classroom behaviors in physical education: A pilot study. *Journal of Reality Therapy, 13*(2), 40–44.

Evans, D. B. (1982). What are you doing? An interview with William Glasser. *Personnel & Guidance Journal, 60,* 460–465.

Author. (1997). Are you a hunter or a preserver? *Executive Strategies, 12*(7), 3.

Fates, M. (1989). A priceless gift. In N. Glasser (Ed.), *Control theory in the practice of reality therapy* (pp. 83–103). New York: HarperCollins.

Feinauer, L., Mitchel, J., Harper, J., & Dane, S. (1996). The impact of hardiness and severity of childhood sexual abuse on adult adjustment. *The American Journal of Family Therapy, 24*(3), 206–214.

Ford, E. (1980). *Permanent love.* Scottsdale, AZ: Brandt.

Ford, E. (1983). *Choosing to love.* Phoenix, AZ: Arrowhead.

Frankl, V. (1984). *Man's search for meaning.* New York: Washington Square Press.

Franklin, M. (1993). Eighty-two reality therapy doctoral dissertations written between 1970 & 1990. *Journal of Reality Therapy, 11*(2), 76–82.

Frazer, M. W. (1996). Cognitive problem solving and aggressive behavior among children. *Families in Society: The Journal of Contemporary Human Services, 77,* 19–28.

Freedman, J., & Combs, G. (1996). *Narrative therapy.* New York: Norton.

Friedman, T. (1999). *The lexus and the olive tree.* New York: Farrar, Straus, & Giroux.

Galindo, J. (1990). *Psychological needs assessment survey.* 1818 Mulberry, Alameda, CA 94501: Private Publication.

Gladding, S. (1998). *Family therapy, history, theory and practice.* Upper Saddle River, NJ: Merrill.

Glasser, C. (1990). *My quality world workbook.* Chatsworth, CA: The William Glasser Institute.

Glasser, C. (1996). *The quality world activity set.* Chatsworth, CA: The William Glasser Institute.

Glasser, N. (Ed.). (1980). *What are you doing?* New York: HarperCollins.

Glasser, N. (Ed.). (1989). *Control theory in the practice of reality therapy.* New York: HarperCollins.

Glasser, W. (1965). *Reality therapy.* New York: HarperCollins.

Glasser, W. (1968). *Schools without failure.* New York: HarperCollins.

Glasser, W. (1972). *Identity society.* New York: HarperCollins.

Glasser, W. (1975). *Woman with psychosomatic problems* (Audio cassette). Series 3, Tape F. Chatsworth, CA: The William Glasser Institute.

Glasser, W. (1976). *Positive addiction.* New York: HarperCollins.

Glasser, W. (1981). *Stations of the mind.* New York: HarperCollins.

Glasser, W. (1985). *Control theory.* New York: HarperCollins.

Glasser, W. (1986). *Basic concepts of reality therapy* (Chart). Chatsworth, CA: The William Glasser Institute.

Glasser, W. (1988). *Difficult couple: Marriage counseling* (Videotape). Chatsworth, CA: The William Glasser Institute.

Glasser, W. (1990a). *A diagram of the brain as a control system* (Chart). Chatsworth, CA: The William Glasser Institute.

Glasser, W. (1990b). The John Dewey Academy: A residential college preparatory therapeutic high school. A dialogue with Tom Bratter. *Journal of Counseling and Development, 68,* 582–585.

Glasser, W. (1990c). *The quality school.* New York: HarperCollins.

Glasser, W. (1991). *The quality school; educational ideas of William Glasser* (Videotape). Culver, IN: Culver Educational Foundation.

Glasser, W. (1992, Spring). Self-evaluation, trust & managing for quality. *Institute for Reality Therapy Newsletter,* 2–5.

Glasser, W. (1993). *The quality school teacher.* New York: HarperCollins.

Glasser, W. (1994). *The choice theory manager.* New York: HarperCollins.

Glasser, W. (1995). *Staying together.* New York: HarperCollins.

Glasser, W. (1996, July). *Address to institute faculty.* International Convention, The William Glasser Institute, Albuquerque.

Glasser, W. (1997). A new look at school failure and school success. *Phi Delta Kappan, 78*(8), 597–602.

Glasser, W. (1998a). *Choice theory.* New York: HarperCollins.

Glasser, W. (1998b). Reality therapy and choice theory. In H. Rosenthal (Ed.), *Favorite counseling and therapy techniques.* Washington, DC: Taylor and Francis.

Glasser, W. (1999). The William Glasser Institute discipline policy. In *Programs, Policies and procedures of The William Glasser Institute.* Chatsworth, CA: The William Glasser Institute.

Glasser, W. (2000). *Reality therapy in action.* New York: HarperCollins.

Glasser, W., & Glasser, C. (1999). *The language of choice theory.* New York: Harper Collins.

Glasser, W., & Karrass, C. (1980). *Both-win management.* Los Angeles, CA: Institute for Reality Therapy.

Glasser, W., & Wubbolding, R. (1995). Reality therapy. In R. Corsini (Ed.), *Current psychotherapies* (pp. 293–321). Itasca, IL: Peacock.

Goleman, D. (1995). *Emotional intelligence.* New York: Bantam Books.

Gorski, T. (1985). *The developmental model of recovery.* Indianapolis: Access Publications.

Gorter-Cass, S. (1988). Program evaluation of an alternative school using William Glasser's reality therapy model for disruptive youth. *Dissertation Abstracts International, 49,* 1702A.

Goshi, K. (1984). *With respect to the Japanese.* Yarmouth, ME: Intercultural Press.

Granello, P. F., & Granello D. H. (1998). Training counseling students to use outcome research. *Counselor Education and Supervision, 37,* 224–237.

Greene, B. (1994). *New paradigms for creating quality schools.* Chapel Hill, NC: New View Publications.

Greene, B., & Uroff, S. (1991). Quality education and at risk students. *Journal of Reality Therapy, 10*(2), 3–11.

Griffith, C. (1999, June 27). Responsibility room: Sturgis high school, Sturgis, Michigan. (Private Correspondence).

Grimesey, R. (1990). Teacher and student perceptions of their middle school's implementation of reality therapy. *Journal of Reality Therapy, 10*(1), 42–45.

Hackett, J. (1998). Program description: Victor J. Andrew High School. Orland Park Schools, Conslidated High School District 230, 15100 South 94th Avenue, Orland Park, IL 60462: Private publication.

Haley, J. (1996). *The brief, brief therapy of Milton Erickson.* Phoenix, AZ: The Milton Erickson Foundation.

Hallock-Bannigan, S. (1994). Intervention with the chemical dependent individual. *Journal of Reality Therapy, 13*(2), 17–19.

Hammel, B. (1989). *So good at acting bad.* In N. Glasser (Ed.), *Control theory in the practice of reality therapy* (pp. 205–223). New York: HarperCollins.

Hammond, W., & Romney, D. (1995). Cognitive factors contributing to adolescent depression. *Journal of Youth and Adolescence, 24*(6), 667–682.

Harris, K. (1995). A study of control theory effect on attitudes, anxiety, computer knowledge, and locus of control of adult vocational learners in Kansas (reality control theory). *Dissertation Abstracts, 56-07A,* 2528.

Hart-Hester, S., Heuchert, C., & Whittier, K. (1989). The effects of teaching reality therapy techniques to elementary students to help change behaviors. *Journal of Reality Therapy, 8*(2), 13–18.

Harvey, V. S., & Retter, K. (1995). The development of the basic needs survey. *Journal of Reality Therapy, 15*(1), 76–80.

Hayes-O'Brien, M. (1998a, Winter). The choice community project: An invitation to faculty. *The William Glasser Institute Newsletter,* p. 4.

Hayes-O'Brien, M. (1998b). Choice community project update. *The William Glasser Institute Northeast Regional News, 4,* 1.

Hemingway, E. (1952). *The old man and the sea.* New York: Scribner.

Hill, C. (1996). The current state of empathy research. *Journal of Counseling Psychology, 45*(3), 261–270.

Ho, D. Y. E. (1985). Cultural values and professional issues in clinical psychology: Implications from the Hong Kong experience. *The American Psychologist, 40*(11), 1212–1218.

Holleran, J. (1981). Effect of group counseling on locus of control and academic achievement: Reality therapy with underachieving junior high students. *Dissertation Abstracts, 41*(12A), 498.

Honeyman, A. (1990). Perceptual changes in addicts as a consequence of reality therapy based on group treatment. *Journal of Reality Therapy, 9*(2), 53–59.

Ingram, J., & Hinkle, S. (1990). Reality therapy and the scientist-practitioner approach: A case study. *Journal of Reality Therapy, 10*(1), 54–58.

Ivey, A. (1980). *Counseling & psychotherapy.* Englewood Cliffs, NJ: Prentice-Hall.

Ivey, A., & Ivey, M. B. (1999). *Intentional interviewing and counseling* (4th ed.). Pacific Grove, CA: Brooks Cole.

Ivey, A., Bradford-Ivey, M., & Simek-Morgan, L. (1999). *Counseling and psychotherapy: A multicultural perspective.* Boston, MA: Allyn and Bacon.

Jacobson, E. (1938). *Progressive relaxation.* Chicago, IL: University of Chicago Press.

Johnson Institute. (1996). *Training families to do a successful intervention.* Minneapolis, MN: Johnson Institute-QVS.

Johnson, V. (1980). *I'll quit tomorrow.* San Francisco: HarperCollins.

Kaiser, H. (1955). The problem of responsibility in psychotherapy. *Psychiatry, 18,* 205–211. Reprinted in Fierman, B. (Ed.). (1965). *Effective psychotherapy.* New York: Free Press.

Kakitani, M. (1999). Punished by rewards. *Japanese Journal of Reality Therapy, 5*(1), 2–7.

Kemp, A. (1994). African-American students' expectations about counseling: A comparative investigation. *Journal of Multicultural Counseling and Development, 22*(5), 257–264.

Kim, H. S. (1997). *The study on the effect of group reality therapy according to the sex factor.* Unpublished masters thesis, Graduate School of Education, Sogang University Seoul, Korea.

Kim, K. S. (1997). *The effect of group reality therapy on the self-esteem and the personality traits of primary students.* Unpublished masters thesis, Graduate School of Education, Sogang University, Seoul, Korea.

Kim, M. S. (1998). *The effect of reality therapy on the locus of control and responsibility of elementary school children.* Unpublished masters thesis, Graduate School of Education, Sogang University, Seoul, Korea.

Kim, R.-I., & Hwang, M. G. (1997). Making the world I want based on reality therapy. *Journal of Reality Therapy, 16*(1), 26–35.

King, V. (1999). *Engaging community members in constructivist learning: Parent involvement in the development of a middle school science curriculum.* Unpublished manuscript.

Kipling, R. (1910). If. In *The collected verse of Rudyard Kipling.* New York: Doubleday.

Kohn, A. (1993). *Punished by rewards.* New York: Houghton-Mifflin.

Kopp, R. (1995). *Metaphor therapy.* New York: Brunner/Mazel.

Lakoff, G., & Johnson, M. (1980). *Metaphors we live by.* Chicago: University of Chicago Press.

Lamarine, R. (1995). Child and adolescent depression. *Journal of School Health, 65*(9), 390–392.

Landis, R. (1995). *Advances in the treatment of post traumatic stress disorder* (Audiotapes). Laguna Niguel, CA: Southern California Society for Ericksonian Psychotherapy and Hypnosis.

Lawson, A., & Lawson, G. (1994, December 17). Gangs and drugs: The new family? *Family Therapy News,* p. 18.

Lennon, B. (1994). The development of reality therapy in Ireland. *Journal of Reality Therapy in Ireland, 13*(2), 3–7.

Lewis, J., & Quatman, J. (1995/1996) *Statistical summaries of disciplinary actions toward students: Cincinnati public schools, 1994–1995 and 1996–1996 school years.* Cincinnati, OH: Cincinnati Public Schools.

Linnenberg, D. (1997). Religion, spirituality and the counseling process. *International Journal of Reality Therapy, 17*(1), 55–59.

Lojk, L. (1986). My experiences using reality therapy. *Journal of Reality Therapy, 5*(2), 28–35.

Lord, B. (1990). *Legacies: A Chinese mosaic.* New York: Knopf.

Louis, G. (1998). The Quality School: Effects on student attitude toward school. *Dissertation Abstracts International, 59*(05), 1415A.

Ludwig, S., & Mentley, K. (1997). *Quality is the key.* Wyoming, MI: KWM Educational Services.

MacColl, L. (1946). *Fundamental theory of servo-mechanisms.* New York: Van Nostrand.

Maisiak, R., Austin, J., & Heck, L. (1995). Health outcomes of two telephone interventions for patients with rheumatoid arthritis or osteoarthritis. *Arthritis and Rheumatism, 39*(8), 1391–1399.

Martin, S., & Thompson, C. (1995). Reality therapy and goal attainment scaling: A program for freshman student athletes. *Journal of Reality Therapy, 14*(2), 45–54.

Martig, R. M. (1978). The behavioral and psychological effects of group reality therapy on male and female college students. *Dissertation Abstracts International, 34*(04B), 1902A.

Maslow, A. (1970). *Motivation and personality* (2nd. ed.). New York: Harper & Row.

Matthews, L. (1996). What do you want? Uncovering basic needs through the lessons of animals. *Journal of Reality Therapy, 15*(2), 46–50.

McGoldrick, M., & Pearce, J. (1981). Family therapy with Irish-Americans. *Family Process, 20,* 223–241.

McNamara, D. (1977). The phantom lurks in the quality world. *International Journal of Reality Therapy, 17*(1), 63–68.

Mickel, E. (1993). Parent assistance workshops (P.A.W.S.). Reality based intervention for the crack exposed child. *Journal of Reality Therapy, 12*(2), 20–28.

Mickel, E. (1994). Violence is a chosen behavior. *Journal of Reality Therapy, 13*(2), 7–13.

Mickel, E. (1995). Andragogy and control theory: Theoretical foundation for family mediation. *Journal of Reality Therapy, 14*(2), 55–62.

Mickel, E. (1996a). Addicting behaviors: Controlling the world we perceive. *Journal of Reality Therapy, 16*(1), 111–116.

Mickel, E. (1996b). Self-evaluation for quality: Method and model. *Journal of Reality Therapy, 15*(2), 71–77.

Mickel, E., & Liddie, B. (1998). Black family therapy: Spirituality, social constructivism and choice theory. *International Journal of Reality Therapy, 18*(1), 29–33.

Mickel, E., & Liddle-Hamilton, B. (1996). Family therapy in transition: Social constructivism and control theory. *Journal of Reality Therapy, 16*(1), 95–100.

Mintz, J. (1992). *Workplace needs survey.* Boca Raton, FL: Institute for Management Development.

Miranda, J. (1998). *Study of the reality therapy model: Development of a questionnaire for the evaluation of its constructs.* Thesis, Malaga University, Malaga, Spain.

Moore, T. (1943). *Personal mental hygiene.* New York: Grune & Stratton.

Morales, M. A. A. (1995). *Why reality therapy works for Puerto Ricans.* Unpublished manuscript; available from Box 4929 Hato Rey, Puerto Rico 00919.

Mosak, H. (1989). Adlerian psychology. In R. Corsini & D. Wedding (Eds.), *Current psychotherapies* (pp. 65–116). Itasca, IL: Peacock.

Murphy, L. (1997). Efficacy of reality therapy in the schools: A review of the research from 1980–1995. *Journal of Reality Therapy, 16*(2), 12–20.

Napan, K. (1996). Teaching and learning as a challenge and need fulfilling activity. *Journal of Reality Therapy, 16*(1), 39–46.

Nashid, N. (1998). *Justice and race, a Muslim perspective.* Unpublished manuscript, Xavier University, Cincinnati, OH.

O'Donnell, D. J. (1987). History of the growth of the Institute for Reality Therapy. *Journal of Reality Therapy, 7*(1), 2–8.

Okonji, J., Ososkie, J., & Pulos, S. (1996). Preferred style and ethnicity of counselors by African American males. *Journal of Black Psychology, 22*(3), 329–339.

Omar, M. (1994). *Effective relaxation techniques* (Audiotape). Kuwait: Al- Nazaer Publishing.

Ornish, D. (1998). *Love and survival.* New York: HarperCollins.

Palmatier, L. (1996). Freud defrauded while Glasser defreuded: From pathologizing to talking solutions. *Journal of Reality Therapy, 16*(1), 75–94.

Palmatier, L. (1998). *Crisis counseling for a quality school community.* Bristol, PA: Accelerated Development.

Parish, T. (1988). Helping teachers take more effective control. *Journal of Reality Therapy, 8*(1), 41–43.

Parish, T. (1988a). Helping college students take control of their lives. *College Student Journal, 22*(1), 64–69.

Parish, T. (1988b). Enhancing college students' social skills and self-concepts. *College Student Journal, 22*(2), 203–205.

Parish, T. (1992a). Using "Quality School" procedures to enhance student enthusiasm and student performance. *Journal of Instructional Psychology, 19*(4), 266–268.

Parish, T. (1992b). Utilizing "Quality School' strategies to enhance enthusiasm for taking statistics. *College Student Journal, 26*, 359–360.

Parish, T., & Parish, J. (1993). Validating a method to identify "at-risk" students. *Journal of Reality Therapy, 12*(2), 65–69.

Parish, T. (1991). Helping students take control via an interactive voice communications system. *Journal of Reality Therapy, 11*(1), 38–40.

Parish, T., Martin, P., & Khramtsova, I. (1992). Enhancing convergence between our real and ideal selves. *Journal of Reality Therapy, 11*(2), 37–40.

Patalano, F. (1997). Developing the working alliance in marital therapy: A psychodynamic perspective. *Contemporary Family Therapy, 19*(4), 497–504.

Pedersen, P. (1988). *A handbook for developing multicultural awareness.* Alexandria, VA: American Counseling Association.

Peterson, A., Chang, C., & Collins, P. (1997). The effects of reality therapy on locus of control among students in Asian universities. *Journal of Reality Therapy, 16*(2), 80–87.

Peterson, A., Chang, C., & Collins, P. (1998). Taiwanese University students meet their basic needs through studying choice theory/reality therapy. *International Journal of Reality Therapy, 17*(2), 27–29.

Peterson, A., & Parr, G. (1982). Pathogram: A visual aid to obtain focus and commitment. *Journal of Reality Therapy, 2*(1), 18–22.

Peterson, A., & Woodward, G. (1993). Quantitative analysis of the CHOICE drug education program for sixth grade students. *Journal of Reality Therapy, 13*(1), 40–45.

Peterson, A., & Woodward, G. (1994). Pete's pathogram as a tool to measure the success of the CHOICE Drug Education Program. *Journal of Reality Therapy, 14*(1), 86–91.

Peterson, A., Woodward, G., & Kissko, R. (1991). A comparison of basic week students and introduction to counseling graduate students on four basic need factors. *Journal of Reality Therapy, 11*(1), 31–37.

Pina, P. (1995, November 6). Blindness doesn't dim ability of man named top teacher. *USA Today,* p. 21.

Pinderhughes, E. (1982). Afro-American families and the victim system. In M. McGoldrick, J. K. Pearce, & J. Giordano (Eds.), *Ethnicity and family therapy* (pp. 109–122). New York: Guilford Press.

Powers, W. (1973). *Behavior: The control of perception.* New York: Aldine Press.

Prediger, D. (1993). *Multicultural Assessment Standards: A compilation for counselors.* Alexandria, VA: American Counselor Association.

Rachor, R. (1995). An evaluation of the first step PASSAGES domestic violence program. *Journal of Reality Therapy, 14*(2), 29–36.

Radtke, L., Sapp, M., & Farrell, W. (1997). Reality therapy: A meta-analysis. *International Journal of Reality Therapy, 17*(1), 4–9.

Rehak, A. T. (1996). Deming's management obligations and control theory. *Journal of Reality Therapy, 15*(2), 51–60.

Rehak, A. T. (1998). Workers and their capacity. *International Journal of Reality Therapy, 17*(2), 31–33.

Renna, R. (1996). Beyond role play: Why reality therapy is so difficult in the real world. *Journal of Reality Therapy, 15*(2), 18–29.

Renna, R. (1997). Special education and the quality school: Are we above the law? *Journal for Reality Therapy, 16*(2), 3–11.

Renna, R. (1998). Israel: Conflict and the quality world. *International Journal of Reality Therapy, 18*(1), 4–7.

Renna, R., Kimball, P., Brescia, J., & O'Connor, J. (1999). *The use of reality therapy with disabled students and the attainment of competitive employment: A survey of eighty-seven graduates from 1992-1998 with accompanying case study.* Manuscript.

Reuss, N. (1985). Alternatives to cocaining. *Journal of Reality Therapy, 4*(2), 8–11.

Richardson, B. (2000). *Working with challenging youth: Lessons learned along the way.* Bristol, PA: Accelerated Development.

Rogers, C. (1957). The necessary and sufficient conditions of therapeutic personality change. *Journal of Consulting Psychology, 21,* 95–103.

Sansone, D. (1998). Research, internal control and choice theory. Where's the beef? *International Journal of Reality Therapy, 17*(2), 39–43.

Schlesinger, A. (1998). *The disuniting of America.* New York: Norton.

Sewall, K. (1982). A comparing and contrasting of reality therapy and rational emotive therapy. *Journal of Reality Therapy, 1*(2), 18–21.

Silver, E. J., Stein, R. E. K., & Dadds, M. R. (1996). Moderating effects of family structure on the relationship between physical and mental health in urban children with chronic illness. *Journal of Pediatric Psychology, 21*(1), 43–56.

Sleek, S. (1994). Merits of long, short term therapy debated. *Monitor, 25*(7), 41–42.

Small, S. (1977). *Radius, a reality therapy school.* Unpublished master's thesis, University of Saskatchewan, Saskatchewan, Canada.

Song, J. E. (1997). *A study in the effect of reality therapy upon the ego of unemployed youth who do not enter a higher school.* Unpublished masters thesis, Graduate School of Education, Sogang University, Seoul, Korea.

Sowell, T. (1994). *Race and culture, a world view.* New York: Basic Books.

Sowell, T. (1996). *Migrations and cultures, a world view.* New York: Basic Books.

Sowell, T. (1998). *Conquests & cultures.* New York: Basic Books.

Stivers, C. (1998). Parent-adolescent communication and its relationship to adolescent depression and suicide proneness. *Adolescence, 23*(90), 291–295.

Storti, C. (1991). *The art of crossing cultures.* Yarmouth, ME: Intercultural Press.

Sullo, R. (1997). *Inspiring quality in your school.* West Haven, CT: NEA Professional Library.

Swenson, S. (1995). *Benjamin Franklin High School: What we are learning about teaching/learning strategies.* Orland Park, IL: Consolidated High School District 230.

Tabata, M. (1999). The usefulness of reality therapy for biblical counseling. *Japanese Journal of Reality Therapy, 5*(1), 30–34.

Teachman, J. D. & Paasch, K. (1998). The family and educational aspirations. *Journal of Marriage and Family, 60,* 704–714.

Thernstrom, S., & Thernstrom, A. (1997). *America in black and white.* New York: Simon & Schuster.

Thompson, F. (1947). *The hound of heaven.* Wilton, CT: Morehouse-Barlow.

Thomson, B. (1990). Appropriate and inappropriate use of humor in psychotherapy as perceived by certified reality therapists: A Delhi study. *Journal of Reality Therapy, 10*(1), 59–65.

Tollefson, W. (1980). Coming out of the corner. In N. Glasser (Ed.), *What are you doing?*(pp. 236–244). New York: HarperCollins.

Vontress, C. (1999). Culture and counseling. *Counseling Today, 41*(8), 8ff.

Watanabe, Y. (1999). Choice theory and stress control. *Japanese Journal of Reality Therapy, 5*(1), 8–17.

Watson, M., & Fetter, P. (1994). The application of control theory for exercise initiation and compliance. *Journal of Reality Therapy, 14*(1), 81–87.

Watzlawick, P. (1988). *Ultra-solutions.* New York: Norton.

Webster's new world dictionary of the American language. (1980). New York: Simon & Schuster, Second College Edition.

Weinberg, G. (1985). *Secrets of consulting.* New York: Dorset House.

Wesley, J. (1988). Group reality therapy intervention for substance abuse with the severely and chronically mentally ill. *Masters Abstracts International,* 2701-59.

Whisnant, P., Hammond, R., & Tilmon, R. (1999). Comparing methods of counseling among Arkansas CADCs. *The Counselor, 17*(4), 33–36.

White, W. (1990). *The culture of addiction; the culture of recovery.* Center City, MN: Hazelden.

Whitehouse, D. G. (1984). Adlerian antecedents to reality therapy and control theory. *Journal of Reality Therapy, 3*(2), 10–14.

Wiener, N. (1948). *Cybernetics.* New York: MIT Press and Wiley.

Wiener, N. (1952). *Nonlinear problems in random theory.* New York: MIT Press and Wiley.

Wigle, S. (1996). Transforming a teacher education course: Helping to make the transition to quality schools. *Journal of Reality Therapy, 16*(1), 58–62.

The William Glasser Insitute. (1999). *Programs, policies and procedures of the William Glasser Institute.* Chatsworth, CA: Author.

Wilson, L., & Stith, S. (1991). Culturally sensitive therapy with black client. *Journal of Multicultural Counseling and Development, 19*(1), 32–43.

Witmer, M. (1985). *Pathways to personal growth.* Muncie, IN: Accelerated Development.

Woo, A. (1998). *A developmental study of a group social work program using reality therapy.* Unpublished doctoral dissertation, Department of Social Work. Yonsei University, Seoul, Korea.

Wooden, C. (1998). For Asian catholics, cultural context is important. *The Catholic Messenger,* p. 12.

Wrenn, C. G. (1962). *The counselor in a changing world.* Washington, DC: APGA.

Wubbolding, R. (1984). How to motivate yourself and your children. *Landmark (Indo American Society, Bombay, India), 2*(9), 5–7.

Wubbolding, R. (1985a). Characteristics of the inner picture album. *Journal of Reality Therapy, 5*(1), 28–30.

Wubbolding, R. (1985b). Reality therapy applied to alcoholism. *The Counselor, 3,* 5–6.

Wubbolding, R. (1988). *Using reality therapy.* New York: HarperCollins.

Wubbolding, R. (1989). Pictures in conflict. In N. Glasser (Ed.), *Control theory in the practice of reality therapy* (pp. 239–254). New York: HarperCollins.

Wubbolding, R. (1990). Evaluation: The cornerstone in the practice of reality therapy. *Omar Psychology Practitioner Series, 2,* 6–27.

Wubbolding, R. (1991a). *Understanding reality therapy.* New York: HarperCollins.

Wubbolding, R. (1991b). *Using reality therapy in group counseling* (Videotape). Cincinnati, OH: Center for Reality Therapy.

Wubbolding, R. (1992). *You steer* (Audiocassette). Kansas City, MO: Credence Cassettes.

Wubbolding, R. (1994). The early years of control theory: Forerunners Marcus Aurelius & Norbert Wiener. *Journal of Reality Therapy, 13*(2), 51–54.

Wubbolding, R. (1996a). *Employee motivation.* Knoxville, TN: SPC Press.

Wubbolding, R. (1996b). Professional issues: The use of questions in reality therapy. *Journal of Reality Therapy, 16*(1), 122–126.

Wubbolding, R. (1998a). Client inner self-evaluation: A necessary prelude to change. In H. Rosenthal (Ed.), *Favorite counseling and therapy techniques* (pp. 197–198). Washington, DC: Taylor and Francis.

Wubbolding, R. (1998b). DEGREES: Who Needs Them? The William Glasser Institute Does!! *International Journal of Reality Therapy, 18*(1), 54–55.

Wubbolding, R. (1998c). *The WDEP system for effective management.* Cincinnati, OH: Center for Reality Therapy.

Wubbolding, R. (1999a). Creating intimacy through reality therapy. In J. Carlson & L. Sperry (Eds.), *The intimate couple.* Levittown, PA: Brunner/Mazel.

Wubbolding, R. (1999b). *Cycle of managing, supervising, counseling and coaching* (Chart, 11th revision). Cincinnati, OH: Center for Reality Therapy.

Wubbolding, R. (2000a). Reality therapy. In A. Horne (Eds.), *Family counseling and therapy* (3rd ed., pp. 420–453). Itasca, IL: Peacock.

Wubbolding, R. (2000b). *Reality therapy training manual* (11th revision). Cincinnati, OH: Center for Reality Therapy.

Wubbolding, R., Al-Rashidi, B., Brickell, J., Kakitani, M., Kim R. I., Lennon, B., Lojk, L., Ong, K. H., Honey, I., Stijacic, D., & Tham, E. (1998). Multicultural awareness: Implications for reality therapy and choice theory. *International Journal of Reality Therapy, 17*(2), 4–6.

Wubbolding, R., & Brickell, J. (1995). Reality therapy and addiction. *One to One, 7*(5), 1–5. (Published by National Association of Alcohol and Drug Abuse Counsellors, United Kingdom.)

Wubbolding, R. & Brickell, J. (1998). Qualities of the reality therapist. *International Journal of Reality Therapy, 17*(2), 47–49.

Wubbolding, R., & Glasser, C. (1992). Chartalk: A valuable tool for learning. *Journal of Reality Therapy, 11*(2), 47–50.

Yamashiro, G., & Matsuoka, J. (1997). Help-seeking among Asian and Pacific Americans: A multiperspective analysis. *Social Work, 42*(2), 176–186.

Zeig, J. (1985). *Experiencing Erickson: An introduction to the man and his work.* New York: Brunner/Mazel.

INDEX

ABOUT THE AUTHOR

Robert E. Wubbolding, EdD, counselor, psychologist, international presenter, teacher, and author, is professor of counseling at Xavier University in Cincinnati, Ohio as well as Director of the Center for Reality Therapy. For The William Glasser Institute in Chatsworth, California Bob is both Senior Faculty and Director of Training. Teaching a wide variety of reality therapy applications he presents compassionate and skillful demonstrations to audiences around the world. His latest book *Reality Therapy for the 21st Century* represents many years of personal training with Dr. Glasser and Bob's own personal interpretation and extensions of these life enhancing ideas. *Reality Therapy for the 21st Century* includes an in depth interview with Dr. Glasser in which readers gain new insights into the founder of Reality Therapy as well as his relentless quest to help people get what they want out of life and contribute to the lives of others.

Dr. Wubbolding offers his readers the opportunity to think more globally and become more culturally aware through the use of anecdotal experiences gleaned from working in North America, Asia, Europe, and the Middle East. Bob illustrates how reality therapy is used to help people discover, clarify, and act on their inner motivations. His entertaining, straight forward and thought provoking style will educate, inspire and motivate the reader. He writes to fulfill his passion for teaching and to offer solace, knowledge and hope. Dr. Wubbolding works with schools, businesses, corrections personnel, mental health agencies, and religious institutions, teaching them how to become more effective, not only as individuals but also as teams using the tenets of reality therapy. Besides teaching reality therapy, he enjoys reading, history, travel, and Xavier University basketball. He resides in Cincinnati with his wife, best friend, and colleague Sandie.

For more information about the theory and practice of reality therapy and for information about training opportunities, please contact:

Robert E. Wubbolding, Ed.D.
Center for Reality Therapy
PMB 383
7672 Montgomery Road
Cincinnati, OH 45236, USA
Phone: (513) 561-1911; Fax: (513) 561-3568

The William Glasser Institute
22024 Lassen Street, #118
Chatsworth, CA 91311, USA
Phone: (818) 700-8000; Fax: (818) 700-0555

ENDORSEMENTS

The long-awaited book from the master of reality therapy. This easy-to-read volume provides both clinical insight and empirical evidence. It is must reading for therapists in the second century of therapy and for educators at any level.

Jon Carlson, Psy.D., Ed.D.
Professor, Governors State University

Reality Therapy for the 21st Century *is an easy-to-read, useful, and comprehensive text that represents significant extensions of reality therapy. Dr. Wubbolding presents a series of thought-provoking questions designed to help readers apply his WDEP system of reality therapy to counseling practice. I particularly appreciate his guidelines for assisting clients in taking inventory of their current behavior to determine the degree to which what they are doing is working for them. His questions that are designed to challenge clients in making a self-evaluation and to develop a plan for change are excellent. The author draws on his professional experience in giving workshops in many countries as a way of translating key concepts and procedures of reality therapy for diverse cultural groups.*

Gerald Corey, Ed.D., ABPP
Professor of Human Services and Counseling
California State University, Fullerton

Reality Therapy for the 21st Century *is essential reading for anyone who works with children and youth. Dr. Wubbolding has the insight and experience to understand how important reality therapy is as a tool for all educators.*

Dr. Phillip Harris, Director
Phi Delta Kappa International
Center for Professional Development and Services

Counselors, psychotherapists, teachers and managers outside North America who practice or teach reality therapy and choice theory have always appreciated Dr. Wubbolding for his efforts to introduce Dr. William Glasser's ideas to different cultures by showing the universal applicability of them. They were an important revelation for those of us who lived almost all our lives in totalitarian regimes. In this book, Dr. Wubbolding brings the ideas to the 21st century, enriching them as a university professor with his own erudite ideas and vast practical experience as a counselor and psychologist.

Leon Lojk, Psychologist, Slovenia
Member, European Association for Psychotherapy

As his previous book, Using Reality Therapy, *has made a great impact on us in Japan, I am sure that his new book,* Reality Therapy for the 21st Century, *will receive even greater acceptance here in Japan.*

Masaki Kakitani, President of Kakitani Counseling Center
President, The William Glasser Institute, Japan

261

In terms of depth and breadth, the most comprehensive source currently available in its coverage of reality therapy and choice theory. The attention paid to the impact of culture and the need for and existence of research fill a vacuum in the literature. An important book for educators, mental health practitioners, and organizational personnel.

Lawrence Litwack, Ed.D, ABPP
Chairman, Department of Counseling Psychology
Northeastern University
Editor-in-Chief, *International Journal of Reality Therapy*

Bob Wubbolding's latest, Reality Therapy for the 21st Century, *is an excellent guide to reality therapy: user-friendly, practical, and comprehensive—an indispensable companion in every counselling office! It's a delight to find choice theory so lucidly explained and so logically applied.*

Sr. Elizabeth Tham, fdcc
International Coordinator, Education
Canossian Sisters

Reality Therapy for the 21st Century *integrates the core of reality therapy with advances in research and multicultural issues. Robert Wubbolding, an innovative contributor to reality therapy for over 30 years, shows his skill through his knowledge and application of techniques and principles of reality therapy to counseling, therapy, education, and business as they evolve into the next century.*

Richard S. Sharf, Ph.D.
Counseling Psychologist
Center for Counseling and Student Development
University of Delaware

In his years in reality therapy and the choice therapy world, Dr. Wubbolding has made marvelous connections between Dr. Glasser's teachings and numerous people all over the world. Now, Bob is foreseeing and suggesting that Reality Therapy for the 21st Century *will embrace more academic support and deal with cultural differences. Through his clear teachings and his gentle invitations, many will choose to become motivated for the quality change!*

Rose In-Za Kim, Ph.D.
Korea Counselling Center
Dean, Retired, Sogang University, Seoul, Korea
Director, The William Glasser Institute, Korea

Dr. Wubbolding's latest book, Reality Therapy for the 21st Century, *is one I strongly recommend to everyone interested in pursuing reality therapy. Chapter 3, "Other Systems: How Is Reality Therapy Different?", serves as an enlightening explanation for both the student and the professional. Chapter 12, summarizing research on reality therapy, provides much needed credibility for reality therapy. Of particular interest to me, as a member of the international community, is the chapter on multicultural counseling. This book is a must for my professional library.*

Kerry Panitz, Director
The William Glasser Institute, Australia
President, Kerry Panitz and Associates
Outstanding Business Achiever Award from Logan Business Achiever Awards
Shailer Park, Queensland, Australia

Reality Therapy has long been recognized as an effective therapeutic approach used in dealing with human behavior. Dr. Wubbolding, in Reality Therapy for the 21st Century, *has provided us with a book that is filled with valuable information and insight. This book, with its emphasis on theory, proven effectiveness, and results, will be very useful to educators, psychologists, social workers, youth counselors, and administrators.*

Michael Reese, M.S.
Associate Director, Boys' Haven
Louisville, Kentucky

In Reality Therapy for the 21st Century, *Robert Wubbolding again offers stunningly simple and sensible thoughts for counselors and therapists from all orientations and settings. This landmark work firmly places reality therapy in a nexus of techniques, theory, and research that are necessary to meet the challenges facing the helping industry in an increasingly complex, interrelated world. For practitioners looking for solid practical, and efficient methods for working with a full spectrum of clients, Dr. Wubbolding's newest book is like having a road map into the future.*

Lauretta Omeltschenko, Ed.D., LPCC
Private practitioner with trauma victims
Adjunct Professor,
Counselor Education and
School Psychologist training programs
Xavier University, Cincinnati, Ohio
Miami University in Ohio

Bob Wubbolding's treatment of reality therapy can be used in many cultures. He demonstrates that the method is not merely Euro-American. It is used by people from a multitude of backgrounds. This book can be used not only by therapists, but by educators, both administrators and classroom teachers.

Kwee Hiong Ong, Ph.D.
Educational Psychologist
Ministry of Education
Singapore

This is a truly significant work. Dr. Wubbolding does an excellent job of taking reality therapy into the 21st century by exploring such cutting edge issues as cross-cultural counseling and research. This book brims with practical tools and persuasive ideas on how to be an effective helper to others. I highly recommend you read and reread this work.

Barbara McFarland, Ed.D.
Psychologist
Author of *Brief Therapy and Eating Disorders,
Shame and Body Image,* and *My Mother Was Right*

For 30 years, I have watched Robert Wubbolding move through the ranks of reality therapy and quality schools, so now, in my opinion, his statue is second only to William Glasser. I believe Wubbolding is the heir apparent. Having read the rough draft, I believe this book is essential reading for not only all reality therapists but also educators and psychotherapists as we enter the millennium. My staff already has read it and await the final copy.

Thomas Edward Bratter, Ed.D.
President and Founder
The John Dewey Academy

Robert Wubbolding's book on choice theory and reality therapy is a definitive statement that straddles the pivotal point of two millennia and promises to serve therapists through this temporal transition and well into the 21st century. Therapists and nontherapists alike can apply the practical ideas in this book to free up their personal lives and enjoy their relationships to the hilt.

Larry L. Palmatier, Ph.D.
Counseling Psychology Department
University of San Francisco

Teachers, administrators and anyone who deals with students will find this book eminently useful. I highly recommend the works of Dr. Wubbolding, especially this definitive book.

J. Robert Cockrum, Ed.D.
Emeritus Professor of Educational Psychology
Kentucky Wesleyan College

This book describes what happens when we merge current research and sensible practice: Professionals grow as they teach responsible behavior; students flourish as they learn the habit of behaving responsibly.
Stuart Swenson, Ed.D.
Director of Program Assessment and Student Services
Consolidated High School District 230
Orland Park, Illinois

Given the ongoing increase in the popularity of Dr. Glasser's ideas and Dr. Wubbolding's well-established reputation, I believe this book will be well received by persons wishing to learn reality therapy. The emphasis on research and transcultural work is most timely because of the remarkable spread of these ideas in many countries and cultures.
Brian Lennon, M.Sc.
Chair, The William Glasser Institute, Ireland

Our experiences in our schools with the study and use of choice theory, reality therapy, and the quality school has been an exciting journey. Reality Therapy for the 21st Century *will help us grow in competence as we attempt to communicate more effectively with each other and with our students.*
Jack Davis, Ed.S.
Assistant Superintendent
Plymouth Community School Corporation
Plymouth, Indiana

With a student contact of approximately 10 per day in the Responsibility Room, I can say, for sure, that reality therapy works in this setting. It has also created a positive sense of unity among our staff and the entire school community. "Educational fads" come and go, but this theory works. Bob Wubbolding's book, Reality Therapy for the 21st Century, *adds immensely to the theory and practice of reality therapy.*
Carol Griffith, B.A.
Supervisor of the Responsibility Room
Sturgis High School

Besides being a skilled practitioner, Bob Wubbolding is an internationally known authority on reality therapy, choice theory and lead management. These qualities, enhanced by his warmth and wonderful sense of humor have had a significant impact in introducing and strengthening William Glasser's ideas in the United Kingdom over the last 10 years. I highly recommend this book for anyone wanting to learn more about reality therapy and those already well versed or qualified in the theory and practice.
John Brickell, D.C.
Senior Faculty, The William Glasser Institute
Director, Centre for Reality Therapy, United Kingdom
Director of Training, The Reality Therapy Association, United Kingdom

It has been a pleasure for me to be involved in reality therapy and a personal privilege to know and work with Bob Wubbolding. His new book, Reality Therapy for the 21st Century, *is well timed and will provide up-to-date information that both students and experts will find invaluable as well as useful to people from many cultures who wish to learn reality therapy.*
Dr. Basheer Al-Rashidi
Chairman, Social Development Office
Professor, Kuwait University

I would like to personally recommend Dr. Wubbolding's latest book. He has made a significant contribution to the growing body of literature on choice theory and reality therapy. Dr. Wubbolding has succeeded in writing a book that is accessible, while comprehensive.
Elijah Mickel, DSW, LICSW, CRT
Professor and BSW Program Director
Delaware State University
Dover Delaware

Robert Wubbolding, for many years a leader in reality therapy, has written a book designed to meet the needs of clinicians and consumers of mental health services at the turn of the century. Reality Therapy for the 21st Century *addresses the important concerns in psychotherapy today: moral, legal, and psychological responsibility; accountability; research documenting effectiveness; treatment planning; managed care; process and outcome; and others. Underlying the broad scope of this book is a strong appreciation of relationships, human development and the individual. Bob Wubbolding has added another important work to his long list of valuable writings on reality therapy.*

Linda Seligman, Ph.D.
Licensed Psychologist and Counselor
Professor, George Mason University
Author of Selecting Effective Treatments, Diagnosis and Treatment Planning in Counseling

When I first met William Glasser I decided to pursue credentialing in Reality Therapy. After the first phase of this process I began to change my behavior in my daily work. With my new experiences and with the close contact with Bob Wubbolding's personality, professional teaching and therapeutic skills, I realized that my decision was correct. And I enjoyed my work much more. (Or as I would have said before: It was Bob who <u>made</u> me feel that my decision was right!). Even after the psychotherapeutic qualification within the German medical system, I can consider that nothing influenced my therapeutic and personal life more than the ideas and tools of reality therapy including the personal relationship to Bob Wubbolding.

Dr. Med Lothar Imhof
Ahrensburg, Germany